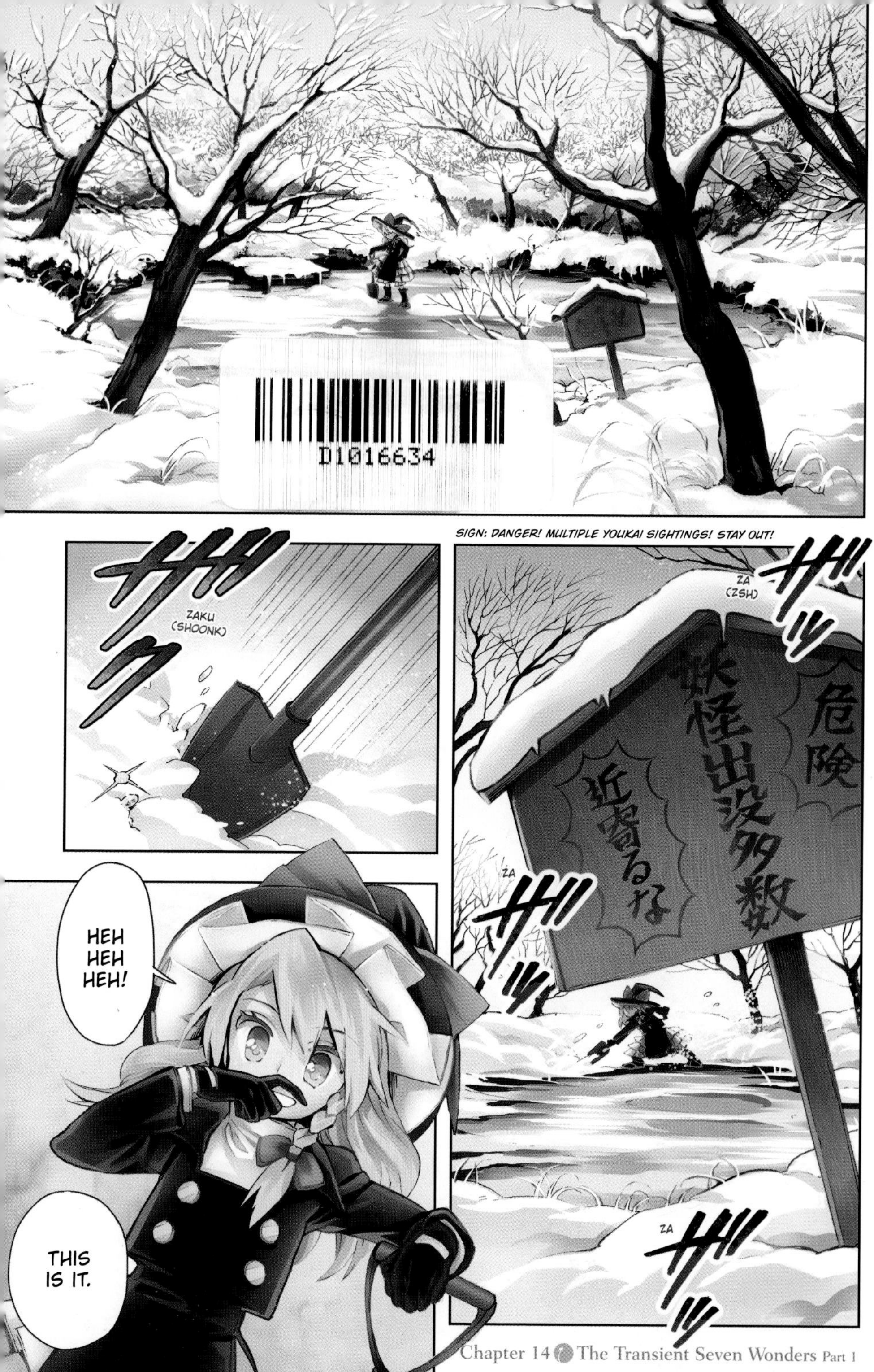
SIGN: DANGER! MULTIPLE YOUKAI SIGHTINGS! STAY OUT!
ZA (ZSH)
危険
妖怪出没多数
近寄るな
ZA
ZA
ZAKU (SHOONK)
HEH HEH HEH!
THIS IS IT.



Chapter 14 The Transient Seven Wonders Part 1

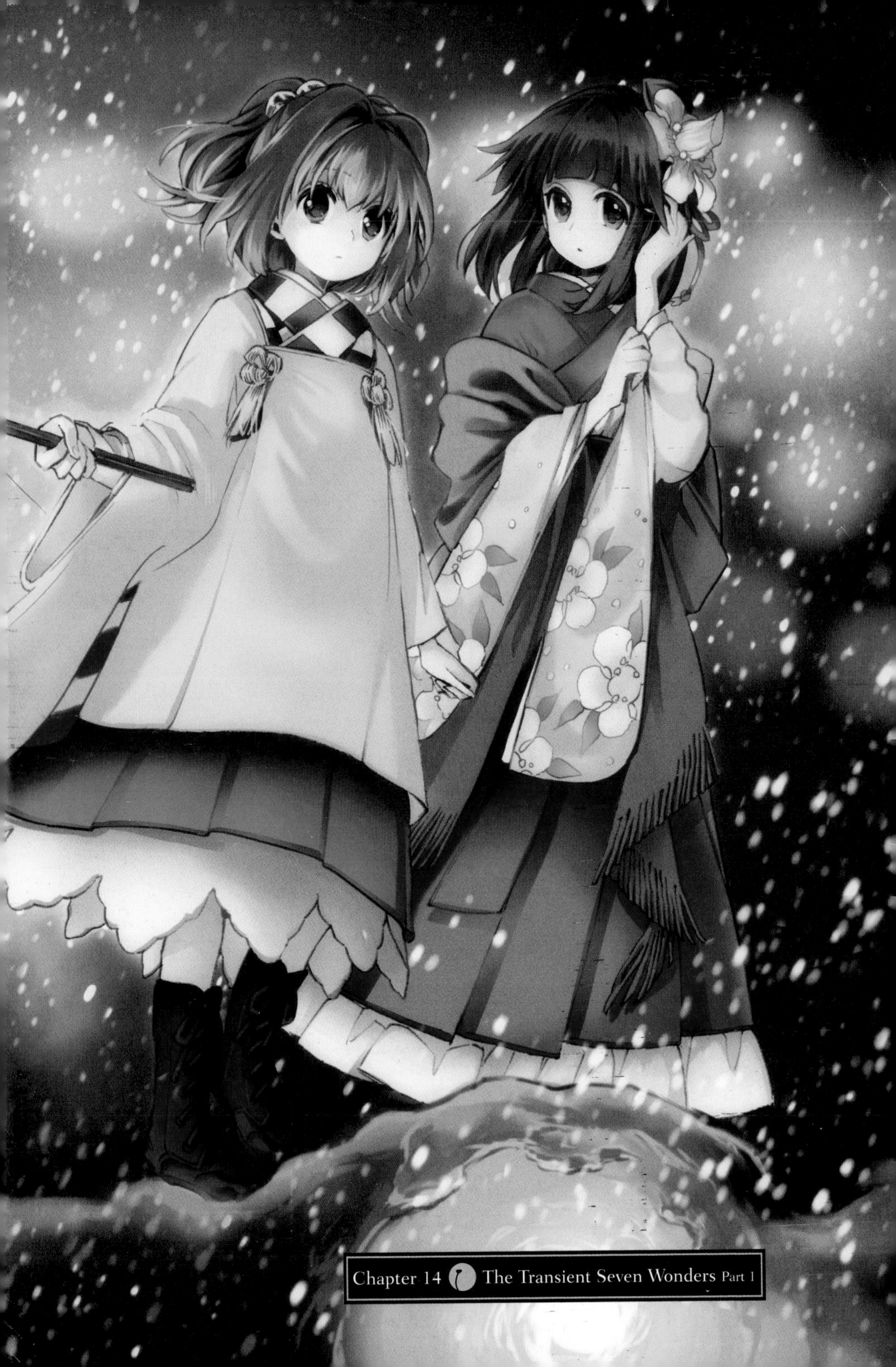

# Chapter 14 The Transient Seven Wonders Part 1

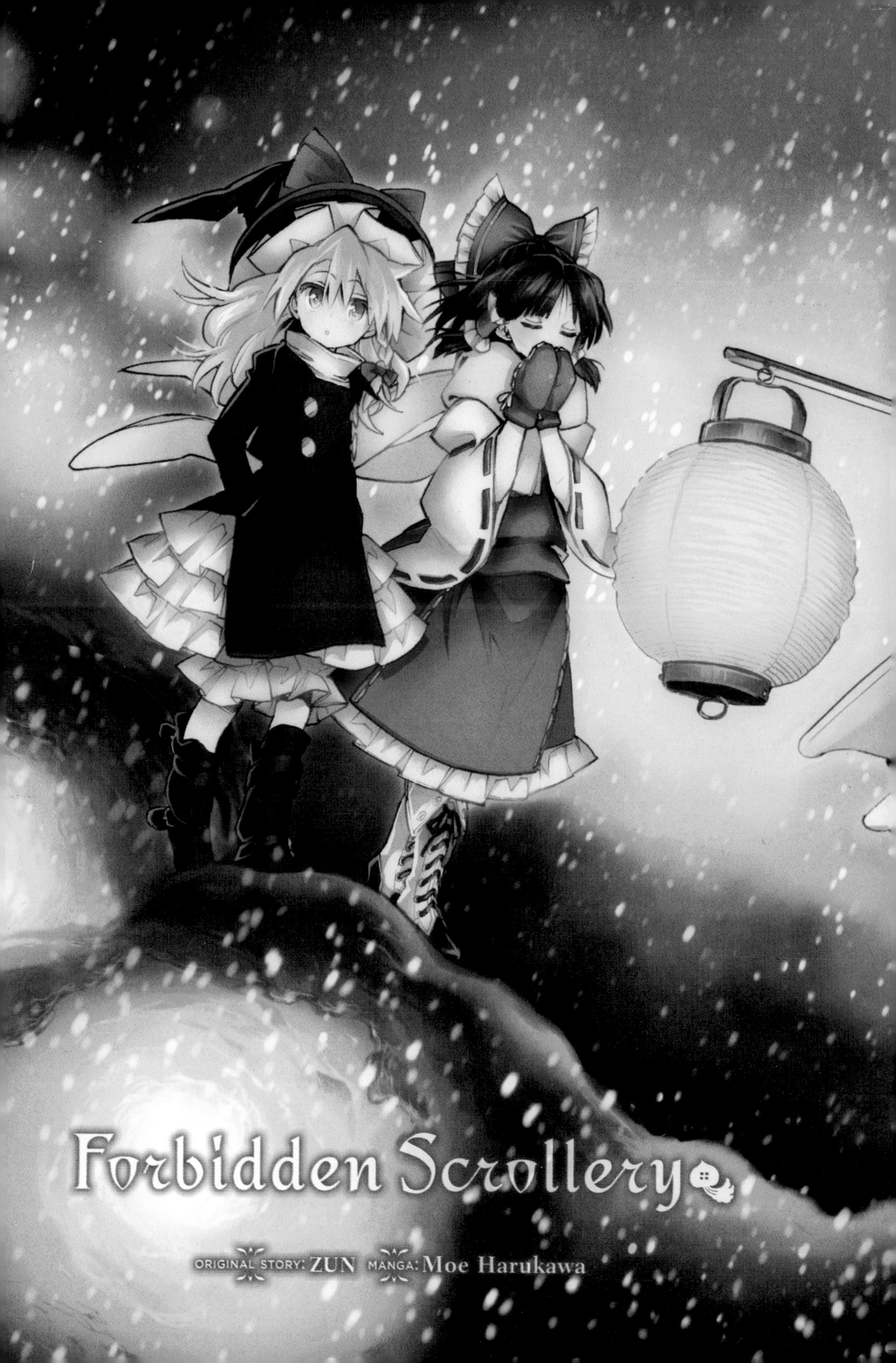
Forbidden Scrollery
ORIGINAL STORY: ZUN MANGA: Moe Harukawa

# CONTENTS

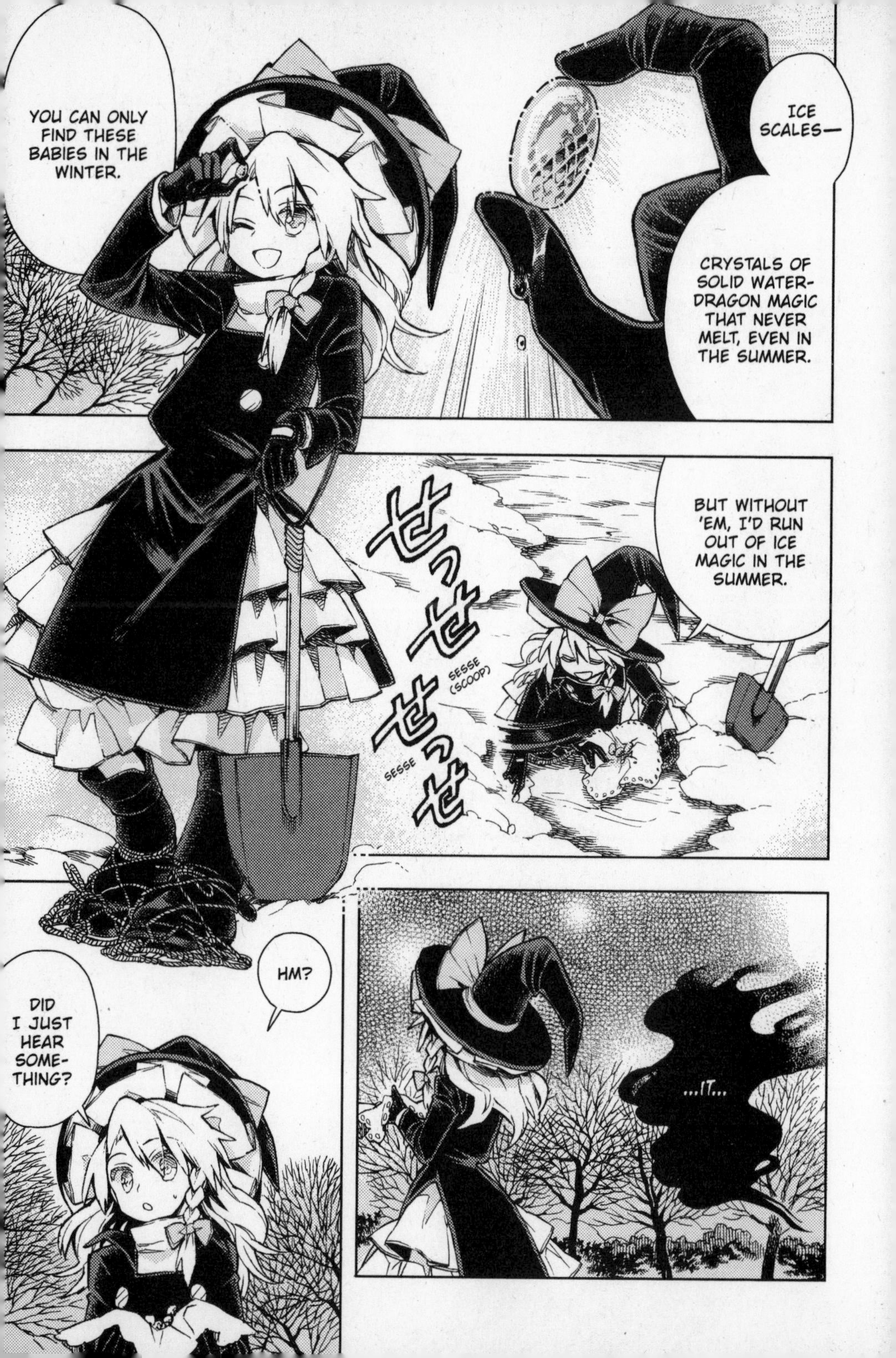
ICE SCALES—
CRYSTALS OF SOLID WATER-DRAGON MAGIC THAT NEVER MELT, EVEN IN THE SUMMER.
YOU CAN ONLY FIND THESE BABIES IN THE WINTER.
BUT WITHOUT 'EM, I'D RUN OUT OF ICE MAGIC IN THE SUMMER.
せっせ
SESSE (SCOOP)
せっせ
SESSE
...IT...
HM?
DID I JUST HEAR SOME-THING?

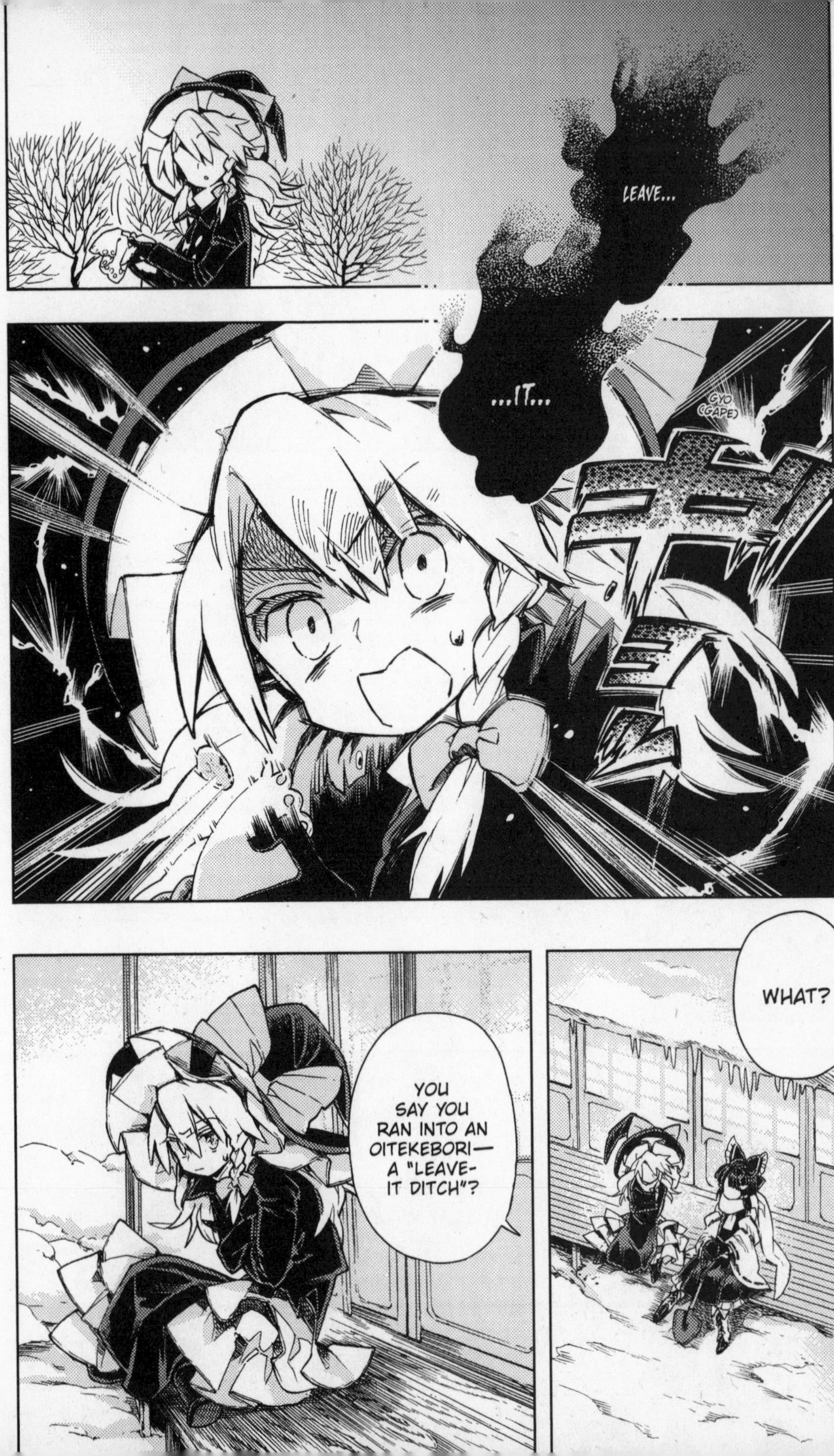
LEAVE...
...IT...
GYO (GAPE)
WHAT?
YOU SAY YOU RAN INTO AN OITEKEBORI— A "LEAVE-IT DITCH"?

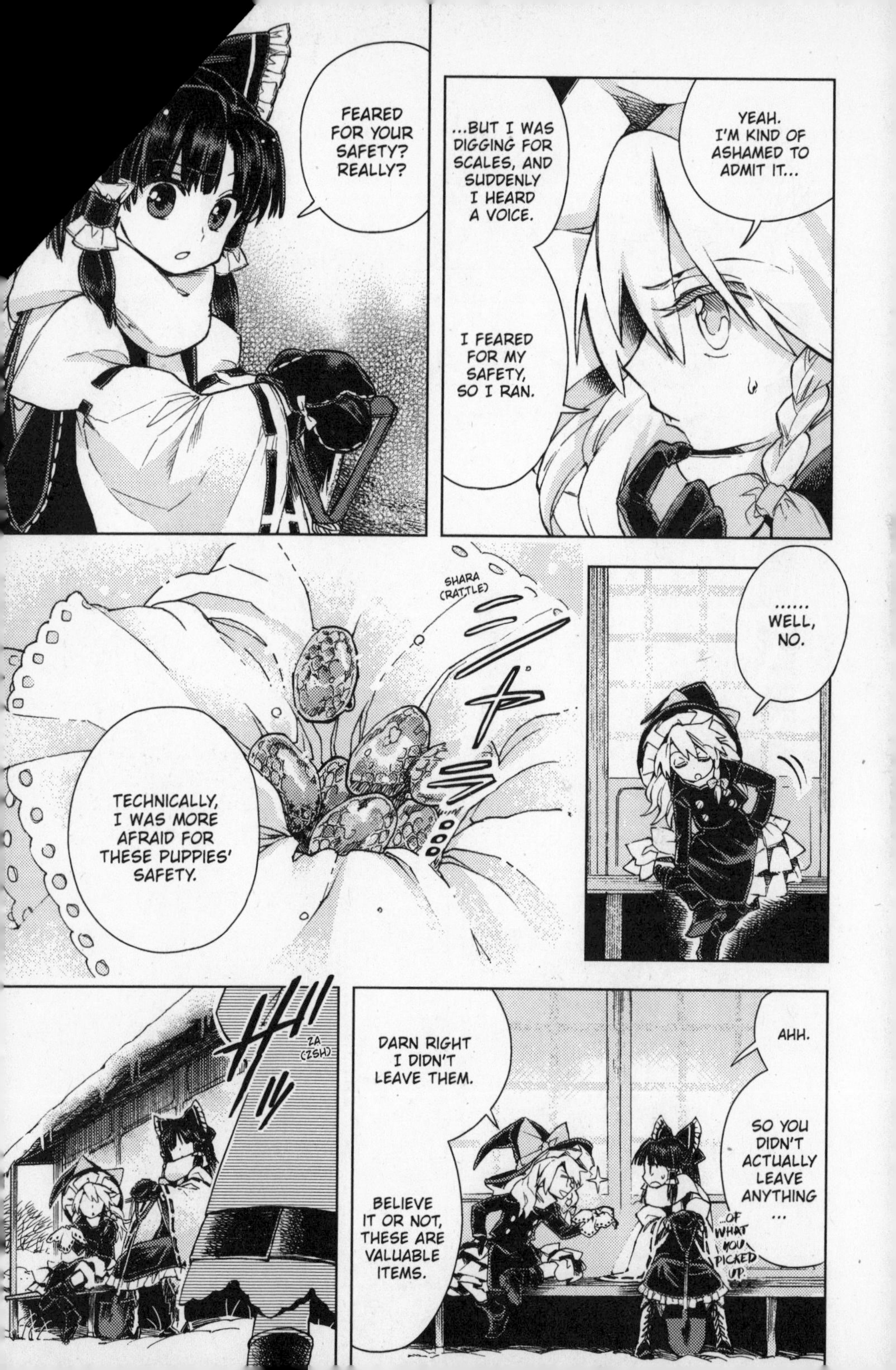
YEAH. I'M KIND OF ASHAMED TO ADMIT IT...
...BUT I WAS DIGGING FOR SCALES, AND SUDDENLY I HEARD A VOICE.
I FEARED FOR MY SAFETY, SO I RAN.
FEARED FOR YOUR SAFETY? REALLY?
......
WELL, NO.
SHARA (RATTLE)
TECHNICALLY, I WAS MORE AFRAID FOR THESE PUPPIES' SAFETY.
AHH.
SO YOU DIDN'T ACTUALLY LEAVE ANYTHING...
...OF WHAT YOU PICKED UP.
DARN RIGHT I DIDN'T LEAVE THEM.
BELIEVE IT OR NOT, THESE ARE VALUABLE ITEMS.
ZA (ZSH)

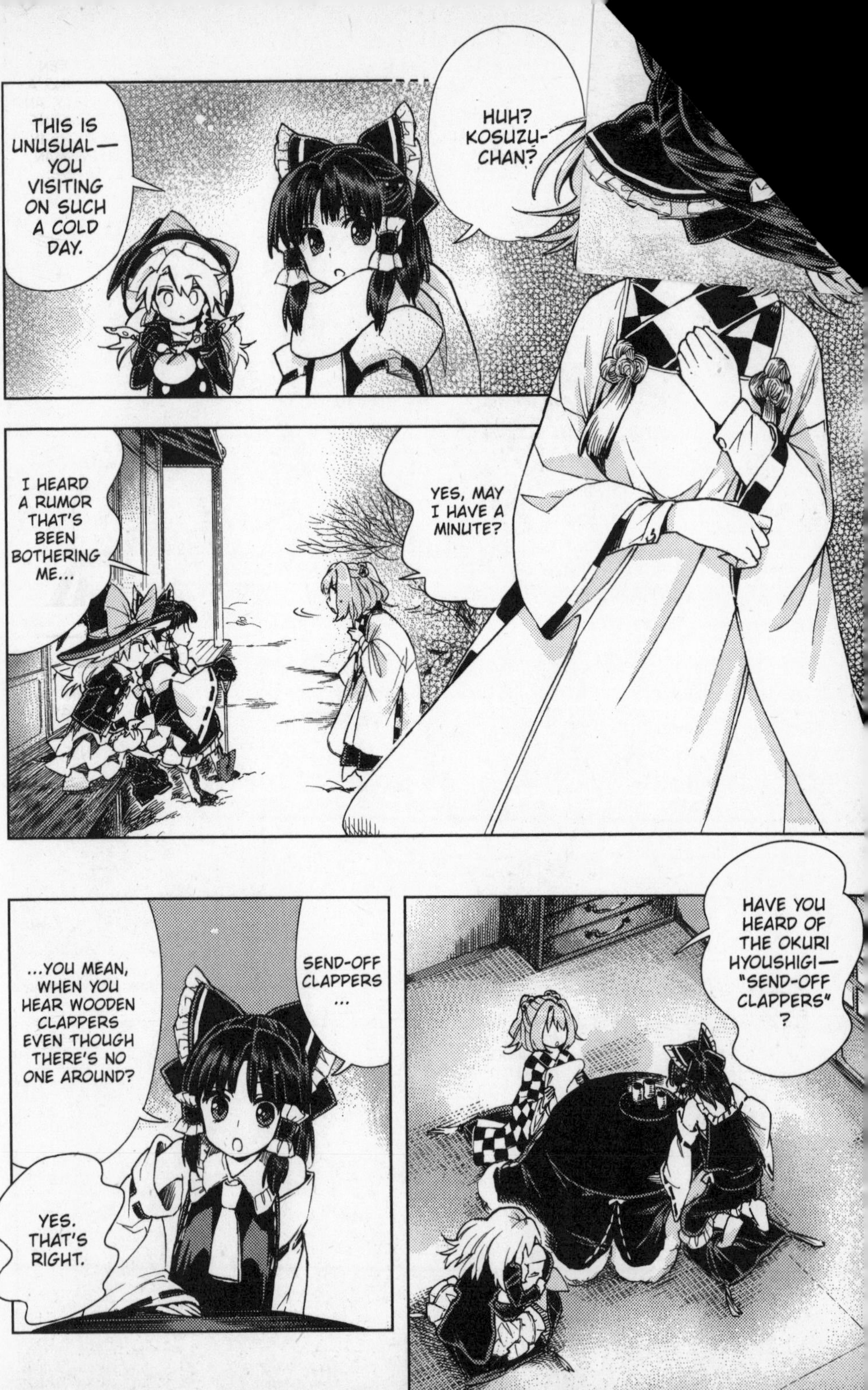
HUH? KOSUZU-CHAN?
THIS IS UNUSUAL—YOU VISITING ON SUCH A COLD DAY.
YES, MAY I HAVE A MINUTE?
I HEARD A RUMOR THAT'S BEEN BOTHERING ME...
HAVE YOU HEARD OF THE OKURI HYOUSHIGI—"SEND-OFF CLAPPERS"?
SEND-OFF CLAPPERS...
...YOU MEAN, WHEN YOU HEAR WOODEN CLAPPERS EVEN THOUGH THERE'S NO ONE AROUND?
YES. THAT'S RIGHT.

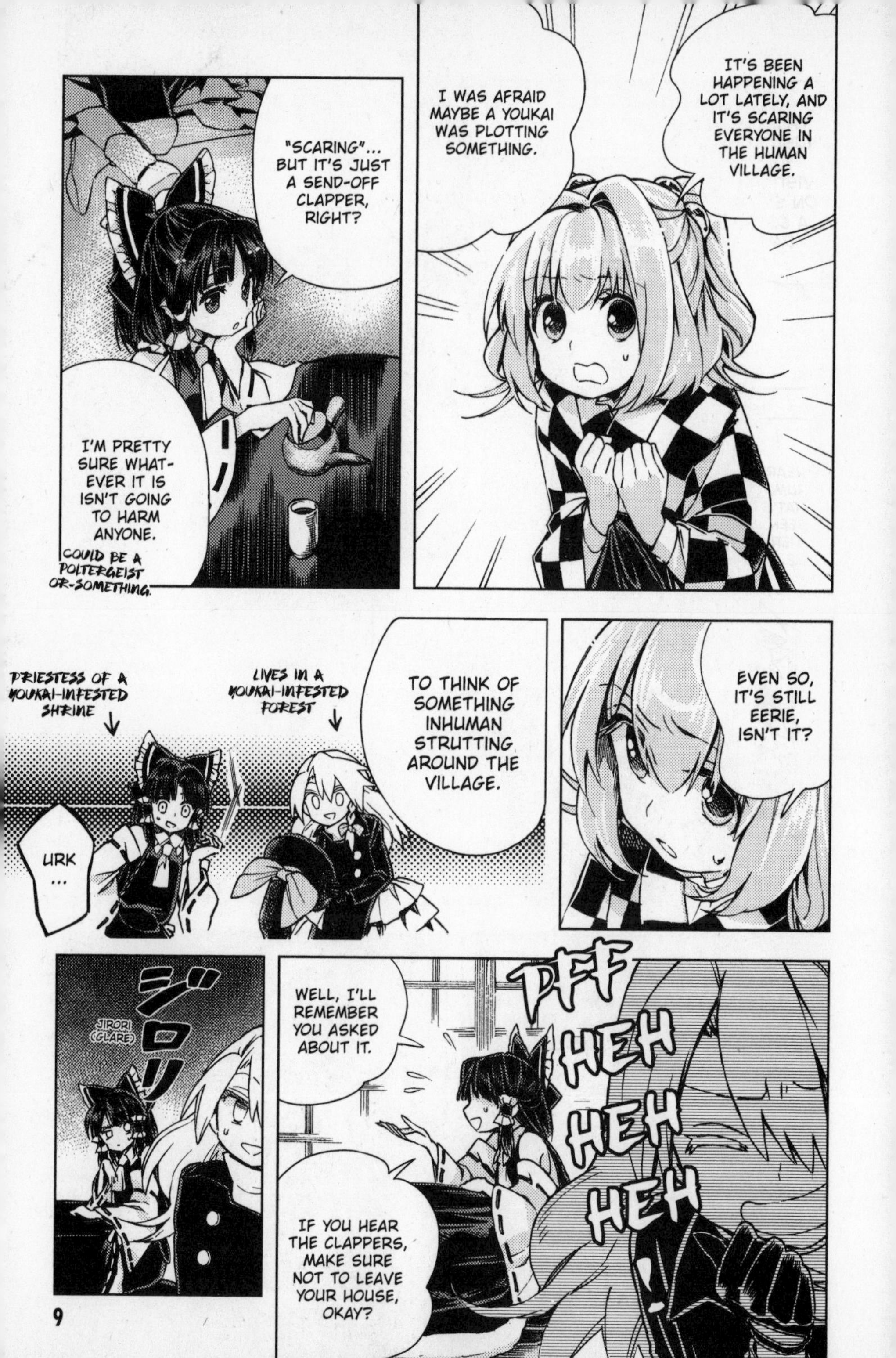
IT'S BEEN HAPPENING A LOT LATELY, AND IT'S SCARING EVERYONE IN THE HUMAN VILLAGE.
I WAS AFRAID MAYBE A YOUKAI WAS PLOTTING SOMETHING.
"SCARING"... BUT IT'S JUST A SEND-OFF CLAPPER, RIGHT?
I'M PRETTY SURE WHAT-EVER IT IS ISN'T GOING TO HARM ANYONE.
COULD BE A POLTERGEIST OR SOMETHING.
EVEN SO, IT'S STILL EERIE, ISN'T IT?
TO THINK OF SOMETHING INHUMAN STRUTTING AROUND THE VILLAGE.
LIVES IN A YOUKAI-INFESTED FOREST
PRIESTESS OF A YOUKAI-INFESTED SHRINE
URK...
PFF HEH HEH HEH HEH
WELL, I'LL REMEMBER YOU ASKED ABOUT IT.
IF YOU HEAR THE CLAPPERS, MAKE SURE NOT TO LEAVE YOUR HOUSE, OKAY?
ジロリ
JIRORI (GLARE)

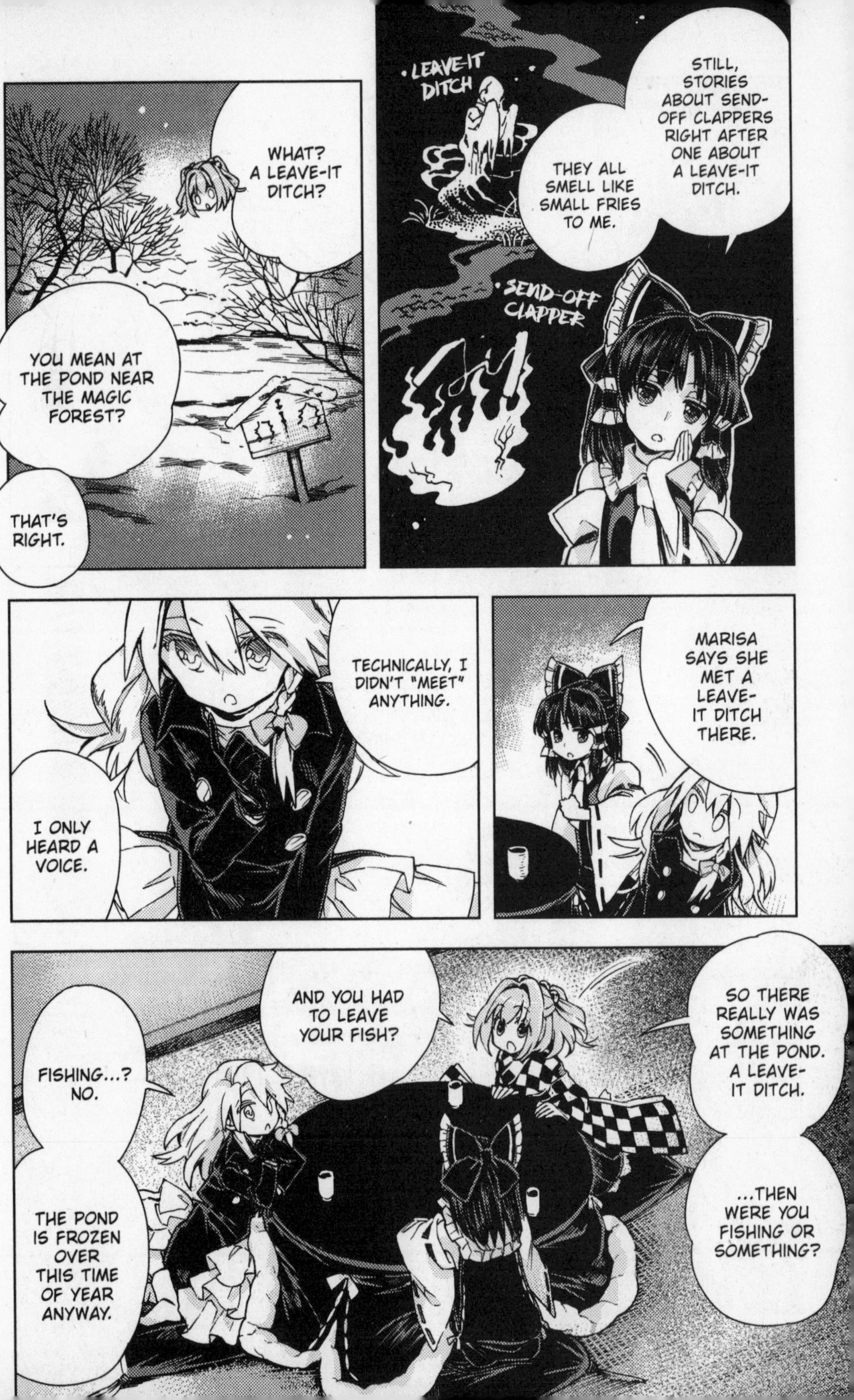
STILL, STORIES ABOUT SEND-OFF CLAPPERS RIGHT AFTER ONE ABOUT A LEAVE-IT DITCH.
THEY ALL SMELL LIKE SMALL FRIES TO ME.
• LEAVE-IT DITCH
• SEND-OFF CLAPPER
WHAT? A LEAVE-IT DITCH?
YOU MEAN AT THE POND NEAR THE MAGIC FOREST?
THAT'S RIGHT.
MARISA SAYS SHE MET A LEAVE-IT DITCH THERE.
TECHNICALLY, I DIDN'T "MEET" ANYTHING.
I ONLY HEARD A VOICE.
SO THERE REALLY WAS SOMETHING AT THE POND. A LEAVE-IT DITCH.
...THEN WERE YOU FISHING OR SOMETHING?
AND YOU HAD TO LEAVE YOUR FISH?
FISHING...? NO.
THE POND IS FROZEN OVER THIS TIME OF YEAR ANYWAY.

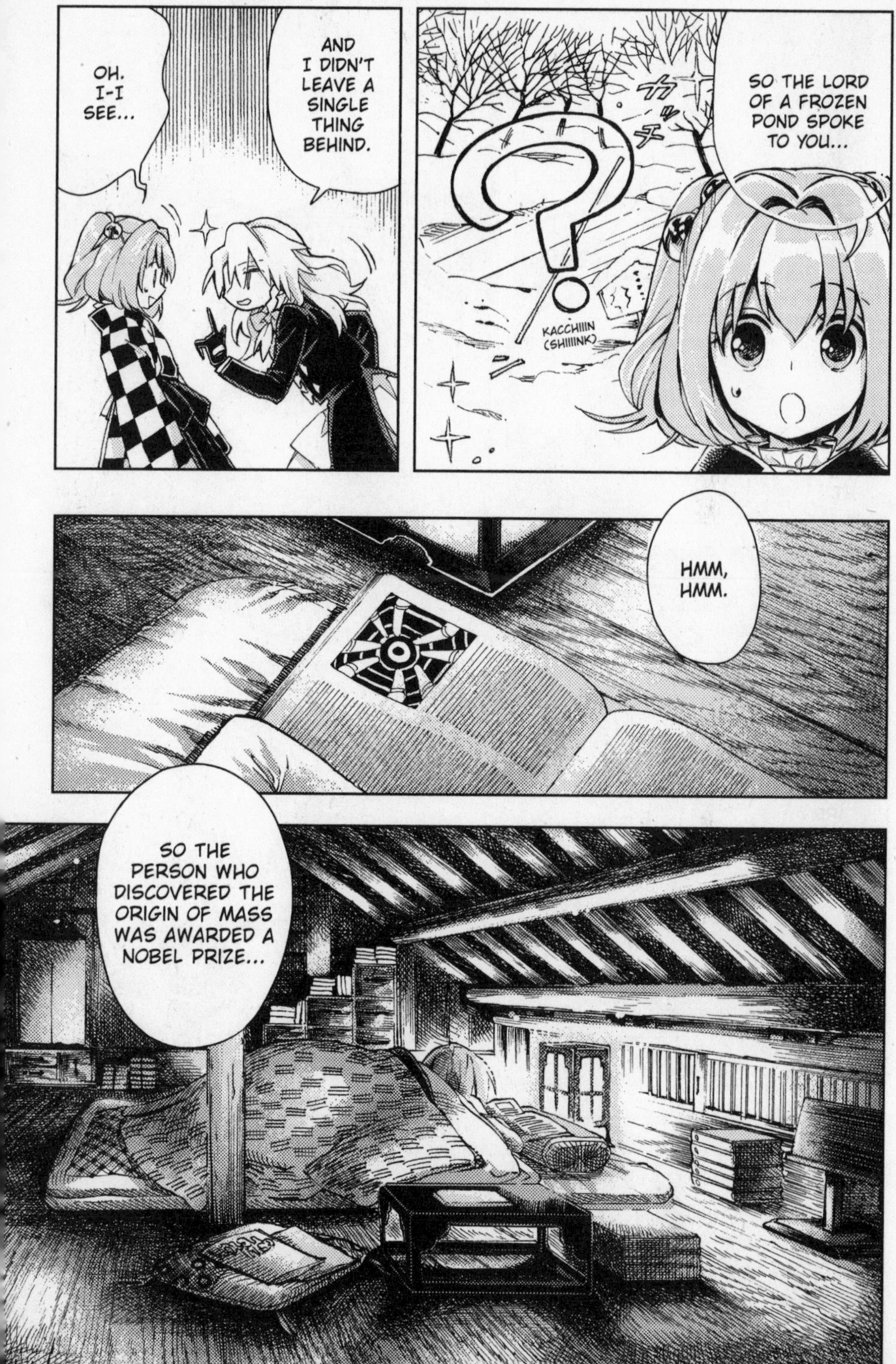
SO THE LORD OF A FROZEN POND SPOKE TO YOU...
KACCHIIIN (SHIIIINK)
AND I DIDN'T LEAVE A SINGLE THING BEHIND.
OH. I-I SEE...
HMM, HMM.
SO THE PERSON WHO DISCOVERED THE ORIGIN OF MASS WAS AWARDED A NOBEL PRIZE...

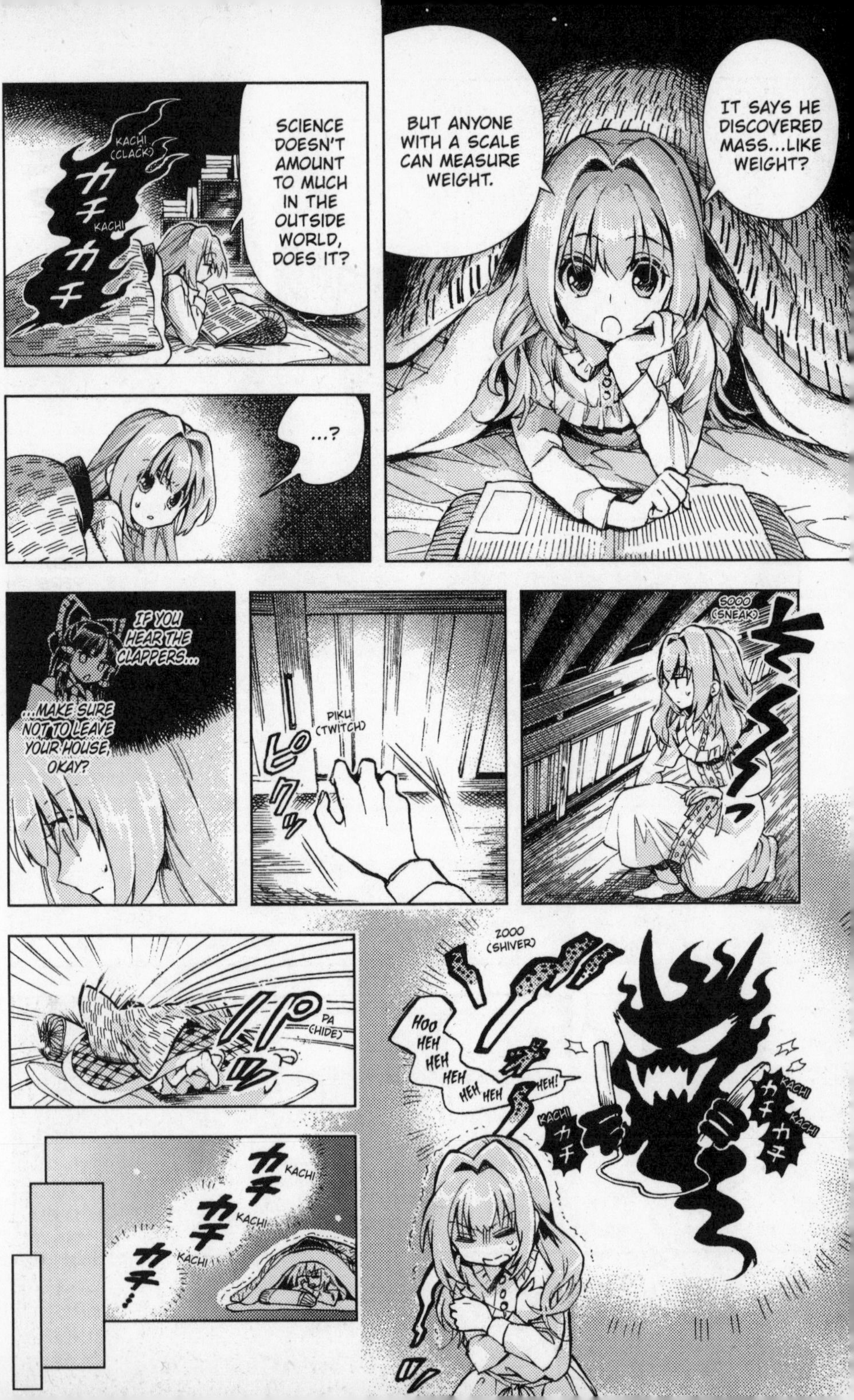
IT SAYS HE DISCOVERED MASS...LIKE WEIGHT?
BUT ANYONE WITH A SCALE CAN MEASURE WEIGHT.
KACHI (CLACK)
カチ
KACHI
カチカチ
SCIENCE DOESN'T AMOUNT TO MUCH IN THE OUTSIDE WORLD, DOES IT?
...?
SOOO (SNEAK)
PIKU (TWITCH)
ピクッ
IF YOU HEAR THE CLAPPERS...
...MAKE SURE NOT TO LEAVE YOUR HOUSE, OKAY?
ZOOO (SHIVER)
HOO HEH HEH HEH HEH HEH!
KACHI
カチ
KACHI
カチ
KACHI
カチ
PA (HIDE)
パッ
カチ
KACHI
カチ
KACHI
カチ...
KACHI

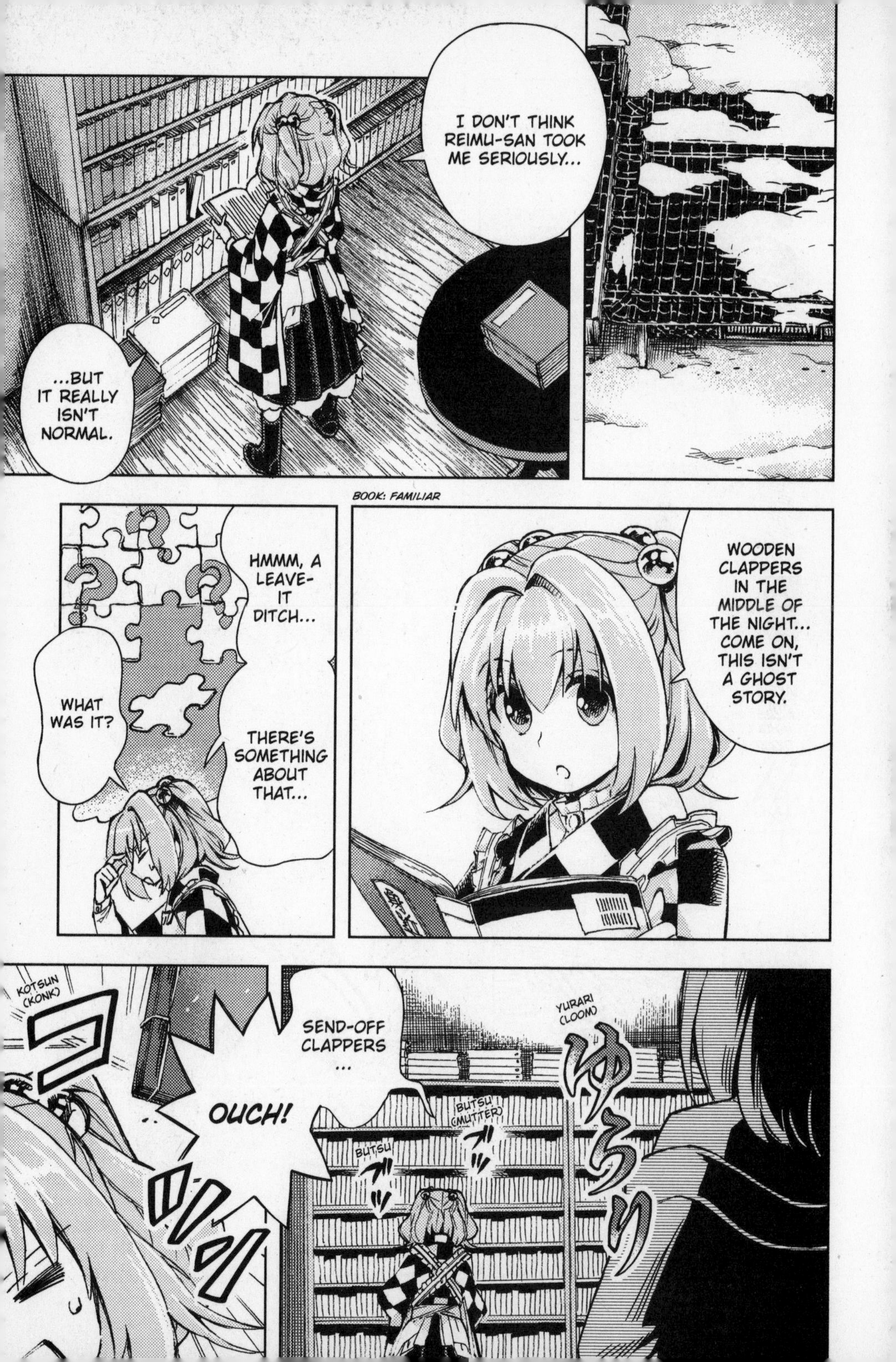
I DON'T THINK REIMU-SAN TOOK ME SERIOUSLY...
...BUT IT REALLY ISN'T NORMAL.
BOOK: FAMILIAR
WOODEN CLAPPERS IN THE MIDDLE OF THE NIGHT... COME ON, THIS ISN'T A GHOST STORY.
HMMM, A LEAVE-IT DITCH...
THERE'S SOMETHING ABOUT THAT...
WHAT WAS IT?
YURARI (LOOM)
BUTSU (MUTTER)
BUTSU
SEND-OFF CLAPPERS...
KOTSUN (KONK)
OUCH!

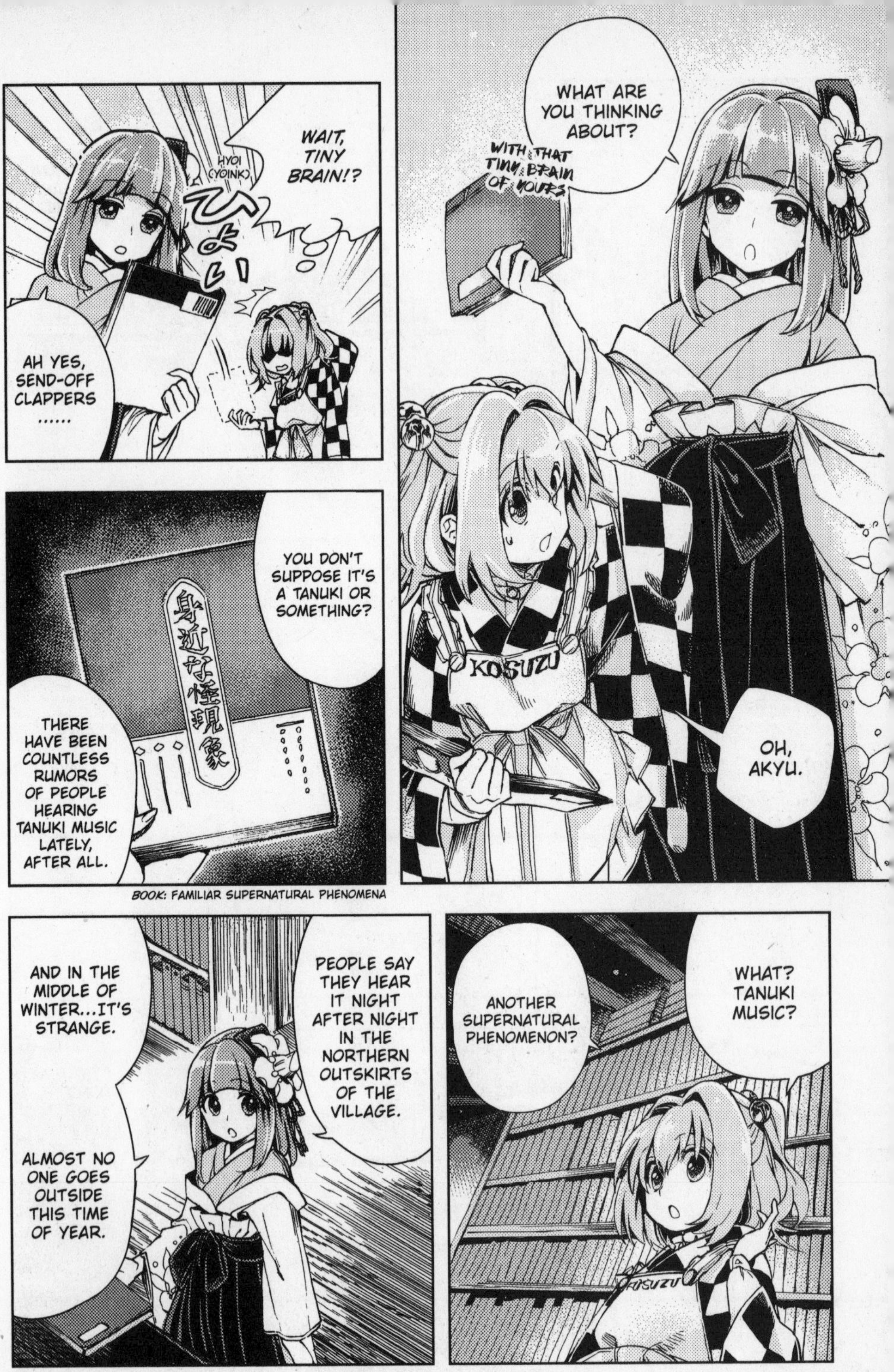
WHAT ARE YOU THINKING ABOUT?
WITH THAT TINY BRAIN OF YOURS
KOSUZU
OH, AKYU.
WAIT, TINY BRAIN!?
HYOI (YOINK)
ひょい
AH YES, SEND-OFF CLAPPERS......
YOU DON'T SUPPOSE IT'S A TANUKI OR SOMETHING?
身近な怪現象
THERE HAVE BEEN COUNTLESS RUMORS OF PEOPLE HEARING TANUKI MUSIC LATELY, AFTER ALL.
BOOK: FAMILIAR SUPERNATURAL PHENOMENA
WHAT? TANUKI MUSIC?
ANOTHER SUPERNATURAL PHENOMENON?
PEOPLE SAY THEY HEAR IT NIGHT AFTER NIGHT IN THE NORTHERN OUTSKIRTS OF THE VILLAGE.
AND IN THE MIDDLE OF WINTER...IT'S STRANGE.
ALMOST NO ONE GOES OUTSIDE THIS TIME OF YEAR.

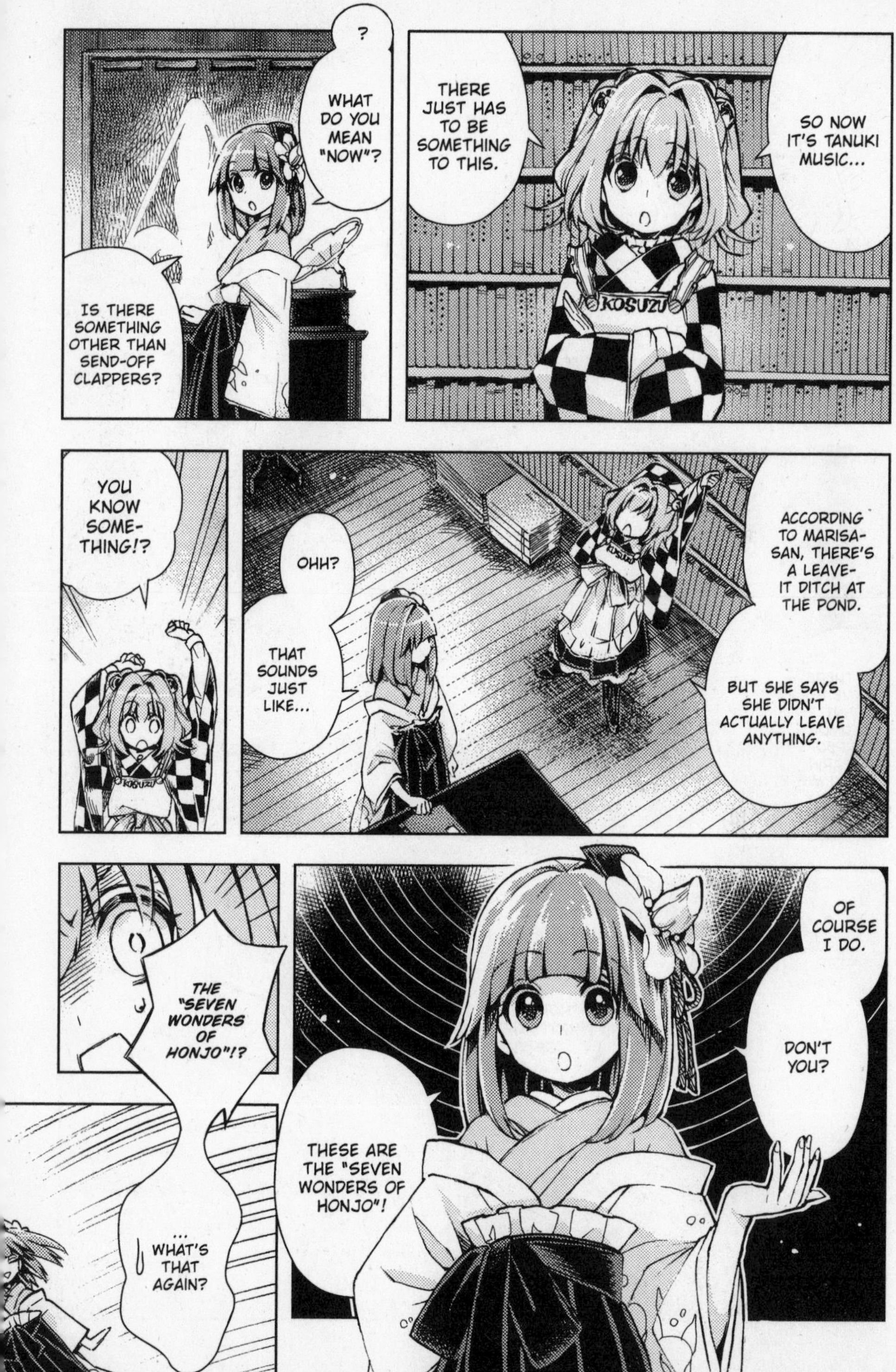
SO NOW IT'S TANUKI MUSIC...
THERE JUST HAS TO BE SOMETHING TO THIS.
?
WHAT DO YOU MEAN "NOW"?
IS THERE SOMETHING OTHER THAN SEND-OFF CLAPPERS?
ACCORDING TO MARISA-SAN, THERE'S A LEAVE-IT DITCH AT THE POND.
BUT SHE SAYS SHE DIDN'T ACTUALLY LEAVE ANYTHING.
OHH?
THAT SOUNDS JUST LIKE...
YOU KNOW SOME-THING!?
OF COURSE I DO.
DON'T YOU?
THESE ARE THE "SEVEN WONDERS OF HONJO"!
THE "SEVEN WONDERS OF HONJO"!?
... WHAT'S THAT AGAIN?

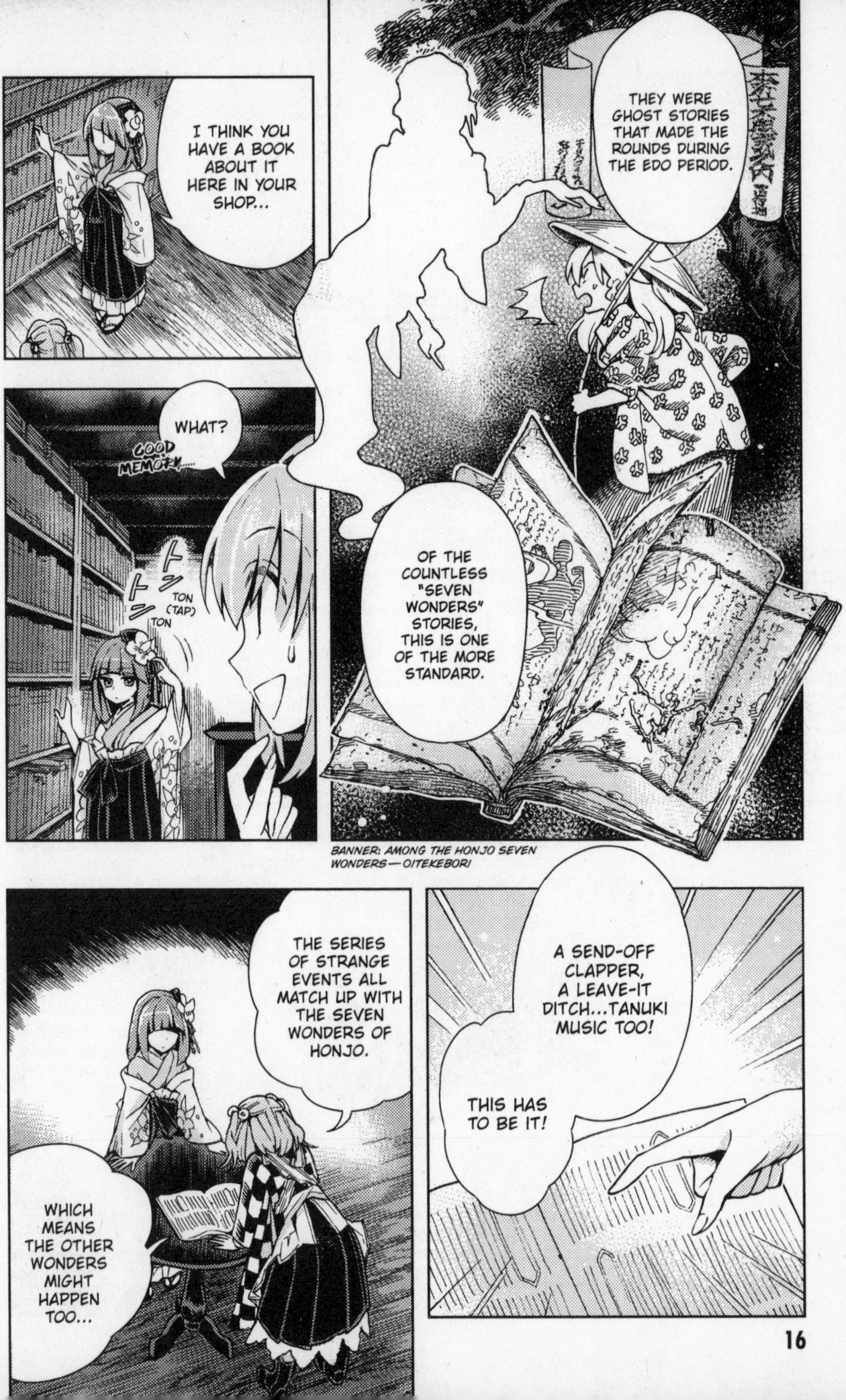
THEY WERE GHOST STORIES THAT MADE THE ROUNDS DURING THE EDO PERIOD.
OF THE COUNTLESS "SEVEN WONDERS" STORIES, THIS IS ONE OF THE MORE STANDARD.
I THINK YOU HAVE A BOOK ABOUT IT HERE IN YOUR SHOP...
WHAT?
GOOD MEMORY......
TON (TAP) TON
A SEND-OFF CLAPPER, A LEAVE-IT DITCH...TANUKI MUSIC TOO!
THIS HAS TO BE IT!
THE SERIES OF STRANGE EVENTS ALL MATCH UP WITH THE SEVEN WONDERS OF HONJO.
WHICH MEANS THE OTHER WONDERS MIGHT HAPPEN TOO...

BANNER: AMONG THE HONJO SEVEN WONDERS—OITEKEBORI

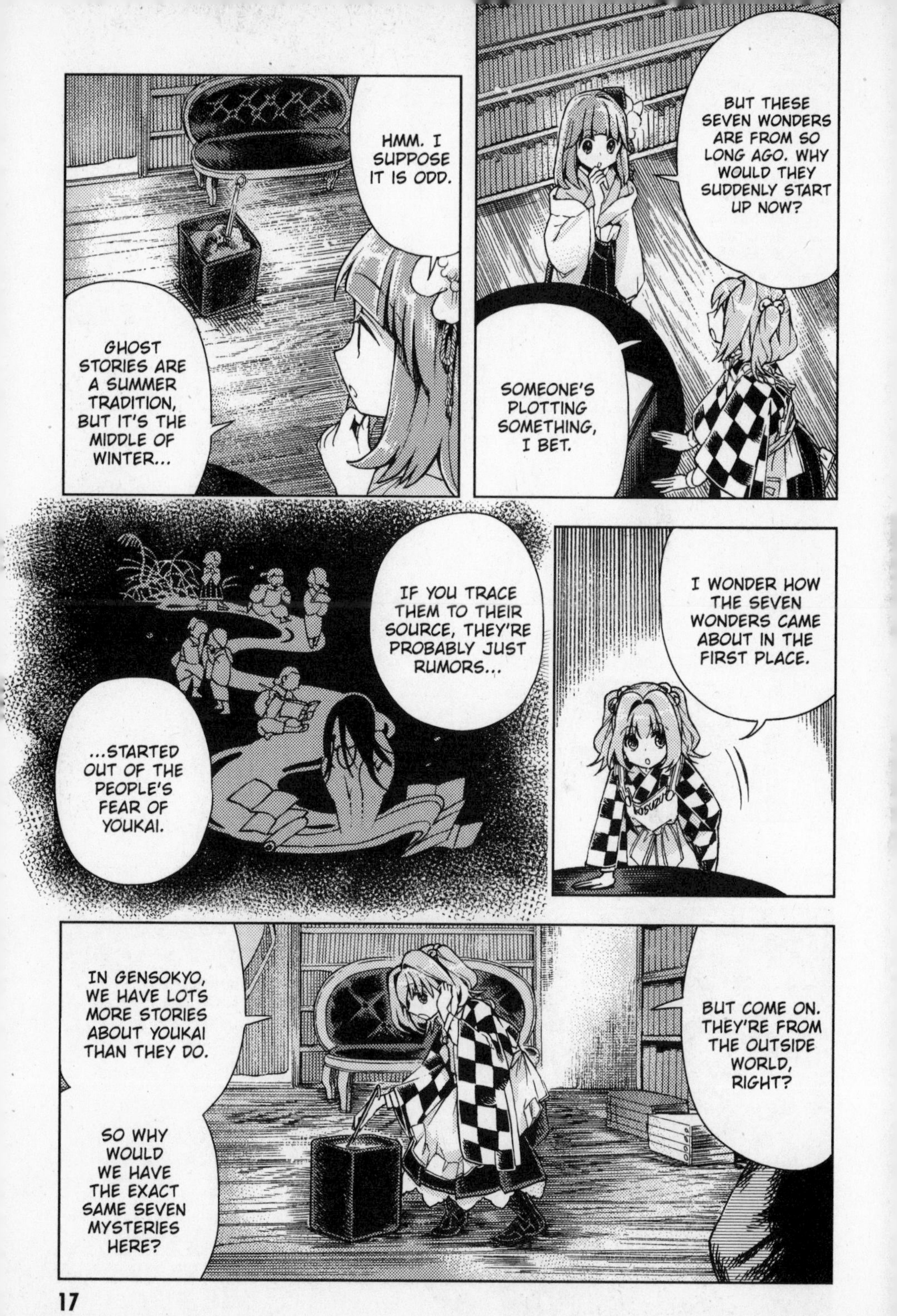
BUT THESE SEVEN WONDERS ARE FROM SO LONG AGO. WHY WOULD THEY SUDDENLY START UP NOW?
SOMEONE'S PLOTTING SOMETHING, I BET.
HMM. I SUPPOSE IT IS ODD.
GHOST STORIES ARE A SUMMER TRADITION, BUT IT'S THE MIDDLE OF WINTER...
I WONDER HOW THE SEVEN WONDERS CAME ABOUT IN THE FIRST PLACE.
IF YOU TRACE THEM TO THEIR SOURCE, THEY'RE PROBABLY JUST RUMORS...
...STARTED OUT OF THE PEOPLE'S FEAR OF YOUKAI.
BUT COME ON. THEY'RE FROM THE OUTSIDE WORLD, RIGHT?
IN GENSOKYO, WE HAVE LOTS MORE STORIES ABOUT YOUKAI THAN THEY DO.
SO WHY WOULD WE HAVE THE EXACT SAME SEVEN MYSTERIES HERE?

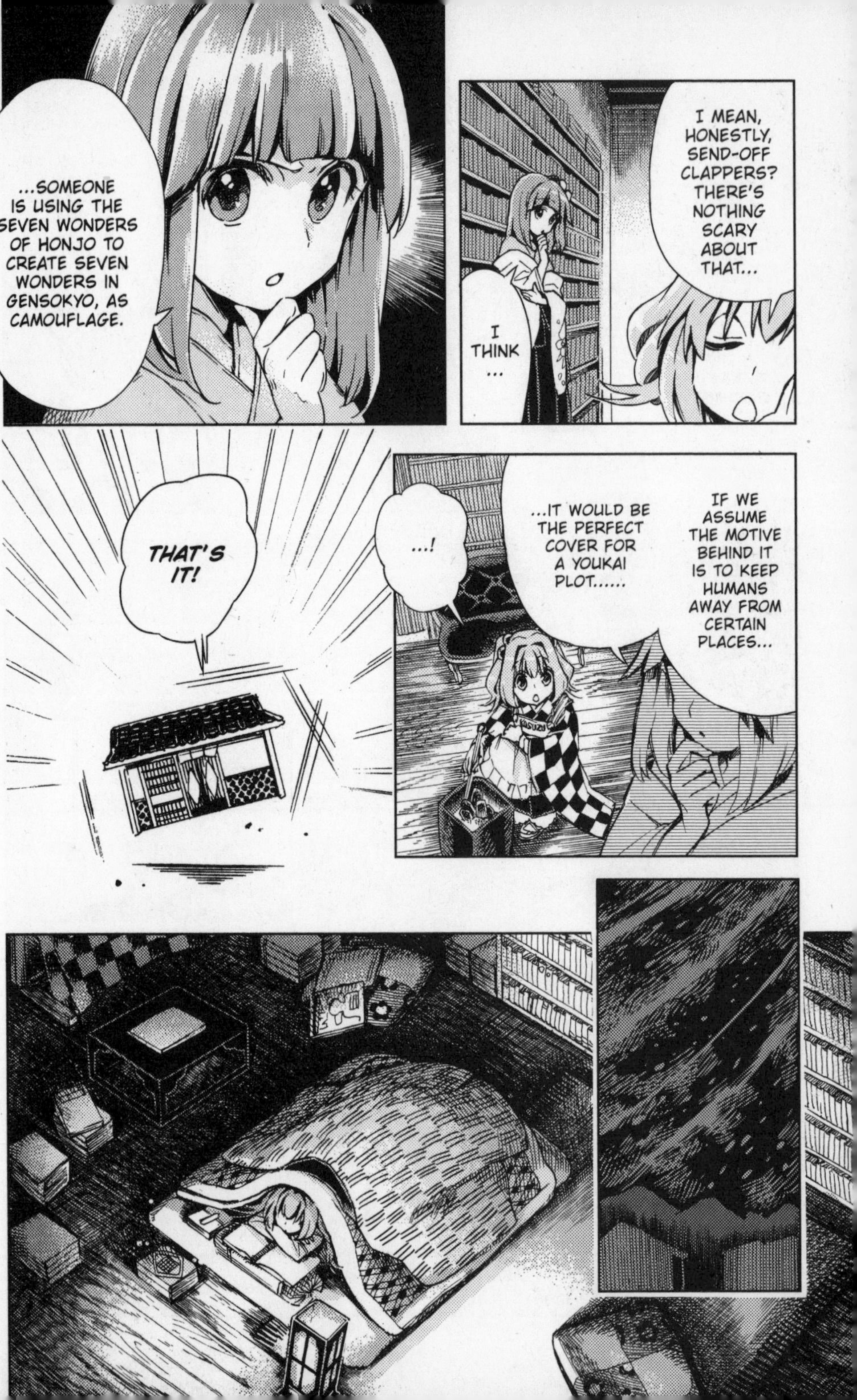
I MEAN, HONESTLY, SEND-OFF CLAPPERS? THERE'S NOTHING SCARY ABOUT THAT...
I THINK...
...SOMEONE IS USING THE SEVEN WONDERS OF HONJO TO CREATE SEVEN WONDERS IN GENSOKYO, AS CAMOUFLAGE.
IF WE ASSUME THE MOTIVE BEHIND IT IS TO KEEP HUMANS AWAY FROM CERTAIN PLACES...
...IT WOULD BE THE PERFECT COVER FOR A YOUKAI PLOT......
...!
THAT'S IT!

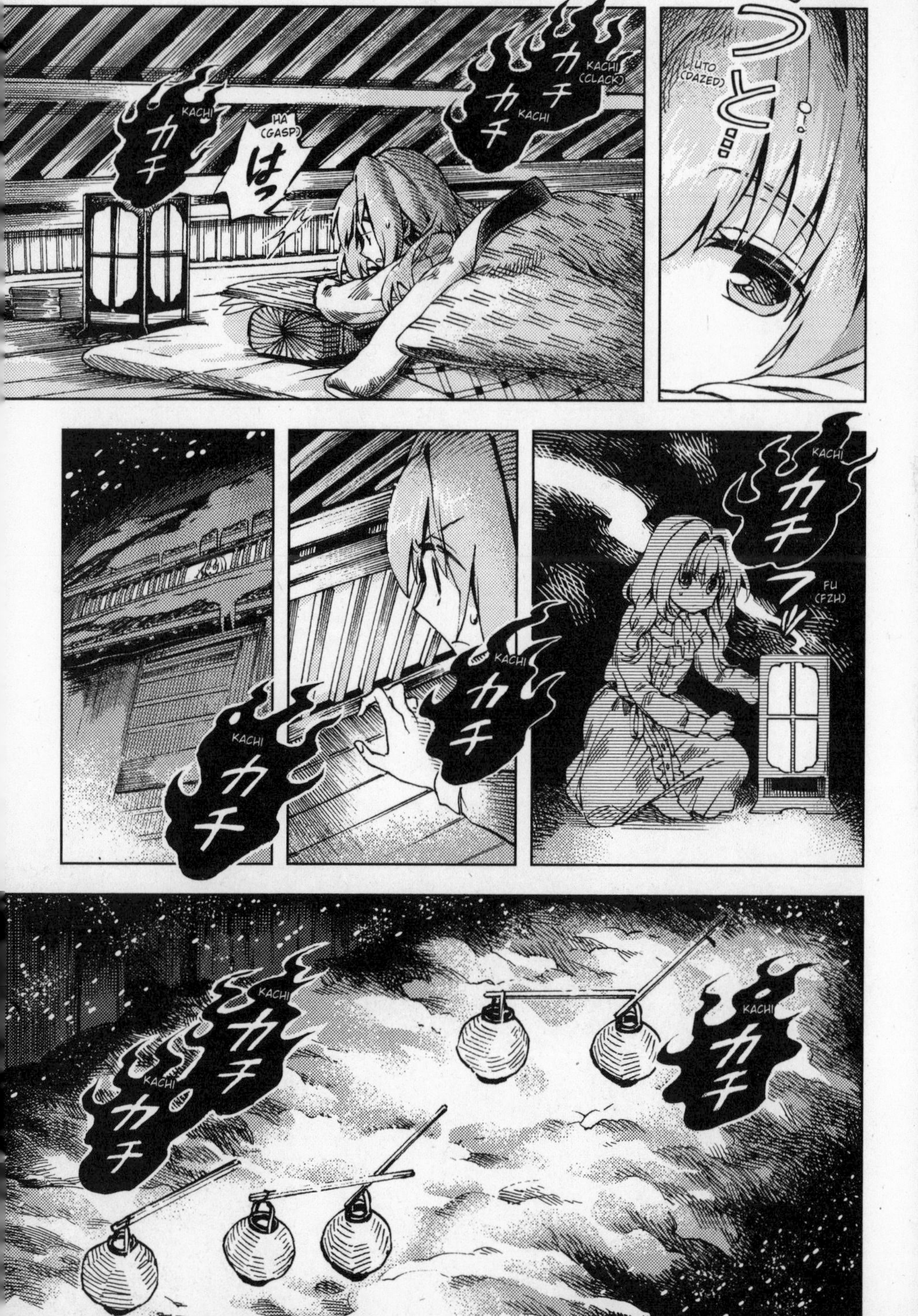

うと…
UTO (DAZED)
カチ カチ
KACHI (CLACK)
KACHI
はっ
HA (GASP)
KACHI
カチ
カチ
KACHI
フ
FU (FZH)
KACHI
カチ
KACHI
カチ
KACHI
カチ
KACHI
カチ
KACHI
カチ

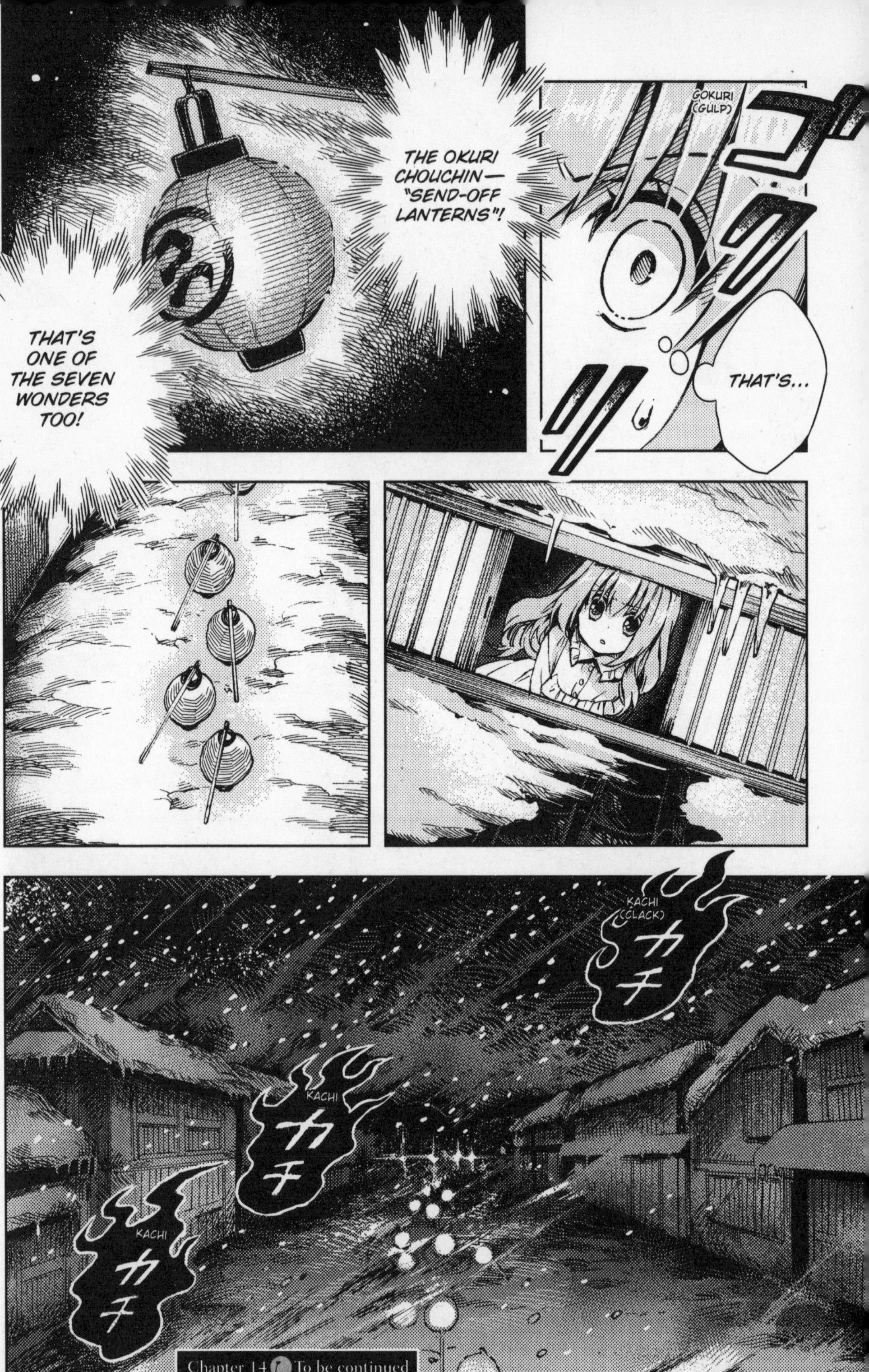
GOKURI (GULP)
THAT'S...
THE OKURI CHOUCHIN— "SEND-OFF LANTERNS"!
THAT'S ONE OF THE SEVEN WONDERS TOO!
KACHI (CLACK)
KACHI
KACHI
Chapter 14 To be continued

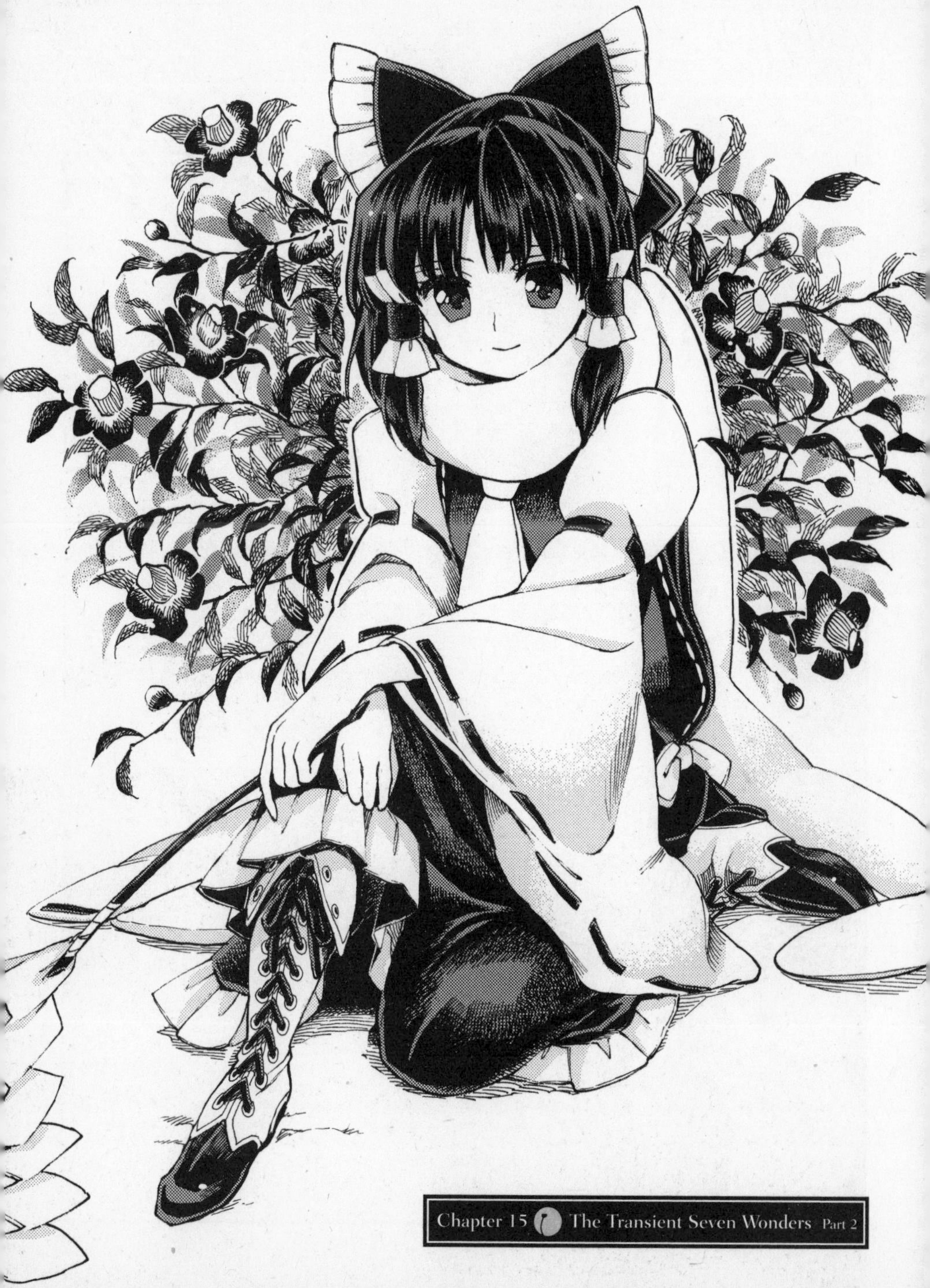

# Chapter 15 The Transient Seven Wonders Part 2

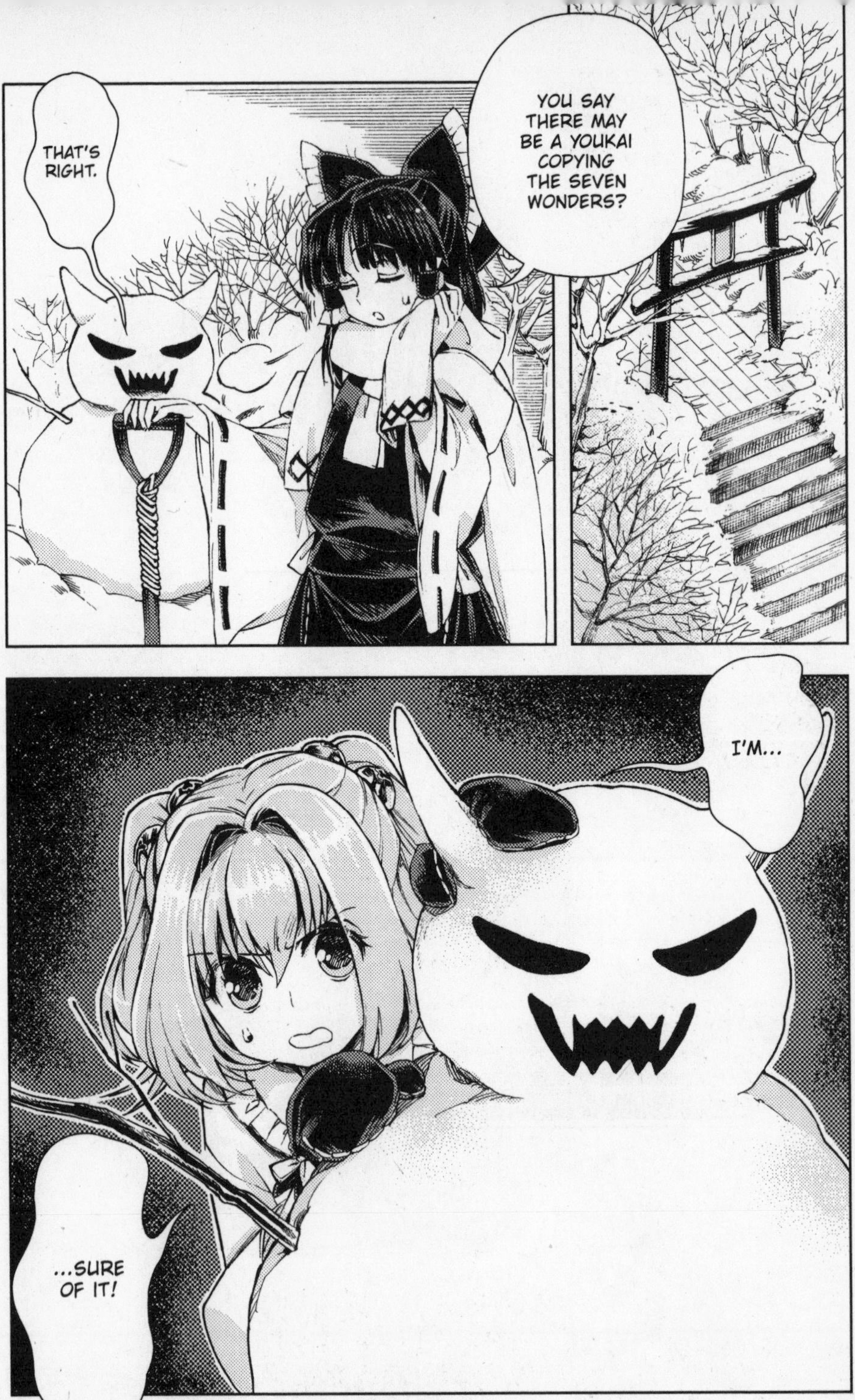
YOU SAY THERE MAY BE A YOUKAI COPYING THE SEVEN WONDERS?
THAT'S RIGHT.
I'M...
...SURE OF IT!

BOOK: FAMILIAR SUPERNATURAL PHENOMENA

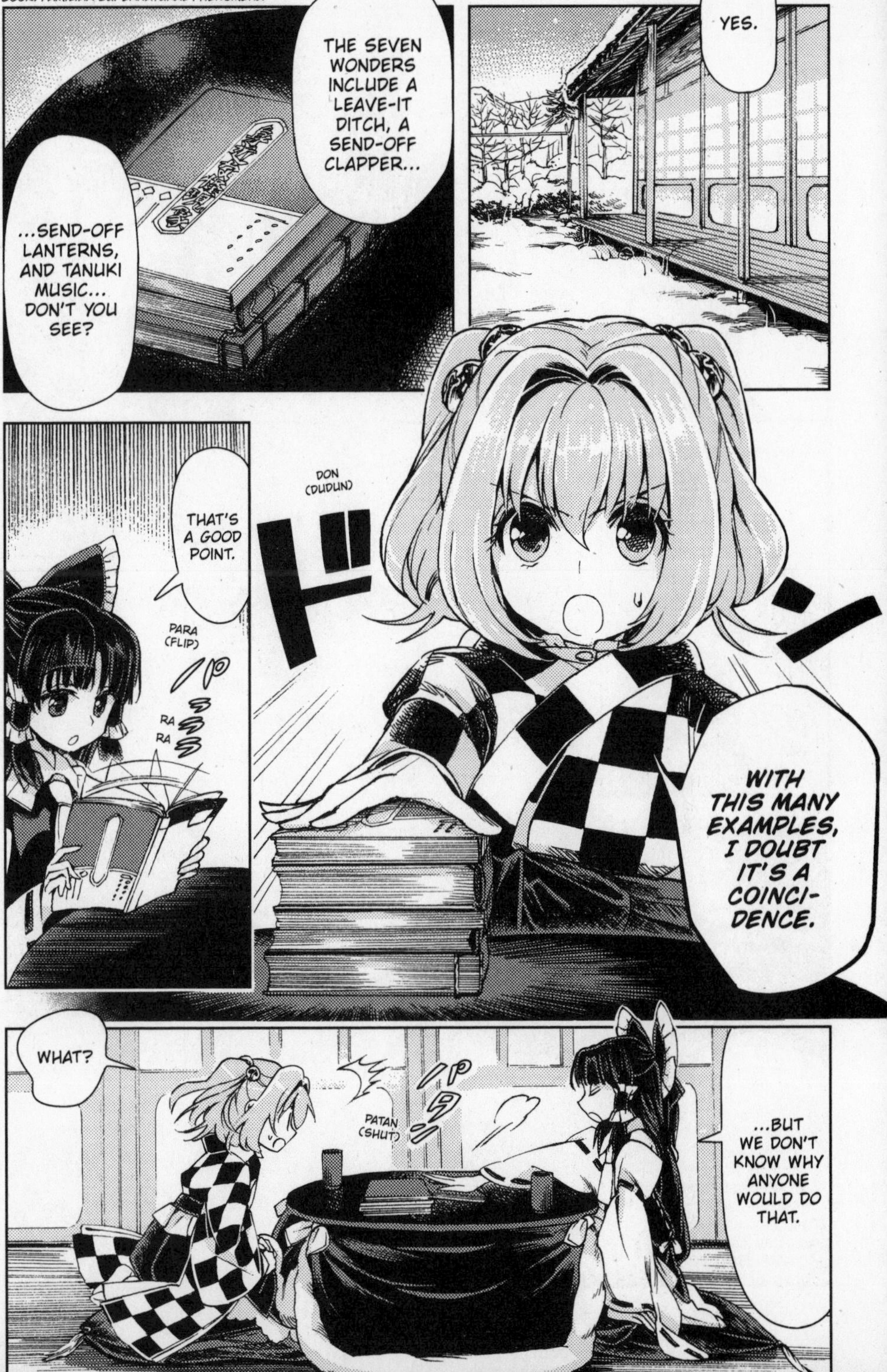
YES.
THE SEVEN WONDERS INCLUDE A LEAVE-IT DITCH, A SEND-OFF CLAPPER...
...SEND-OFF LANTERNS, AND TANUKI MUSIC... DON'T YOU SEE?
WITH THIS MANY EXAMPLES, I DOUBT IT'S A COINCIDENCE.
DON (DUDUN)
THAT'S A GOOD POINT.
PARA (FLIP)
RA RA
...BUT WE DON'T KNOW WHY ANYONE WOULD DO THAT.
PATAN (SHUT)
WHAT?

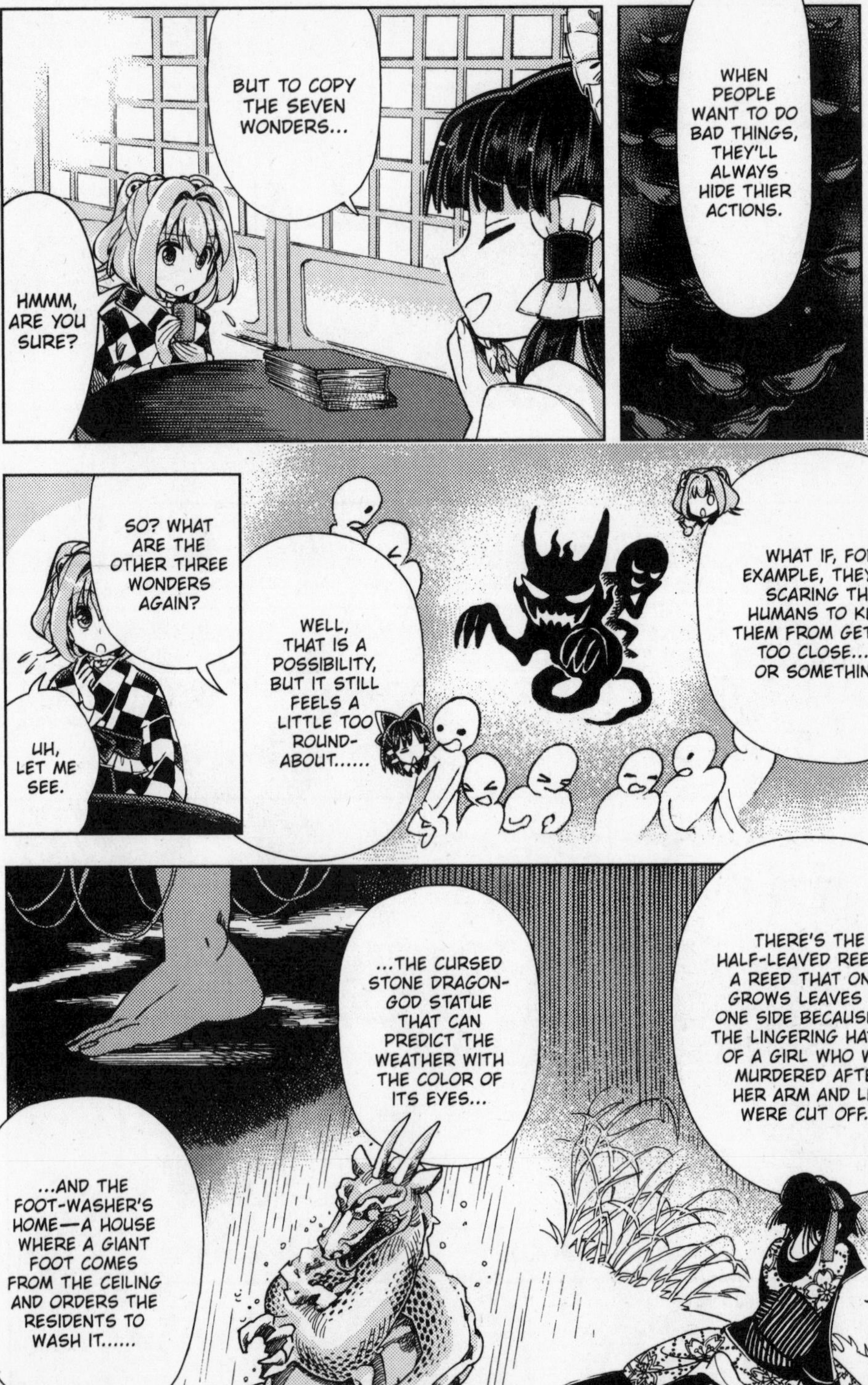
WHEN PEOPLE WANT TO DO BAD THINGS, THEY'LL ALWAYS HIDE THIER ACTIONS.
BUT TO COPY THE SEVEN WONDERS...
HMMM, ARE YOU SURE?
WHAT IF, FOR EXAMPLE, THEY'RE SCARING THE HUMANS TO KEEP THEM FROM GETTING TOO CLOSE...... OR SOMETHING.
WELL, THAT IS A POSSIBILITY, BUT IT STILL FEELS A LITTLE TOO ROUND-ABOUT......
SO? WHAT ARE THE OTHER THREE WONDERS AGAIN?
UH, LET ME SEE.
THERE'S THE HALF-LEAVED REED— A REED THAT ONLY GROWS LEAVES ON ONE SIDE BECAUSE OF THE LINGERING HATRED OF A GIRL WHO WAS MURDERED AFTER HER ARM AND LEG WERE CUT OFF...
...THE CURSED STONE DRAGON-GOD STATUE THAT CAN PREDICT THE WEATHER WITH THE COLOR OF ITS EYES...
...AND THE FOOT-WASHER'S HOME—A HOUSE WHERE A GIANT FOOT COMES FROM THE CEILING AND ORDERS THE RESIDENTS TO WASH IT......

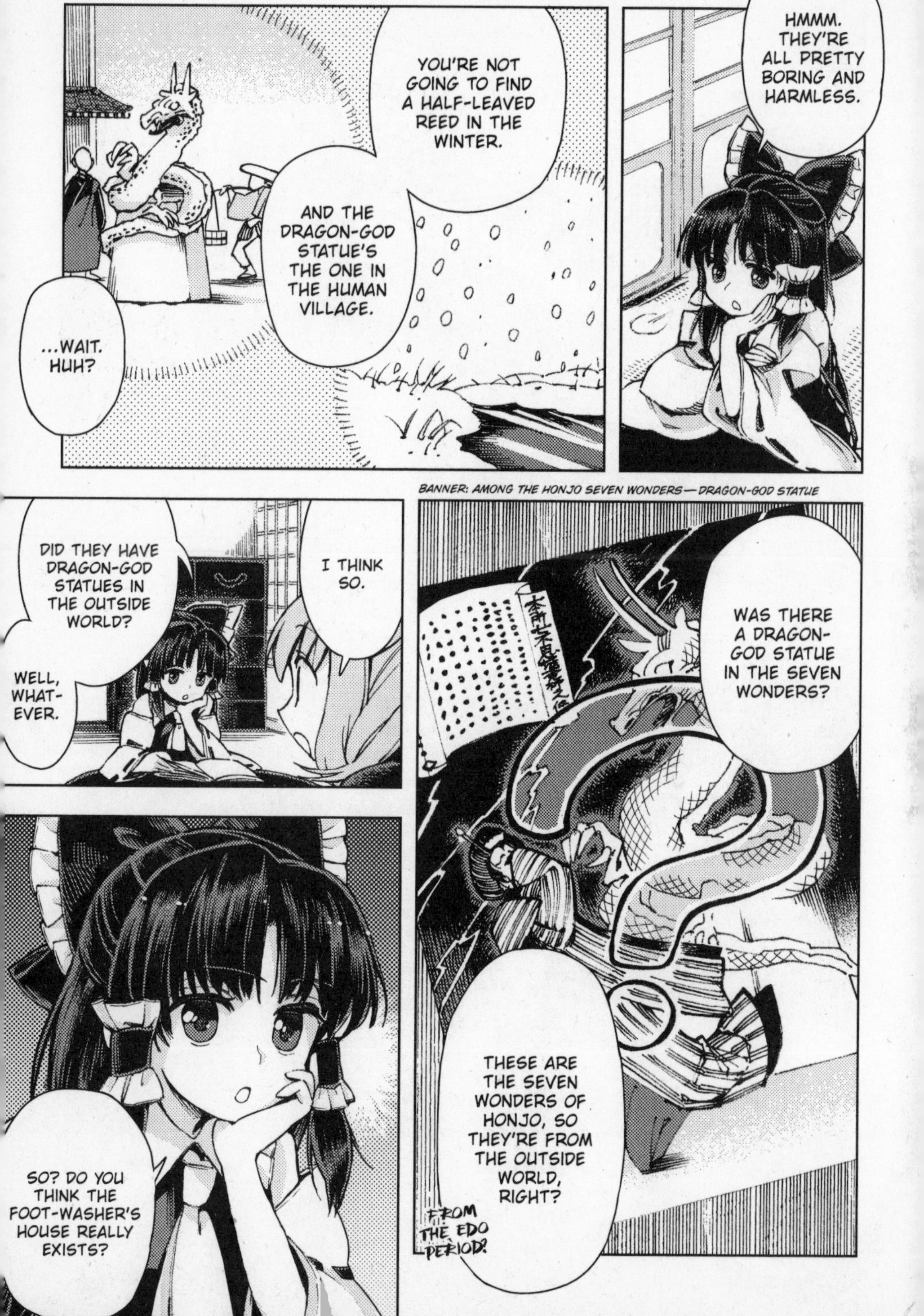
HMMM. THEY'RE ALL PRETTY BORING AND HARMLESS.
YOU'RE NOT GOING TO FIND A HALF-LEAVED REED IN THE WINTER.
AND THE DRAGON-GOD STATUE'S THE ONE IN THE HUMAN VILLAGE.
...WAIT. HUH?
BANNER: AMONG THE HONJO SEVEN WONDERS—DRAGON-GOD STATUE
WAS THERE A DRAGON-GOD STATUE IN THE SEVEN WONDERS?
THESE ARE THE SEVEN WONDERS OF HONJO, SO THEY'RE FROM THE OUTSIDE WORLD, RIGHT?
FROM THE EDO PERIOD!
I THINK SO.
DID THEY HAVE DRAGON-GOD STATUES IN THE OUTSIDE WORLD?
WELL, WHATEVER.
SO? DO YOU THINK THE FOOT-WASHER'S HOUSE REALLY EXISTS?

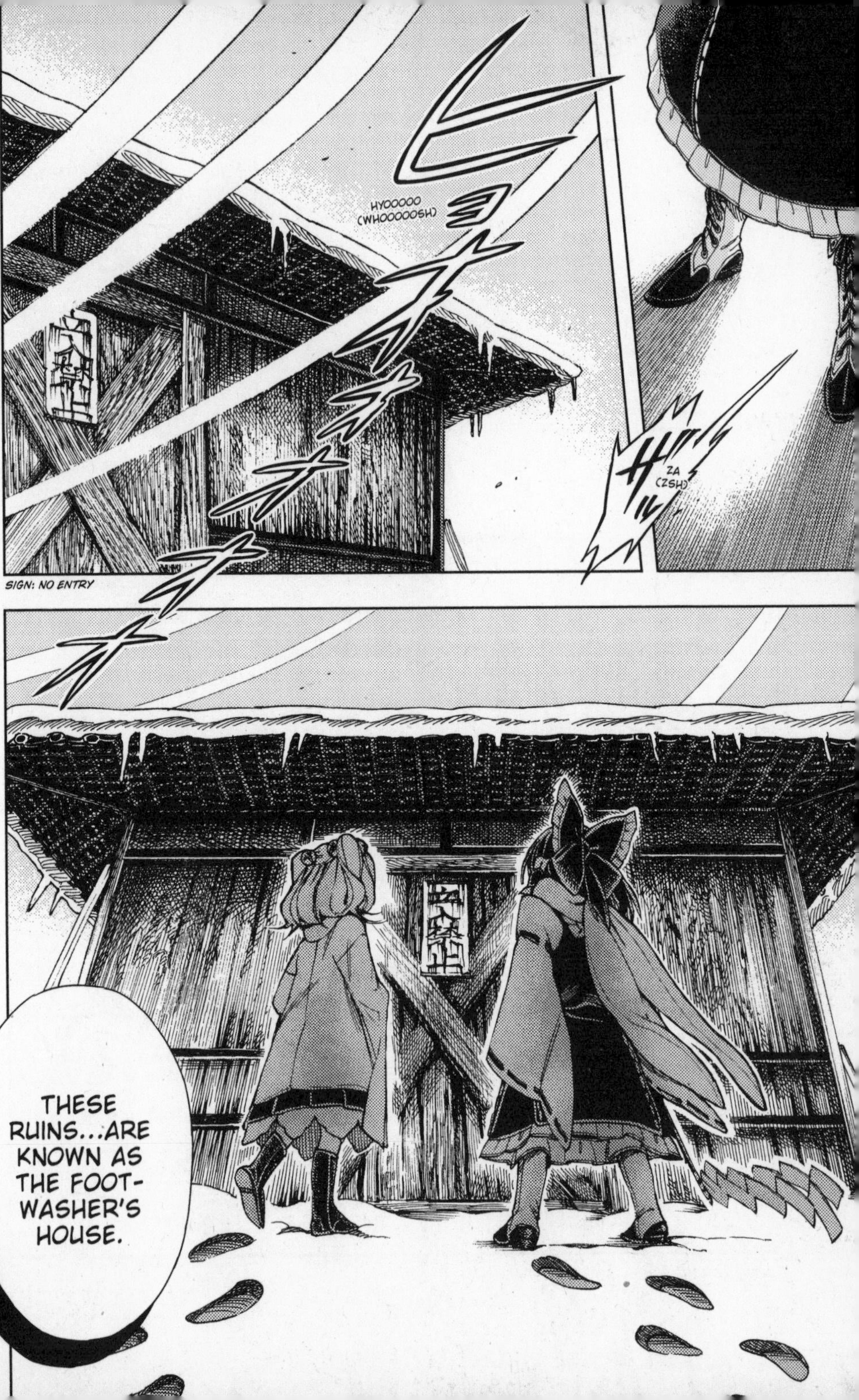
ZA (ZSH)
HYOOOOO (WHOOOOOSH)
SIGN: NO ENTRY
THESE RUINS...ARE KNOWN AS THE FOOT-WASHER'S HOUSE.

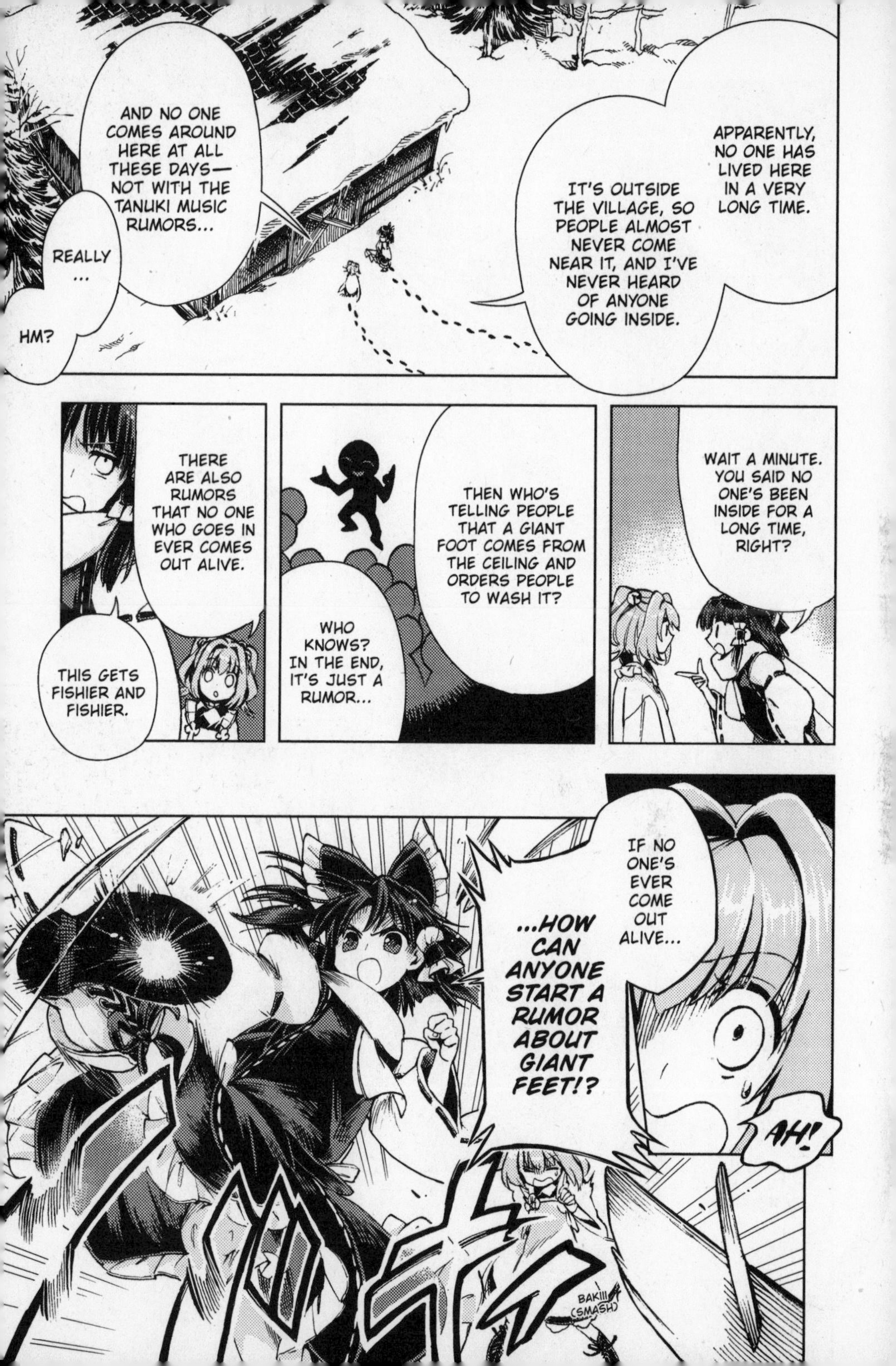
APPARENTLY, NO ONE HAS LIVED HERE IN A VERY LONG TIME.
IT'S OUTSIDE THE VILLAGE, SO PEOPLE ALMOST NEVER COME NEAR IT, AND I'VE NEVER HEARD OF ANYONE GOING INSIDE.
AND NO ONE COMES AROUND HERE AT ALL THESE DAYS— NOT WITH THE TANUKI MUSIC RUMORS...
REALLY ...
HM?
WAIT A MINUTE. YOU SAID NO ONE'S BEEN INSIDE FOR A LONG TIME, RIGHT?
THEN WHO'S TELLING PEOPLE THAT A GIANT FOOT COMES FROM THE CEILING AND ORDERS PEOPLE TO WASH IT?
WHO KNOWS? IN THE END, IT'S JUST A RUMOR...
THERE ARE ALSO RUMORS THAT NO ONE WHO GOES IN EVER COMES OUT ALIVE.
THIS GETS FISHIER AND FISHIER.
IF NO ONE'S EVER COME OUT ALIVE...
...HOW CAN ANYONE START A RUMOR ABOUT GIANT FEET!?
AH!
BAKIII (SMASH)

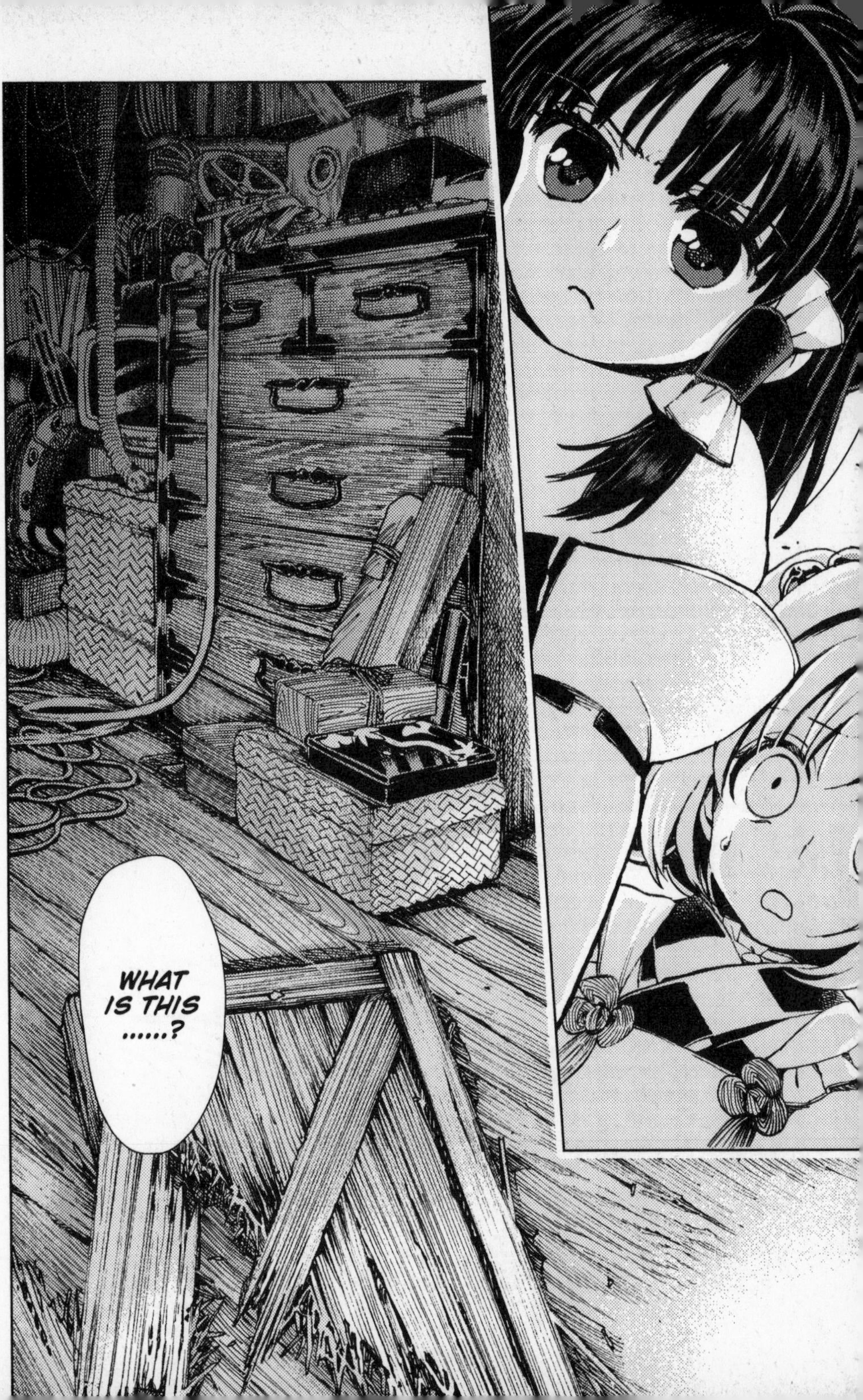
WHAT IS THIS ......?

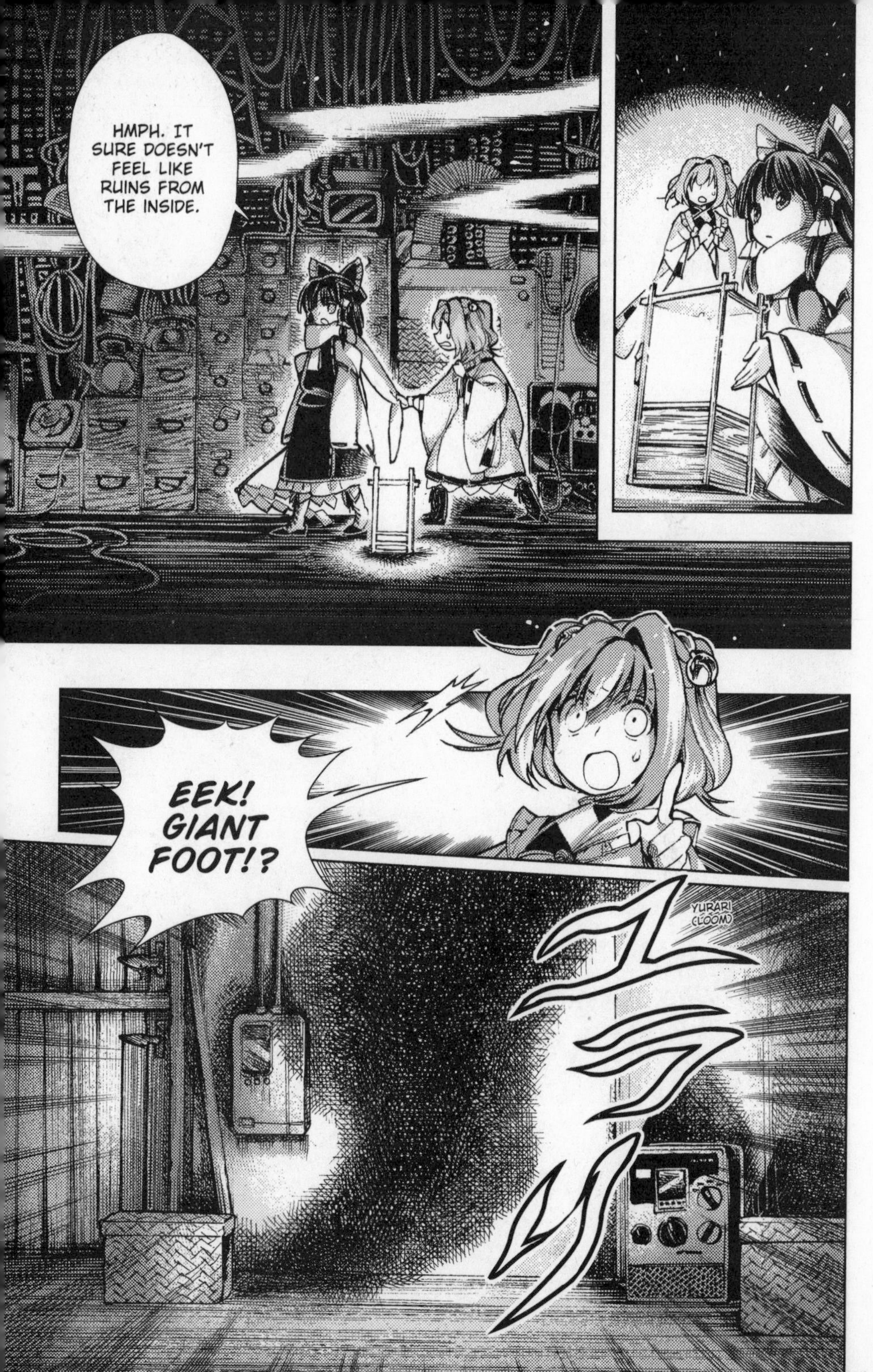
HMPH. IT SURE DOESN'T FEEL LIKE RUINS FROM THE INSIDE.
EEK! GIANT FOOT!?
YURARI (LOOM)

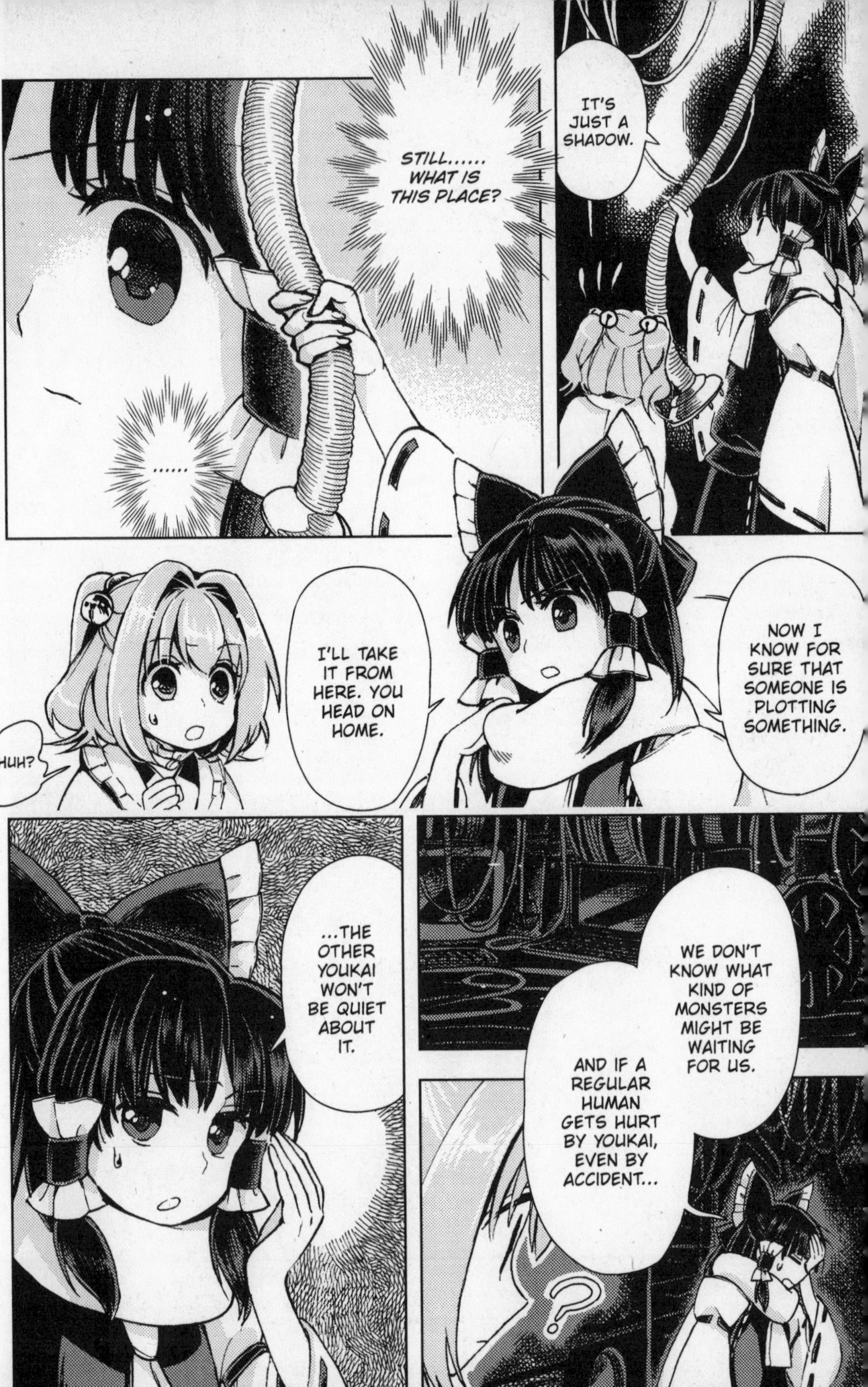
IT'S JUST A SHADOW.
STILL...... WHAT IS THIS PLACE?
......
NOW I KNOW FOR SURE THAT SOMEONE IS PLOTTING SOMETHING.
I'LL TAKE IT FROM HERE. YOU HEAD ON HOME.
HUH?
WE DON'T KNOW WHAT KIND OF MONSTERS MIGHT BE WAITING FOR US.
AND IF A REGULAR HUMAN GETS HURT BY YOUKAI, EVEN BY ACCIDENT...
?
...THE OTHER YOUKAI WON'T BE QUIET ABOUT IT.

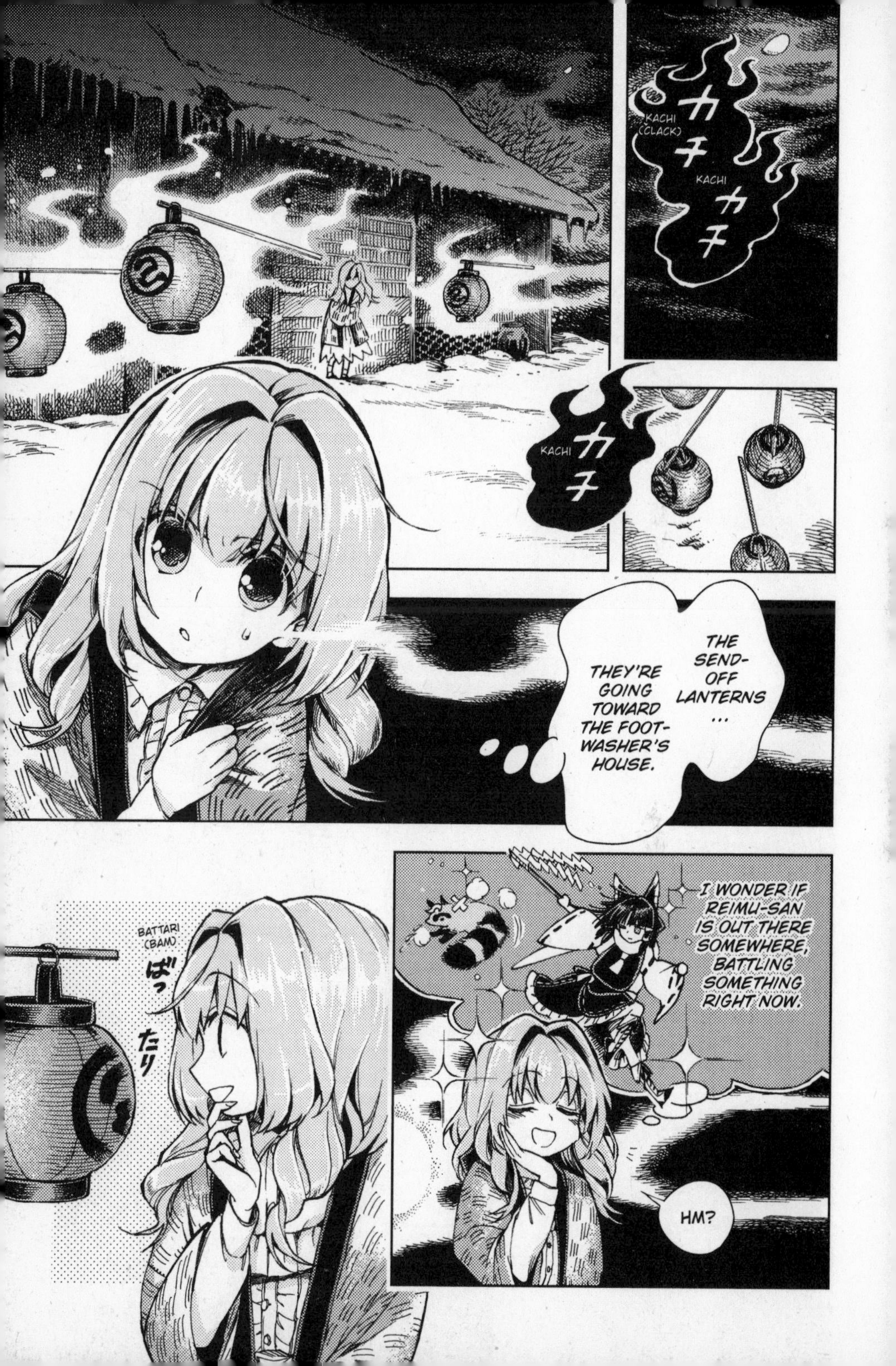

KACHI (CLACK)
カチ
KACHI
カチ
KACHI
カチ
THE SEND-OFF LANTERNS...
THEY'RE GOING TOWARD THE FOOT-WASHER'S HOUSE.
I WONDER IF REIMU-SAN IS OUT THERE SOMEWHERE, BATTLING SOMETHING RIGHT NOW.
HM?
BATTARI (BAM)
ばったり

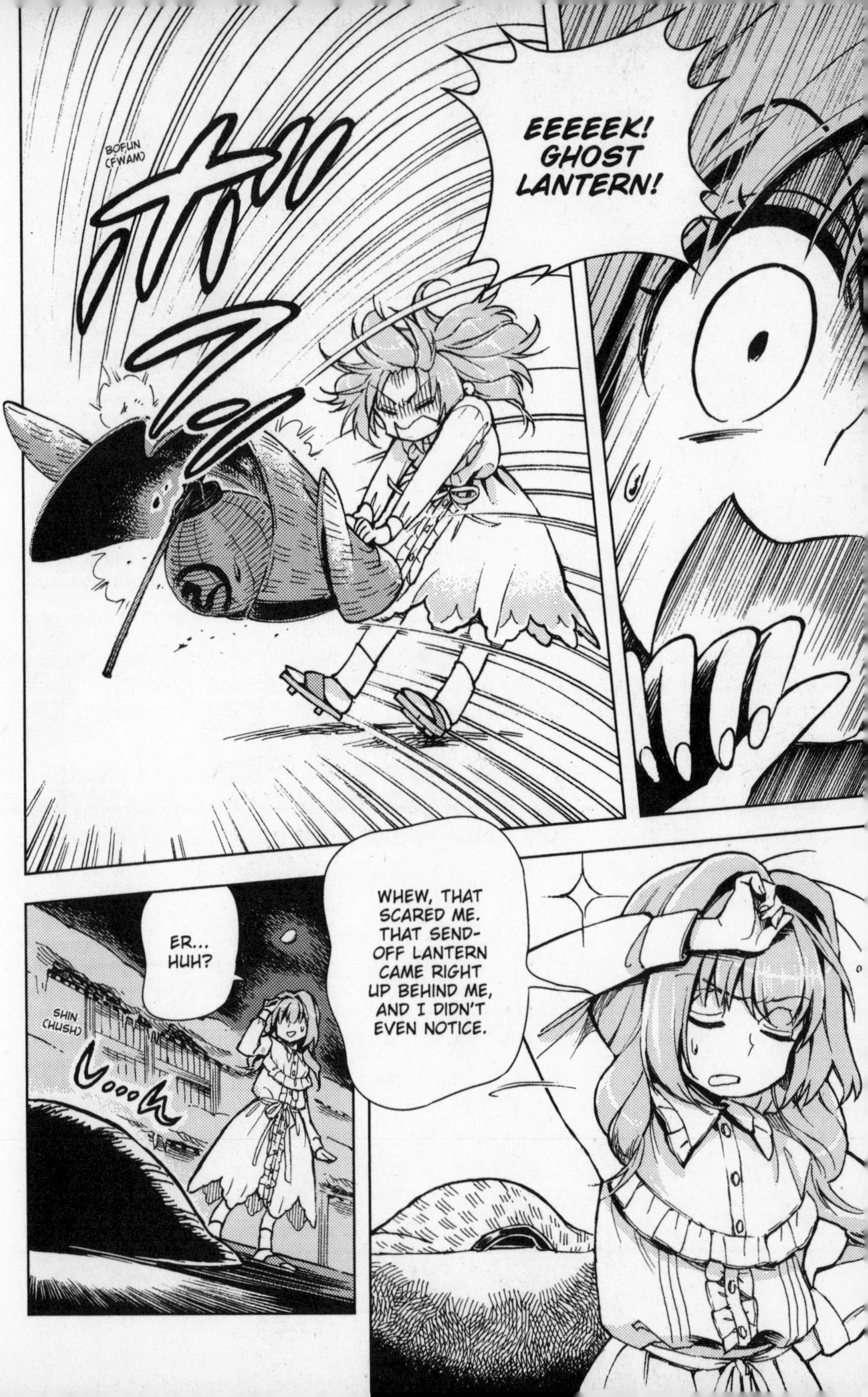
EEEEEK! GHOST LANTERN!
BOFUN (FWAM)
WHEW, THAT SCARED ME. THAT SEND-OFF LANTERN CAME RIGHT UP BEHIND ME, AND I DIDN'T EVEN NOTICE.
ER... HUH?
SHIN (CHUSH)

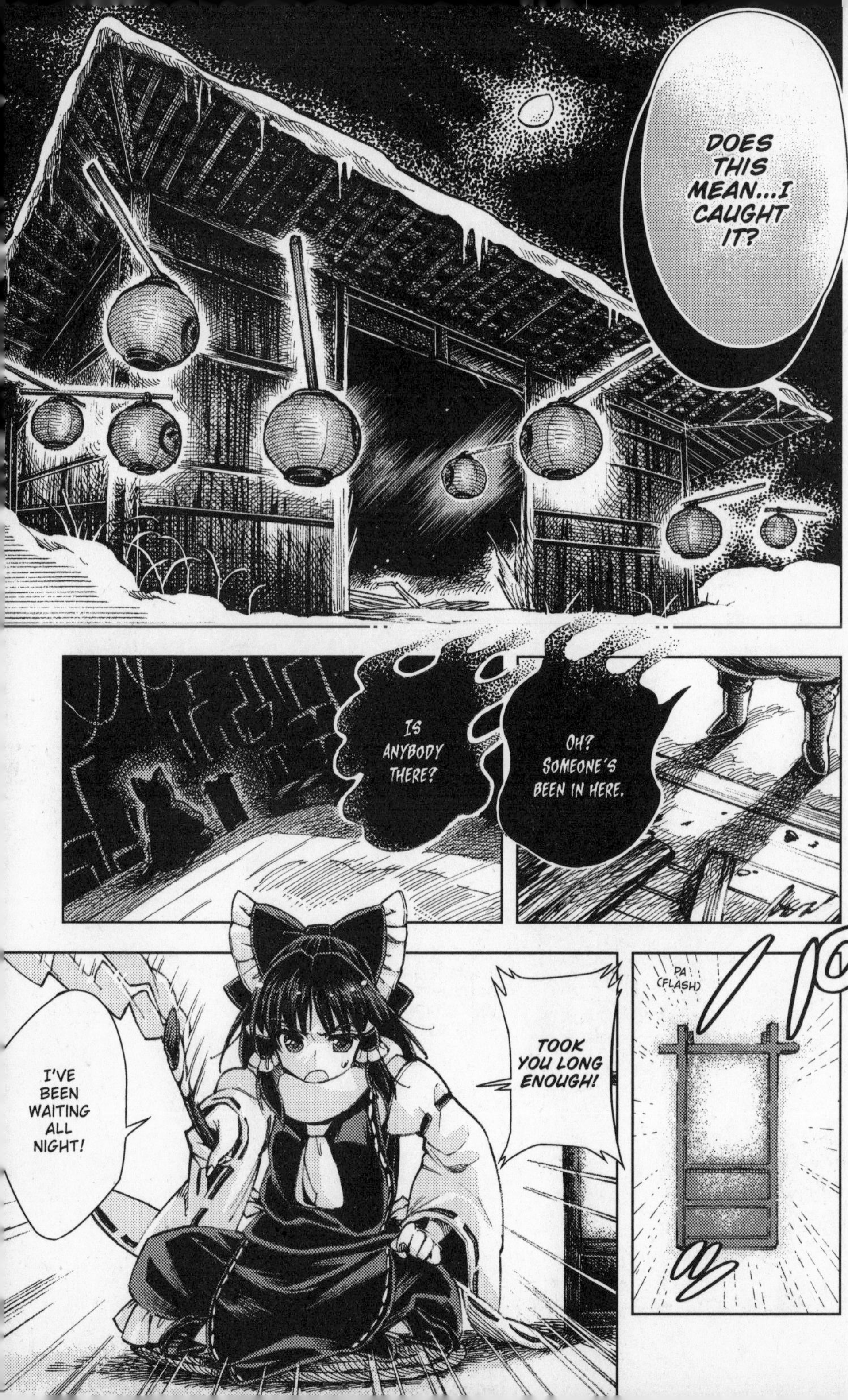
DOES THIS MEAN...I CAUGHT IT?
OH? SOMEONE'S BEEN IN HERE.
IS ANYBODY THERE?
PA (FLASH)
TOOK YOU LONG ENOUGH!
I'VE BEEN WAITING ALL NIGHT!

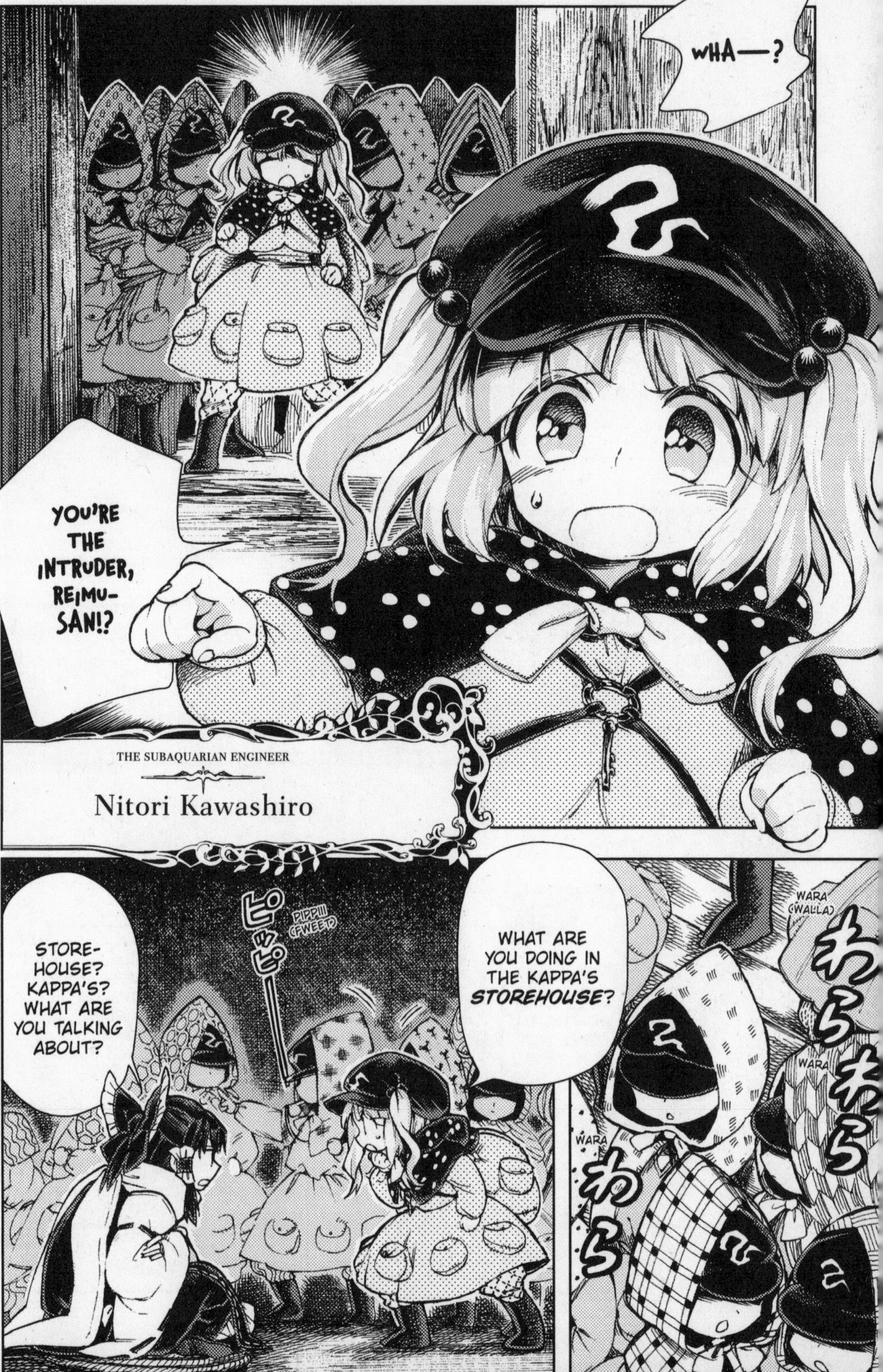
WHA—?
YOU'RE THE INTRUDER, REIMU-SAN!?
THE SUBAQUARIAN ENGINEER
Nitori Kawashiro
わらわら
WARA (WALLA)
WARA
わらわら
WARA
WHAT ARE YOU DOING IN THE KAPPA'S STOREHOUSE?
ピッピ
PIPPI!! (FWEET)
STORE-HOUSE? KAPPA'S? WHAT ARE YOU TALKING ABOUT?

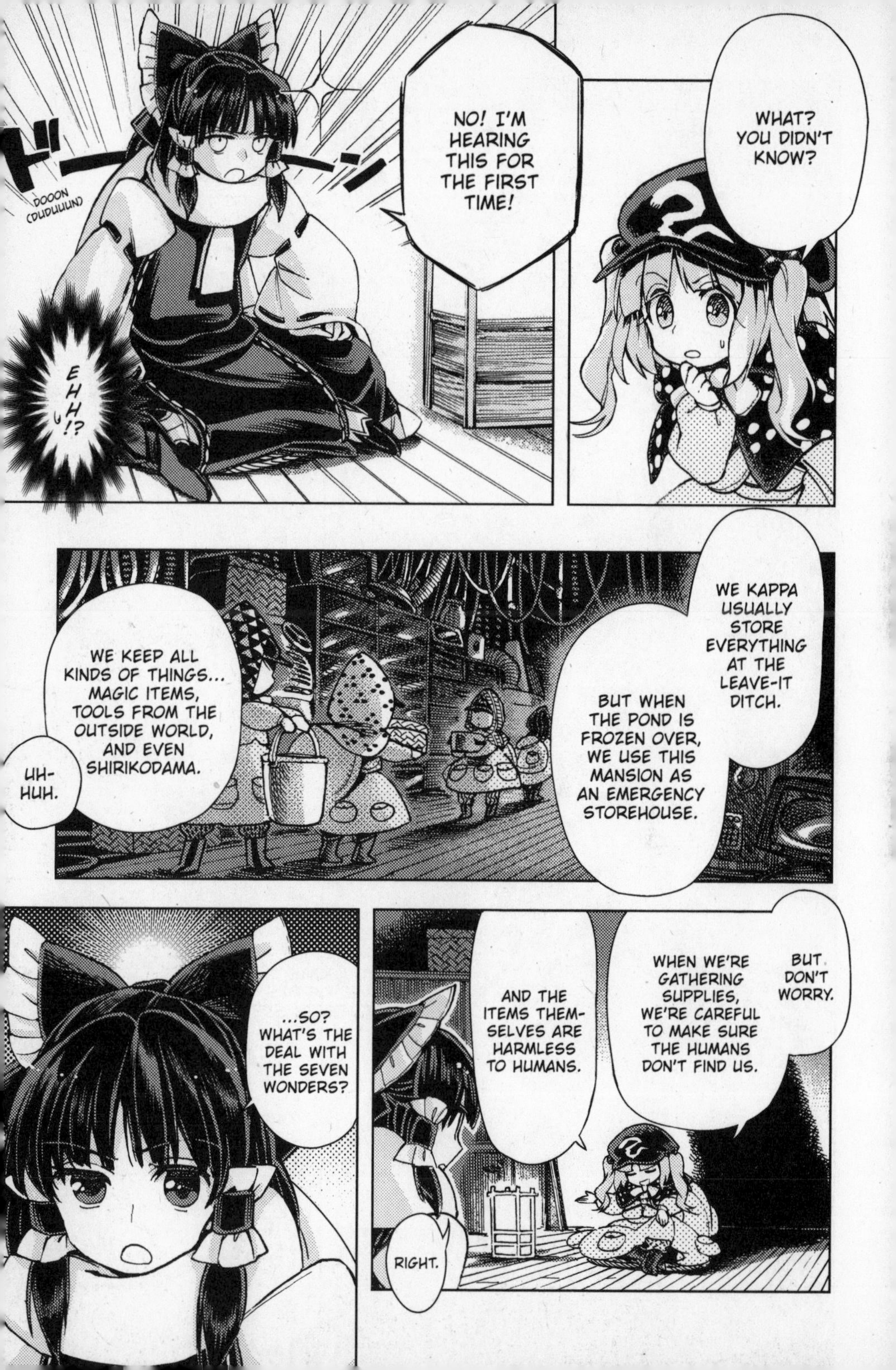
WHAT? YOU DIDN'T KNOW?
NO! I'M HEARING THIS FOR THE FIRST TIME!
DOOON (DUDUUUN)
EHH!?
WE KAPPA USUALLY STORE EVERYTHING AT THE LEAVE-IT DITCH.
BUT WHEN THE POND IS FROZEN OVER, WE USE THIS MANSION AS AN EMERGENCY STOREHOUSE.
WE KEEP ALL KINDS OF THINGS... MAGIC ITEMS, TOOLS FROM THE OUTSIDE WORLD, AND EVEN SHIRIKODAMA.
UH-HUH.
BUT DON'T WORRY.
WHEN WE'RE GATHERING SUPPLIES, WE'RE CAREFUL TO MAKE SURE THE HUMANS DON'T FIND US.
AND THE ITEMS THEMSELVES ARE HARMLESS TO HUMANS.
RIGHT.
...SO? WHAT'S THE DEAL WITH THE SEVEN WONDERS?

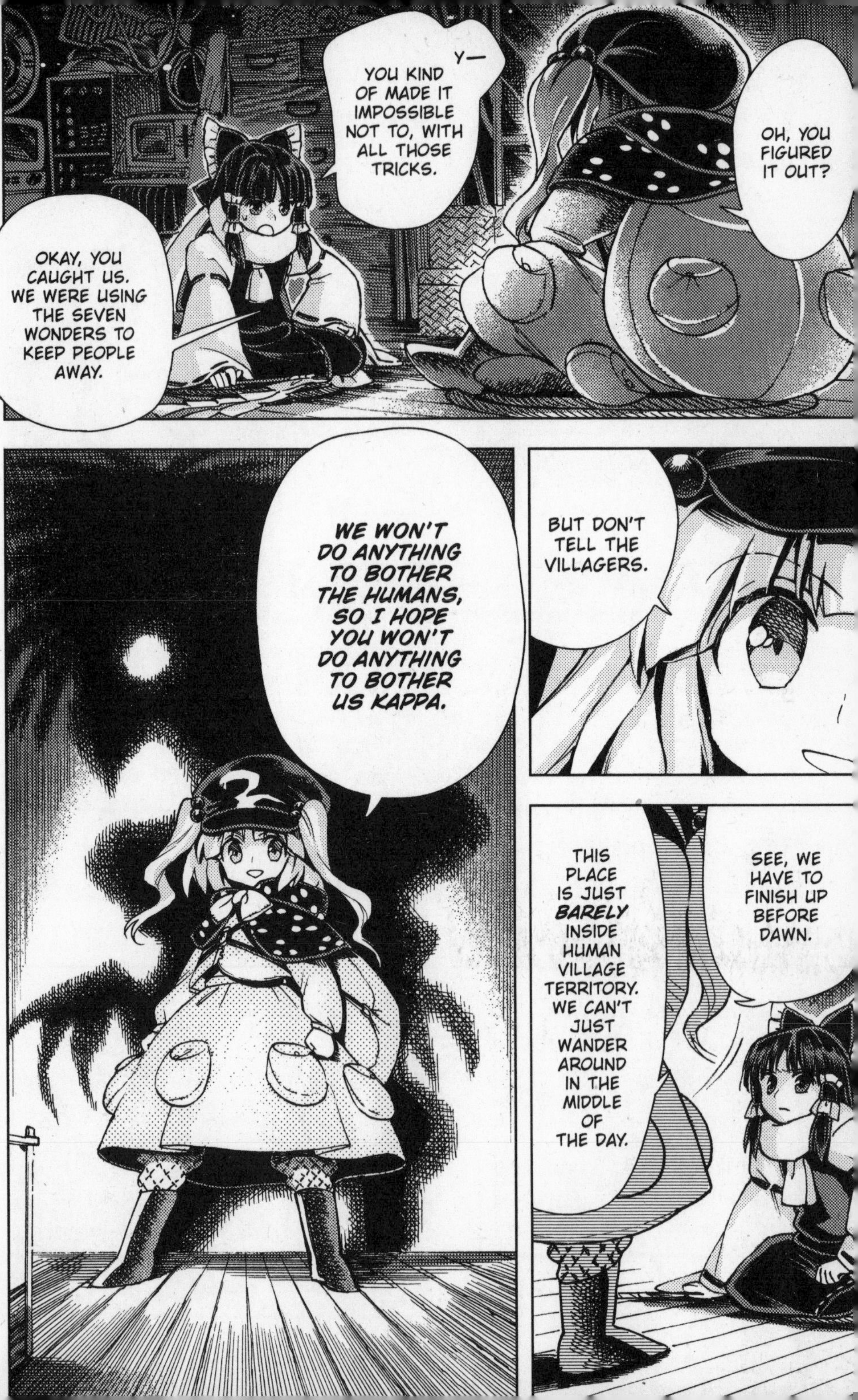
OH, YOU FIGURED IT OUT?
Y— YOU KIND OF MADE IT IMPOSSIBLE NOT TO, WITH ALL THOSE TRICKS.
OKAY, YOU CAUGHT US. WE WERE USING THE SEVEN WONDERS TO KEEP PEOPLE AWAY.
BUT DON'T TELL THE VILLAGERS.
SEE, WE HAVE TO FINISH UP BEFORE DAWN.
THIS PLACE IS JUST *BARELY* INSIDE HUMAN VILLAGE TERRITORY. WE CAN'T JUST WANDER AROUND IN THE MIDDLE OF THE DAY.
*WE WON'T DO ANYTHING TO BOTHER THE HUMANS, SO I HOPE YOU WON'T DO ANYTHING TO BOTHER US KAPPA.*

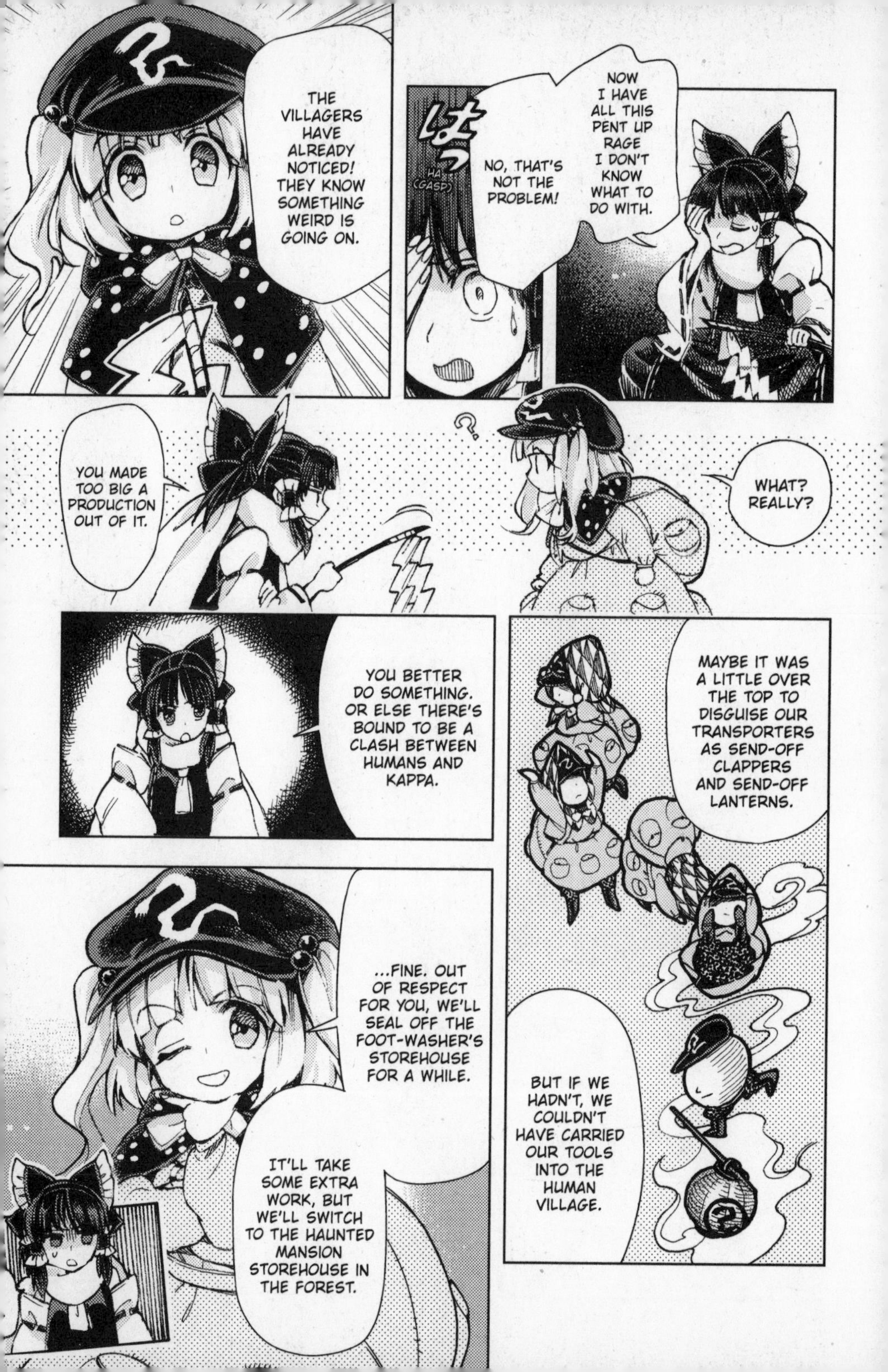
NOW I HAVE ALL THIS PENT UP RAGE I DON'T KNOW WHAT TO DO WITH.
はっ
HA (GASP)
NO, THAT'S NOT THE PROBLEM!
THE VILLAGERS HAVE ALREADY NOTICED! THEY KNOW SOMETHING WEIRD IS GOING ON.
WHAT? REALLY?
YOU MADE TOO BIG A PRODUCTION OUT OF IT.
MAYBE IT WAS A LITTLE OVER THE TOP TO DISGUISE OUR TRANSPORTERS AS SEND-OFF CLAPPERS AND SEND-OFF LANTERNS.
BUT IF WE HADN'T, WE COULDN'T HAVE CARRIED OUR TOOLS INTO THE HUMAN VILLAGE.
YOU BETTER DO SOMETHING. OR ELSE THERE'S BOUND TO BE A CLASH BETWEEN HUMANS AND KAPPA.
...FINE. OUT OF RESPECT FOR YOU, WE'LL SEAL OFF THE FOOT-WASHER'S STOREHOUSE FOR A WHILE.
IT'LL TAKE SOME EXTRA WORK, BUT WE'LL SWITCH TO THE HAUNTED MANSION STOREHOUSE IN THE FOREST.

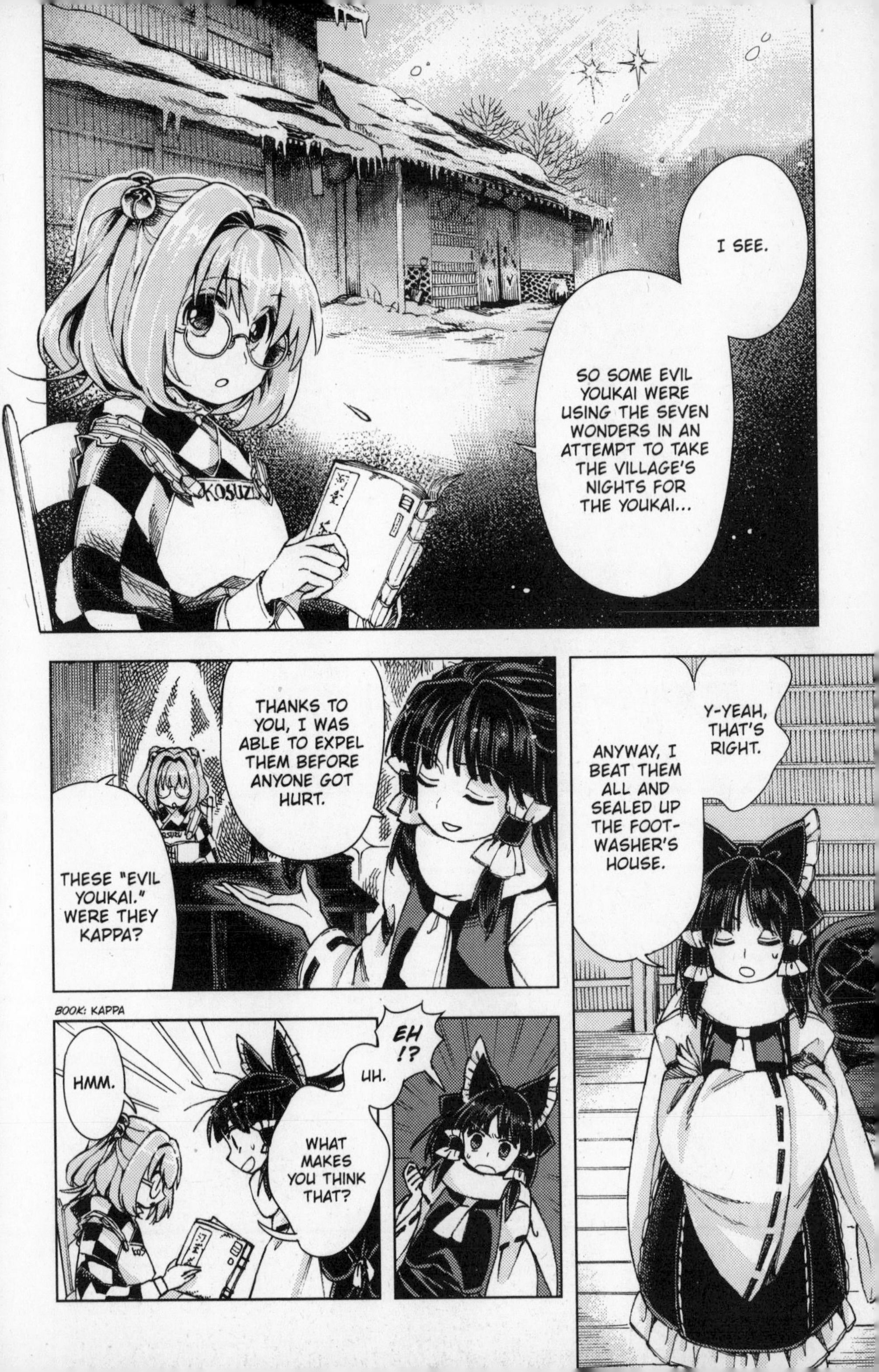
I SEE.
SO SOME EVIL YOUKAI WERE USING THE SEVEN WONDERS IN AN ATTEMPT TO TAKE THE VILLAGE'S NIGHTS FOR THE YOUKAI...
Y-YEAH, THAT'S RIGHT.
ANYWAY, I BEAT THEM ALL AND SEALED UP THE FOOT-WASHER'S HOUSE.
THANKS TO YOU, I WAS ABLE TO EXPEL THEM BEFORE ANYONE GOT HURT.
THESE "EVIL YOUKAI." WERE THEY KAPPA?
BOOK: KAPPA
EH!?
UH.
WHAT MAKES YOU THINK THAT?
HMM.

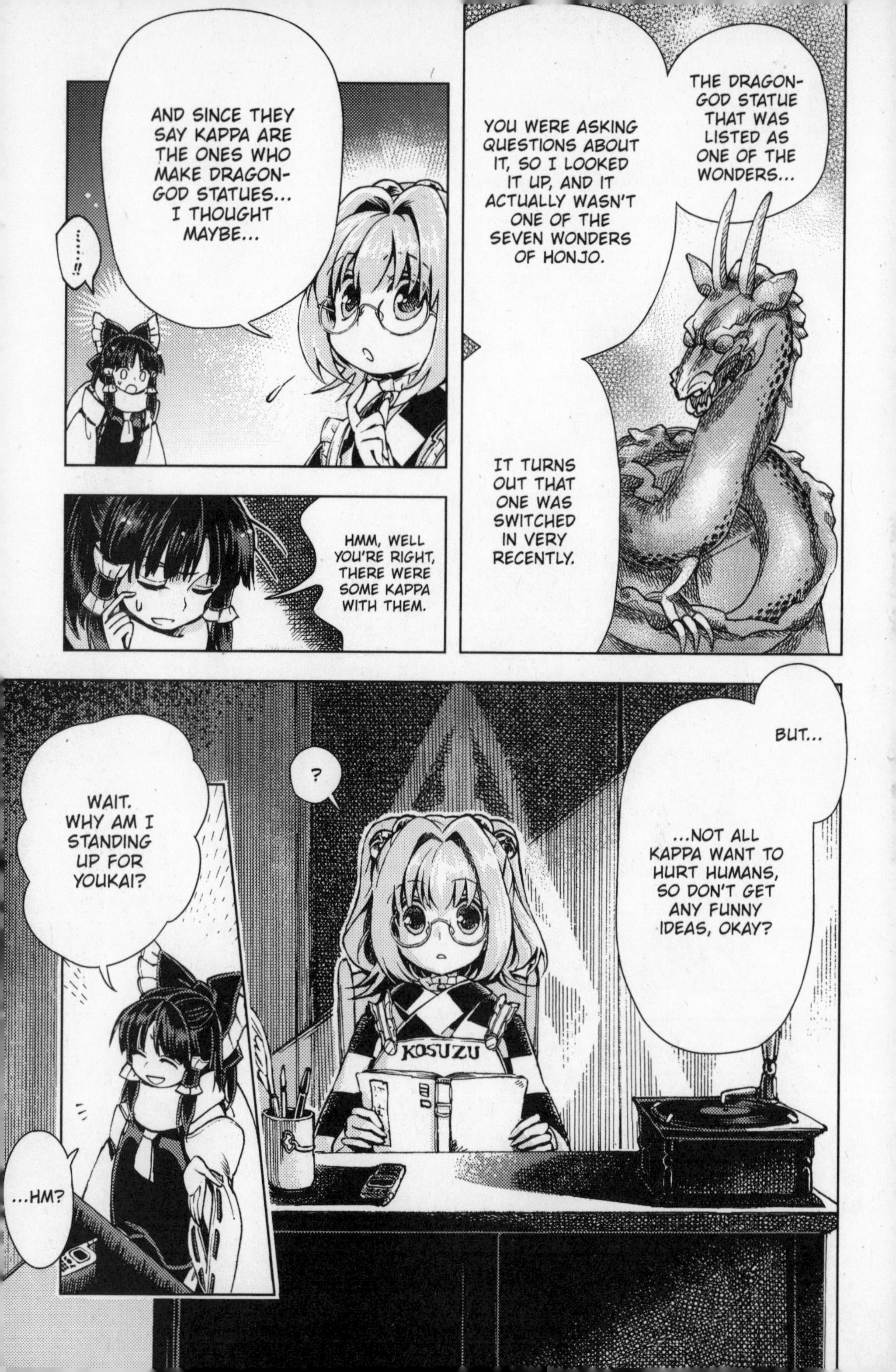
THE DRAGON-GOD STATUE THAT WAS LISTED AS ONE OF THE WONDERS...
YOU WERE ASKING QUESTIONS ABOUT IT, SO I LOOKED IT UP, AND IT ACTUALLY WASN'T ONE OF THE SEVEN WONDERS OF HONJO.
IT TURNS OUT THAT ONE WAS SWITCHED IN VERY RECENTLY.
AND SINCE THEY SAY KAPPA ARE THE ONES WHO MAKE DRAGON-GOD STATUES... I THOUGHT MAYBE...
......!!
HMM, WELL YOU'RE RIGHT, THERE WERE SOME KAPPA WITH THEM.
BUT...
...NOT ALL KAPPA WANT TO HURT HUMANS, SO DON'T GET ANY FUNNY IDEAS, OKAY?
?
KOSUZU
WAIT. WHY AM I STANDING UP FOR YOUKAI?
...HM?

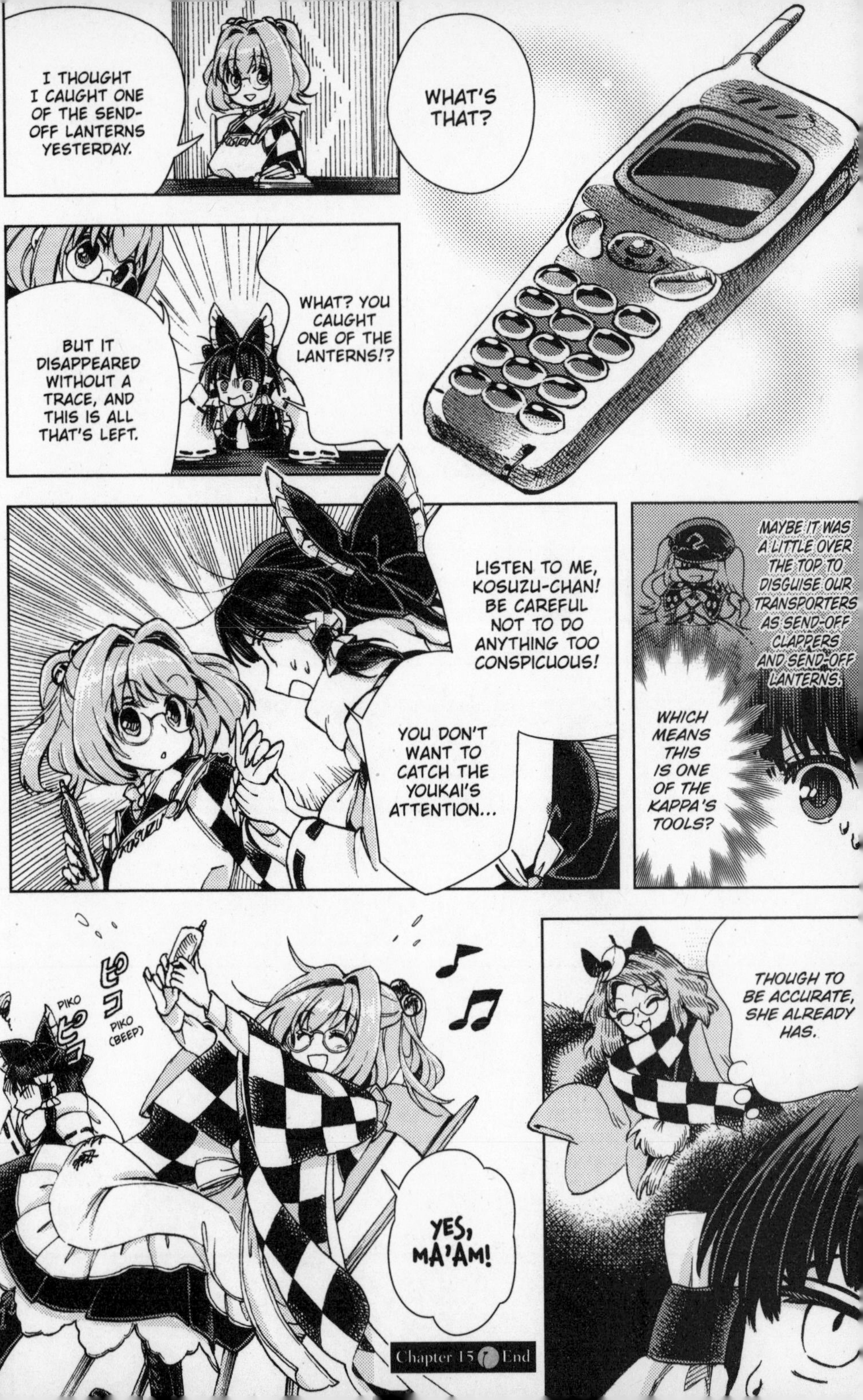
WHAT'S THAT?
I THOUGHT I CAUGHT ONE OF THE SEND-OFF LANTERNS YESTERDAY.
WHAT? YOU CAUGHT ONE OF THE LANTERNS!?
BUT IT DISAPPEARED WITHOUT A TRACE, AND THIS IS ALL THAT'S LEFT.
MAYBE IT WAS A LITTLE OVER THE TOP TO DISGUISE OUR TRANSPORTERS AS SEND-OFF CLAPPERS AND SEND-OFF LANTERNS.
WHICH MEANS THIS IS ONE OF THE KAPPA'S TOOLS?
LISTEN TO ME, KOSUZU-CHAN! BE CAREFUL NOT TO DO ANYTHING TOO CONSPICUOUS!
YOU DON'T WANT TO CATCH THE YOUKAI'S ATTENTION...
THOUGH TO BE ACCURATE, SHE ALREADY HAS.
PIKO PIKO (BEEP)
YES, MA'AM!
Chapter 15 End

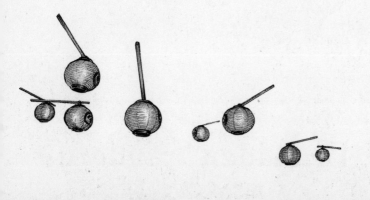

Forbidden Scrollery

## Chapter 16 Love Letters with a Past Part 1

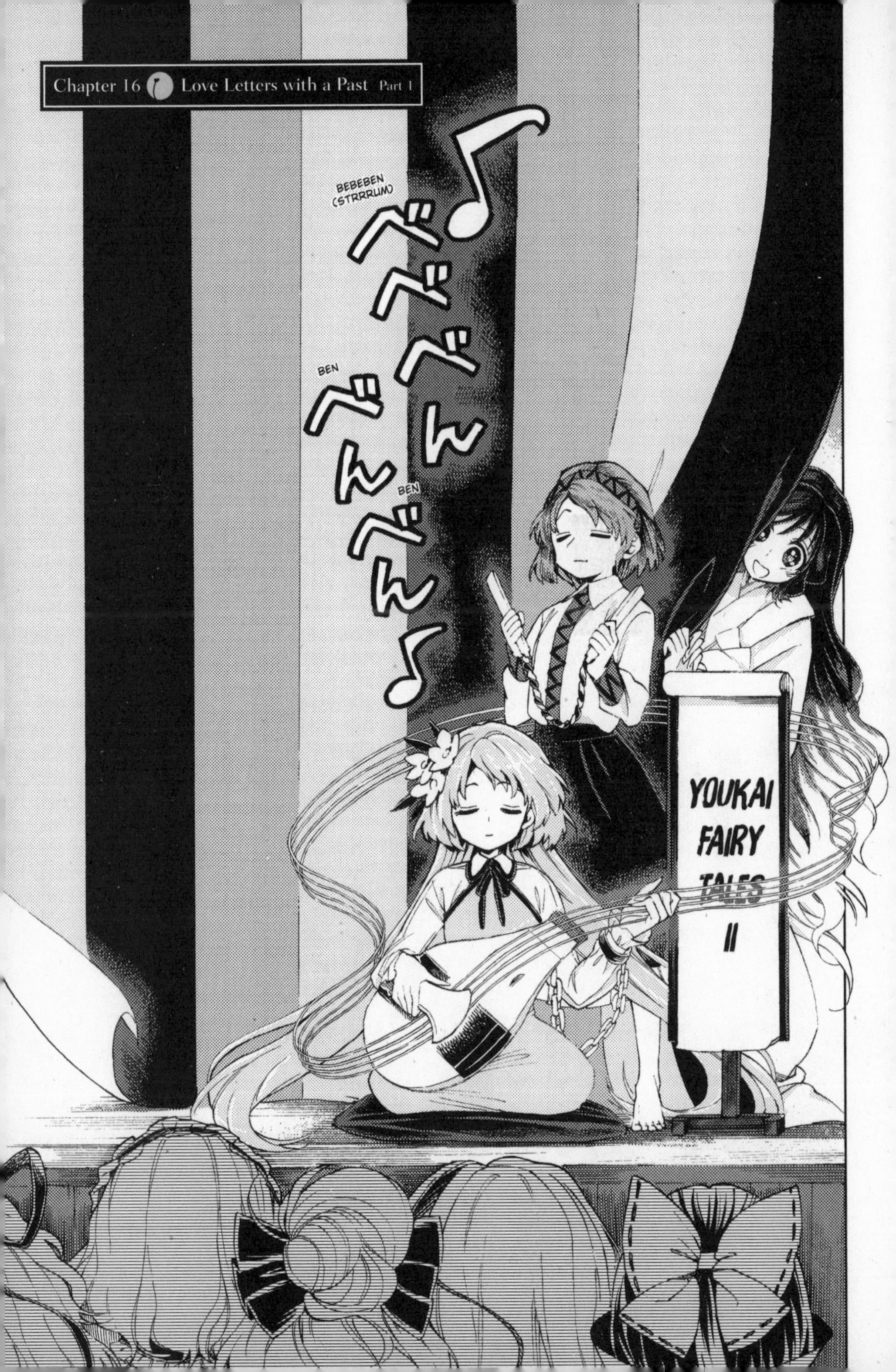
べべべん
BEBEBEN (STRRRUM)
べんべん
BEN
BEN
YOUKAI FAIRY TALES II

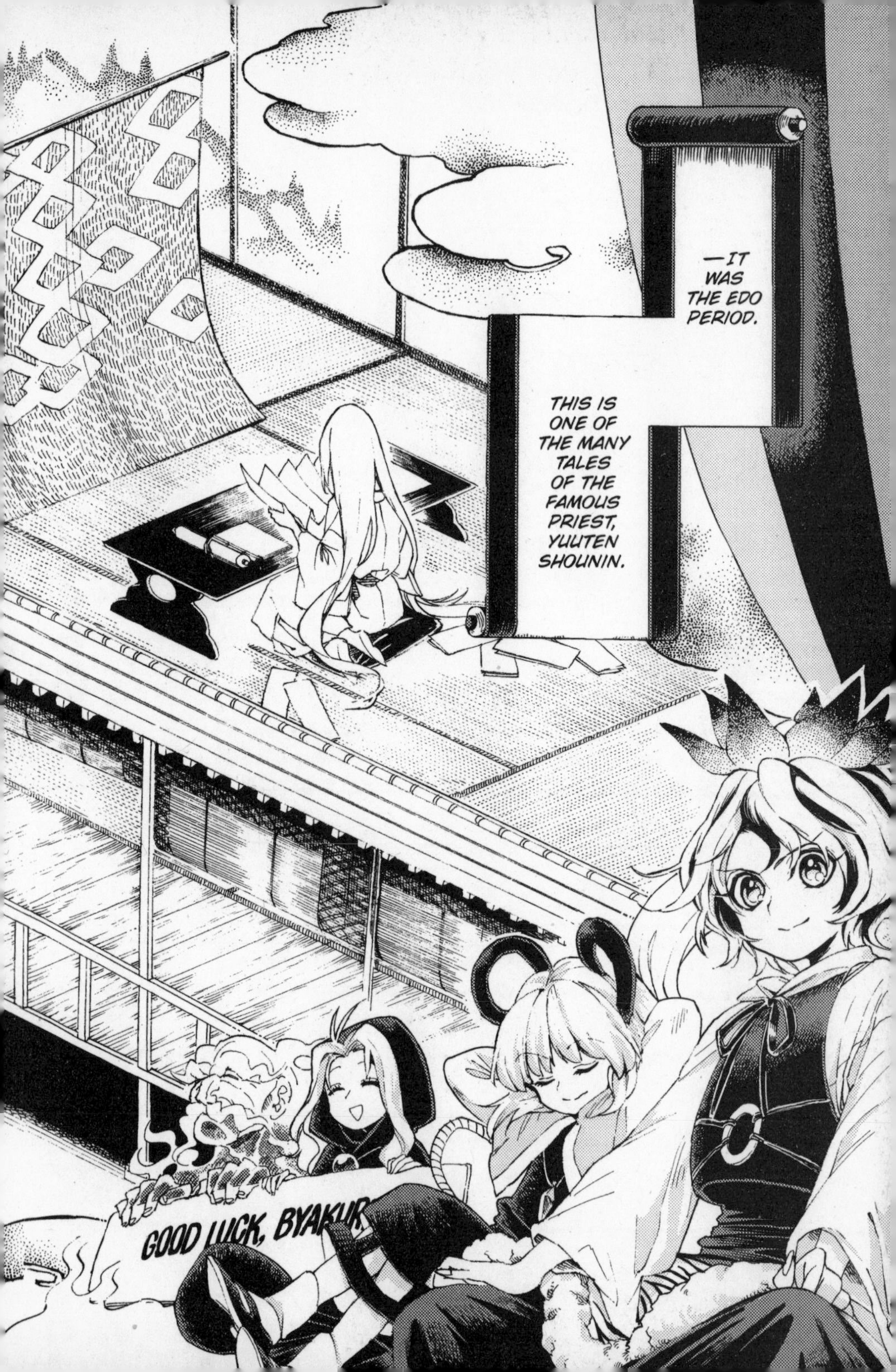
—IT WAS THE EDO PERIOD.
THIS IS ONE OF THE MANY TALES OF THE FAMOUS PRIEST, YUUTEN SHOUNIN.
GOOD LUCK, BYAKUR

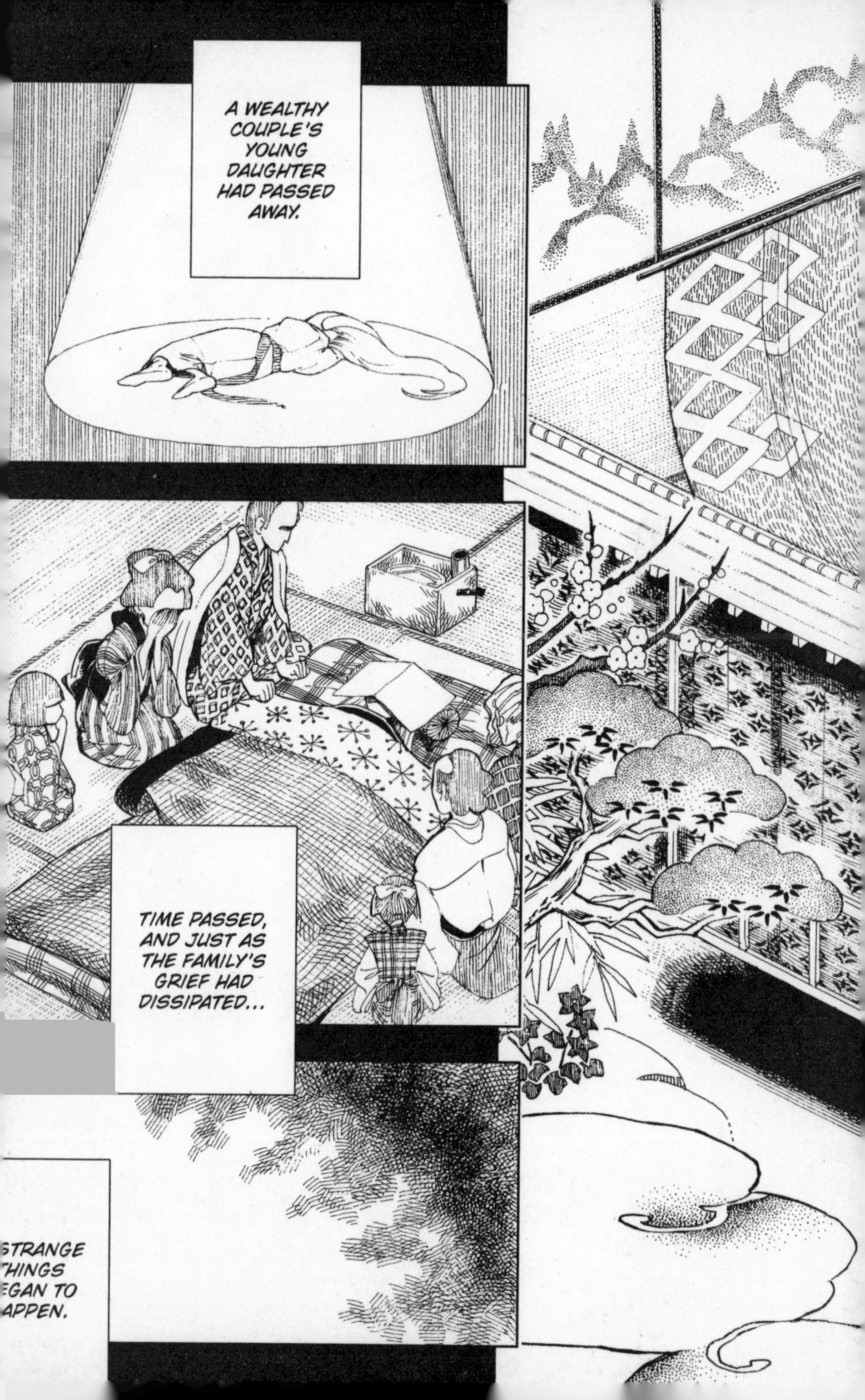
A WEALTHY COUPLE'S YOUNG DAUGHTER HAD PASSED AWAY.
TIME PASSED, AND JUST AS THE FAMILY'S GRIEF HAD DISSIPATED...
STRANGE THINGS EGAN TO APPEN.

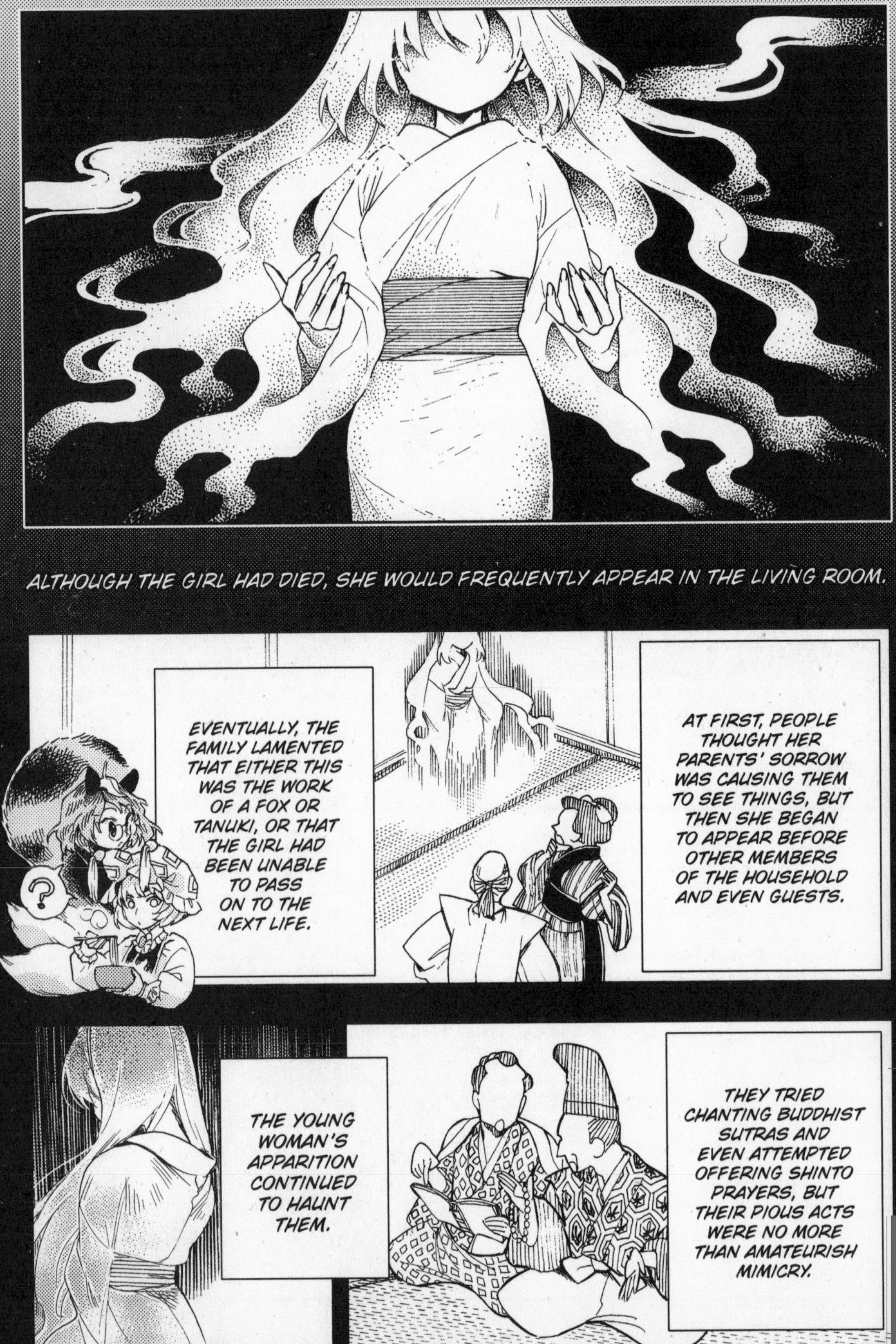
ALTHOUGH THE GIRL HAD DIED, SHE WOULD FREQUENTLY APPEAR IN THE LIVING ROOM.
AT FIRST, PEOPLE THOUGHT HER PARENTS' SORROW WAS CAUSING THEM TO SEE THINGS, BUT THEN SHE BEGAN TO APPEAR BEFORE OTHER MEMBERS OF THE HOUSEHOLD AND EVEN GUESTS.
EVENTUALLY, THE FAMILY LAMENTED THAT EITHER THIS WAS THE WORK OF A FOX OR TANUKI, OR THAT THE GIRL HAD BEEN UNABLE TO PASS ON TO THE NEXT LIFE.
THEY TRIED CHANTING BUDDHIST SUTRAS AND EVEN ATTEMPTED OFFERING SHINTO PRAYERS, BUT THEIR PIOUS ACTS WERE NO MORE THAN AMATEURISH MIMICRY.
THE YOUNG WOMAN'S APPARITION CONTINUED TO HAUNT THEM.

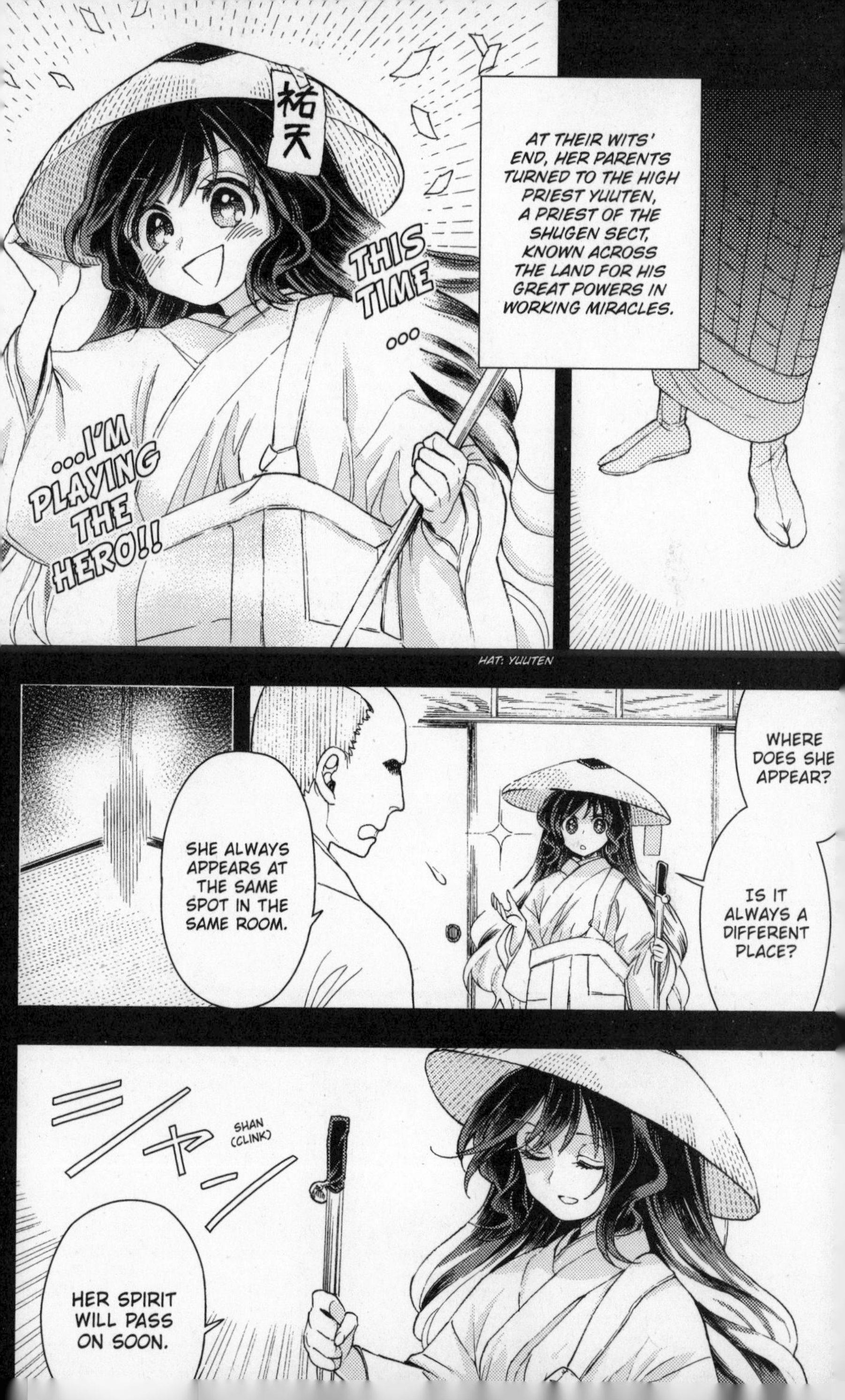
AT THEIR WITS' END, HER PARENTS TURNED TO THE HIGH PRIEST YUUTEN, A PRIEST OF THE SHUGEN SECT, KNOWN ACROSS THE LAND FOR HIS GREAT POWERS IN WORKING MIRACLES.
祐天
THIS TIME ooo
oooI'M PLAYING THE HERO!!
HAT: YUUTEN
WHERE DOES SHE APPEAR?
IS IT ALWAYS A DIFFERENT PLACE?
SHE ALWAYS APPEARS AT THE SAME SPOT IN THE SAME ROOM.
シャーン
SHAN (CLINK)
HER SPIRIT WILL PASS ON SOON.

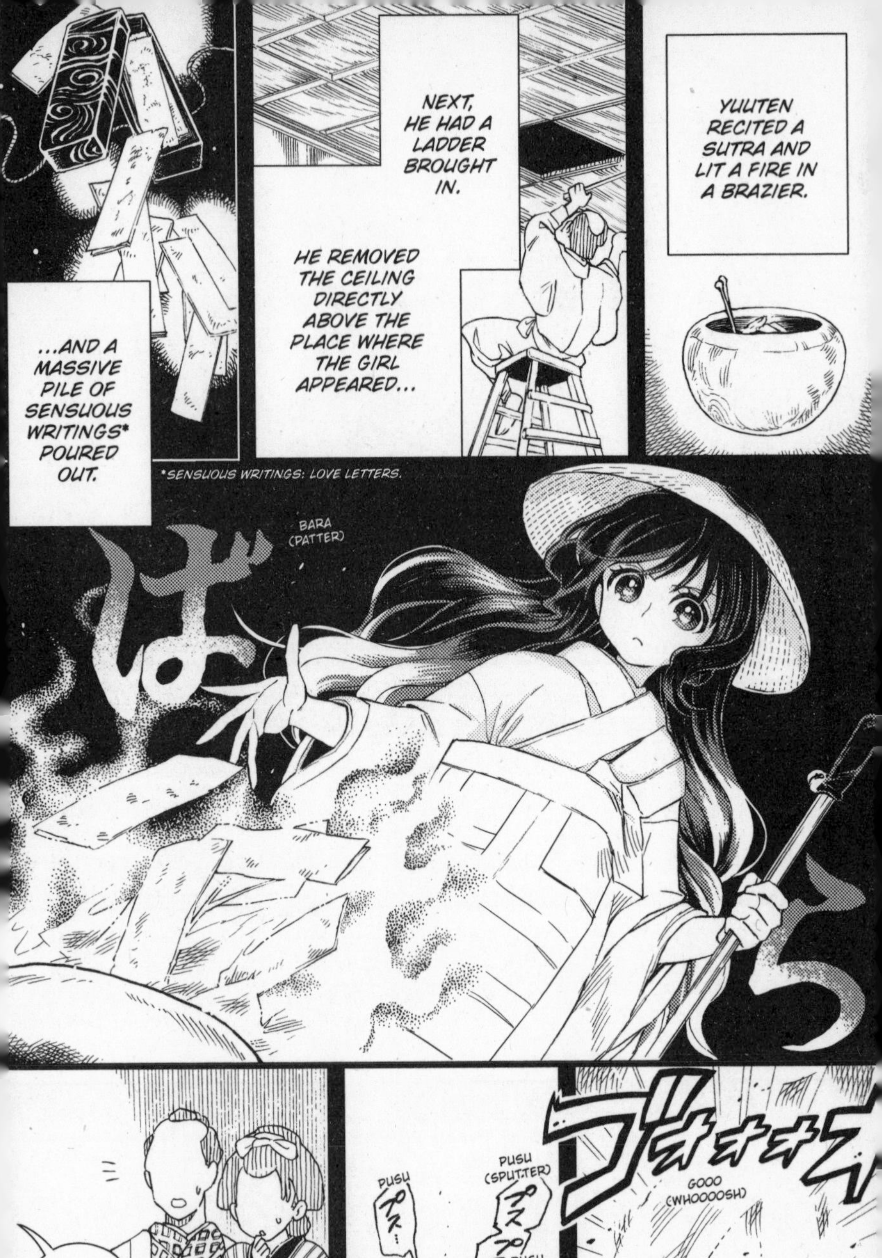
YUUTEN RECITED A SUTRA AND LIT A FIRE IN A BRAZIER.
NEXT, HE HAD A LADDER BROUGHT IN.
HE REMOVED THE CEILING DIRECTLY ABOVE THE PLACE WHERE THE GIRL APPEARED...
...AND A MASSIVE PILE OF SENSUOUS WRITINGS* POURED OUT.
*SENSUOUS WRITINGS: LOVE LETTERS.
ばら
BARA (PATTER)
ゴォォォ
GOOO (WHOOOOSH)
ぷす
PUSU (SPUTTER)
ぷすぷす
PUSU
PUSU
LET YOUR MINDS BE AT EASE.

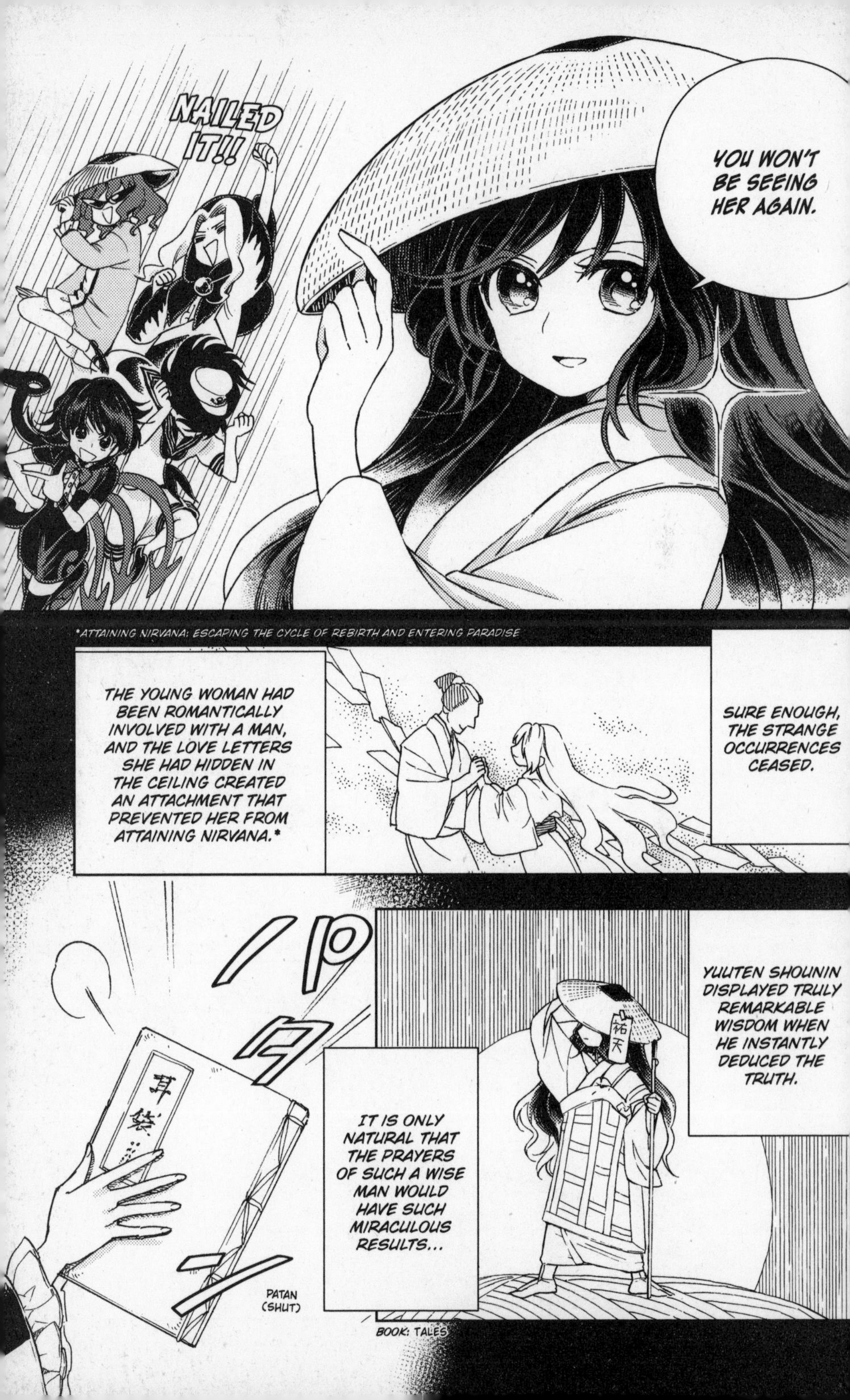
YOU WON'T BE SEEING HER AGAIN.
NAILED IT!!
SURE ENOUGH, THE STRANGE OCCURRENCES CEASED.
THE YOUNG WOMAN HAD BEEN ROMANTICALLY INVOLVED WITH A MAN, AND THE LOVE LETTERS SHE HAD HIDDEN IN THE CEILING CREATED AN ATTACHMENT THAT PREVENTED HER FROM ATTAINING NIRVANA.*
YUUTEN SHOUNIN DISPLAYED TRULY REMARKABLE WISDOM WHEN HE INSTANTLY DEDUCED THE TRUTH.
IT IS ONLY NATURAL THAT THE PRAYERS OF SUCH A WISE MAN WOULD HAVE SUCH MIRACULOUS RESULTS...
PATAN (SHUT)
BOOK: TALES

*ATTAINING NIRVANA: ESCAPING THE CYCLE OF REBIRTH AND ENTERING PARADISE

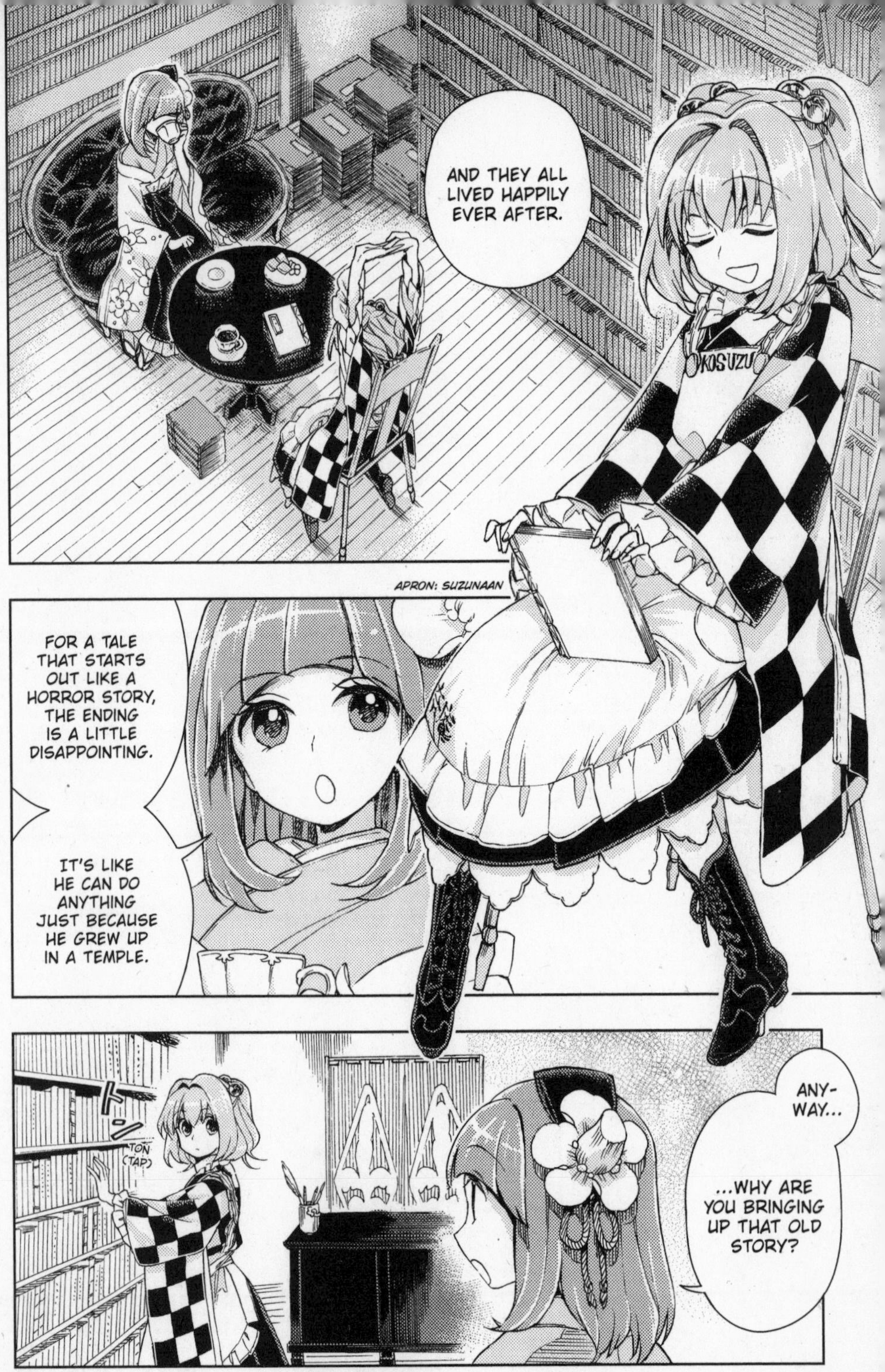
AND THEY ALL LIVED HAPPILY EVER AFTER.
KOSUZU
APRON: SUZUNAAN
FOR A TALE THAT STARTS OUT LIKE A HORROR STORY, THE ENDING IS A LITTLE DISAPPOINTING.
IT'S LIKE HE CAN DO ANYTHING JUST BECAUSE HE GREW UP IN A TEMPLE.
ANY-WAY...
...WHY ARE YOU BRINGING UP THAT OLD STORY?
TON (TAP)

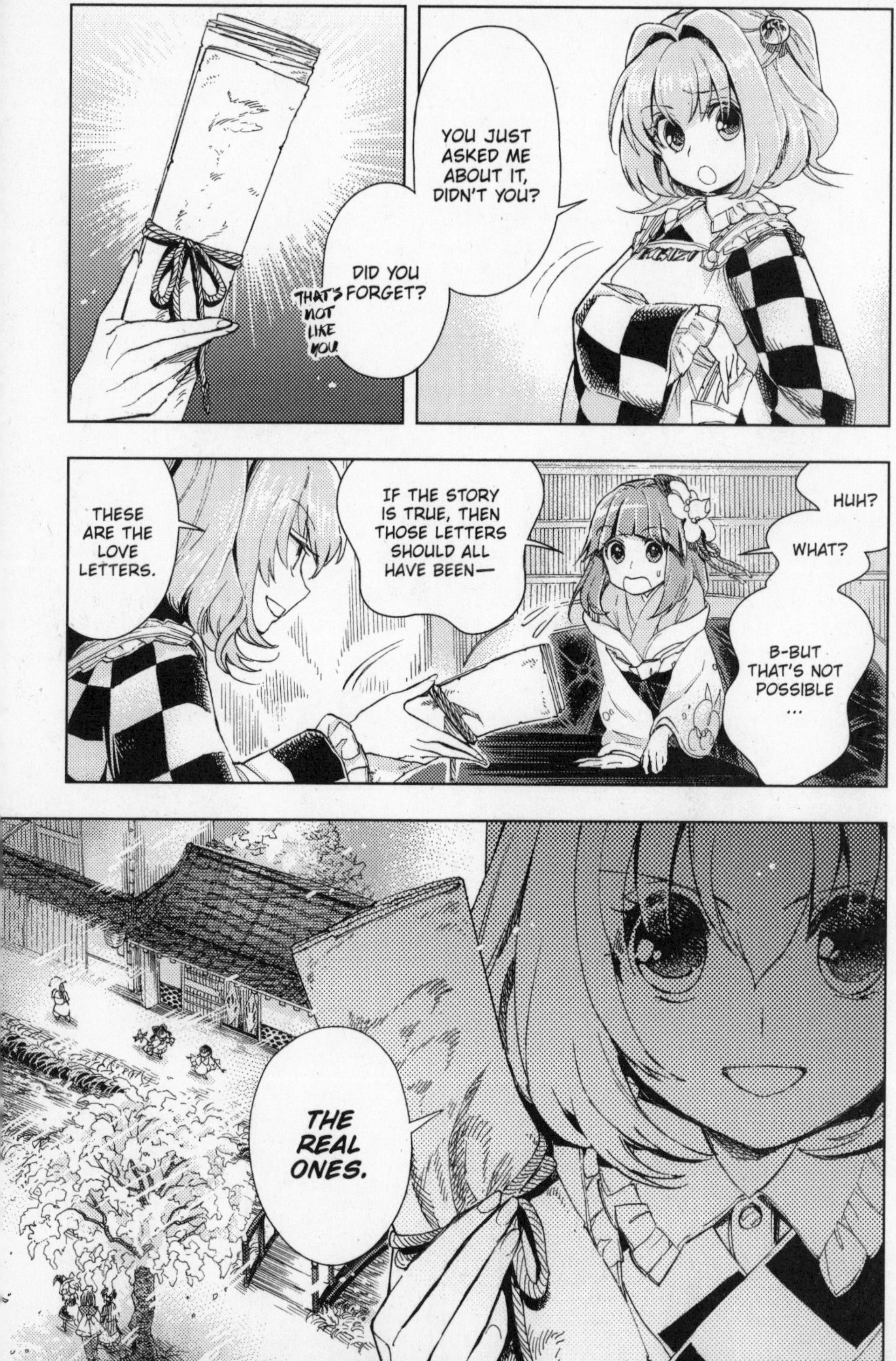
YOU JUST ASKED ME ABOUT IT, DIDN'T YOU?
DID YOU FORGET?
THAT'S NOT LIKE YOU.
HUH?
WHAT?
B-BUT THAT'S NOT POSSIBLE ...
IF THE STORY IS TRUE, THEN THOSE LETTERS SHOULD ALL HAVE BEEN—
THESE ARE THE LOVE LETTERS.
THE REAL ONES.

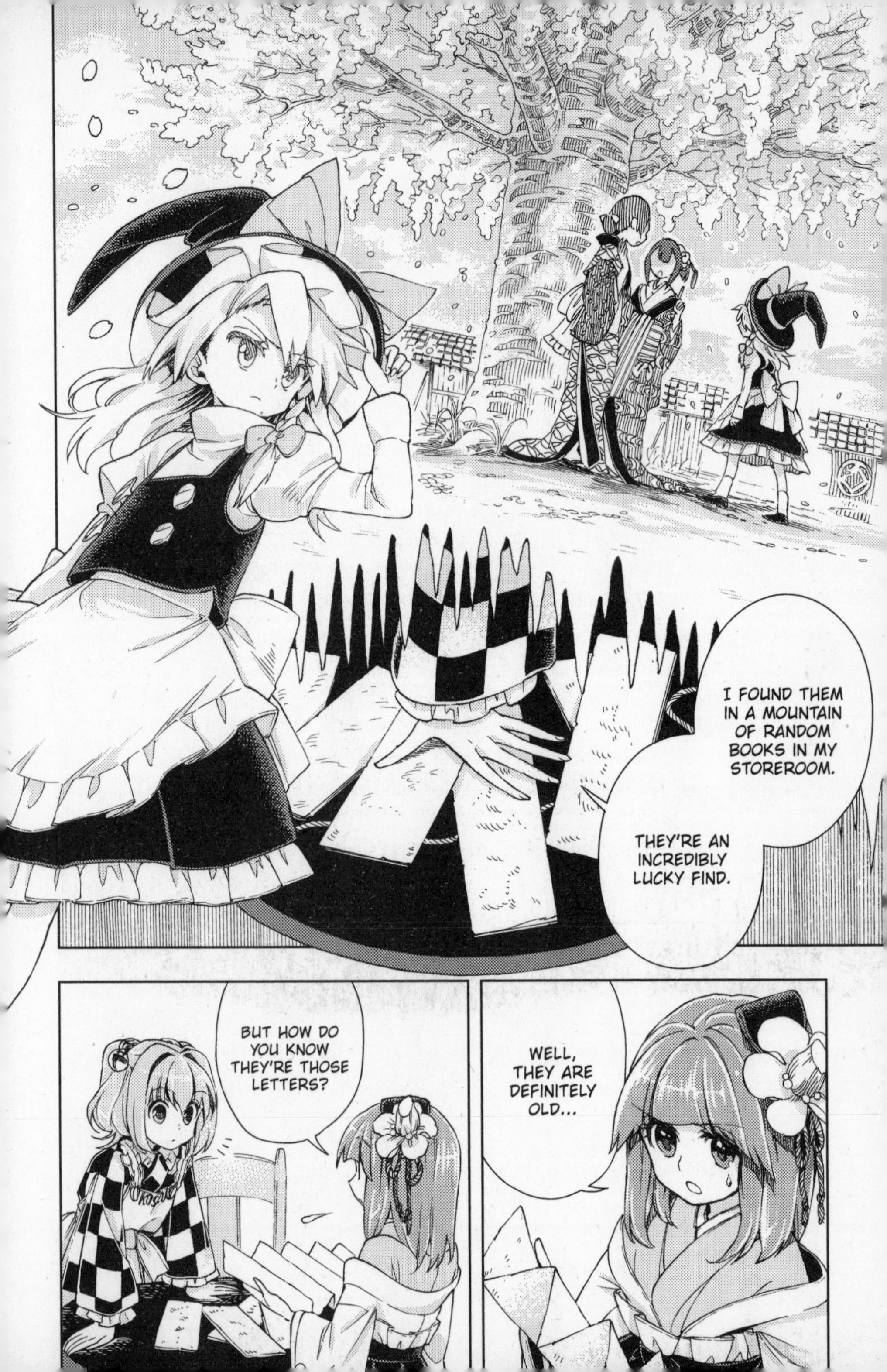
I FOUND THEM IN A MOUNTAIN OF RANDOM BOOKS IN MY STOREROOM.
THEY'RE AN INCREDIBLY LUCKY FIND.
WELL, THEY ARE DEFINITELY OLD...
BUT HOW DO YOU KNOW THEY'RE THOSE LETTERS?

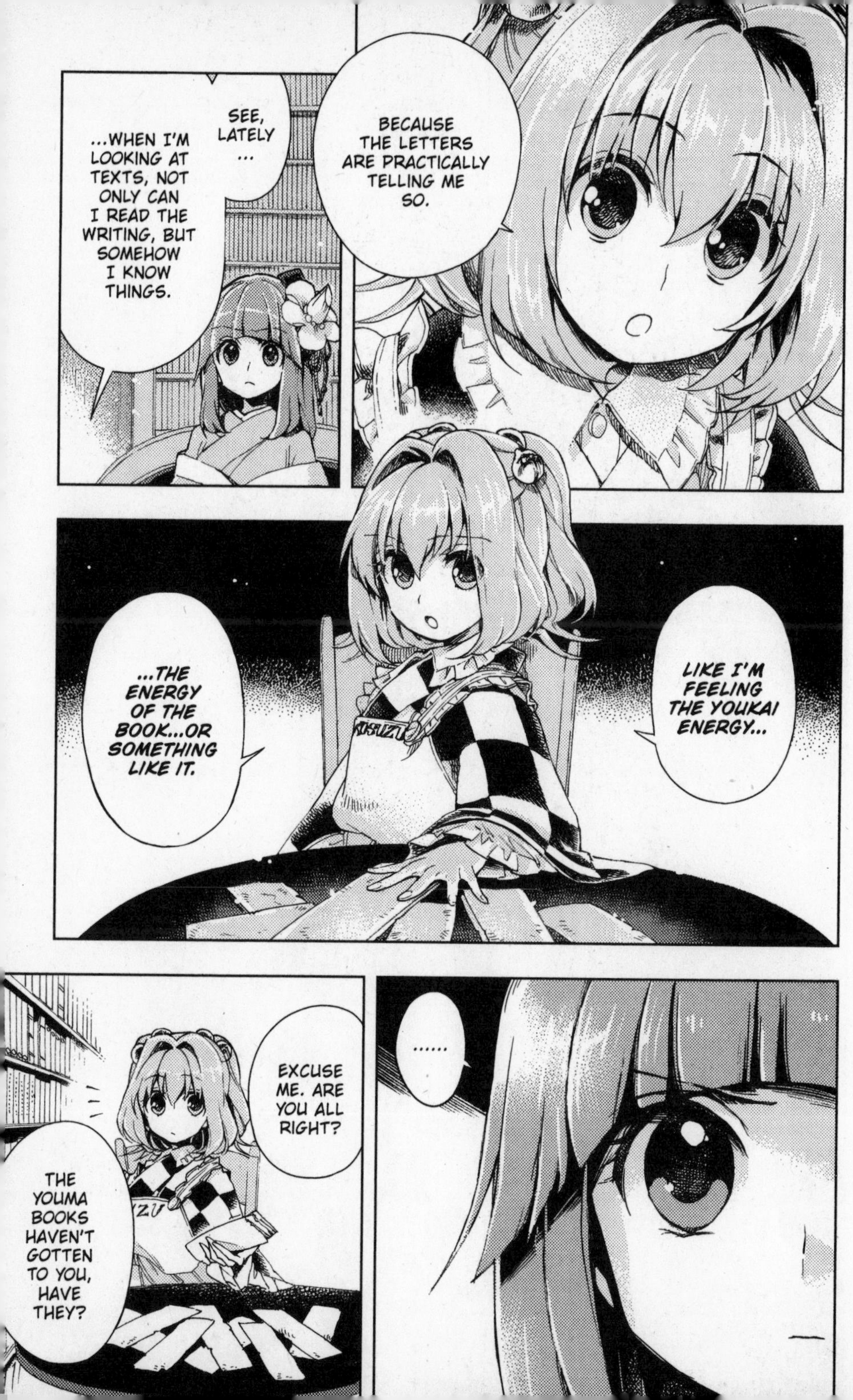
BECAUSE THE LETTERS ARE PRACTICALLY TELLING ME SO.
SEE, LATELY ...
...WHEN I'M LOOKING AT TEXTS, NOT ONLY CAN I READ THE WRITING, BUT SOMEHOW I KNOW THINGS.
LIKE I'M FEELING THE YOUKAI ENERGY...
...THE ENERGY OF THE BOOK...OR SOMETHING LIKE IT.
......
EXCUSE ME. ARE YOU ALL RIGHT?
THE YOUMA BOOKS HAVEN'T GOTTEN TO YOU, HAVE THEY?

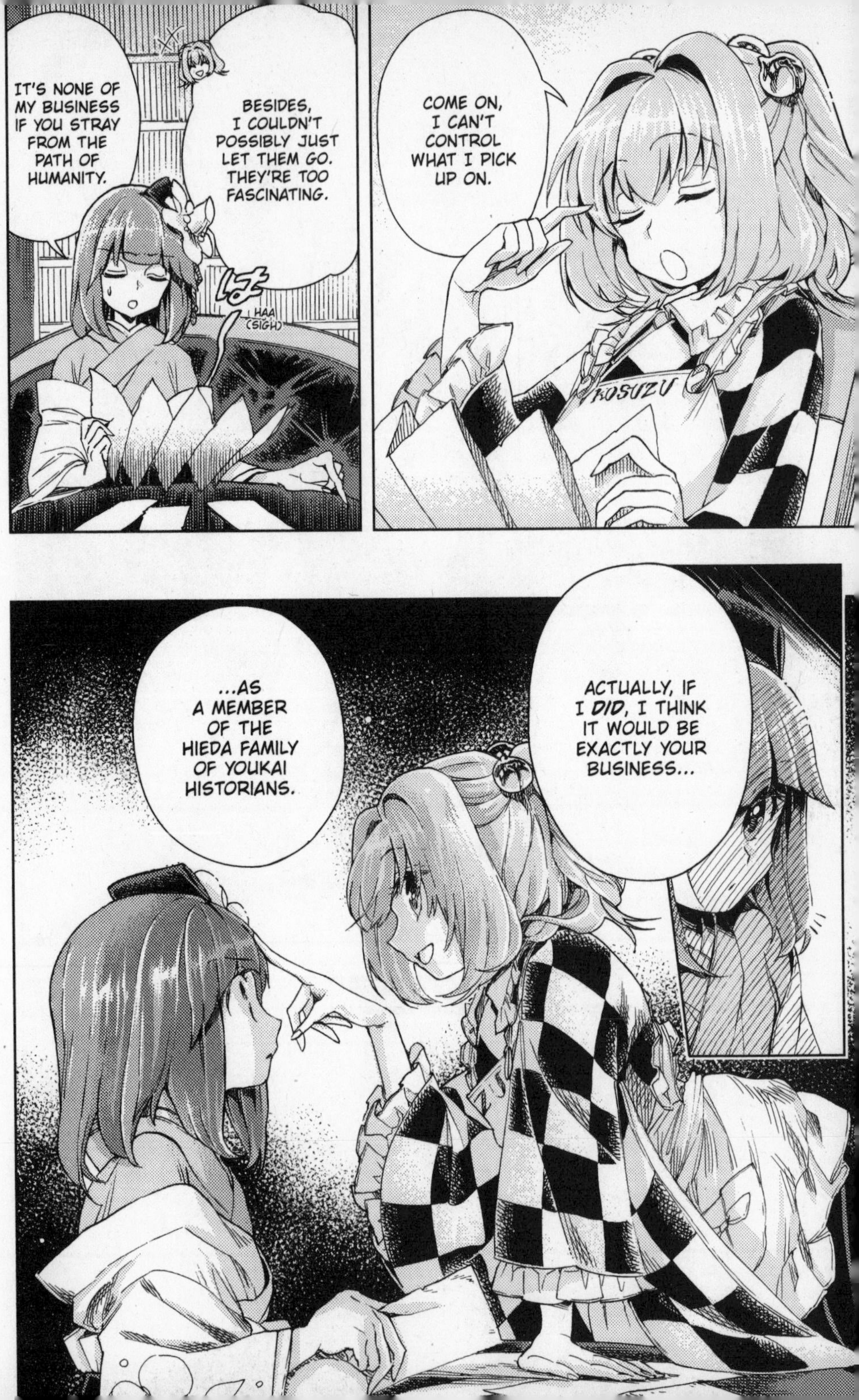
COME ON, I CAN'T CONTROL WHAT I PICK UP ON.
KOSUZU
BESIDES, I COULDN'T POSSIBLY JUST LET THEM GO. THEY'RE TOO FASCINATING.
はぁ
HAA (SIGH)
IT'S NONE OF MY BUSINESS IF YOU STRAY FROM THE PATH OF HUMANITY.
ACTUALLY, IF I *DID*, I THINK IT WOULD BE EXACTLY YOUR BUSINESS...
...AS A MEMBER OF THE HIEDA FAMILY OF YOUKAI HISTORIANS.

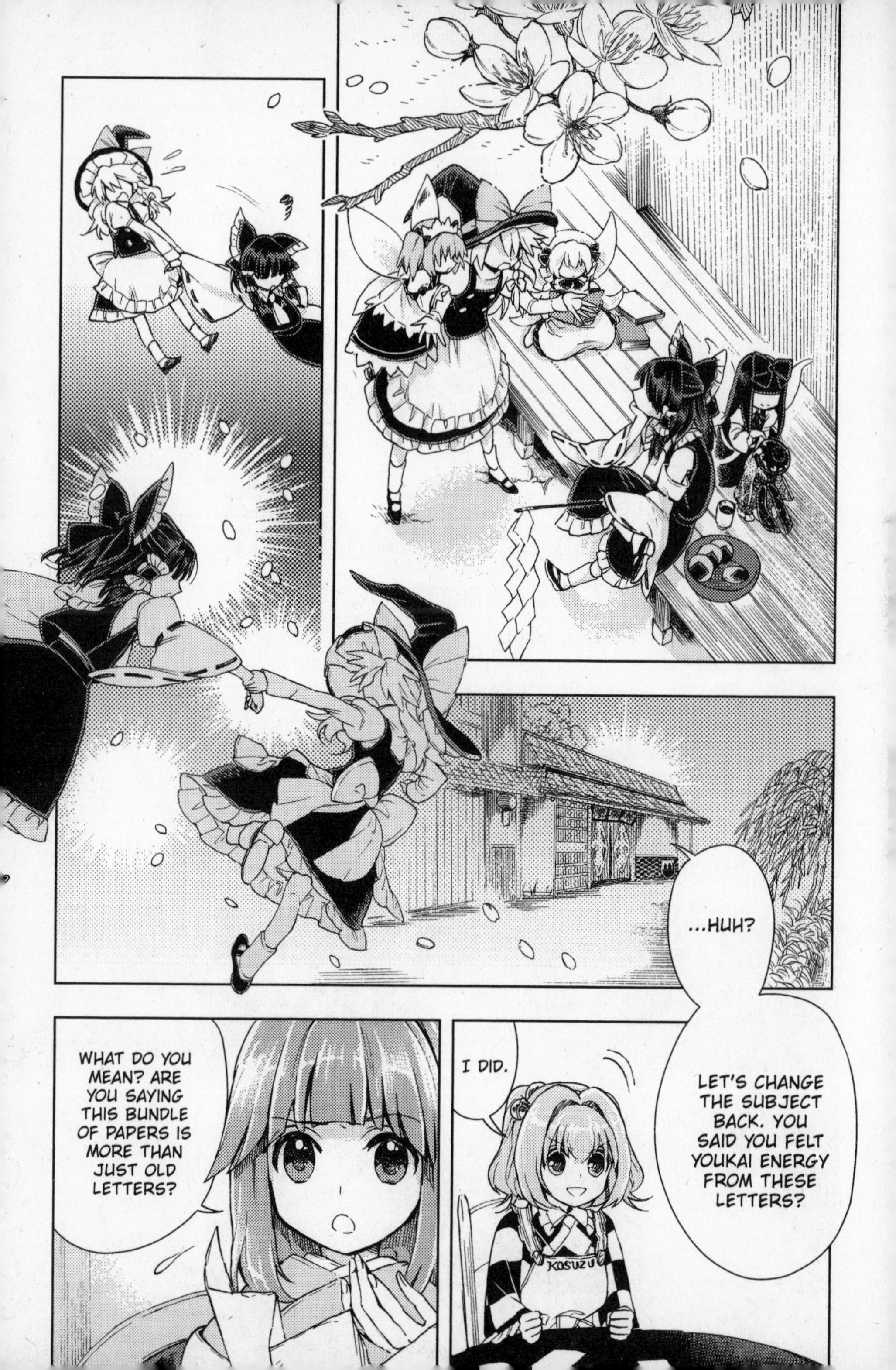
...HUH?
LET'S CHANGE THE SUBJECT BACK. YOU SAID YOU FELT YOUKAI ENERGY FROM THESE LETTERS?
I DID.
KOSUZU
WHAT DO YOU MEAN? ARE YOU SAYING THIS BUNDLE OF PAPERS IS MORE THAN JUST OLD LETTERS?

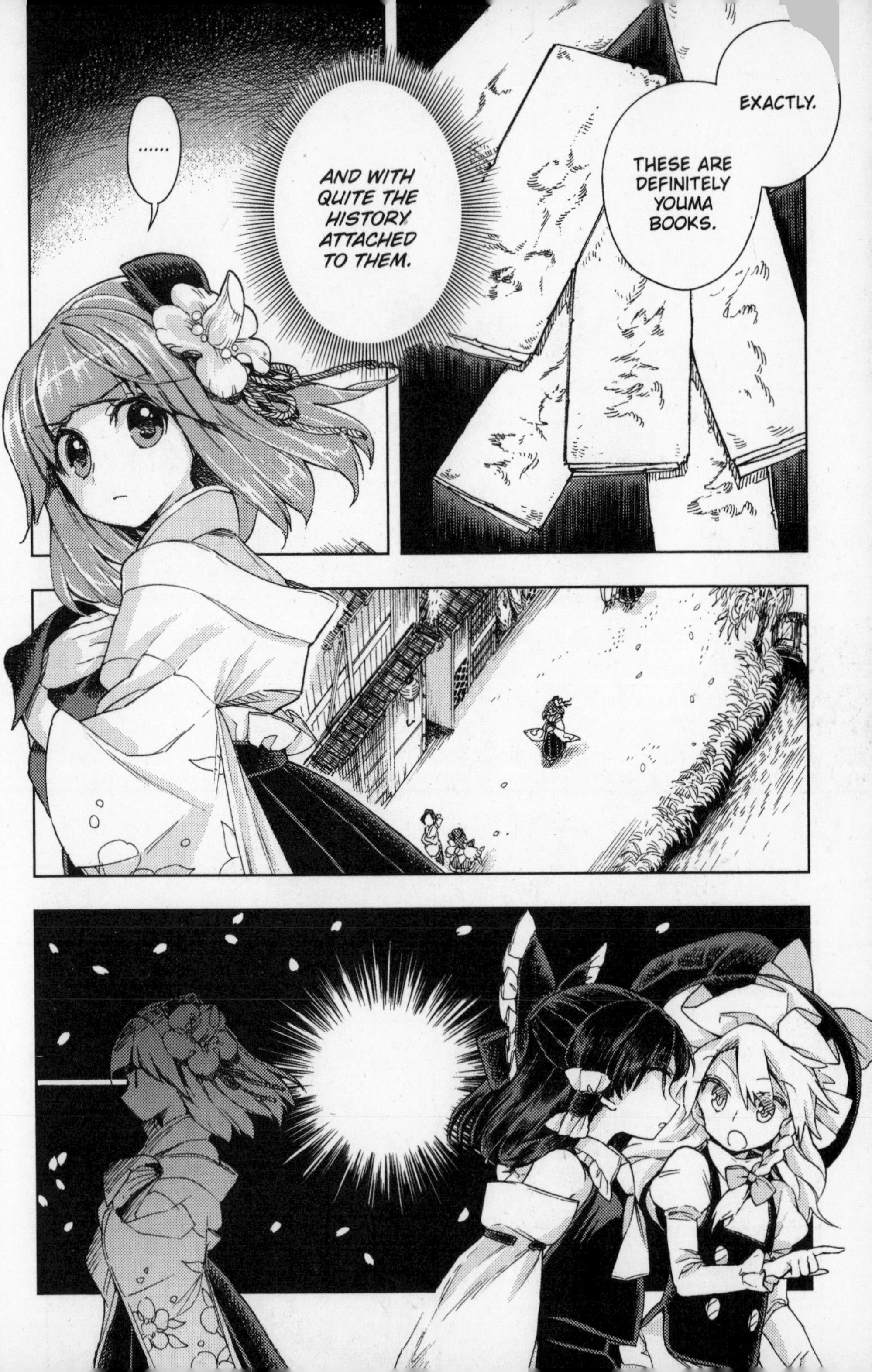
EXACTLY.
THESE ARE DEFINITELY YOUMA BOOKS.
AND WITH QUITE THE HISTORY ATTACHED TO THEM.
......

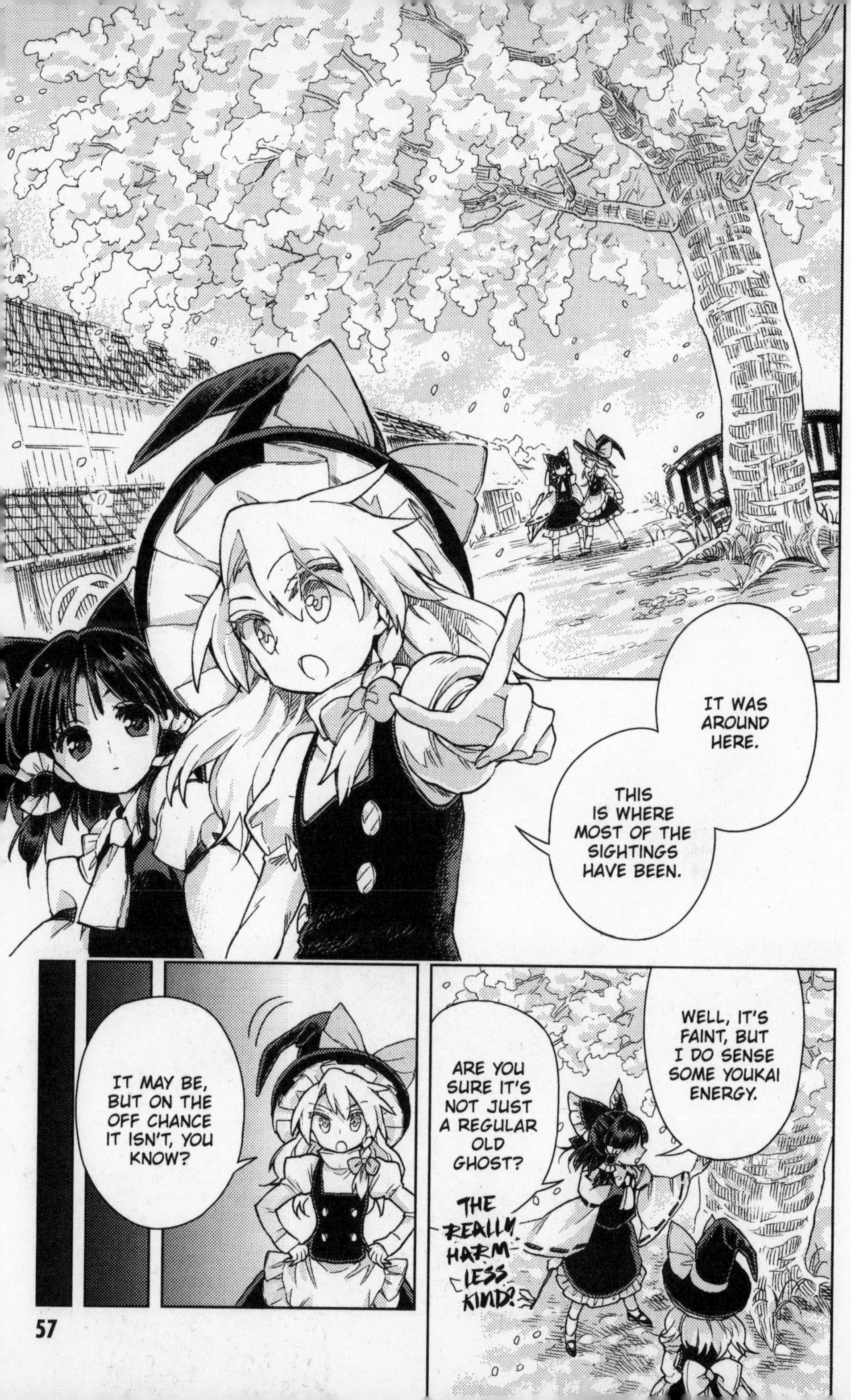
IT WAS AROUND HERE.
THIS IS WHERE MOST OF THE SIGHTINGS HAVE BEEN.
WELL, IT'S FAINT, BUT I DO SENSE SOME YOUKAI ENERGY.
ARE YOU SURE IT'S NOT JUST A REGULAR OLD GHOST?
THE REALLY HARMLESS KIND?
IT MAY BE, BUT ON THE OFF CHANCE IT ISN'T, YOU KNOW?

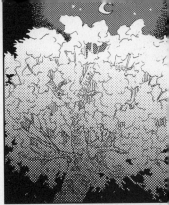

THE WITCHING HOUR DRAWS NEAR.

IS SHE REALLY GOING TO SHOW UP?

KOSO
(SNEAK)

THE NIGHTS ARE STILL COLD.

HM?

KUSU
(CHUCKLE)

AH-CHOO!

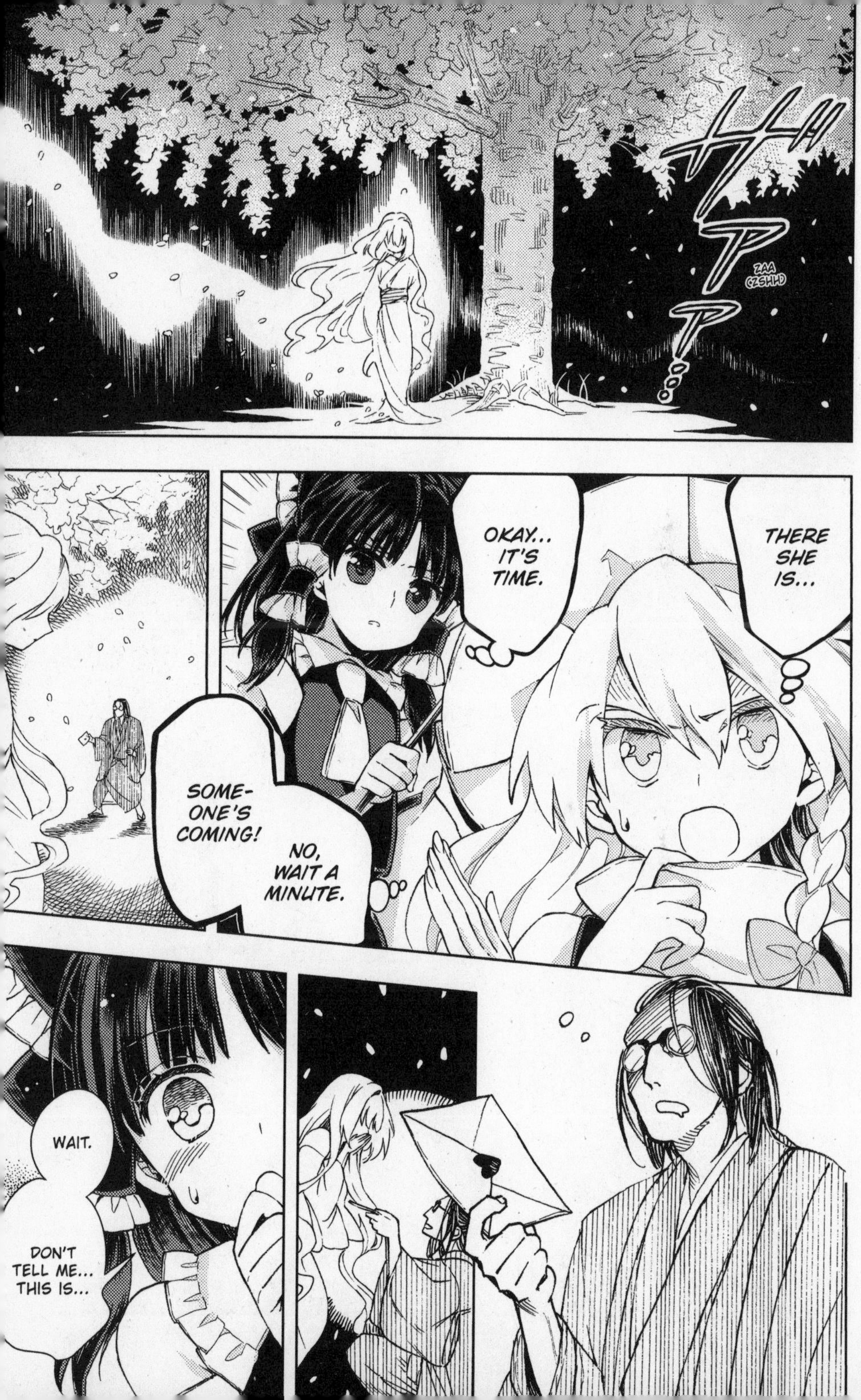
ZAA (ZSHHH)
THERE SHE IS...
OKAY... IT'S TIME.
SOME-ONE'S COMING!
NO, WAIT A MINUTE.
WAIT.
DON'T TELL ME... THIS IS...

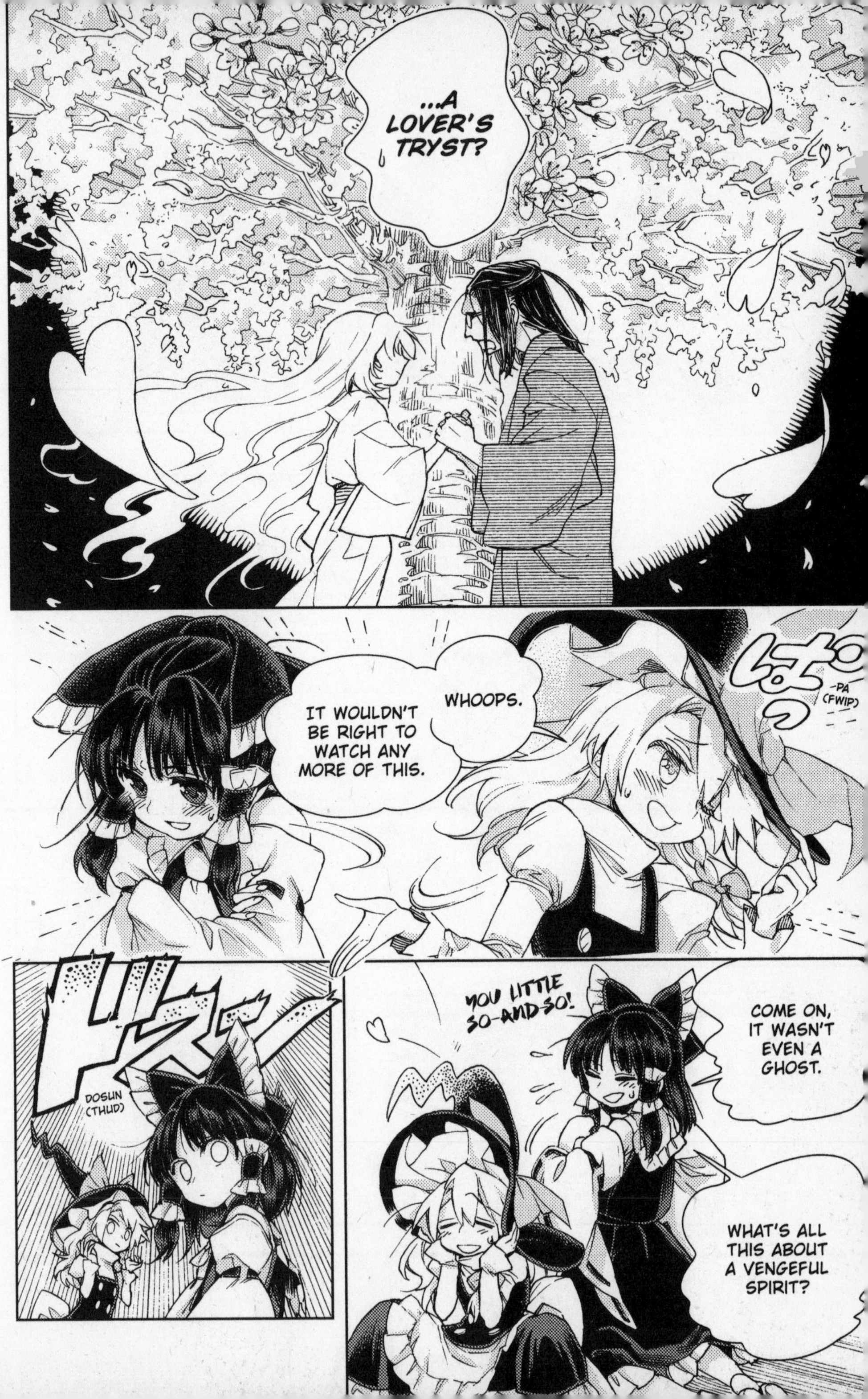
...A LOVER'S TRYST?
-PA (FWIP)
WHOOPS.
IT WOULDN'T BE RIGHT TO WATCH ANY MORE OF THIS.
COME ON, IT WASN'T EVEN A GHOST.
YOU LITTLE SO-AND-SO!
WHAT'S ALL THIS ABOUT A VENGEFUL SPIRIT?
DOSUN (THUD)

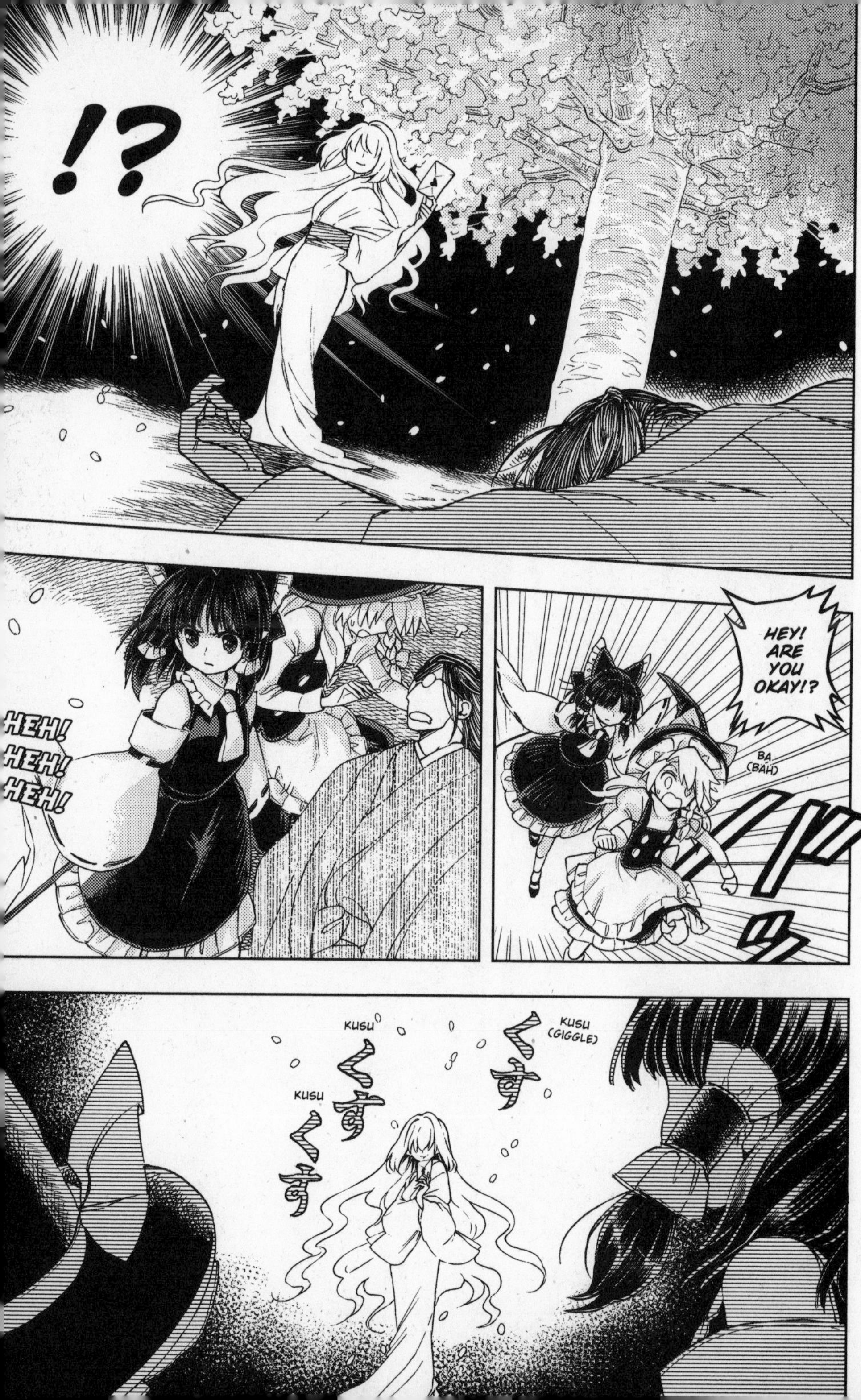
!?
HEY! ARE YOU OKAY!?
BA (BAH)
HEH! HEH! HEH!
KUSU (GIGGLE)
KUSU
KUSU
くすくすくす

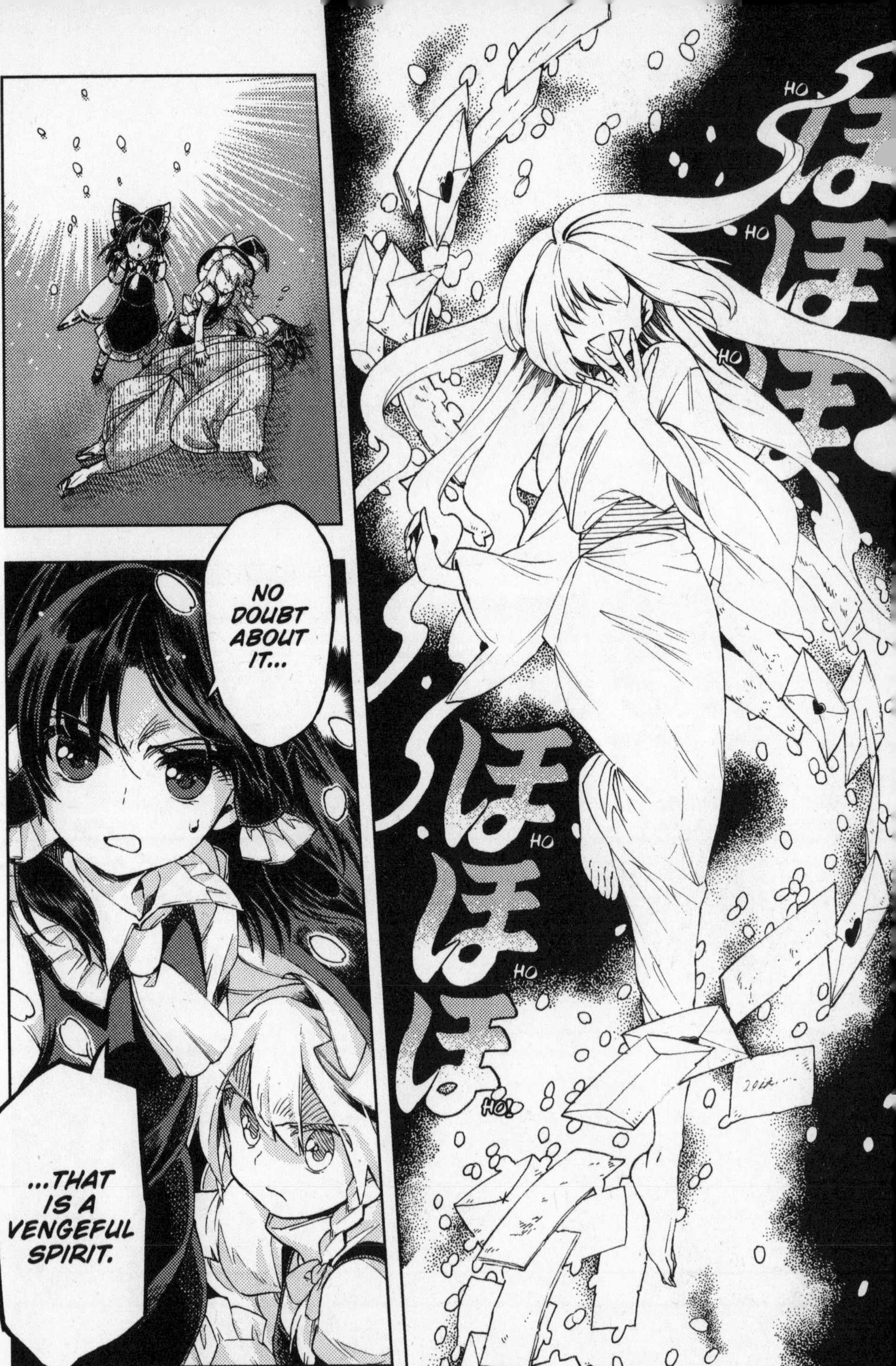
ほほほ
HO HO HO
ほほほ
HO HO HO!
NO DOUBT ABOUT IT...
...THAT IS A VENGEFUL SPIRIT.

Chapter 16 To be continued

# Chapter 17 Love Letters with a Past Part 2

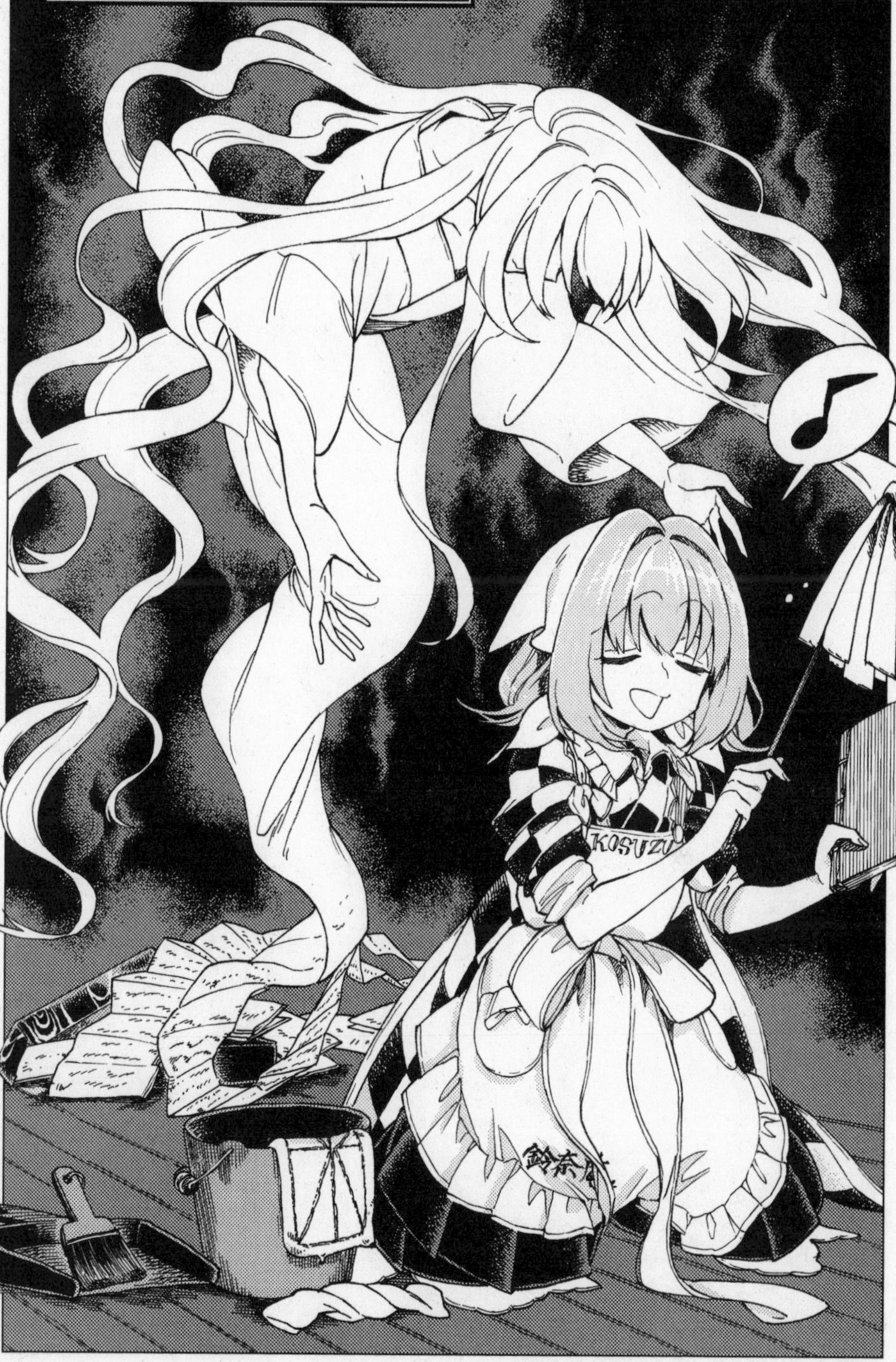
KOSUZU

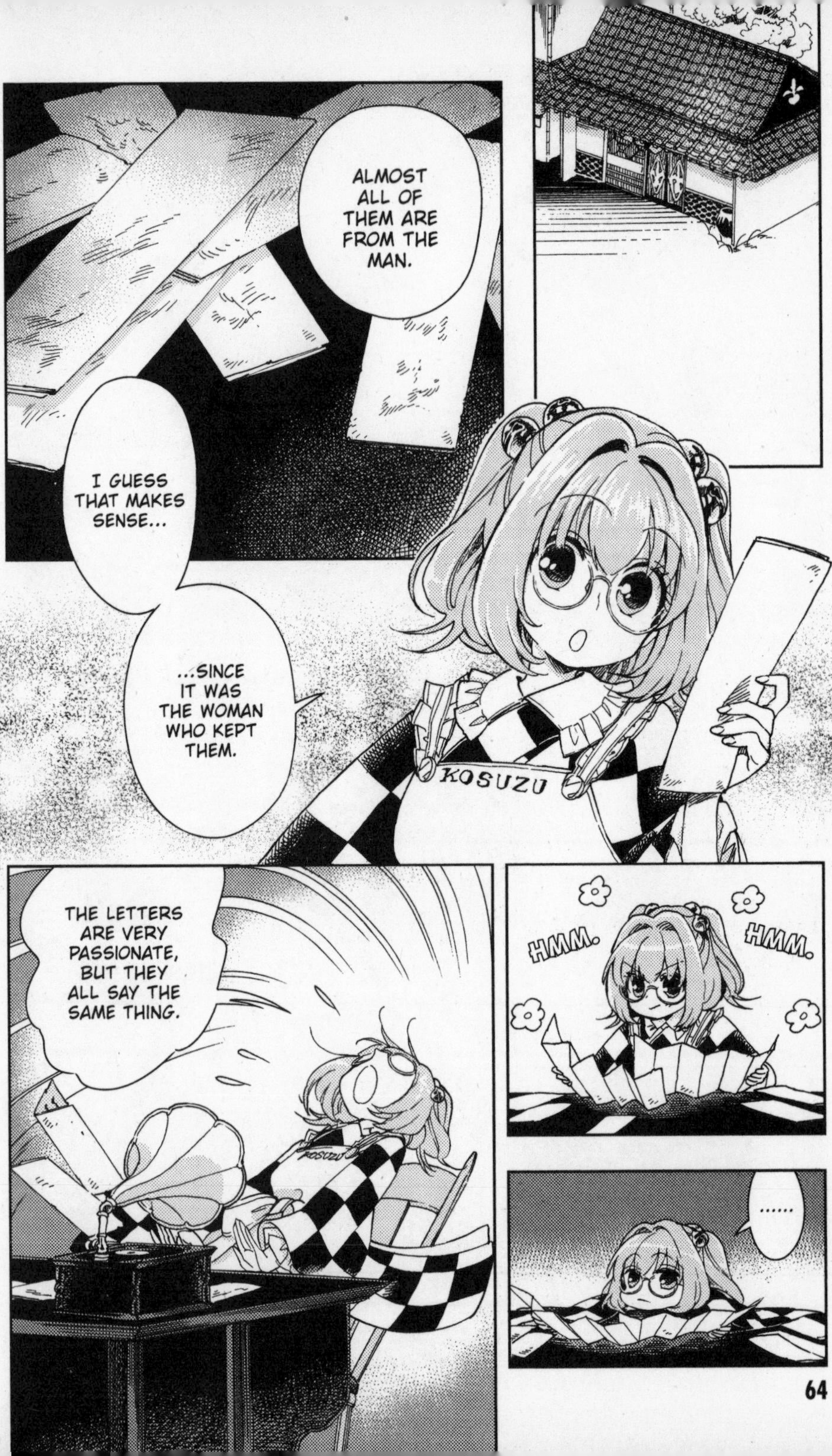
ALMOST ALL OF THEM ARE FROM THE MAN.
I GUESS THAT MAKES SENSE...
...SINCE IT WAS THE WOMAN WHO KEPT THEM.
KOSUZU
HMM.
HMM.
......
THE LETTERS ARE VERY PASSIONATE, BUT THEY ALL SAY THE SAME THING.
KOSUZU

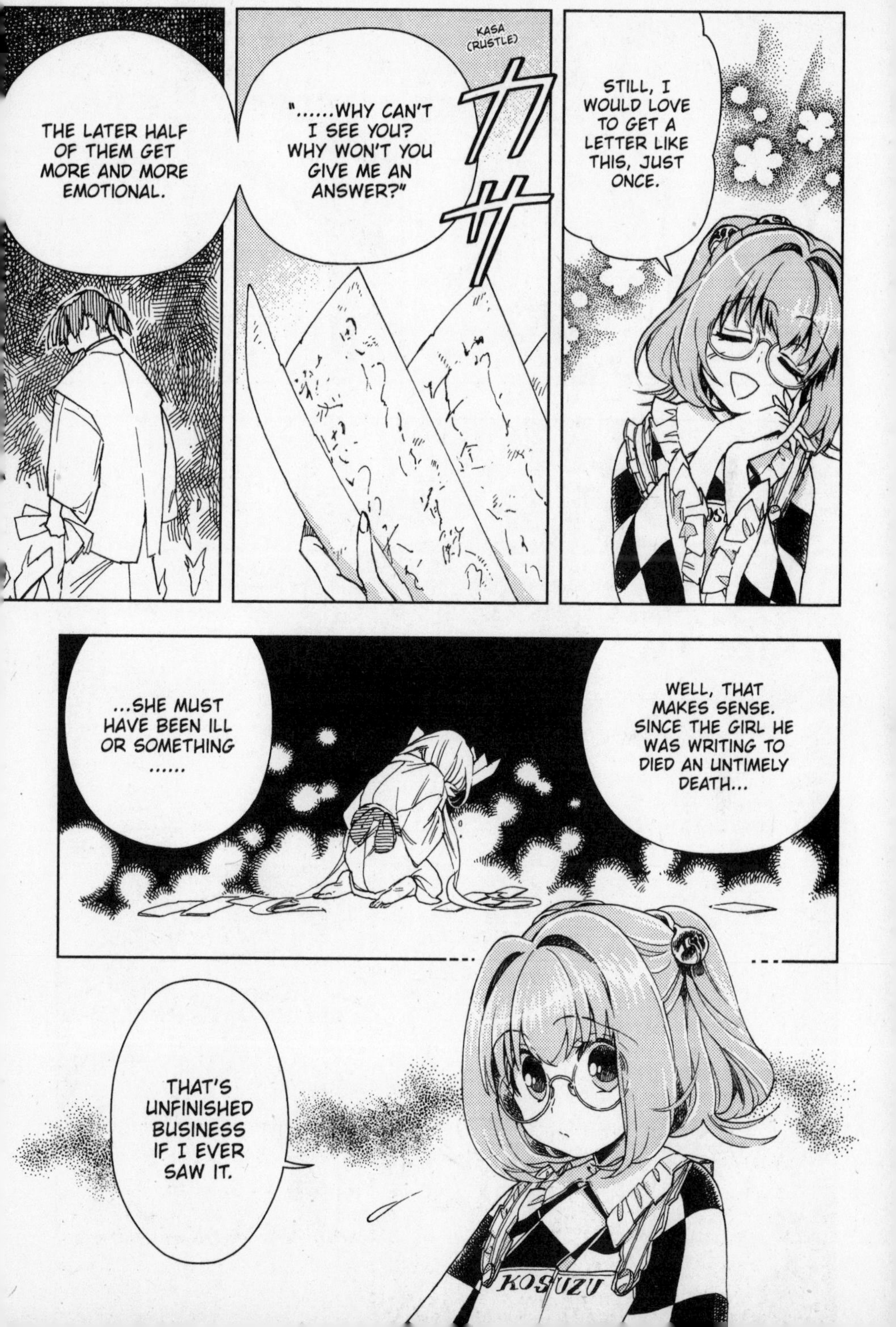
STILL, I WOULD LOVE TO GET A LETTER LIKE THIS, JUST ONCE.
KASA (RUSTLE)
カサ
"......WHY CAN'T I SEE YOU? WHY WON'T YOU GIVE ME AN ANSWER?"
THE LATER HALF OF THEM GET MORE AND MORE EMOTIONAL.
WELL, THAT MAKES SENSE. SINCE THE GIRL HE WAS WRITING TO DIED AN UNTIMELY DEATH...
...SHE MUST HAVE BEEN ILL OR SOMETHING ......
THAT'S UNFINISHED BUSINESS IF I EVER SAW IT.
KOSUZU

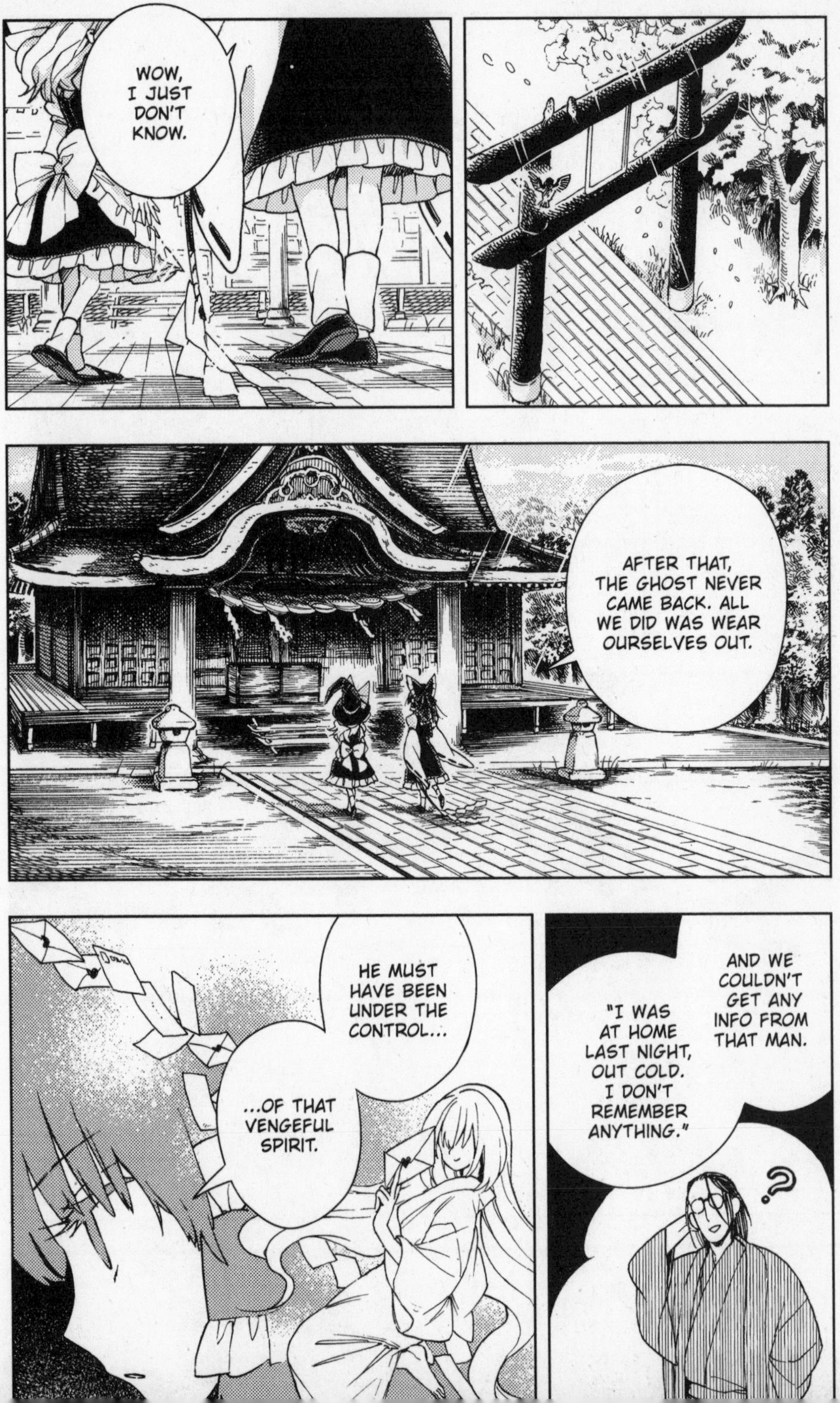
WOW, I JUST DON'T KNOW.
AFTER THAT, THE GHOST NEVER CAME BACK. ALL WE DID WAS WEAR OURSELVES OUT.
AND WE COULDN'T GET ANY INFO FROM THAT MAN.
"I WAS AT HOME LAST NIGHT, OUT COLD. I DON'T REMEMBER ANYTHING."
HE MUST HAVE BEEN UNDER THE CONTROL...
...OF THAT VENGEFUL SPIRIT.

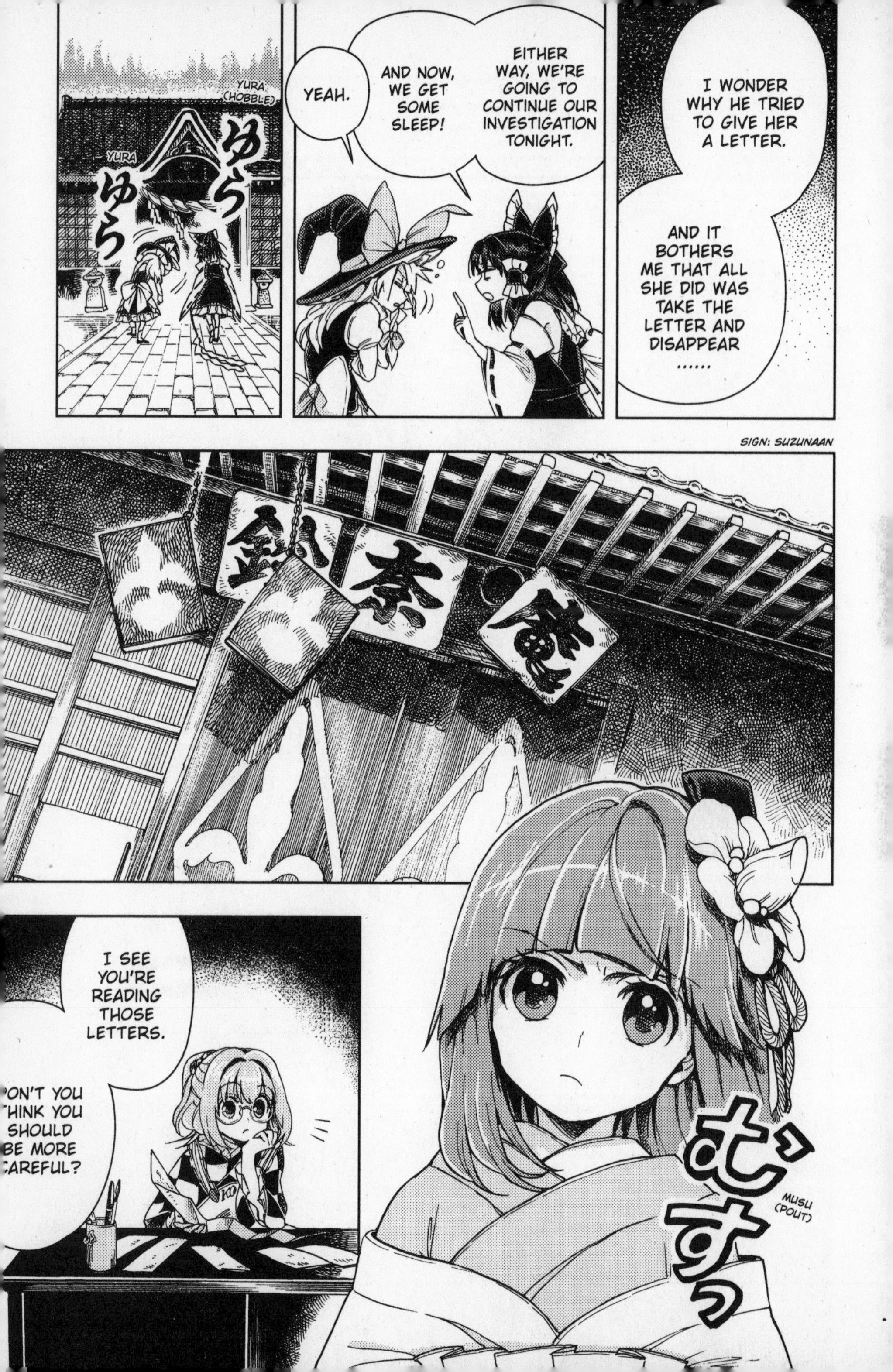
I WONDER WHY HE TRIED TO GIVE HER A LETTER.
AND IT BOTHERS ME THAT ALL SHE DID WAS TAKE THE LETTER AND DISAPPEAR ......
EITHER WAY, WE'RE GOING TO CONTINUE OUR INVESTIGATION TONIGHT.
AND NOW, WE GET SOME SLEEP!
YEAH.
ゆら
YURA (HOBBLE)
ゆら
YURA
SIGN: SUZUNAAN
鈴奈庵
むすっ
MUSU (POUT)
I SEE YOU'RE READING THOSE LETTERS.
ON'T YOU THINK YOU SHOULD BE MORE CAREFUL?

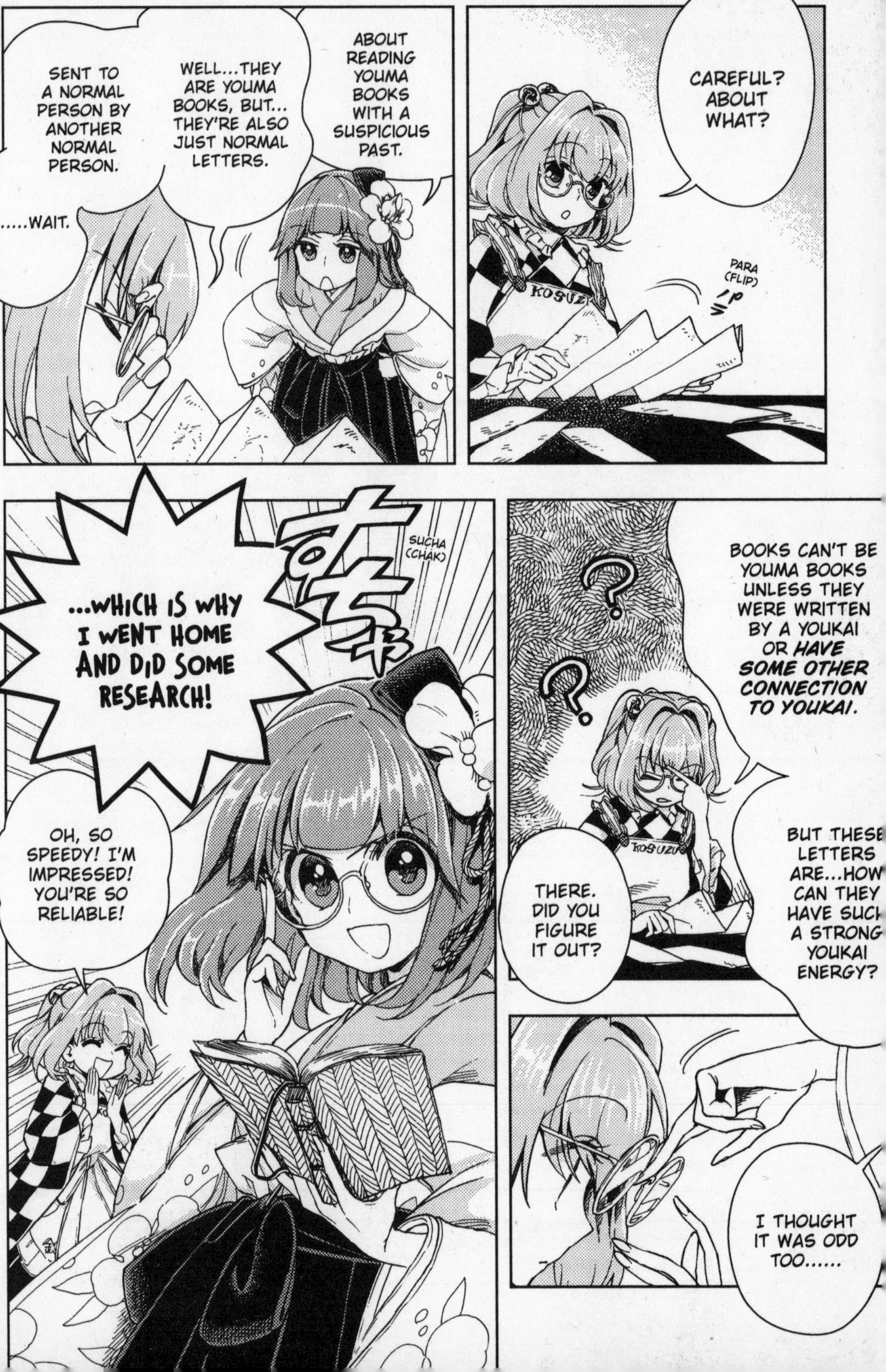
CAREFUL? ABOUT WHAT?
PARA (FLIP)
ABOUT READING YOUMA BOOKS WITH A SUSPICIOUS PAST.
WELL...THEY ARE YOUMA BOOKS, BUT... THEY'RE ALSO JUST NORMAL LETTERS.
SENT TO A NORMAL PERSON BY ANOTHER NORMAL PERSON.
......WAIT.
BOOKS CAN'T BE YOUMA BOOKS UNLESS THEY WERE WRITTEN BY A YOUKAI OR *HAVE SOME OTHER CONNECTION TO YOUKAI.*
BUT THESE LETTERS ARE...HOW CAN THEY HAVE SUCH A STRONG YOUKAI ENERGY?
THERE. DID YOU FIGURE IT OUT?
I THOUGHT IT WAS ODD TOO......
すちゃ
SUCHA (CHAK)
...WHICH IS WHY I WENT HOME AND DID SOME RESEARCH!
OH, SO SPEEDY! I'M IMPRESSED! YOU'RE SO RELIABLE!

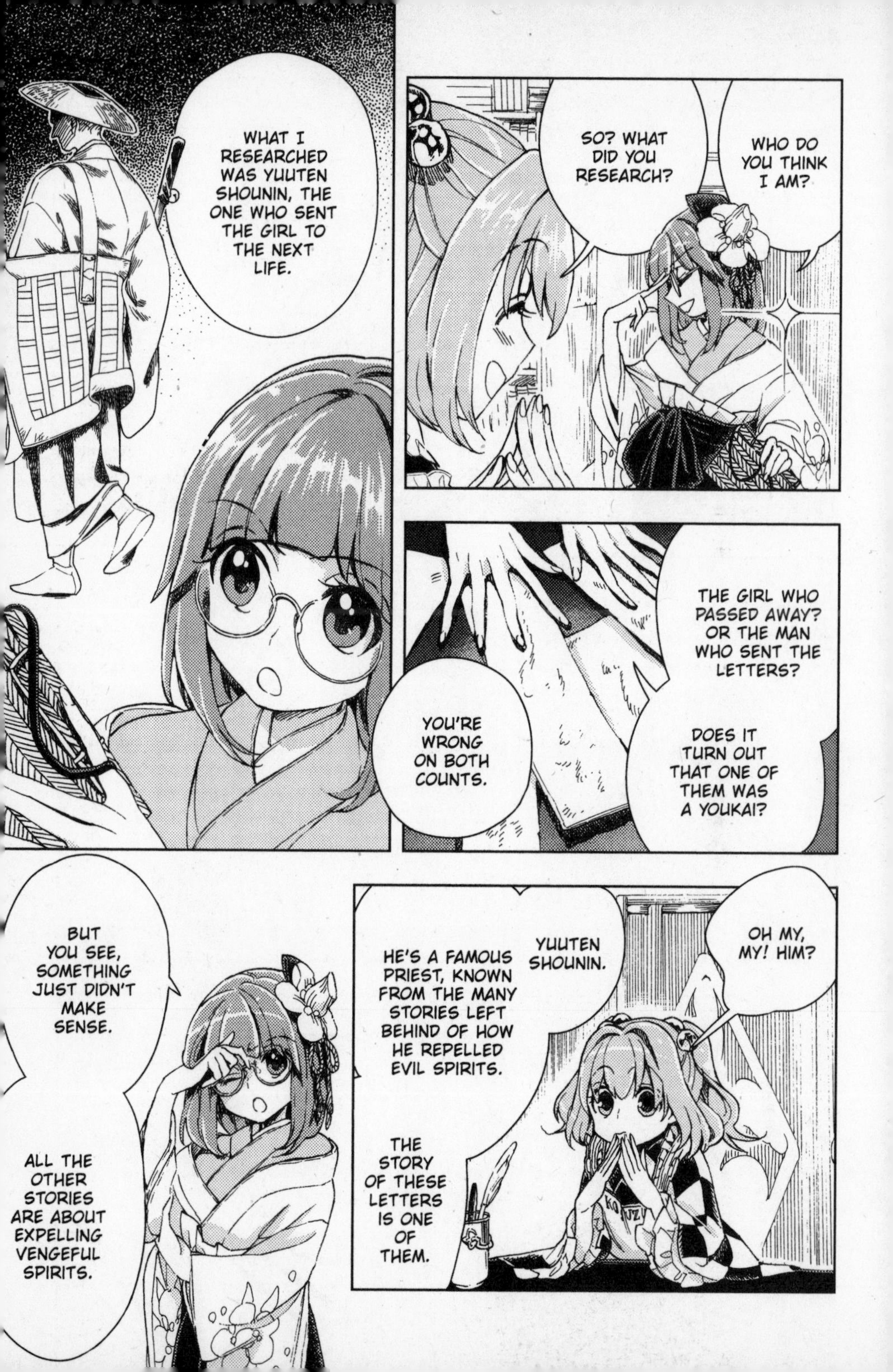

WHO DO YOU THINK I AM?
SO? WHAT DID YOU RESEARCH?
THE GIRL WHO PASSED AWAY? OR THE MAN WHO SENT THE LETTERS?
DOES IT TURN OUT THAT ONE OF THEM WAS A YOUKAI?
YOU'RE WRONG ON BOTH COUNTS.
WHAT I RESEARCHED WAS YUUTEN SHOUNIN, THE ONE WHO SENT THE GIRL TO THE NEXT LIFE.
OH MY, MY! HIM?
YUUTEN SHOUNIN.
HE'S A FAMOUS PRIEST, KNOWN FROM THE MANY STORIES LEFT BEHIND OF HOW HE REPELLED EVIL SPIRITS.
THE STORY OF THESE LETTERS IS ONE OF THEM.
BUT YOU SEE, SOMETHING JUST DIDN'T MAKE SENSE.
ALL THE OTHER STORIES ARE ABOUT EXPELLING VENGEFUL SPIRITS.

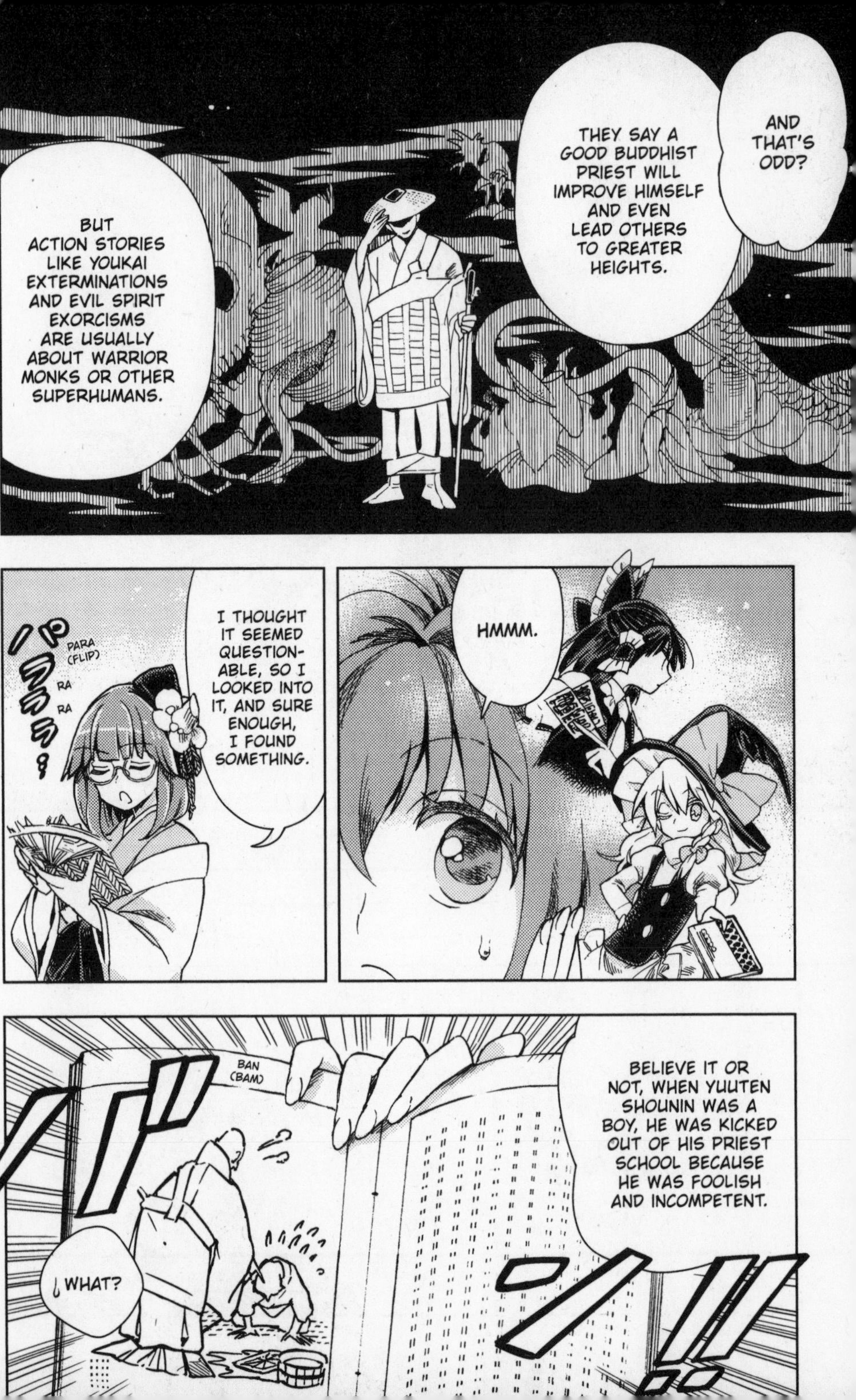

AND THAT'S ODD?
THEY SAY A GOOD BUDDHIST PRIEST WILL IMPROVE HIMSELF AND EVEN LEAD OTHERS TO GREATER HEIGHTS.
BUT ACTION STORIES LIKE YOUKAI EXTERMINATIONS AND EVIL SPIRIT EXORCISMS ARE USUALLY ABOUT WARRIOR MONKS OR OTHER SUPERHUMANS.
HMMM.
I THOUGHT IT SEEMED QUESTION-ABLE, SO I LOOKED INTO IT, AND SURE ENOUGH, I FOUND SOMETHING.
PARA (FLIP)
RA
RA
BELIEVE IT OR NOT, WHEN YUUTEN SHOUNIN WAS A BOY, HE WAS KICKED OUT OF HIS PRIEST SCHOOL BECAUSE HE WAS FOOLISH AND INCOMPETENT.
BAN (BAM)
¿WHAT?

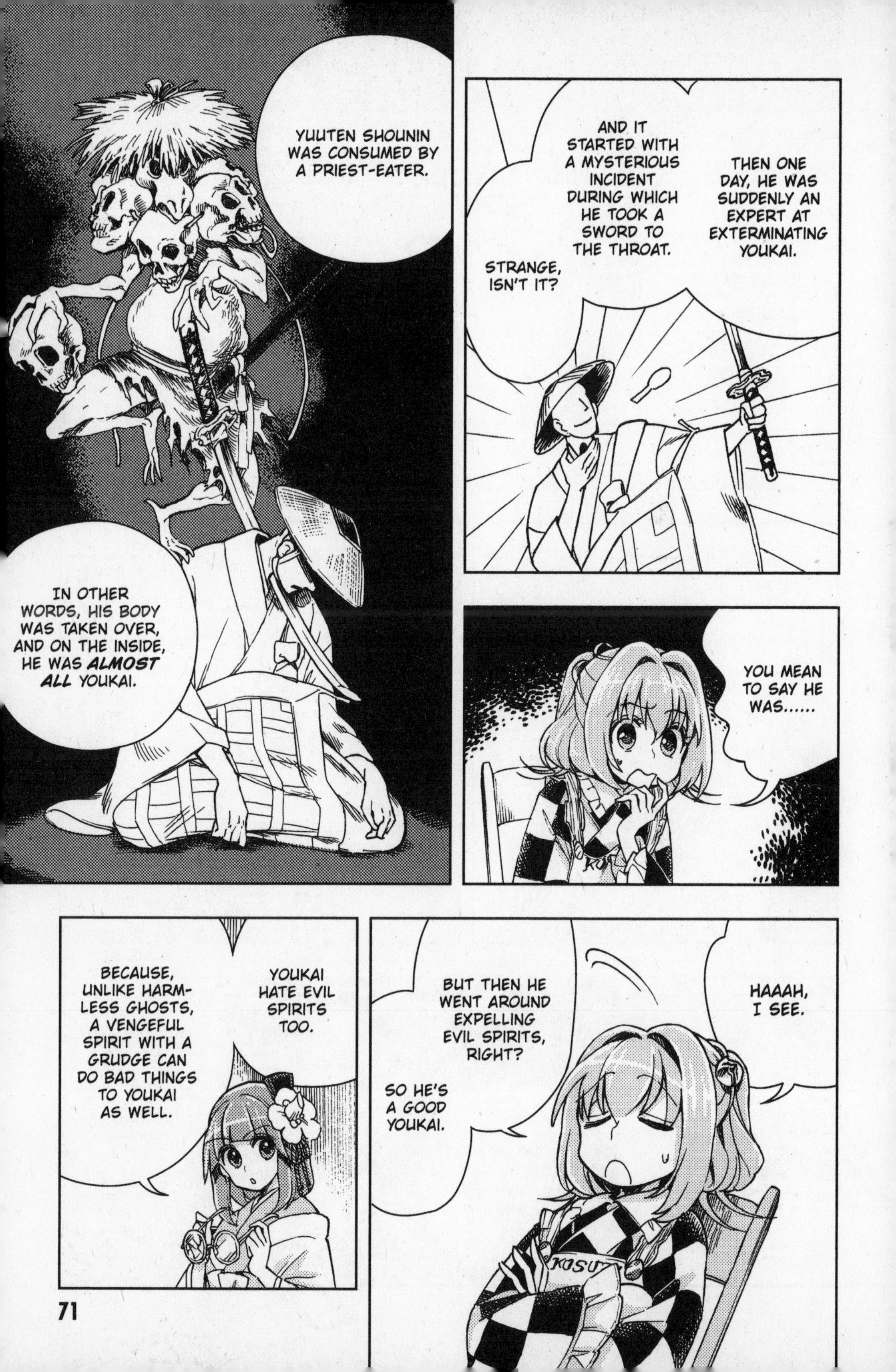
THEN ONE DAY, HE WAS SUDDENLY AN EXPERT AT EXTERMINATING YOUKAI.
AND IT STARTED WITH A MYSTERIOUS INCIDENT DURING WHICH HE TOOK A SWORD TO THE THROAT.
STRANGE, ISN'T IT?
YOU MEAN TO SAY HE WAS......
YUUTEN SHOUNIN WAS CONSUMED BY A PRIEST-EATER.
IN OTHER WORDS, HIS BODY WAS TAKEN OVER, AND ON THE INSIDE, HE WAS ***ALMOST ALL*** YOUKAI.
HAAAH, I SEE.
BUT THEN HE WENT AROUND EXPELLING EVIL SPIRITS, RIGHT?
SO HE'S A GOOD YOUKAI.
YOUKAI HATE EVIL SPIRITS TOO.
BECAUSE, UNLIKE HARM-LESS GHOSTS, A VENGEFUL SPIRIT WITH A GRUDGE CAN DO BAD THINGS TO YOUKAI AS WELL.

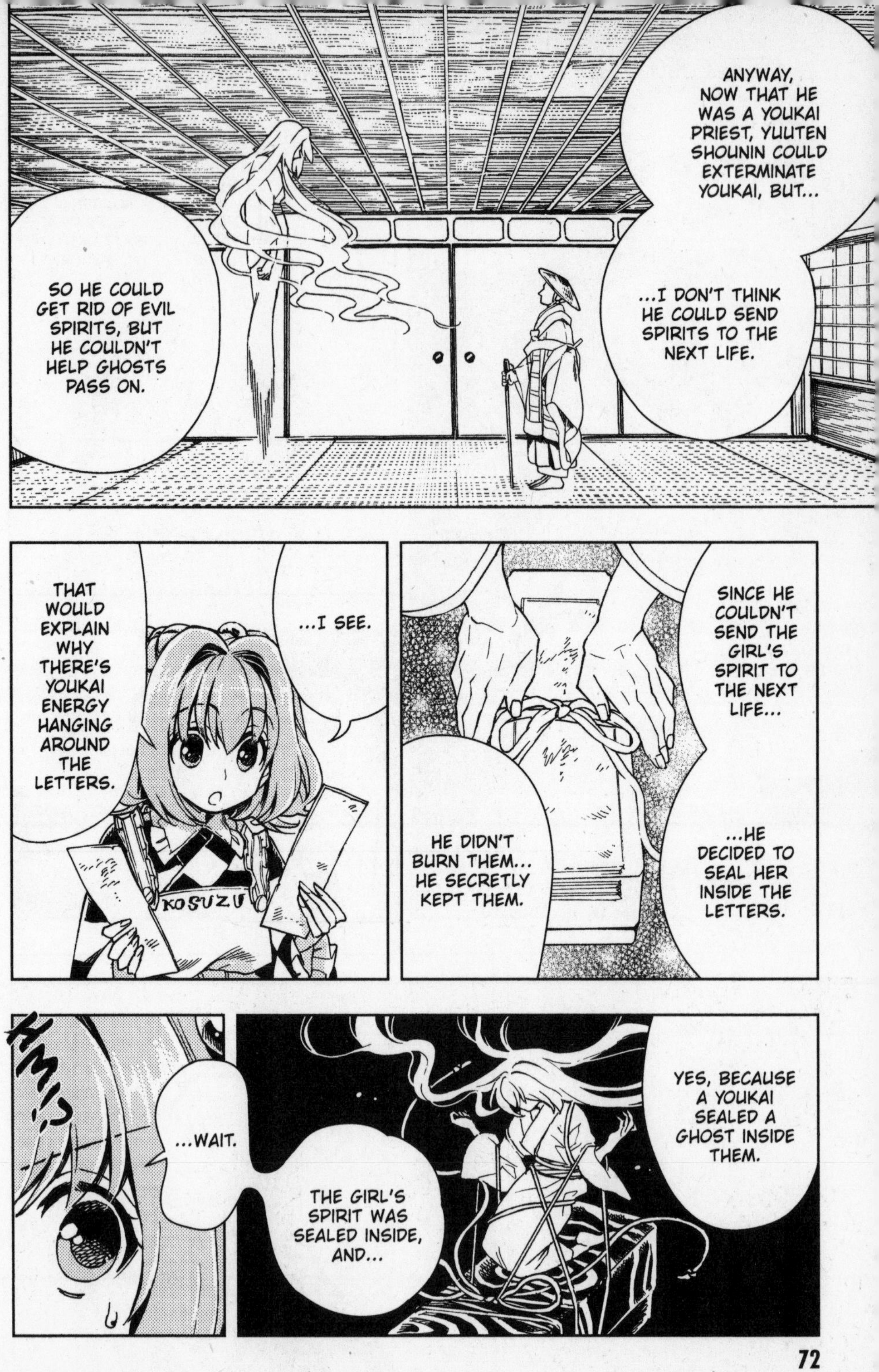
ANYWAY, NOW THAT HE WAS A YOUKAI PRIEST, YUUTEN SHOUNIN COULD EXTERMINATE YOUKAI, BUT...
...I DON'T THINK HE COULD SEND SPIRITS TO THE NEXT LIFE.
SO HE COULD GET RID OF EVIL SPIRITS, BUT HE COULDN'T HELP GHOSTS PASS ON.
SINCE HE COULDN'T SEND THE GIRL'S SPIRIT TO THE NEXT LIFE...
...HE DECIDED TO SEAL HER INSIDE THE LETTERS.
HE DIDN'T BURN THEM... HE SECRETLY KEPT THEM.
...I SEE.
THAT WOULD EXPLAIN WHY THERE'S YOUKAI ENERGY HANGING AROUND THE LETTERS.
KOSUZU
YES, BECAUSE A YOUKAI SEALED A GHOST INSIDE THEM.
HM!?
...WAIT.
THE GIRL'S SPIRIT WAS SEALED INSIDE, AND...

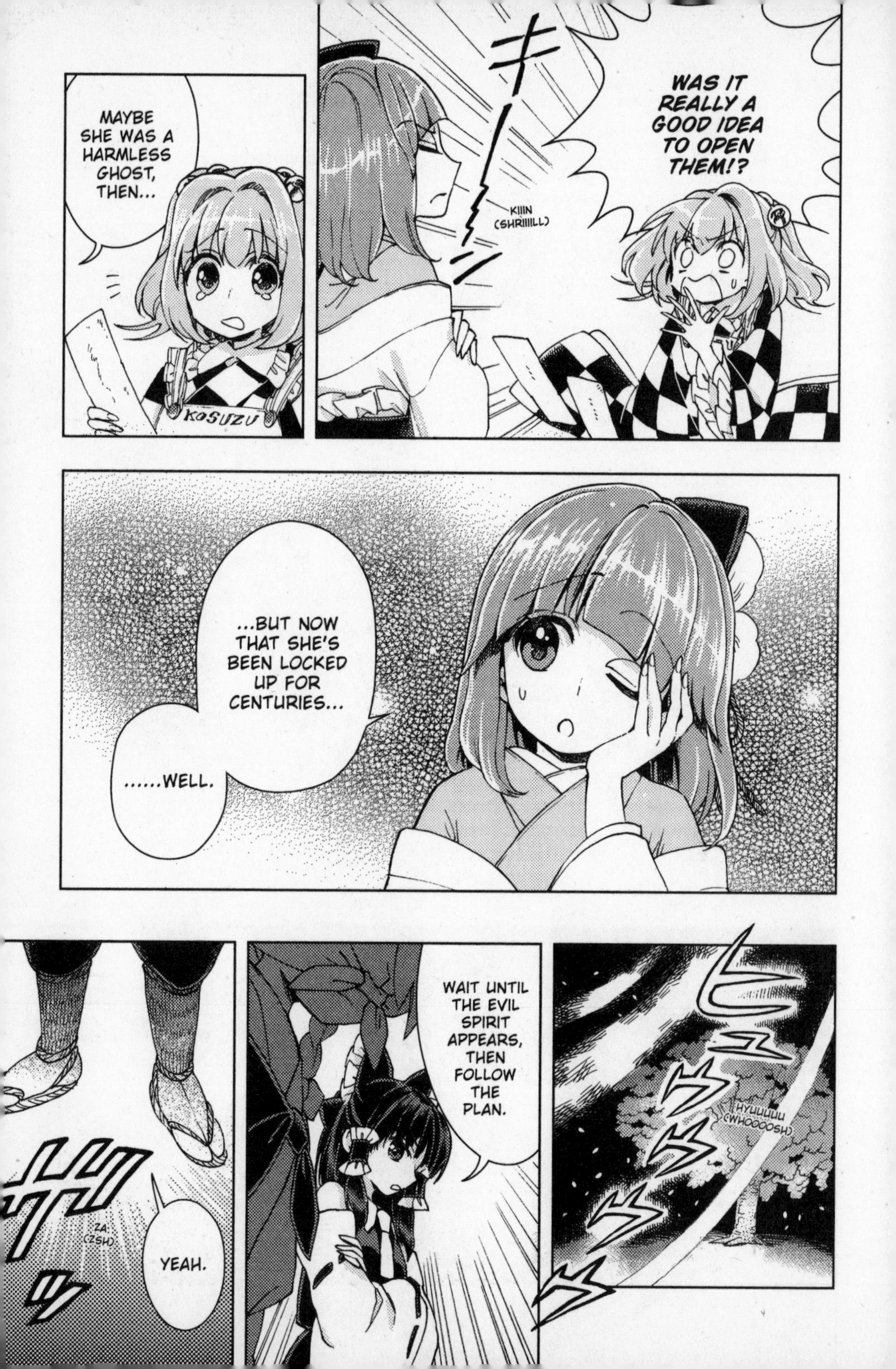
WAS IT REALLY A GOOD IDEA TO OPEN THEM!?
KIIIN (SHRIIIILL)
MAYBE SHE WAS A HARMLESS GHOST, THEN...
KOSUZU
...BUT NOW THAT SHE'S BEEN LOCKED UP FOR CENTURIES...
......WELL.
HYUUUUU (WHOOOOSH)
WAIT UNTIL THE EVIL SPIRIT APPEARS, THEN FOLLOW THE PLAN.
ZA (ZSH)
YEAH.

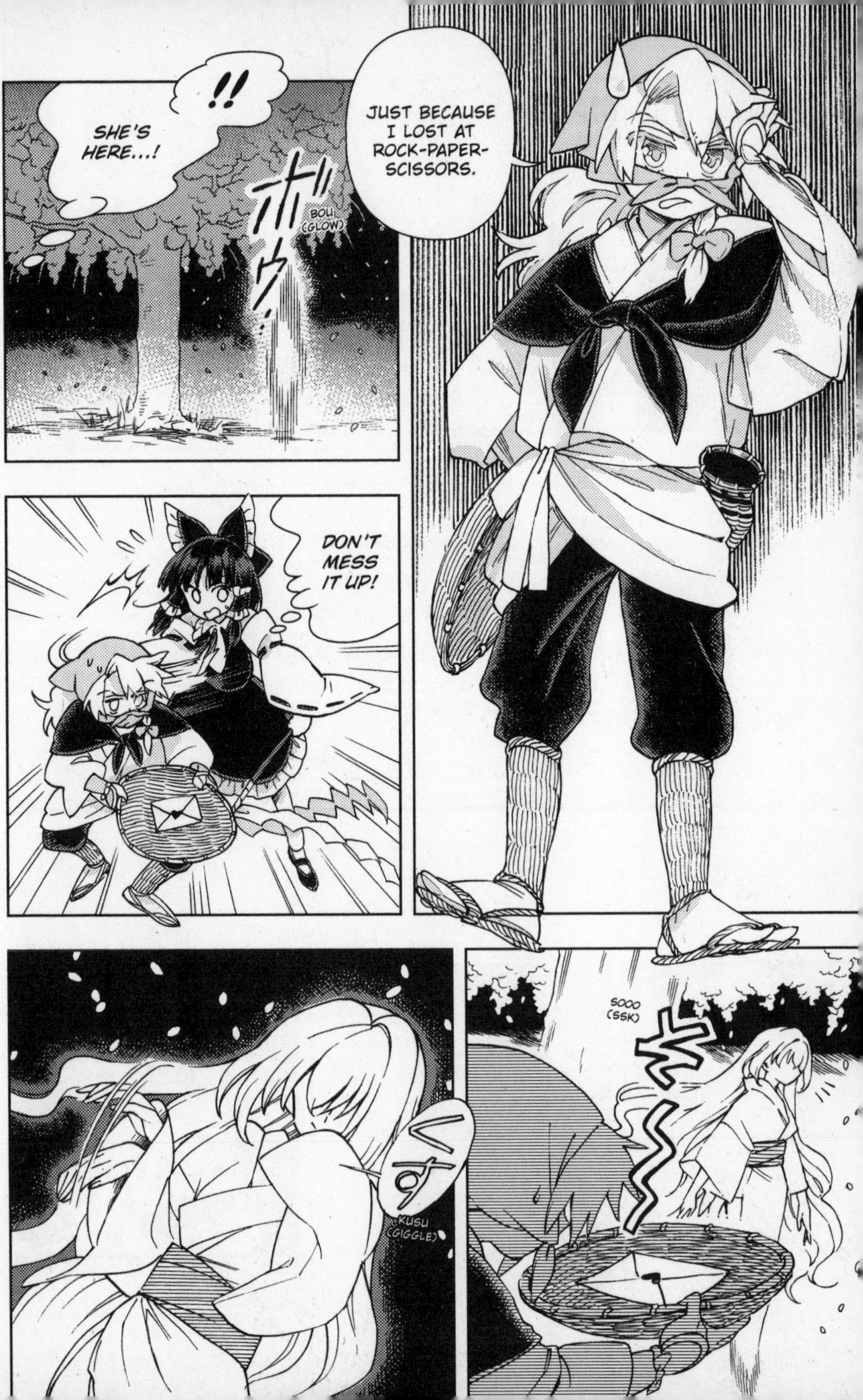
JUST BECAUSE I LOST AT ROCK-PAPER-SCISSORS.
!!
SHE'S HERE...!
BOU (GLOW)
DON'T MESS IT UP!
SOOO (SSK)
KUSU (GIGGLE)

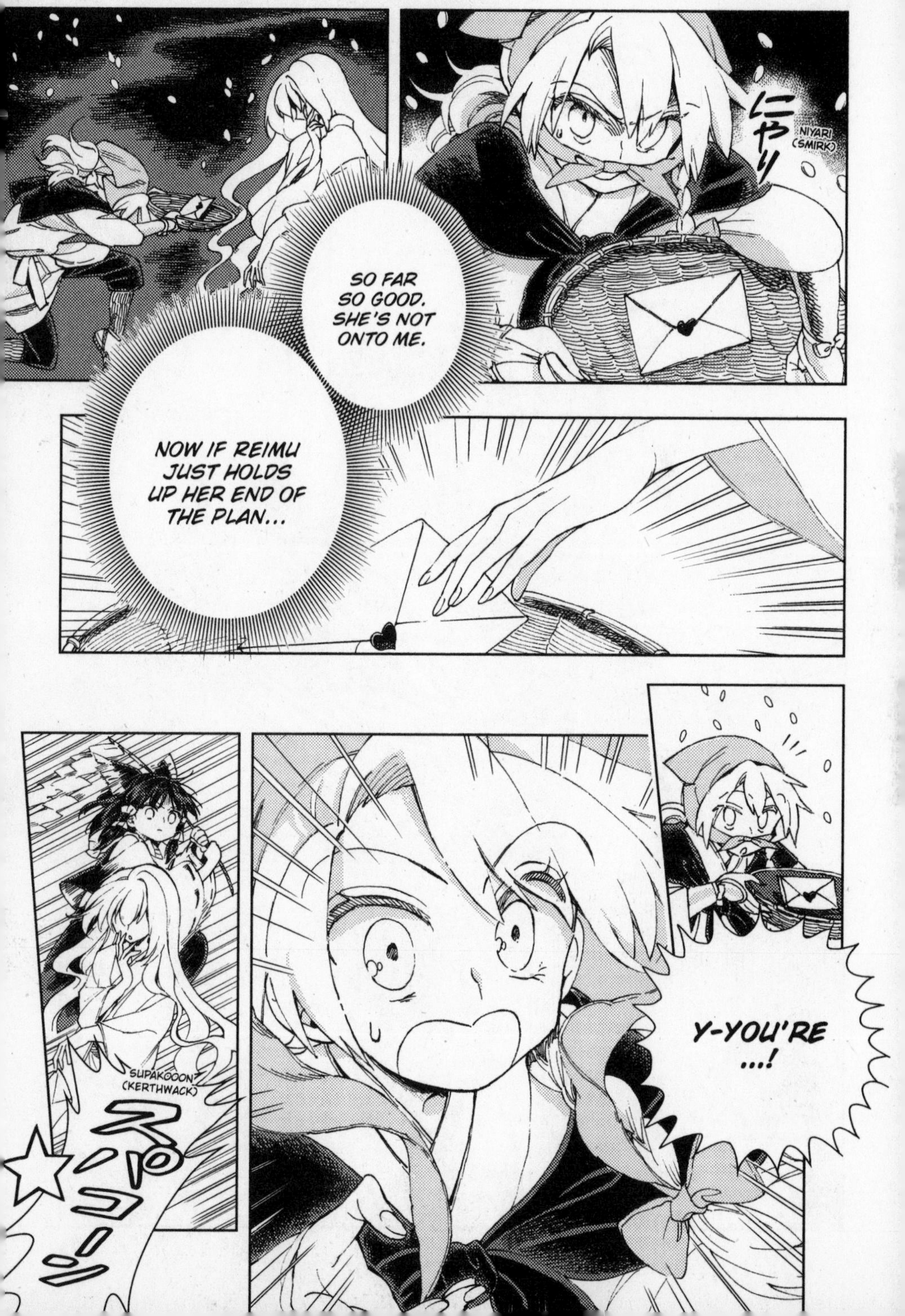
にやり
NIYARI (SMIRK)
SO FAR SO GOOD. SHE'S NOT ONTO ME.
NOW IF REIMU JUST HOLDS UP HER END OF THE PLAN...
Y-YOU'RE ...!
SUPAKOOON (KERTHWACK)

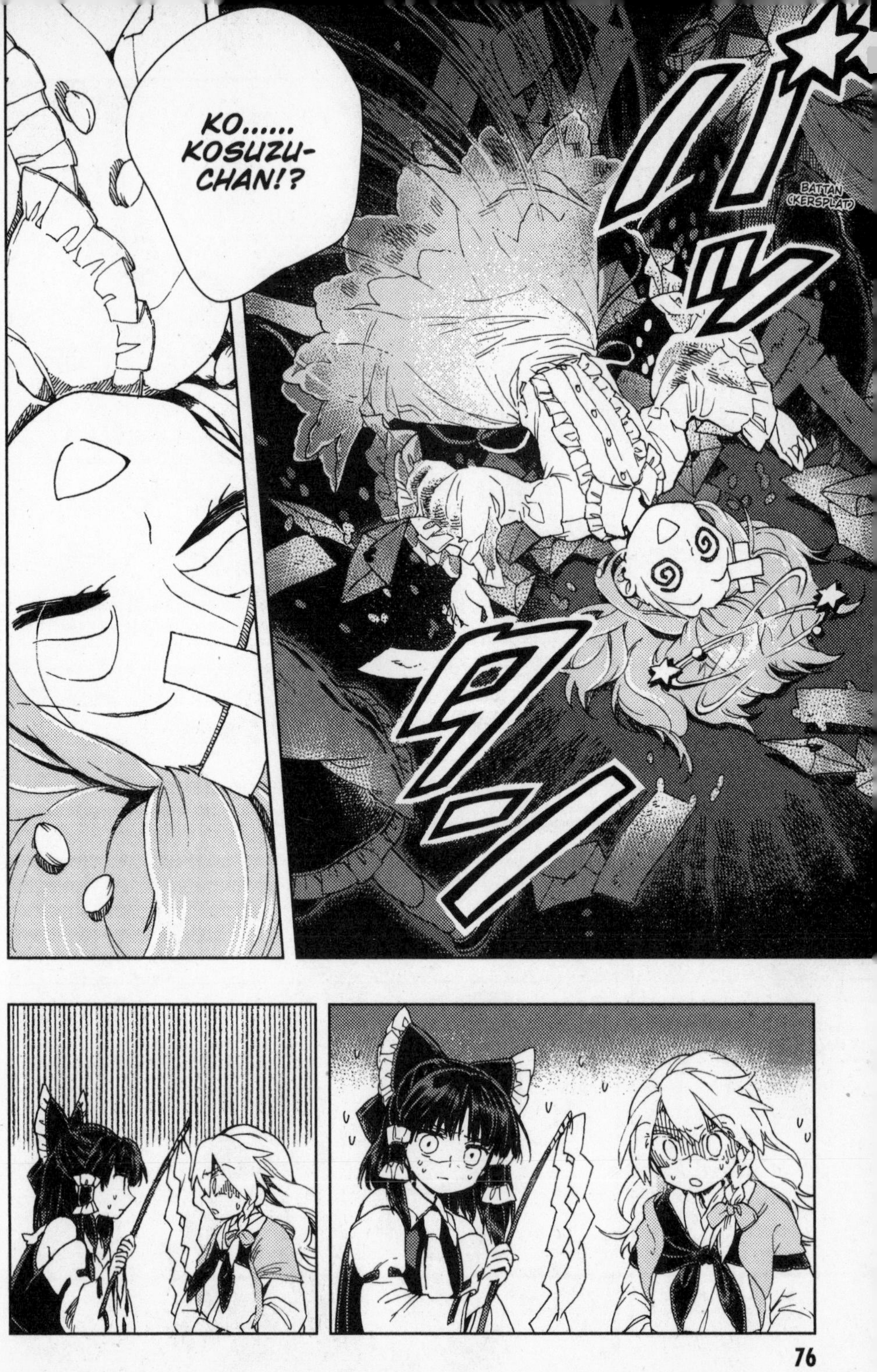
BATTAN (KERSPLAT)
KO...... KOSUZU-CHAN!?

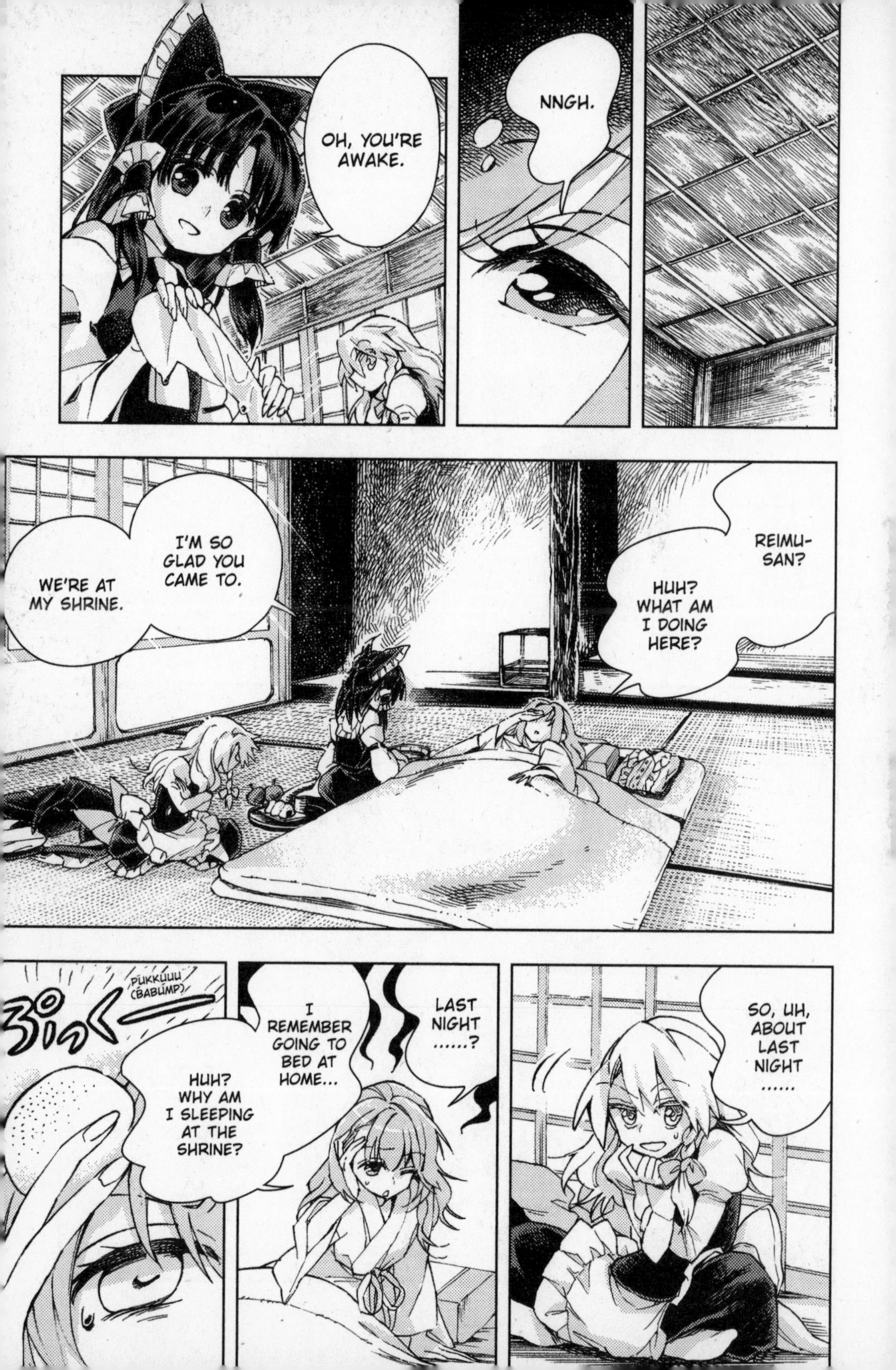
NNGH.
OH, YOU'RE AWAKE.
REIMU-SAN?
HUH? WHAT AM I DOING HERE?
I'M SO GLAD YOU CAME TO.
WE'RE AT MY SHRINE.
SO, UH, ABOUT LAST NIGHT ......
LAST NIGHT ......?
I REMEMBER GOING TO BED AT HOME...
ぷっく
PUKKUUU (BABUMP)
HUH? WHY AM I SLEEPING AT THE SHRINE?

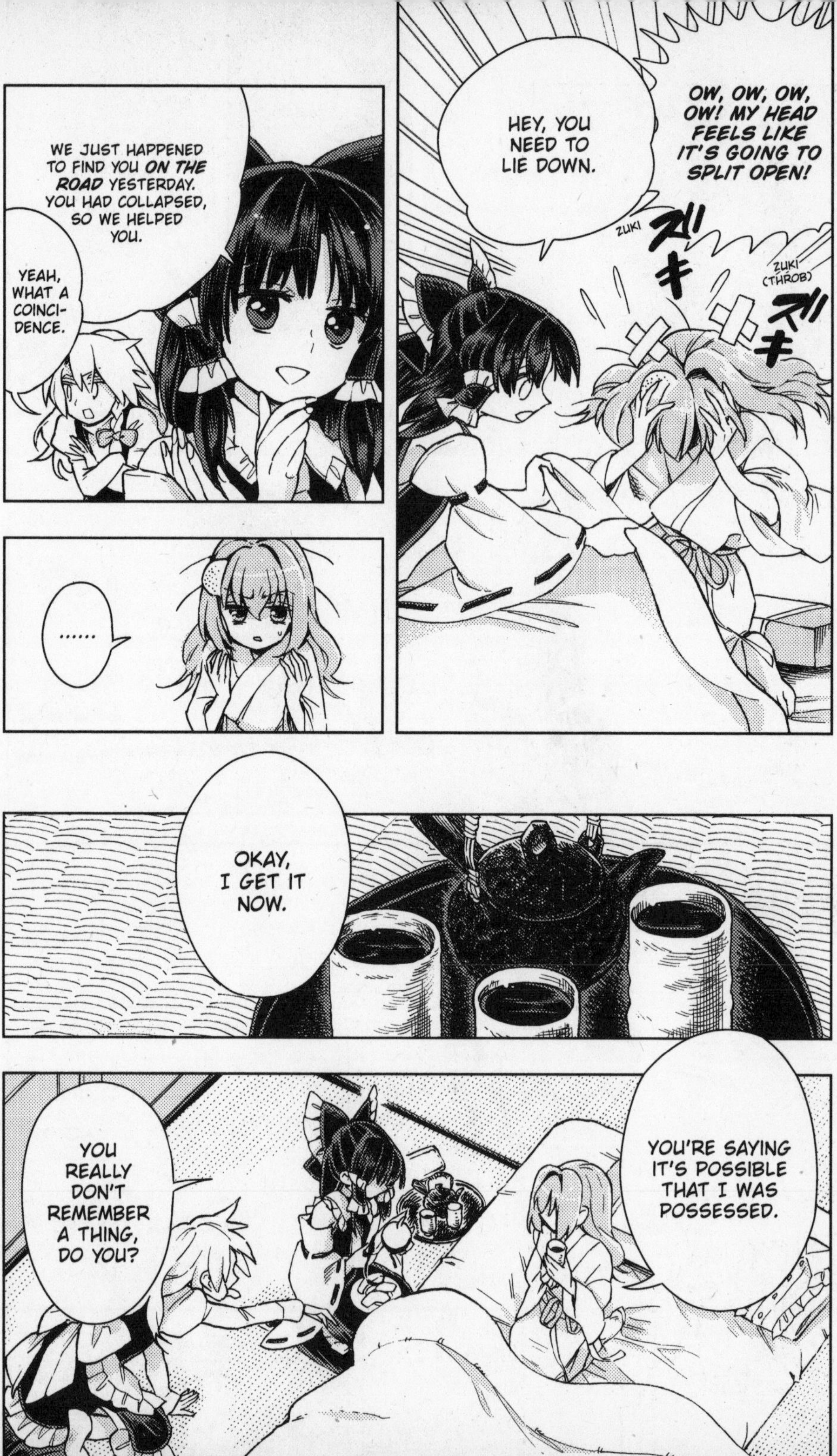
OW, OW, OW, OW! MY HEAD FEELS LIKE IT'S GOING TO SPLIT OPEN!
ZUKI (THROB) ズキ
ZUKI ズキ
HEY, YOU NEED TO LIE DOWN.
WE JUST HAPPENED TO FIND YOU **ON THE ROAD** YESTERDAY. YOU HAD COLLAPSED, SO WE HELPED YOU.
YEAH, WHAT A COINCI-DENCE.
......
OKAY, I GET IT NOW.
YOU'RE SAYING IT'S POSSIBLE THAT I WAS POSSESSED.
YOU REALLY DON'T REMEMBER A THING, DO YOU?

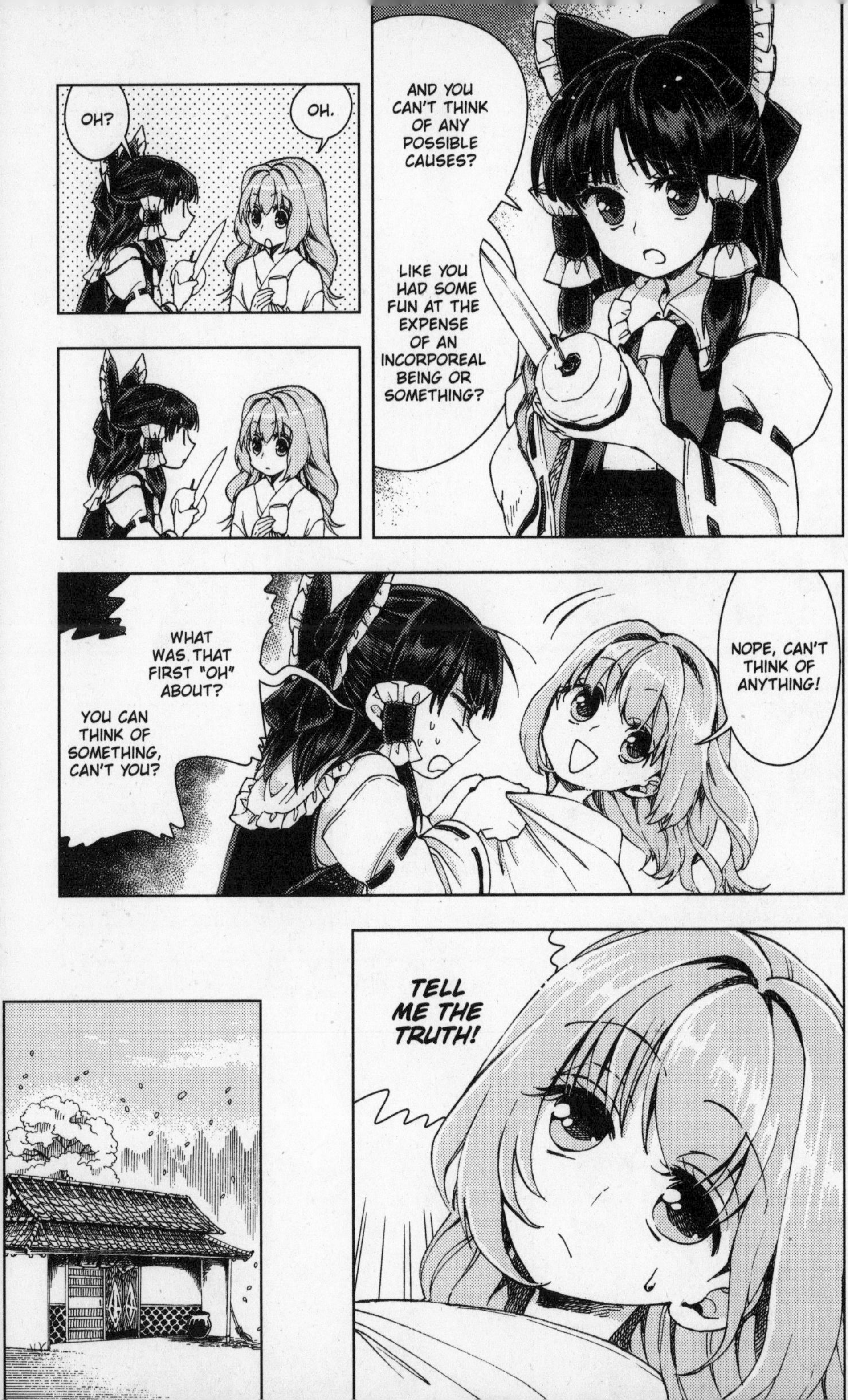
AND YOU CAN'T THINK OF ANY POSSIBLE CAUSES?
LIKE YOU HAD SOME FUN AT THE EXPENSE OF AN INCORPOREAL BEING OR SOMETHING?
OH.
OH?
NOPE, CAN'T THINK OF ANYTHING!
WHAT WAS THAT FIRST "OH" ABOUT?
YOU CAN THINK OF SOMETHING, CAN'T YOU?
TELL ME THE TRUTH!

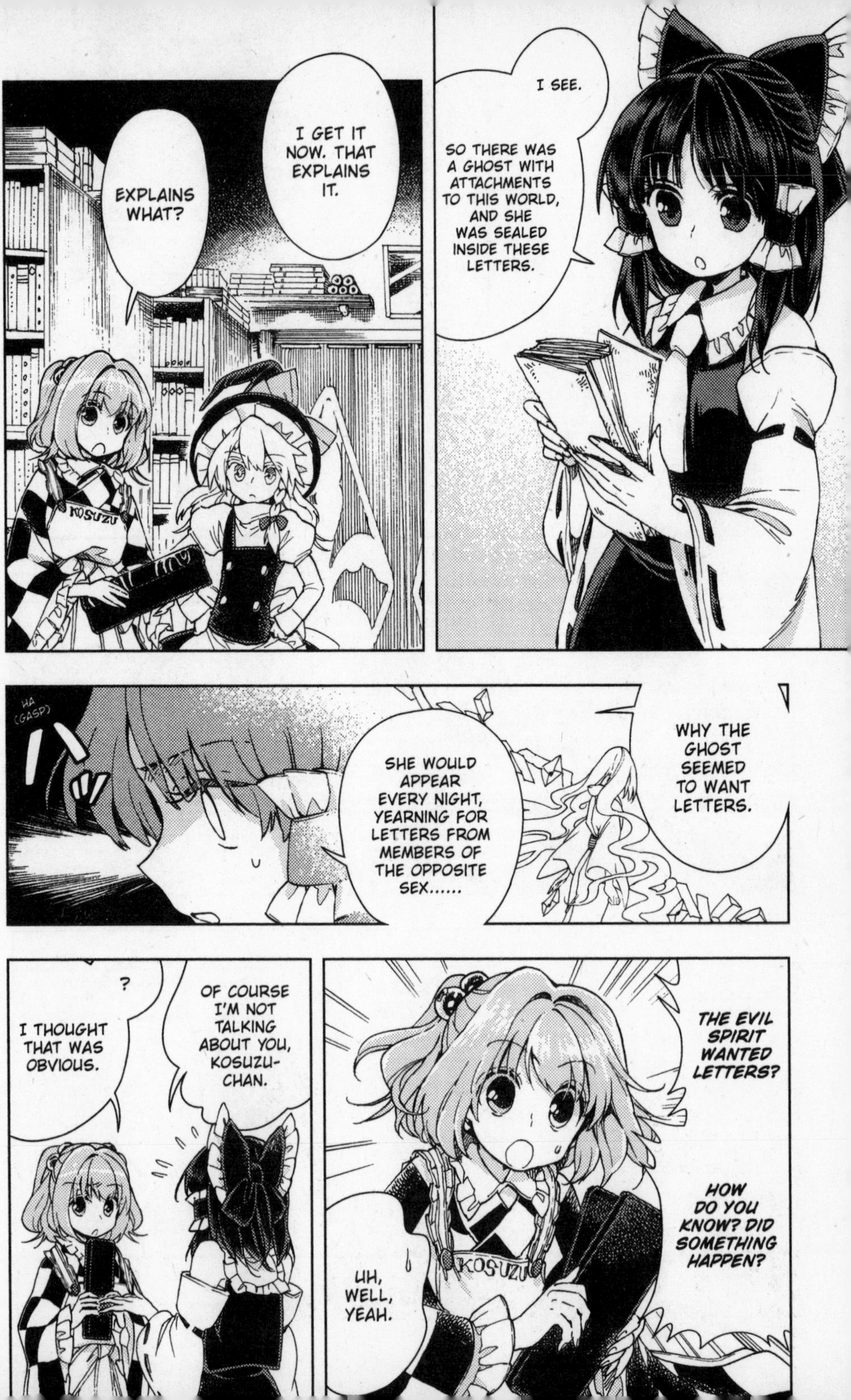

I SEE.
SO THERE WAS A GHOST WITH ATTACHMENTS TO THIS WORLD, AND SHE WAS SEALED INSIDE THESE LETTERS.
I GET IT NOW. THAT EXPLAINS IT.
EXPLAINS WHAT?
WHY THE GHOST SEEMED TO WANT LETTERS.
SHE WOULD APPEAR EVERY NIGHT, YEARNING FOR LETTERS FROM MEMBERS OF THE OPPOSITE SEX......
HA (GASP)
THE EVIL SPIRIT WANTED LETTERS?
HOW DO YOU KNOW? DID SOMETHING HAPPEN?
UH, WELL, YEAH.
?
OF COURSE I'M NOT TALKING ABOUT YOU, KOSUZU-CHAN.
I THOUGHT THAT WAS OBVIOUS.

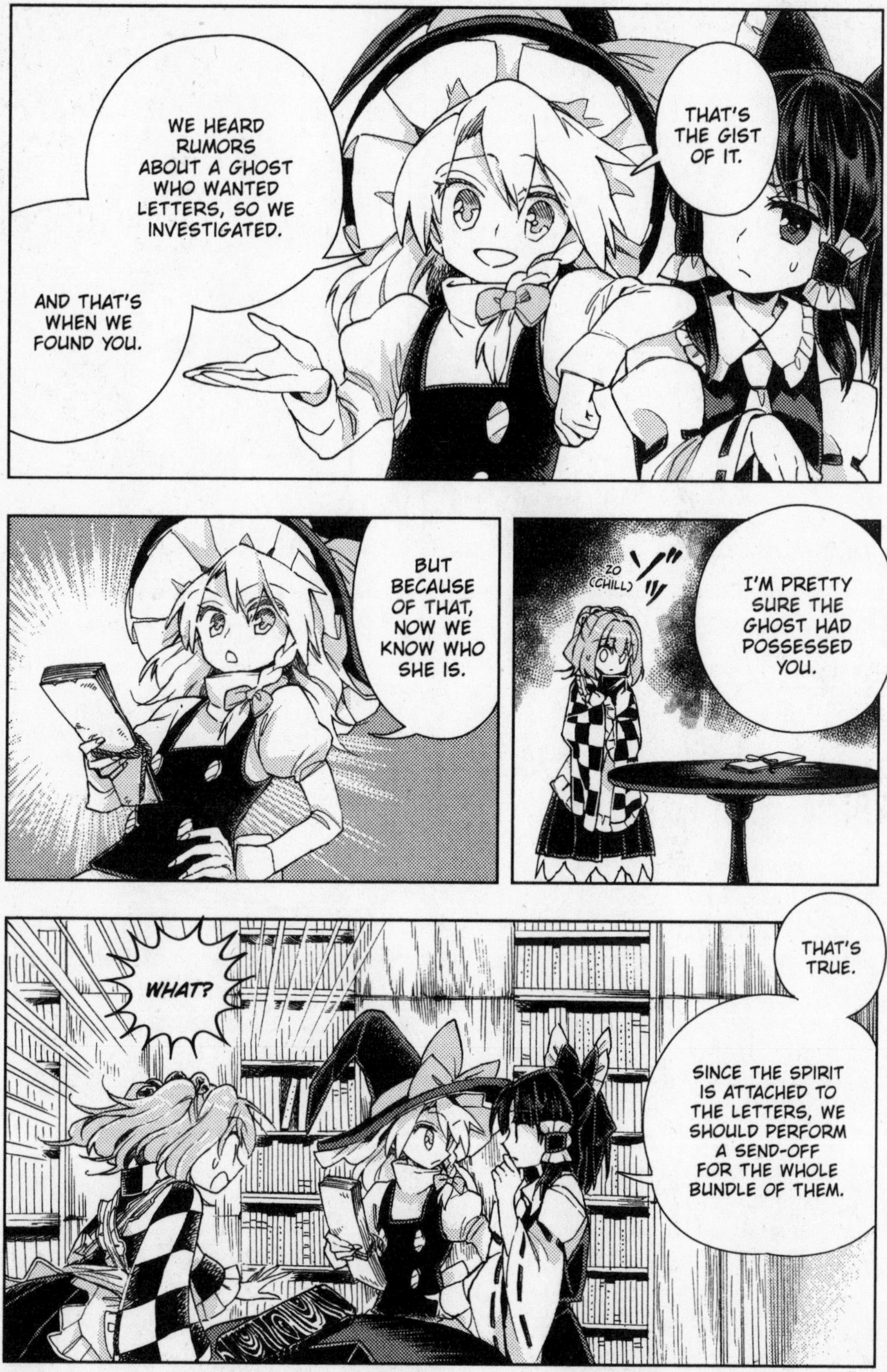
THAT'S THE GIST OF IT.
WE HEARD RUMORS ABOUT A GHOST WHO WANTED LETTERS, SO WE INVESTIGATED.
AND THAT'S WHEN WE FOUND YOU.
I'M PRETTY SURE THE GHOST HAD POSSESSED YOU.
ZO (CHILL)
BUT BECAUSE OF THAT, NOW WE KNOW WHO SHE IS.
THAT'S TRUE.
SINCE THE SPIRIT IS ATTACHED TO THE LETTERS, WE SHOULD PERFORM A SEND-OFF FOR THE WHOLE BUNDLE OF THEM.
WHAT?

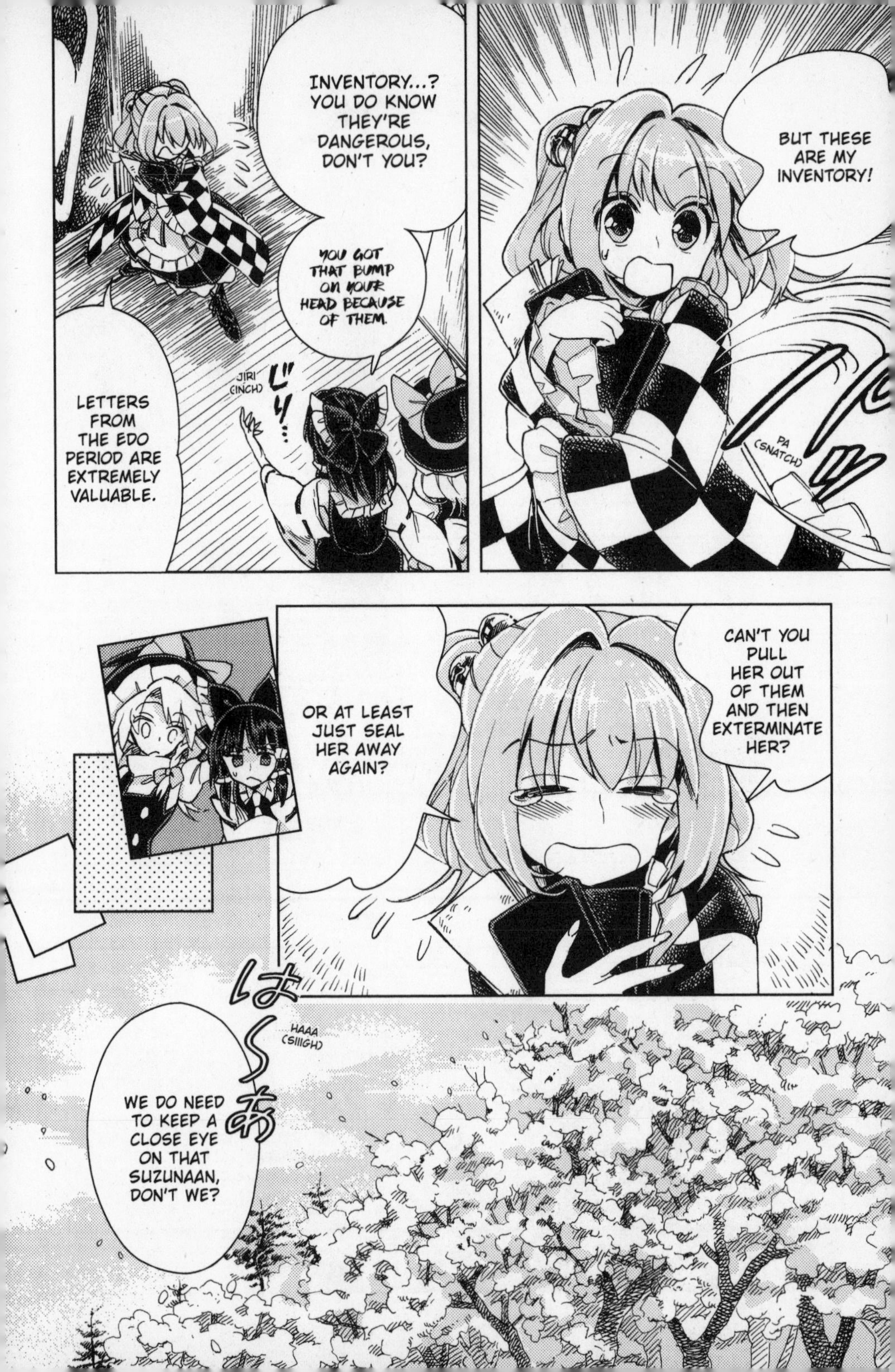

BUT THESE ARE MY INVENTORY!
PA (SNATCH)
INVENTORY...? YOU DO KNOW THEY'RE DANGEROUS, DON'T YOU?
YOU GOT THAT BUMP ON YOUR HEAD BECAUSE OF THEM.
ジリ…
JIRI (INCH)
LETTERS FROM THE EDO PERIOD ARE EXTREMELY VALUABLE.
CAN'T YOU PULL HER OUT OF THEM AND THEN EXTERMINATE HER?
OR AT LEAST JUST SEAL HER AWAY AGAIN?
はぁ
HAAA (SIIIGH)
WE DO NEED TO KEEP A CLOSE EYE ON THAT SUZUNAAN, DON'T WE?

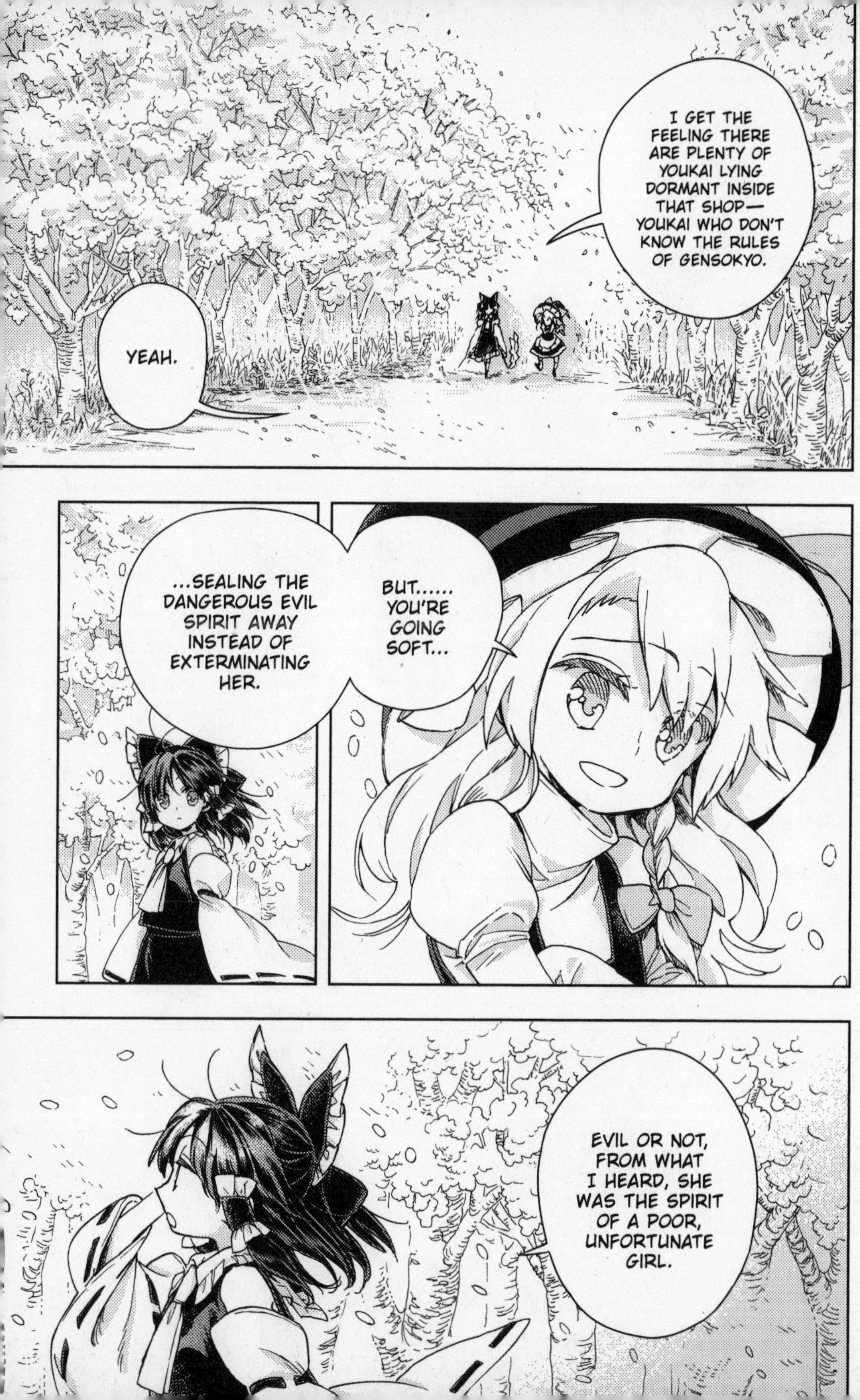
I GET THE FEELING THERE ARE PLENTY OF YOUKAI LYING DORMANT INSIDE THAT SHOP— YOUKAI WHO DON'T KNOW THE RULES OF GENSOKYO.
YEAH.
BUT...... YOU'RE GOING SOFT...
...SEALING THE DANGEROUS EVIL SPIRIT AWAY INSTEAD OF EXTERMINATING HER.
EVIL OR NOT, FROM WHAT I HEARD, SHE WAS THE SPIRIT OF A POOR, UNFORTUNATE GIRL.

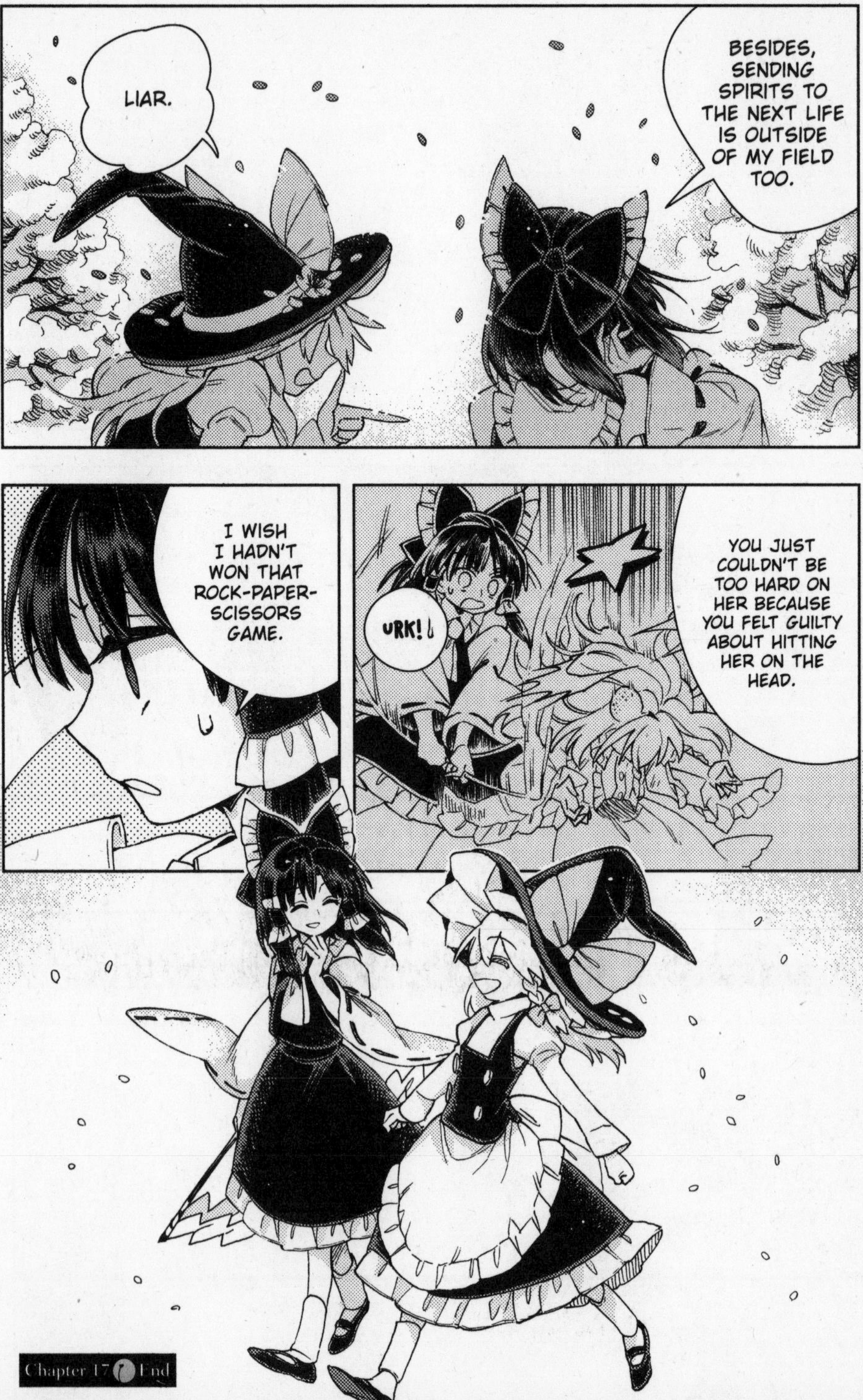
BESIDES, SENDING SPIRITS TO THE NEXT LIFE IS OUTSIDE OF MY FIELD TOO.
LIAR.
YOU JUST COULDN'T BE TOO HARD ON HER BECAUSE YOU FELT GUILTY ABOUT HITTING HER ON THE HEAD.
URK!
I WISH I HADN'T WON THAT ROCK-PAPER-SCISSORS GAME.
Chapter 17 End

# Chapter 18 The Hesitant Book Renter Part 1

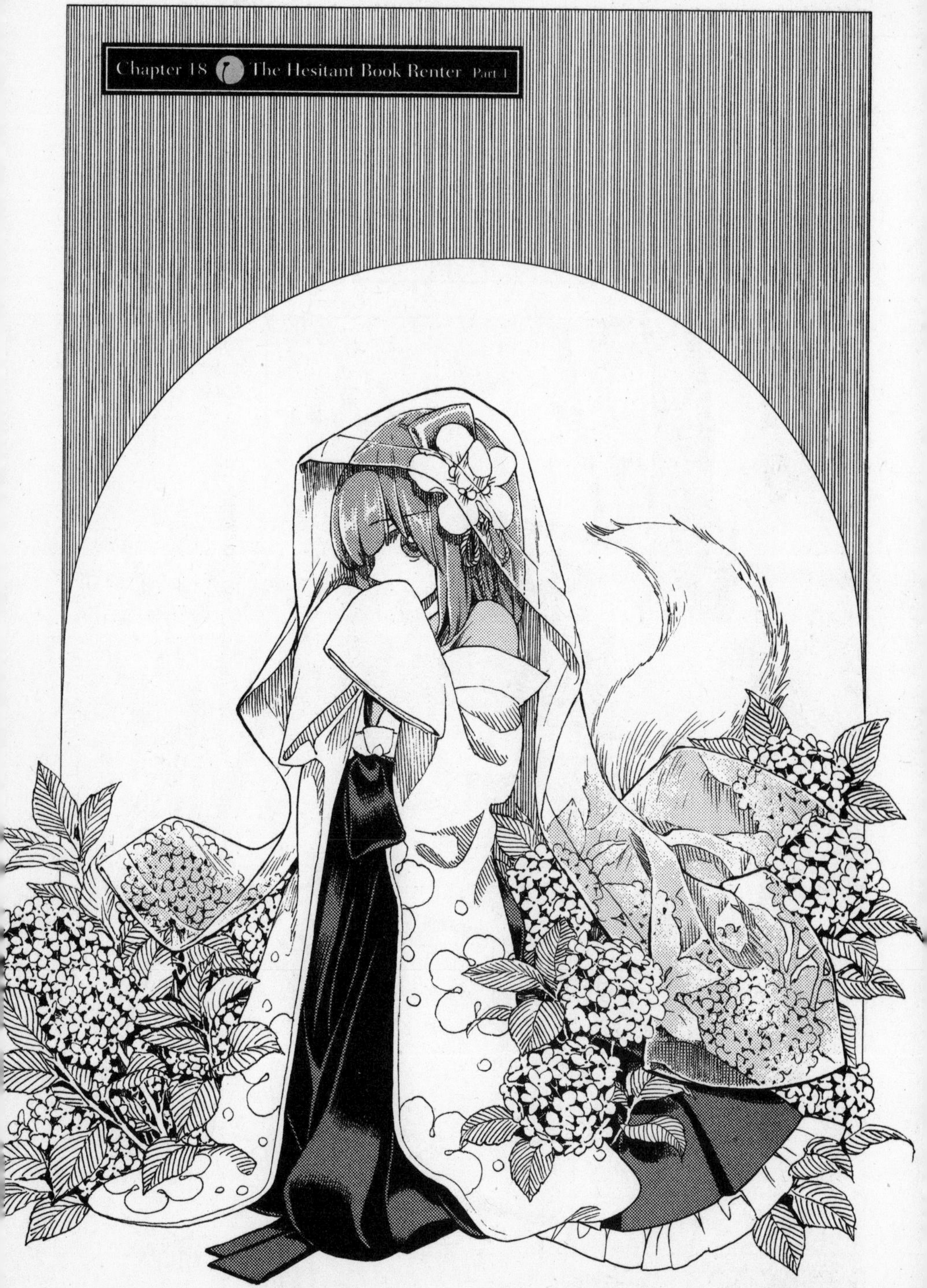

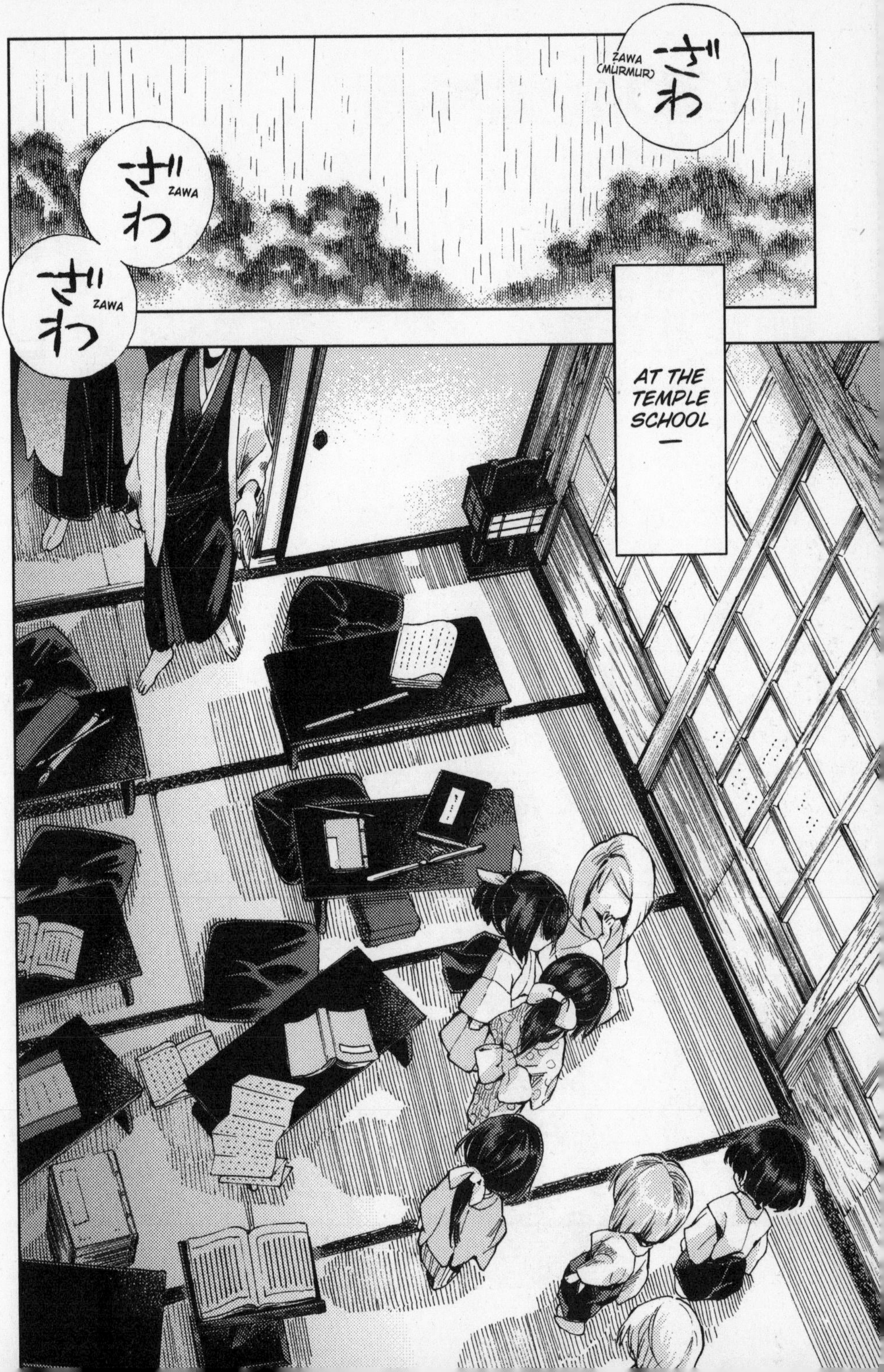
ざわ
ZAWA (MURMUR)
ざわ
ZAWA
ざわ
ZAWA
AT THE TEMPLE SCHOOL —

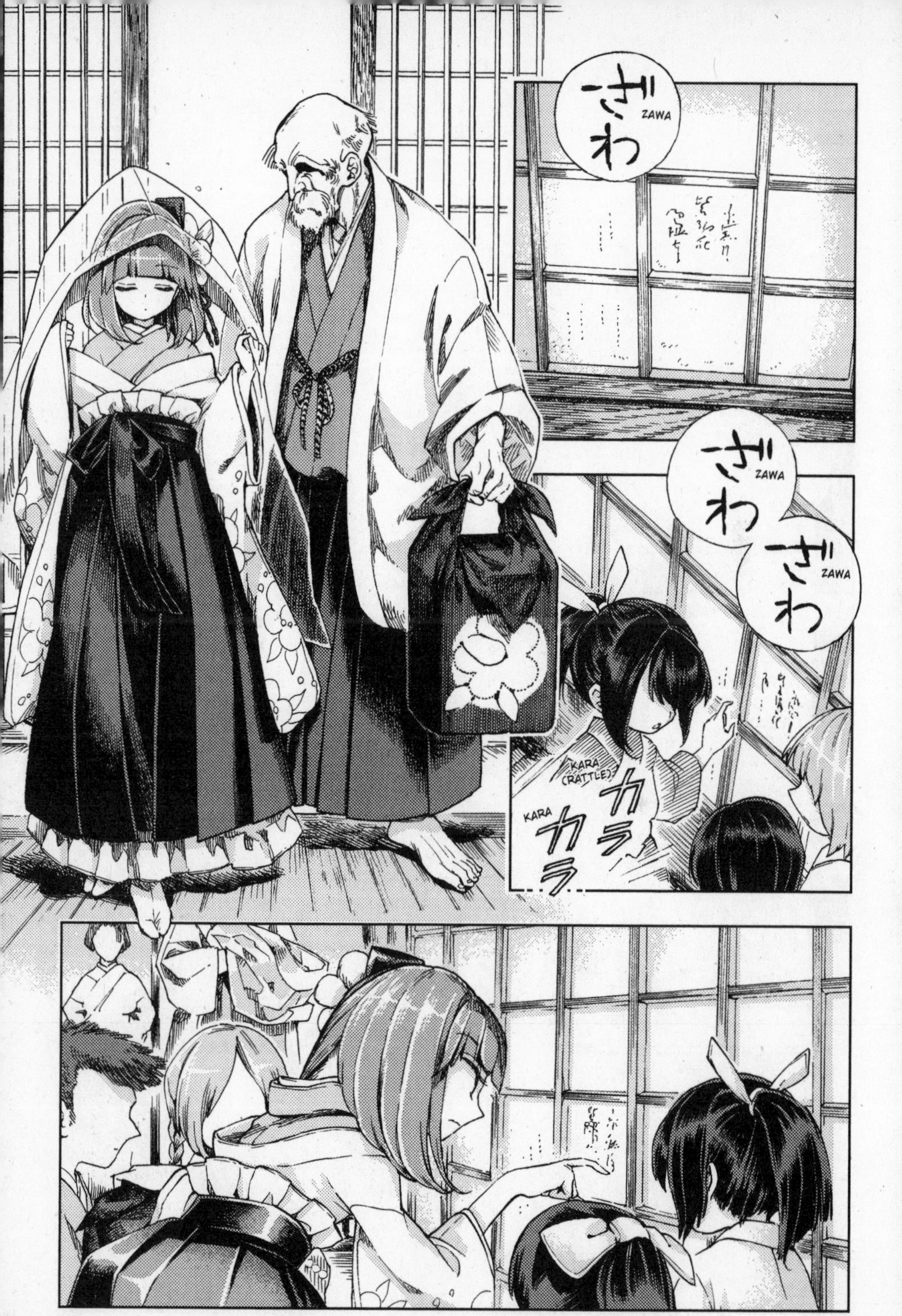
ざわ
ZAWA
ざわ
ZAWA
ざわ
ZAWA
カラ
KARA (RATTLE)
カラ
KARA

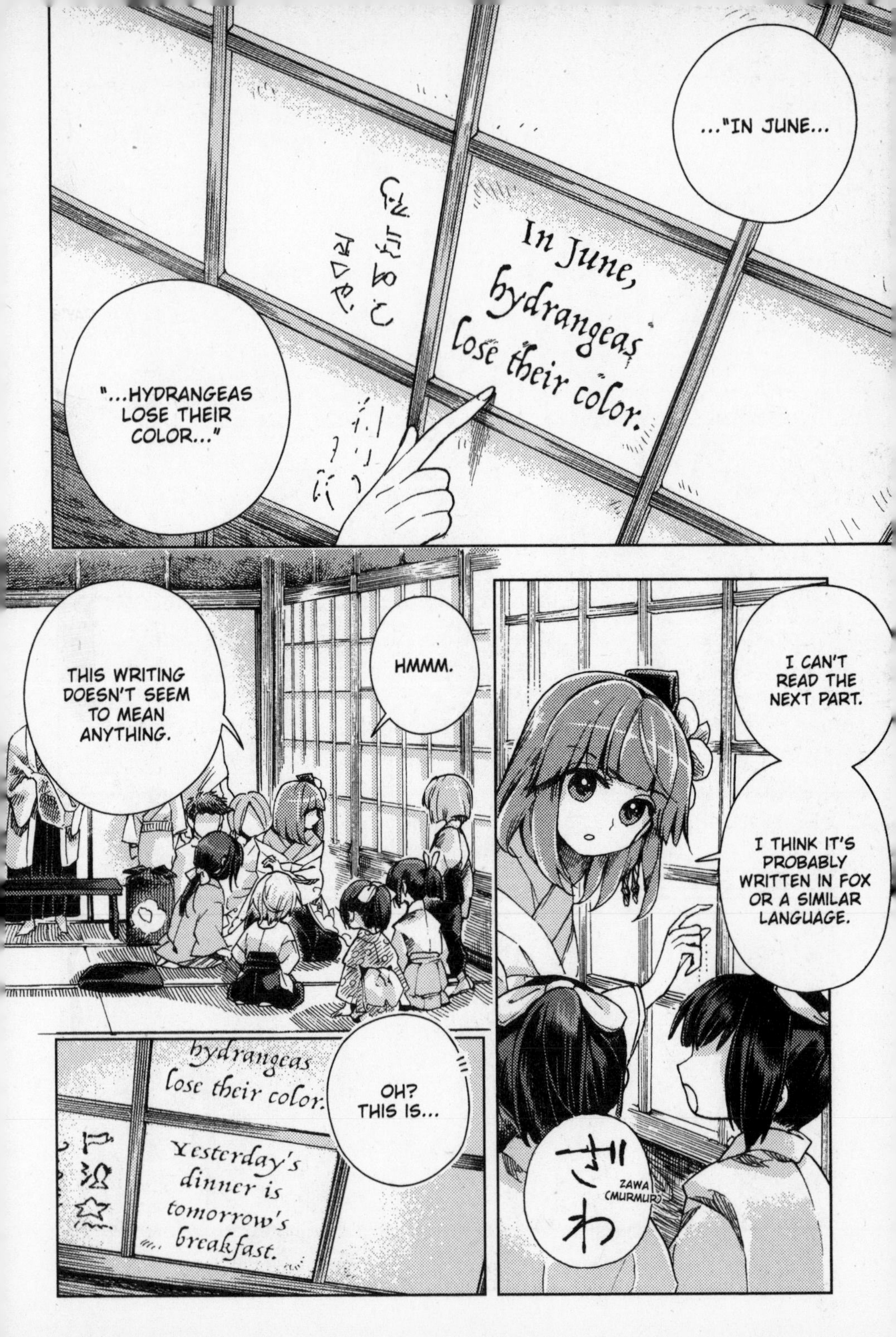
..."IN JUNE...
In June, hydrangeas lose their color.
"...HYDRANGEAS LOSE THEIR COLOR..."
I CAN'T READ THE NEXT PART.
I THINK IT'S PROBABLY WRITTEN IN FOX OR A SIMILAR LANGUAGE.
ざわ
ZAWA (MURMUR)
HMMM.
THIS WRITING DOESN'T SEEM TO MEAN ANYTHING.
OH? THIS IS...
hydrangeas lose their color.
Yesterday's dinner is tomorrow's breakfast.

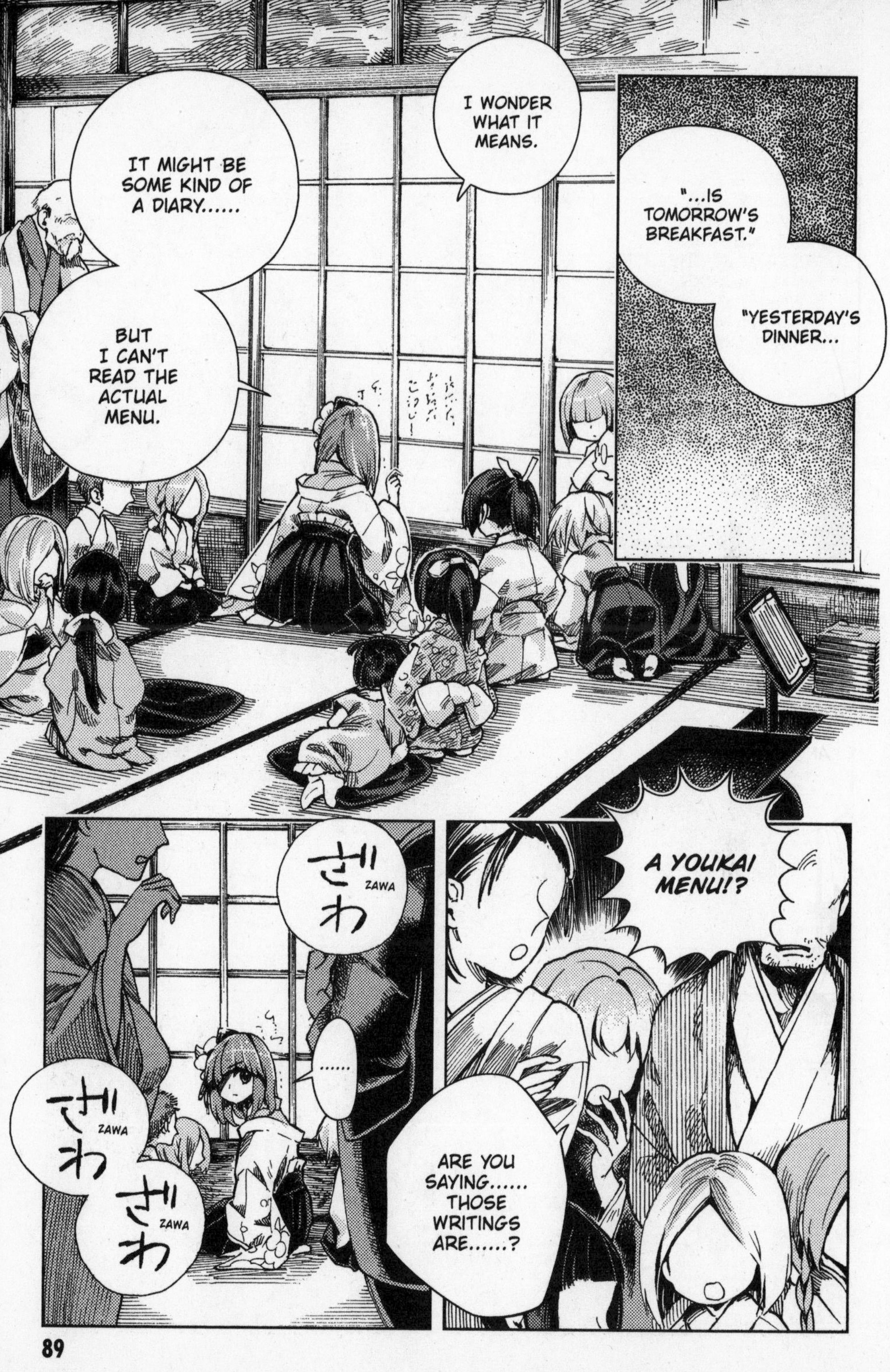
"YESTERDAY'S DINNER...
"...IS TOMORROW'S BREAKFAST."
I WONDER WHAT IT MEANS.
IT MIGHT BE SOME KIND OF A DIARY......
BUT I CAN'T READ THE ACTUAL MENU.
ARE YOU SAYING...... THOSE WRITINGS ARE......?
A YOUKAI MENU!?
ざわ ZAWA
......
ざわ ZAWA
ざわ ZAWA

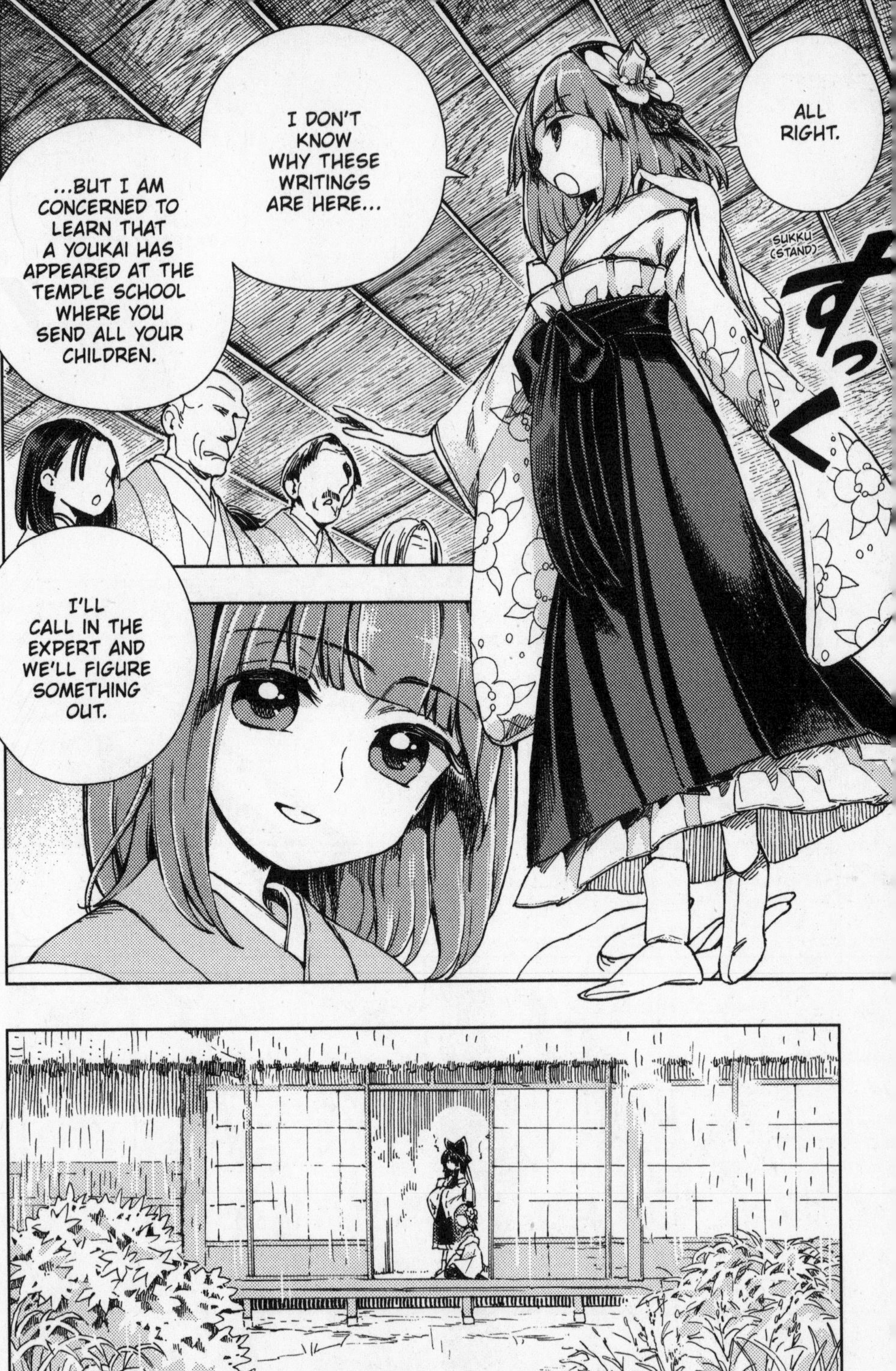
ALL RIGHT.
SUKKU (STAND)
I DON'T KNOW WHY THESE WRITINGS ARE HERE...
...BUT I AM CONCERNED TO LEARN THAT A YOUKAI HAS APPEARED AT THE TEMPLE SCHOOL WHERE YOU SEND ALL YOUR CHILDREN.
I'LL CALL IN THE EXPERT AND WE'LL FIGURE SOMETHING OUT.

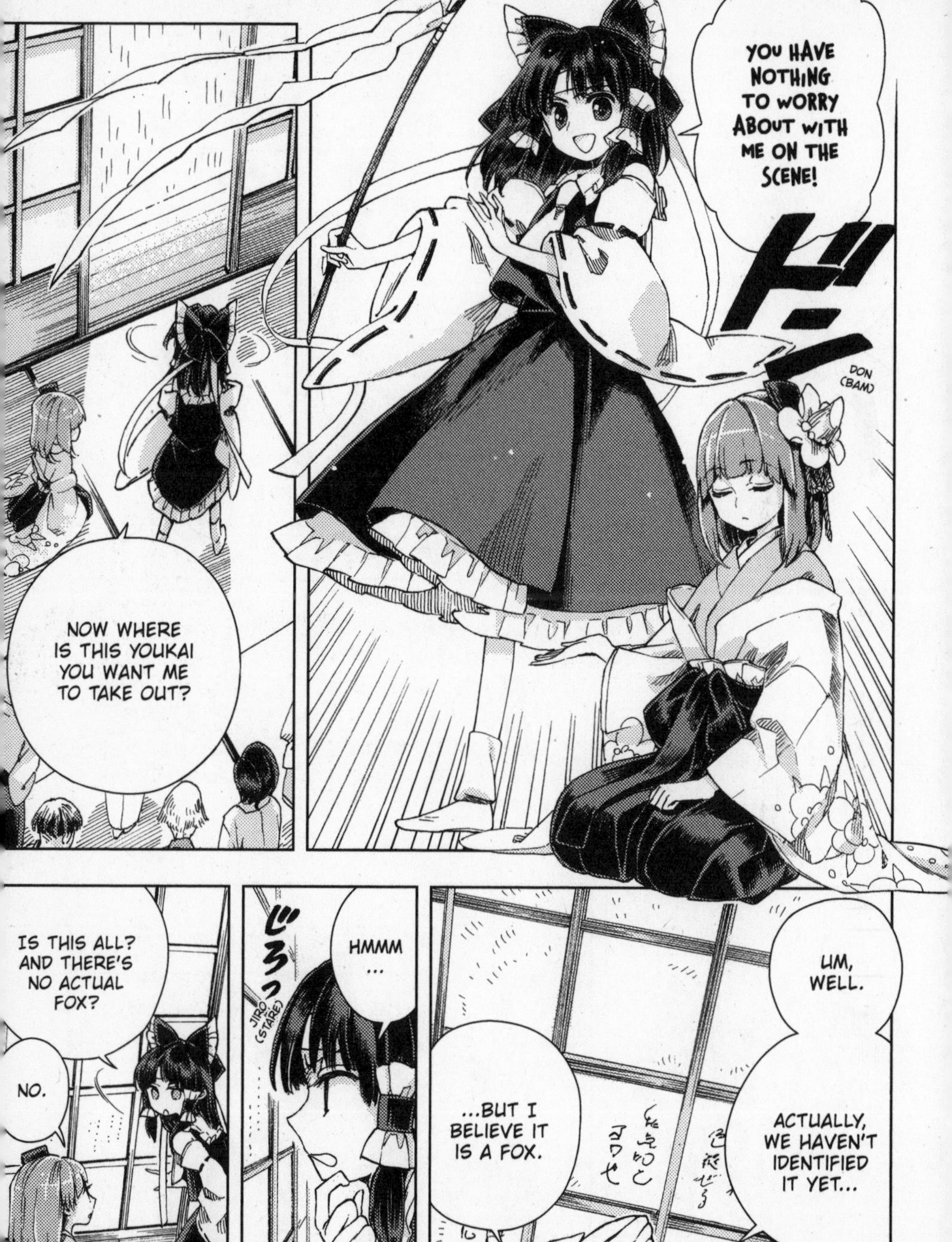
YOU HAVE NOTHING TO WORRY ABOUT WITH ME ON THE SCENE!
DON (BAM)
NOW WHERE IS THIS YOUKAI YOU WANT ME TO TAKE OUT?
UM, WELL.
ACTUALLY, WE HAVEN'T IDENTIFIED IT YET...
HMMM ...
...BUT I BELIEVE IT IS A FOX.
じろっ
JIRO (STARE)
IS THIS ALL? AND THERE'S NO ACTUAL FOX?
NO.

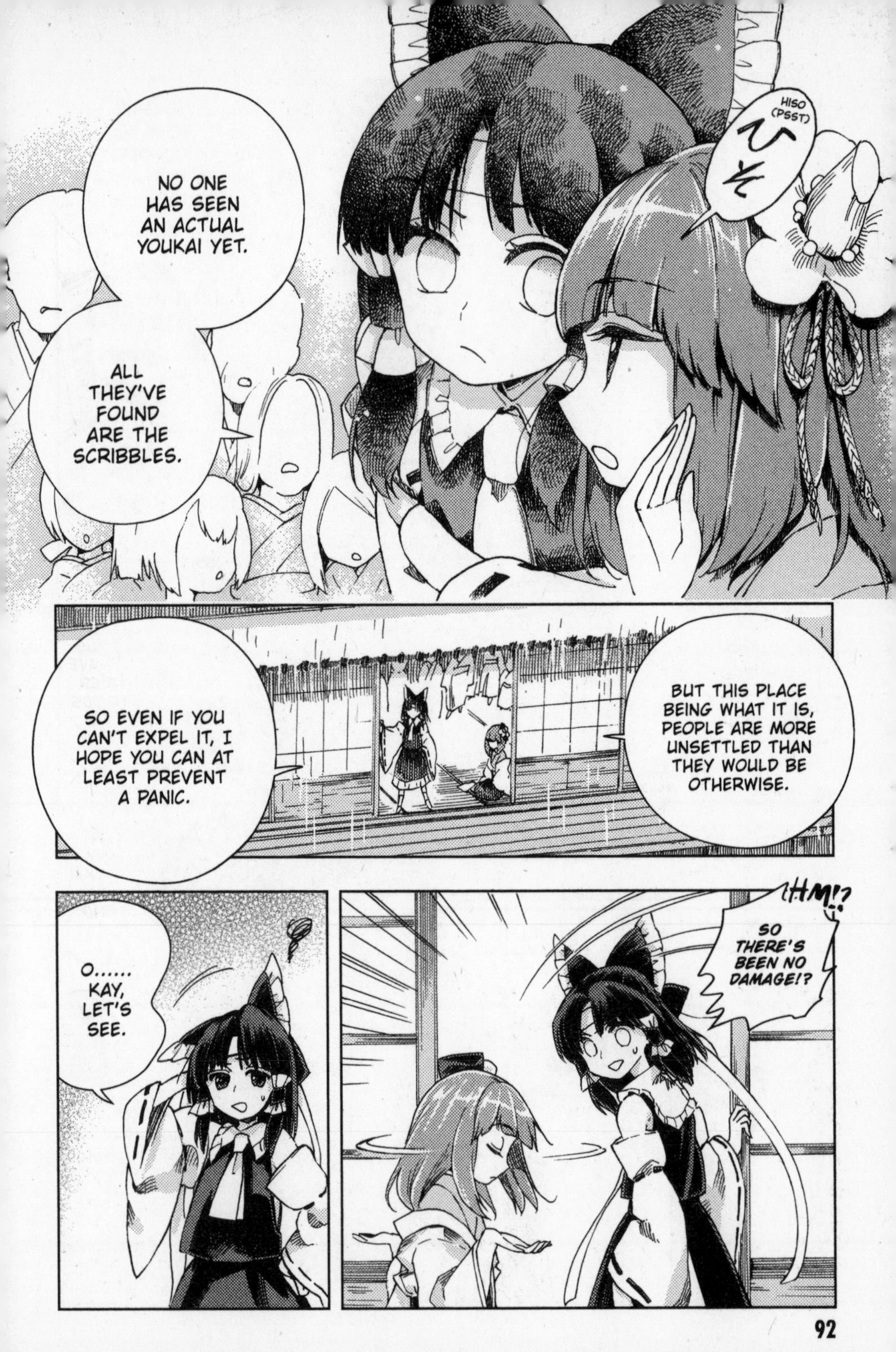
HISO (PSST) ひそ
NO ONE HAS SEEN AN ACTUAL YOUKAI YET.
ALL THEY'VE FOUND ARE THE SCRIBBLES.
BUT THIS PLACE BEING WHAT IT IS, PEOPLE ARE MORE UNSETTLED THAN THEY WOULD BE OTHERWISE.
SO EVEN IF YOU CAN'T EXPEL IT, I HOPE YOU CAN AT LEAST PREVENT A PANIC.
HM!?
SO THERE'S BEEN NO DAMAGE!?
O...... KAY, LET'S SEE.

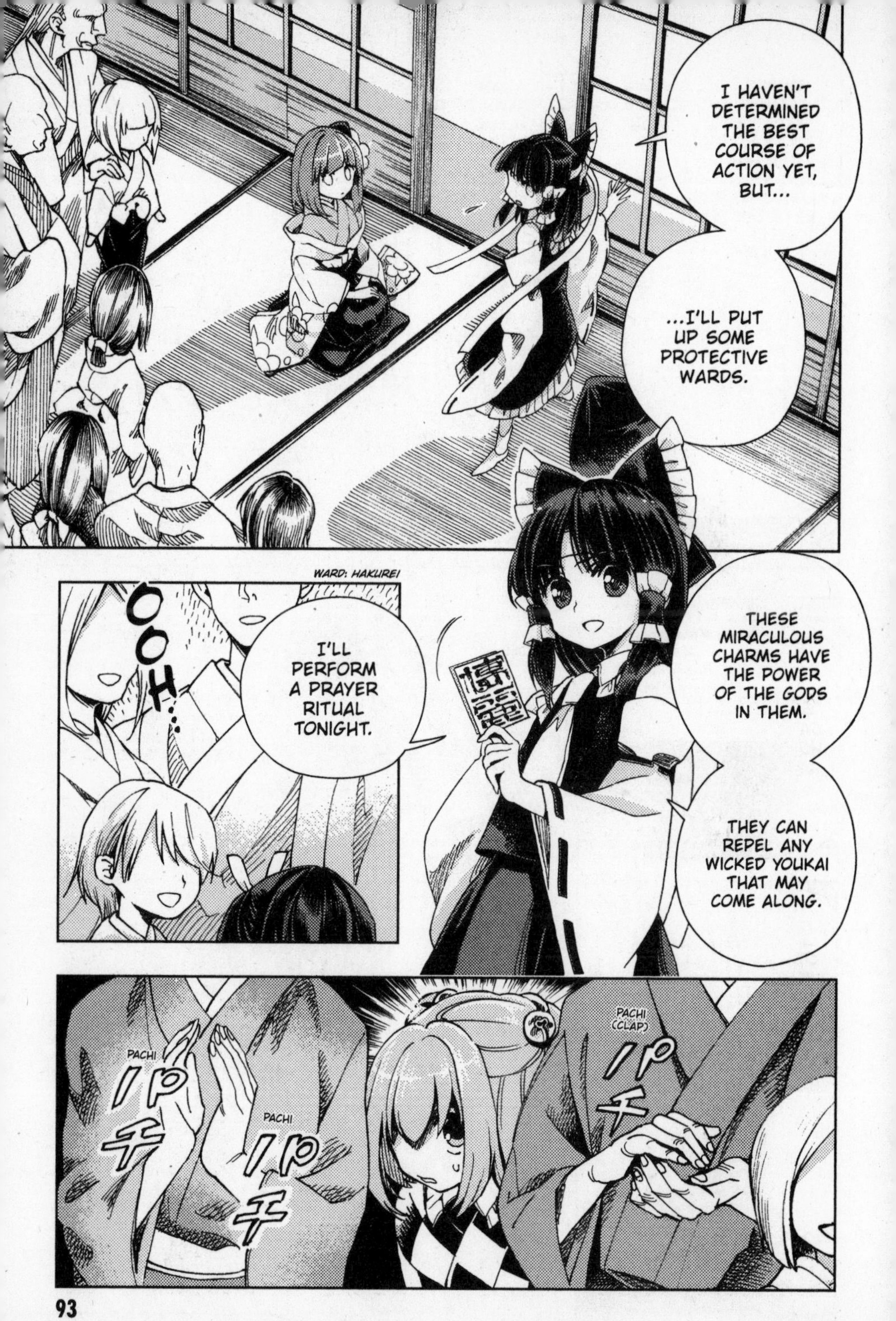
I HAVEN'T DETERMINED THE BEST COURSE OF ACTION YET, BUT...
...I'LL PUT UP SOME PROTECTIVE WARDS.
THESE MIRACULOUS CHARMS HAVE THE POWER OF THE GODS IN THEM.
THEY CAN REPEL ANY WICKED YOUKAI THAT MAY COME ALONG.
WARD: HAKUREI
博麗
I'LL PERFORM A PRAYER RITUAL TONIGHT.
OOH...
PACHI (CLAP)
パチ
PACHI
パチ
PACHI
パチ

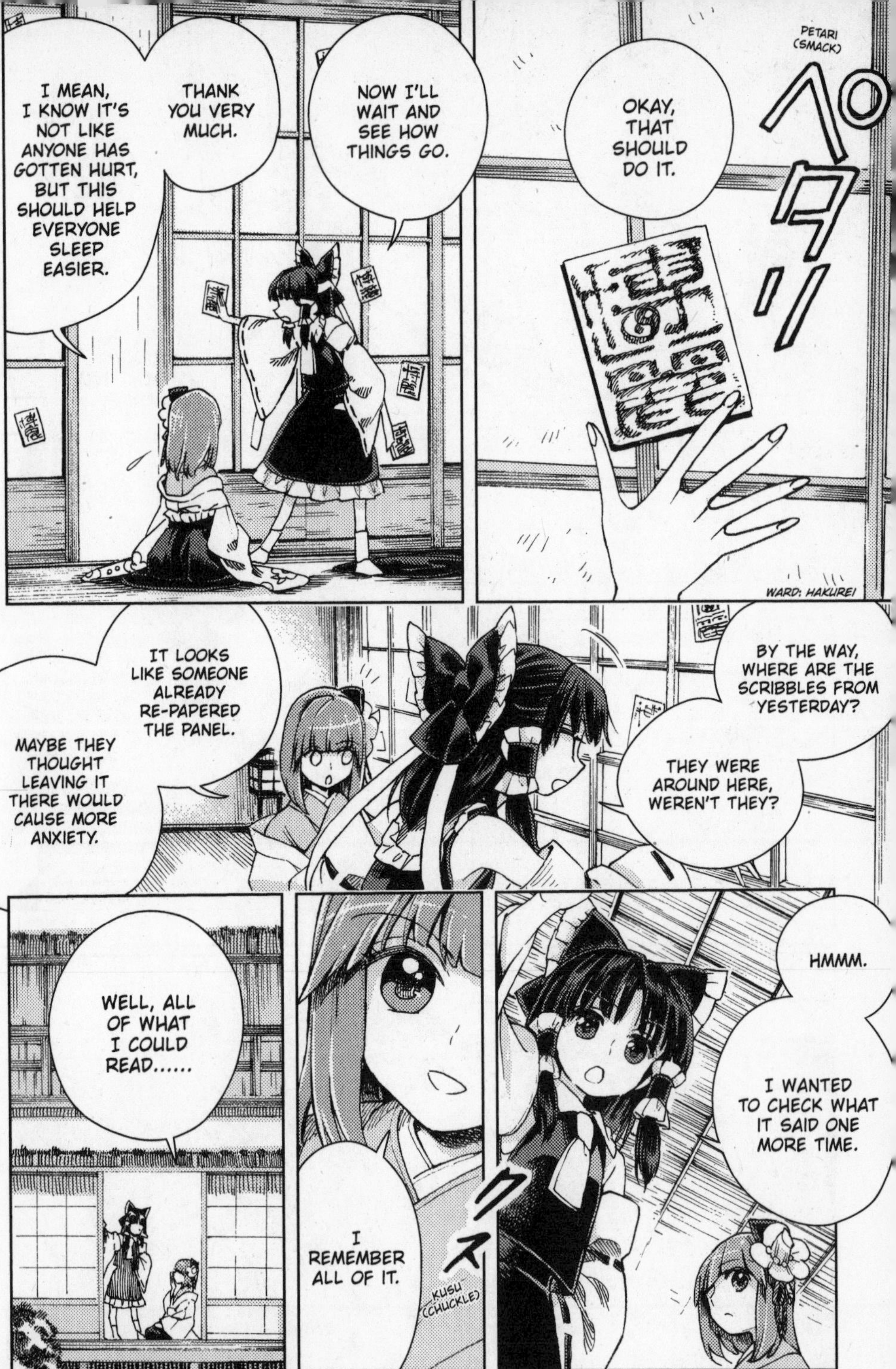
PETARI (SMACK)
OKAY, THAT SHOULD DO IT.
WARD: HAKUREI
NOW I'LL WAIT AND SEE HOW THINGS GO.
THANK YOU VERY MUCH.
I MEAN, I KNOW IT'S NOT LIKE ANYONE HAS GOTTEN HURT, BUT THIS SHOULD HELP EVERYONE SLEEP EASIER.
BY THE WAY, WHERE ARE THE SCRIBBLES FROM YESTERDAY?
THEY WERE AROUND HERE, WEREN'T THEY?
IT LOOKS LIKE SOMEONE ALREADY RE-PAPERED THE PANEL.
MAYBE THEY THOUGHT LEAVING IT THERE WOULD CAUSE MORE ANXIETY.
HMMM.
I WANTED TO CHECK WHAT IT SAID ONE MORE TIME.
I REMEMBER ALL OF IT.
KUSU (CHUCKLE)
WELL, ALL OF WHAT I COULD READ......

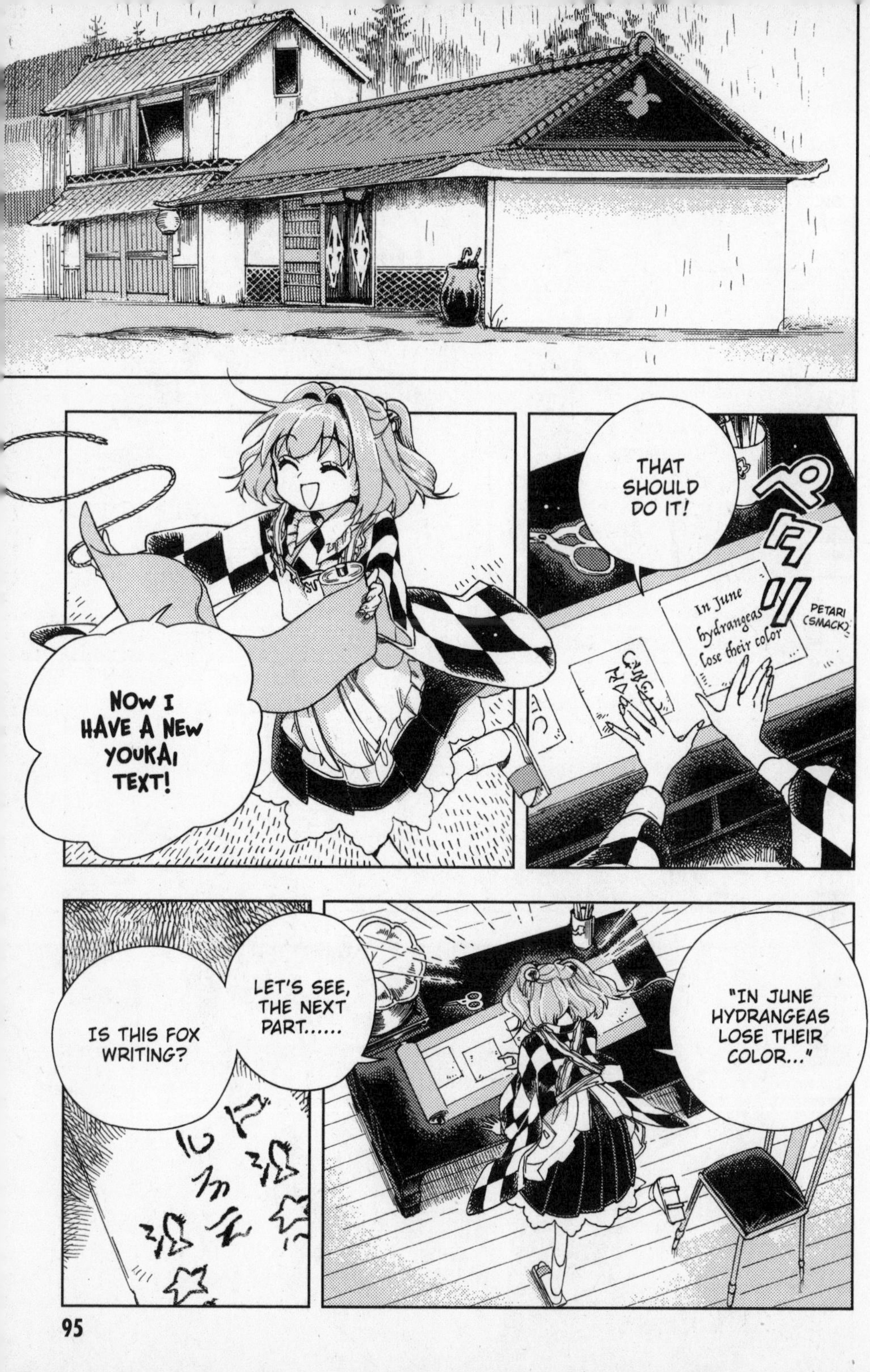
THAT SHOULD DO IT!
PETARI (SMACK)
In June hydrangeas lose their color ...
NOW I HAVE A NEW YOUKAI TEXT!
"IN JUNE HYDRANGEAS LOSE THEIR COLOR..."
LET'S SEE, THE NEXT PART......
IS THIS FOX WRITING?

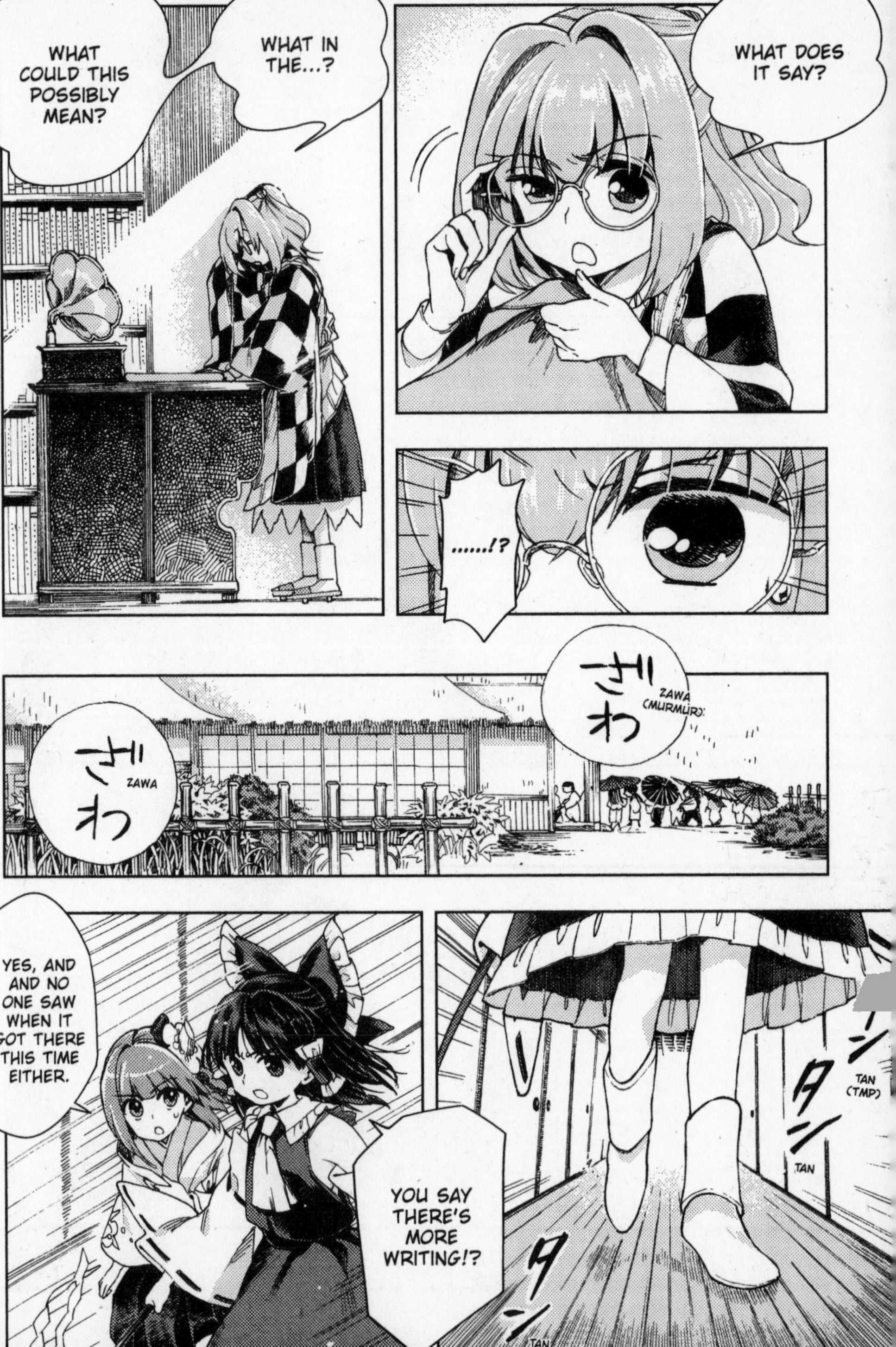
WHAT DOES IT SAY?
......!?
WHAT IN THE...?
WHAT COULD THIS POSSIBLY MEAN?
ざわ
ZAWA (MURMUR)
ざわ
ZAWA
タン
TAN (TMP)
タン
TAN
タン
TAN
YOU SAY THERE'S MORE WRITING!?
YES, AND AND NO ONE SAW WHEN IT GOT THERE THIS TIME EITHER.

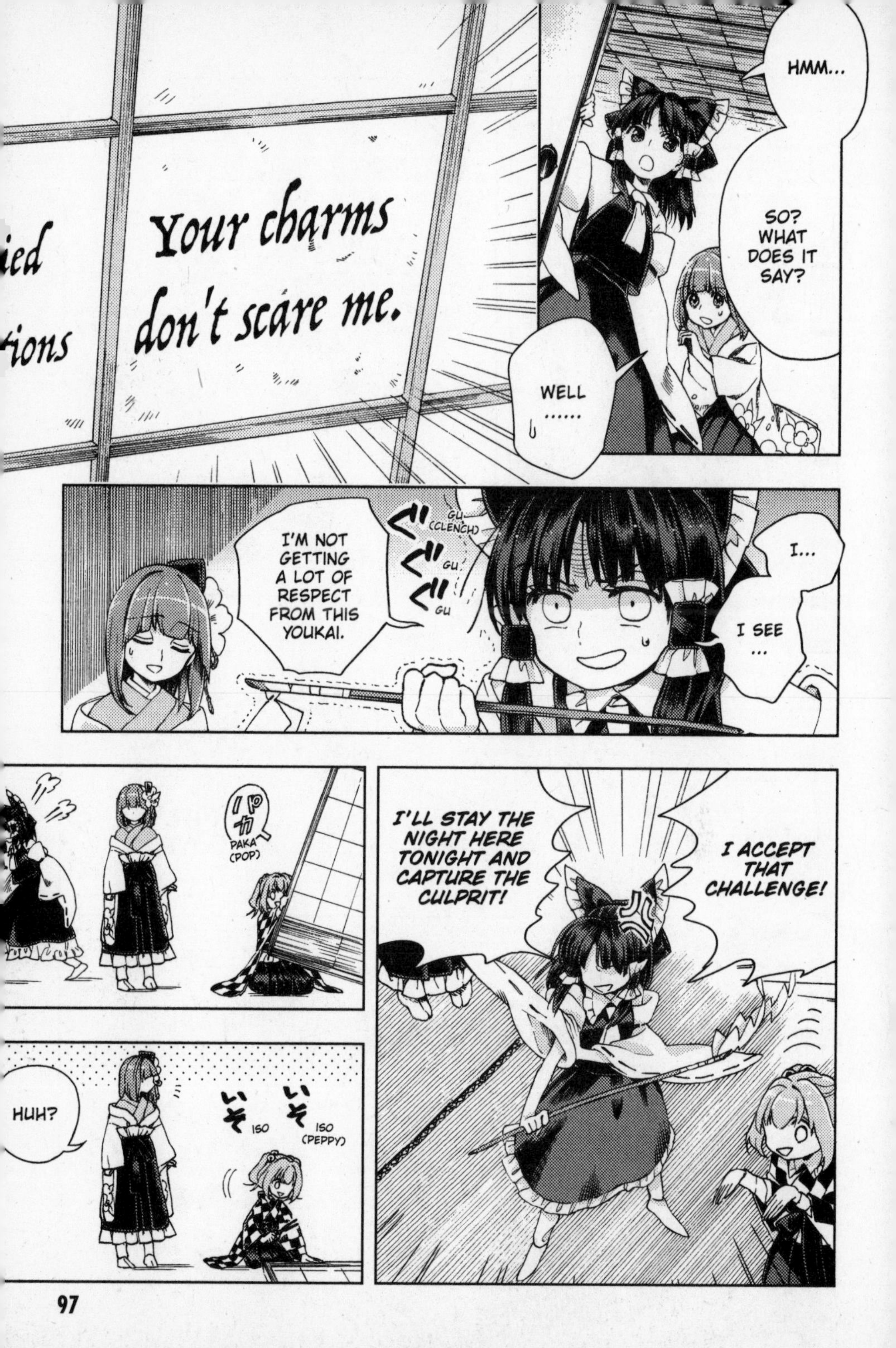
HMM...
SO? WHAT DOES IT SAY?
WELL ......
Your charms don't scare me.
I...
I SEE ...
ぐ GU (CLENCH)
ぐ GU
ぐ GU
I'M NOT GETTING A LOT OF RESPECT FROM THIS YOUKAI.
I ACCEPT THAT CHALLENGE!
I'LL STAY THE NIGHT HERE TONIGHT AND CAPTURE THE CULPRIT!
パカ PAKA (POP)
いそ ISO (PEPPY)
いそ ISO
HUH?

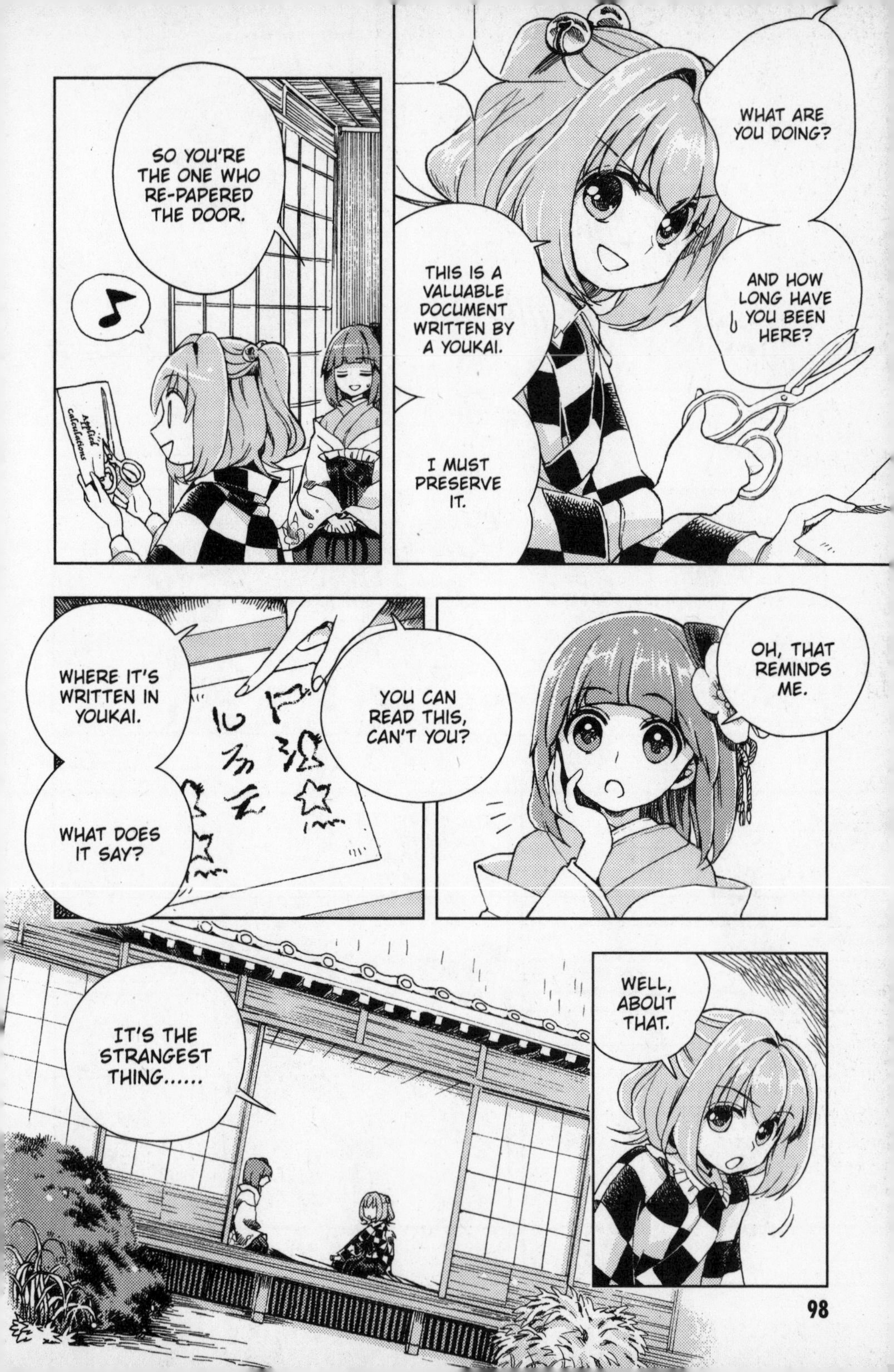
WHAT ARE YOU DOING?
AND HOW LONG HAVE YOU BEEN HERE?
THIS IS A VALUABLE DOCUMENT WRITTEN BY A YOUKAI.
I MUST PRESERVE IT.
SO YOU'RE THE ONE WHO RE-PAPERED THE DOOR.
Applied calculations
OH, THAT REMINDS ME.
YOU CAN READ THIS, CAN'T YOU?
WHERE IT'S WRITTEN IN YOUKAI.
WHAT DOES IT SAY?
WELL, ABOUT THAT.
IT'S THE STRANGEST THING......

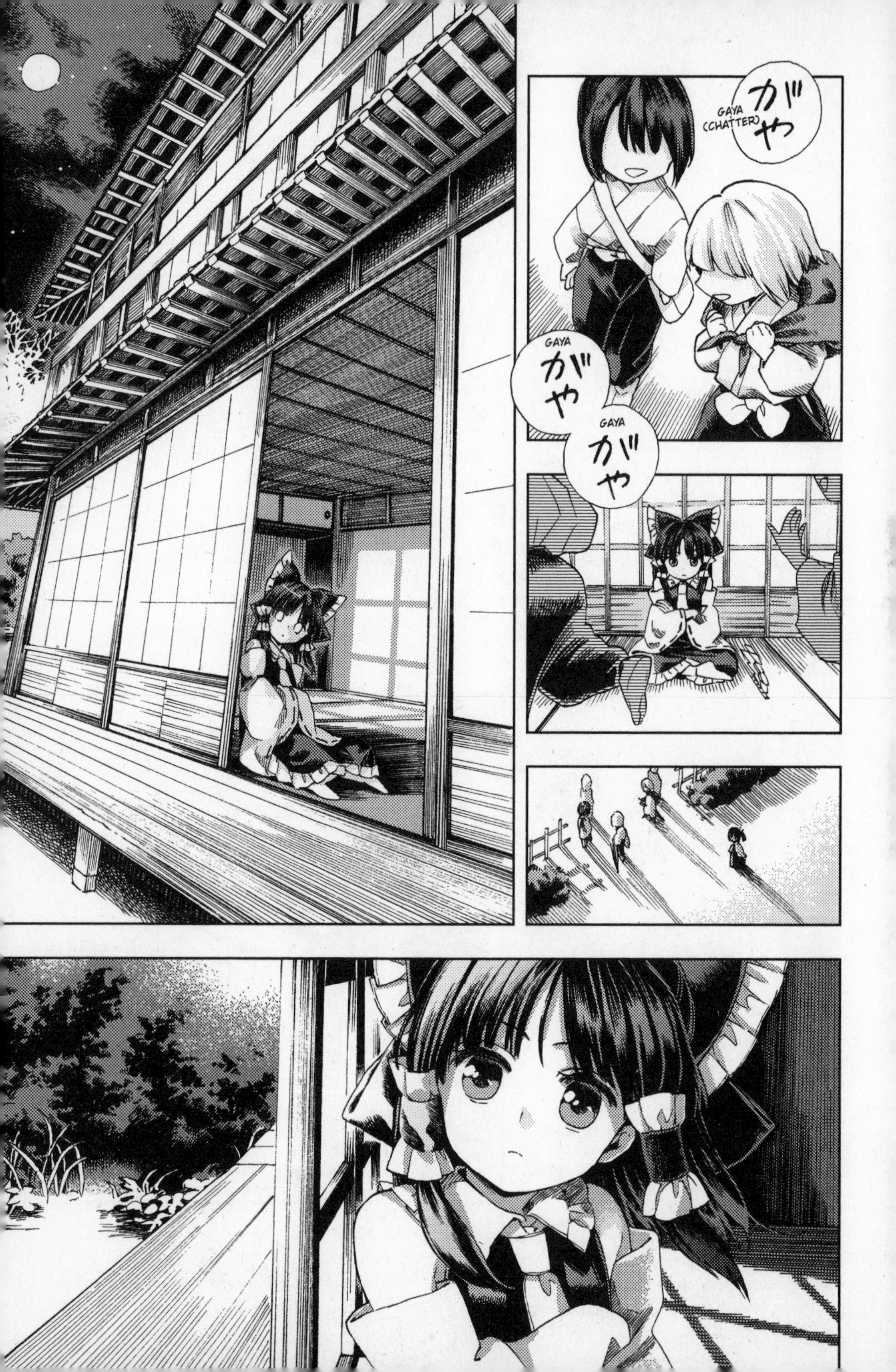
ガヤ
GAYA (CHATTER)
ガヤ
GAYA
ガヤ
GAYA

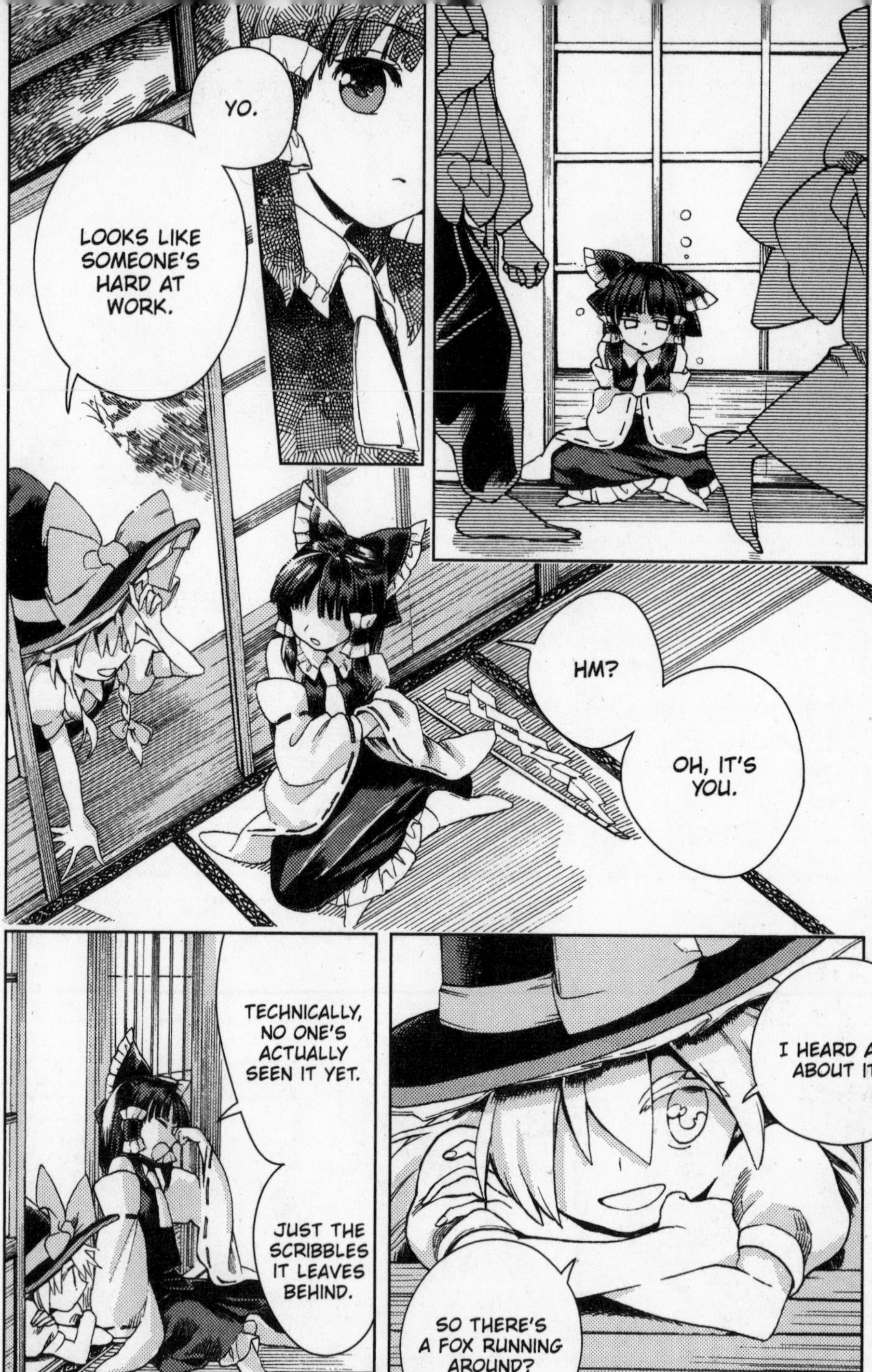
YO.
LOOKS LIKE SOMEONE'S HARD AT WORK.
HM?
OH, IT'S YOU.
I HEARD ALL ABOUT IT.
SO THERE'S A FOX RUNNING AROUND?
TECHNICALLY, NO ONE'S ACTUALLY SEEN IT YET.
JUST THE SCRIBBLES IT LEAVES BEHIND.

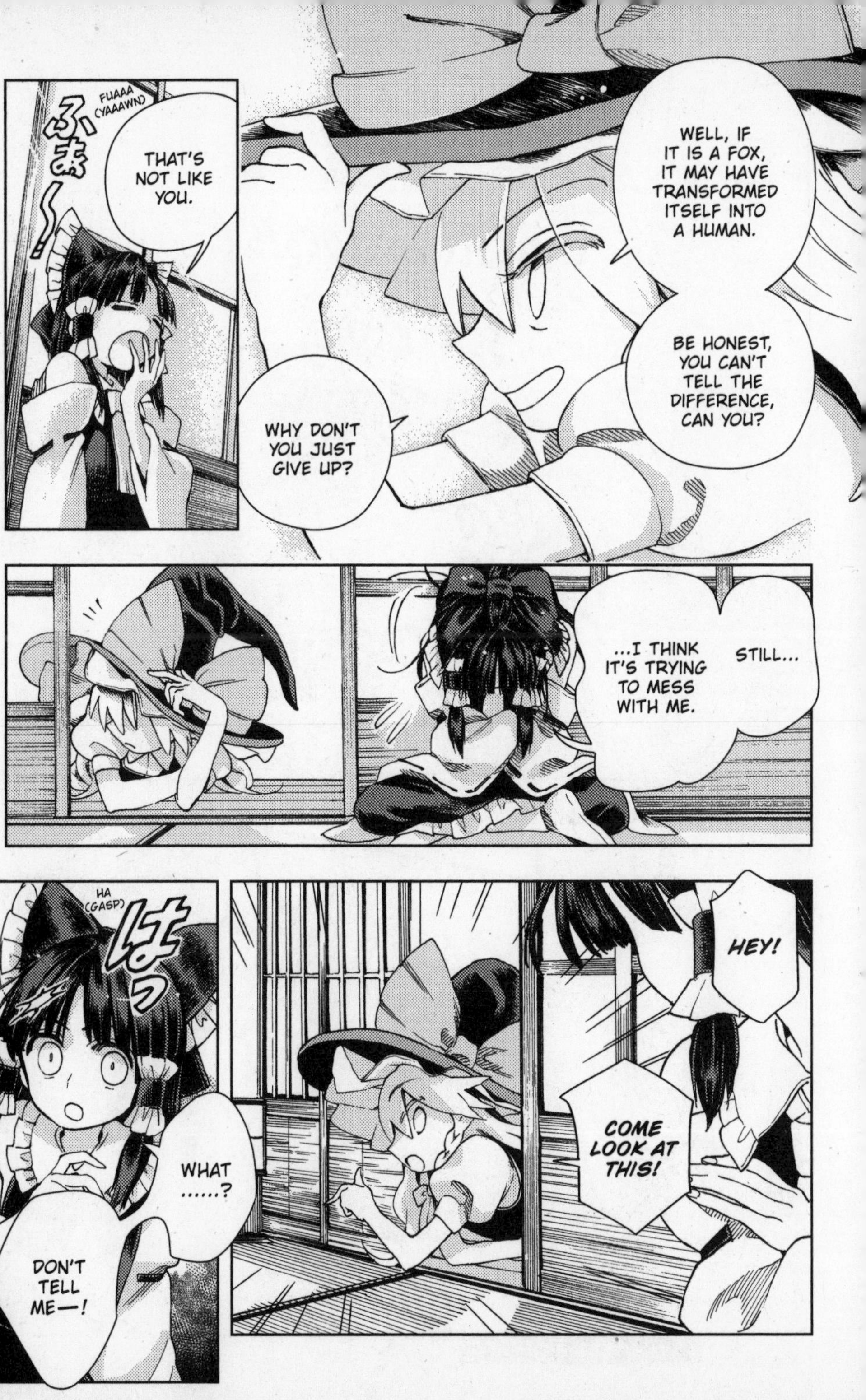
WELL, IF IT IS A FOX, IT MAY HAVE TRANSFORMED ITSELF INTO A HUMAN.
BE HONEST, YOU CAN'T TELL THE DIFFERENCE, CAN YOU?
WHY DON'T YOU JUST GIVE UP?
ふぁ〜
FUAAA (YAAAWN)
THAT'S NOT LIKE YOU.
STILL...
...I THINK IT'S TRYING TO MESS WITH ME.
HEY!
COME LOOK AT THIS!
はっ
HA (GASP)
WHAT ......?
DON'T TELL ME—!

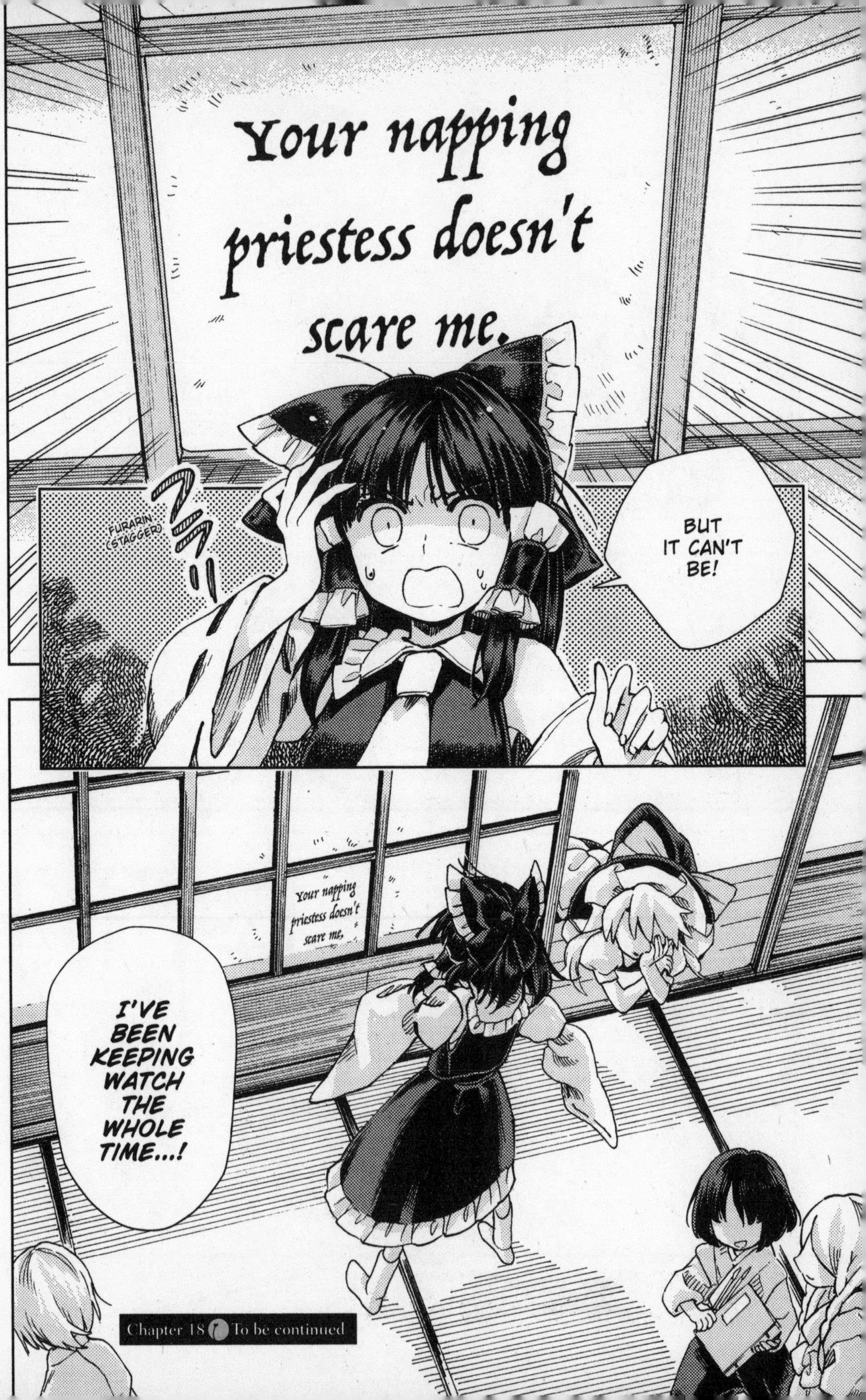
Your napping priestess doesn't scare me.
BUT IT CAN'T BE!
FURARIN (STAGGER)
Your napping priestess doesn't scare me.
I'VE BEEN KEEPING WATCH THE WHOLE TIME...!
Chapter 18 To be continued

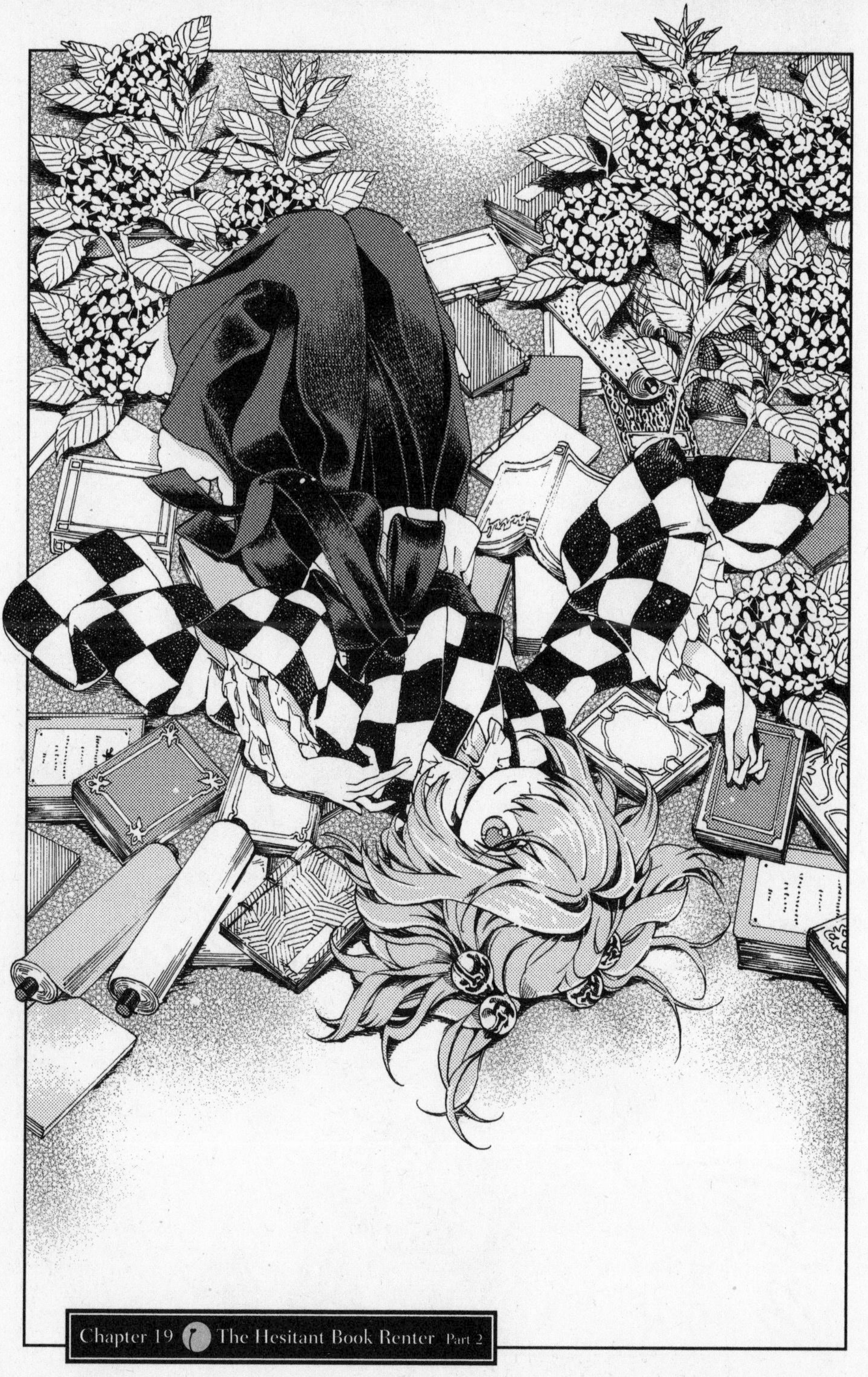

# Chapter 19 The Hesitant Book Renter Part 2

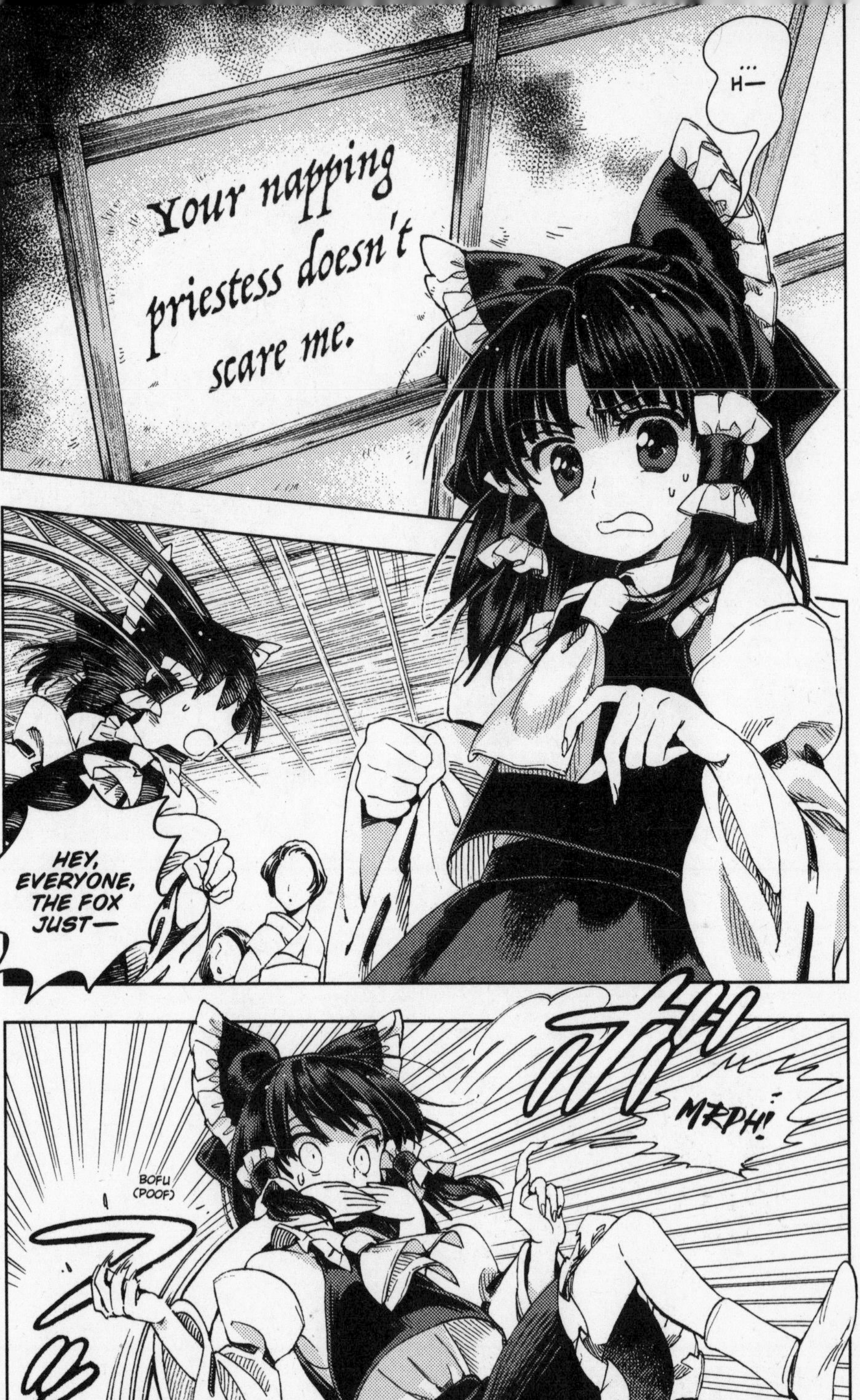
...H—
Your napping priestess doesn't scare me.
HEY, EVERYONE, THE FOX JUST—
MRPH!
BOFU (POOF)

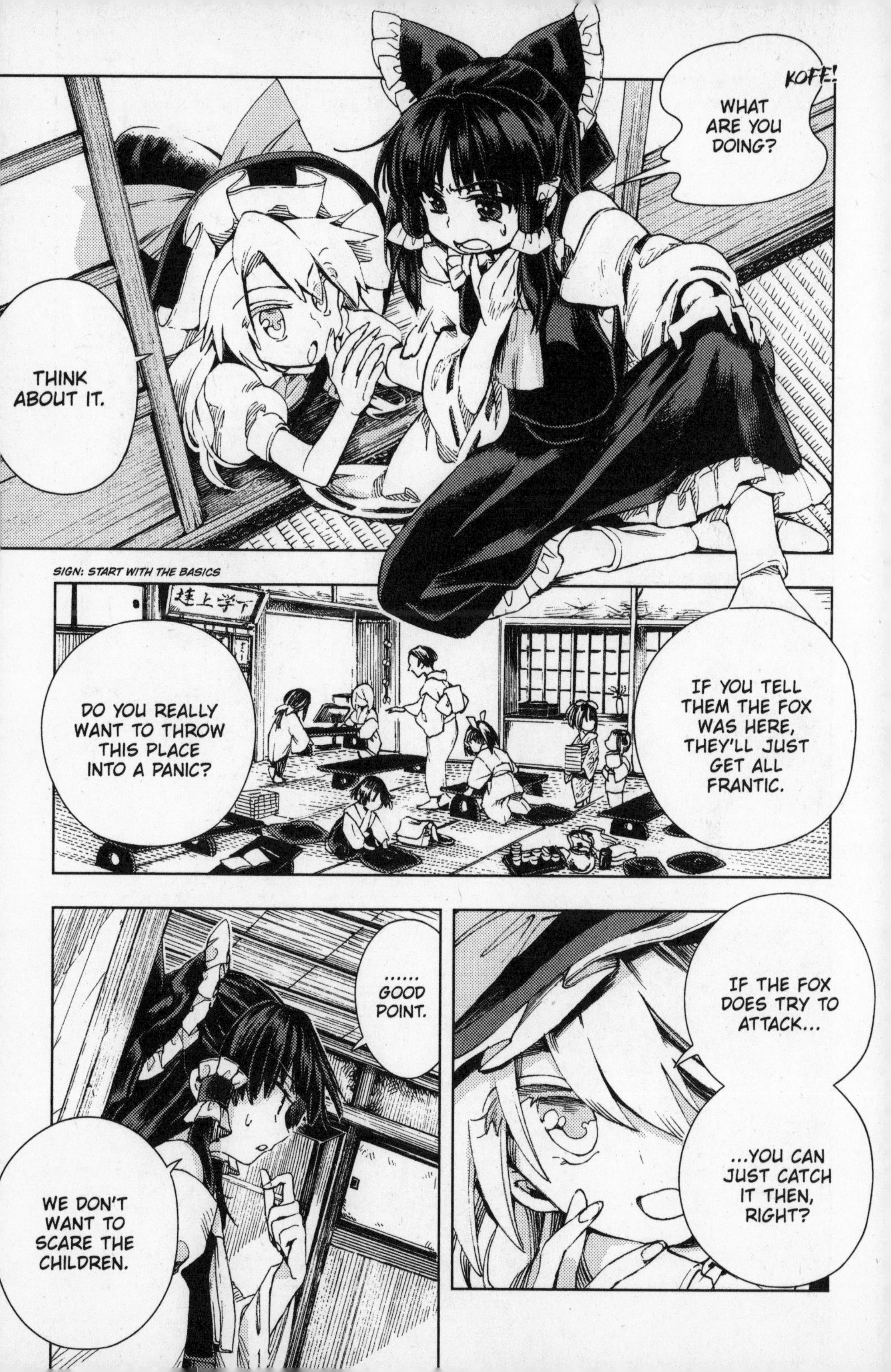
KOFF!
WHAT ARE YOU DOING?
THINK ABOUT IT.
SIGN: START WITH THE BASICS
IF YOU TELL THEM THE FOX WAS HERE, THEY'LL JUST GET ALL FRANTIC.
DO YOU REALLY WANT TO THROW THIS PLACE INTO A PANIC?
IF THE FOX DOES TRY TO ATTACK...
...YOU CAN JUST CATCH IT THEN, RIGHT?
......GOOD POINT.
WE DON'T WANT TO SCARE THE CHILDREN.

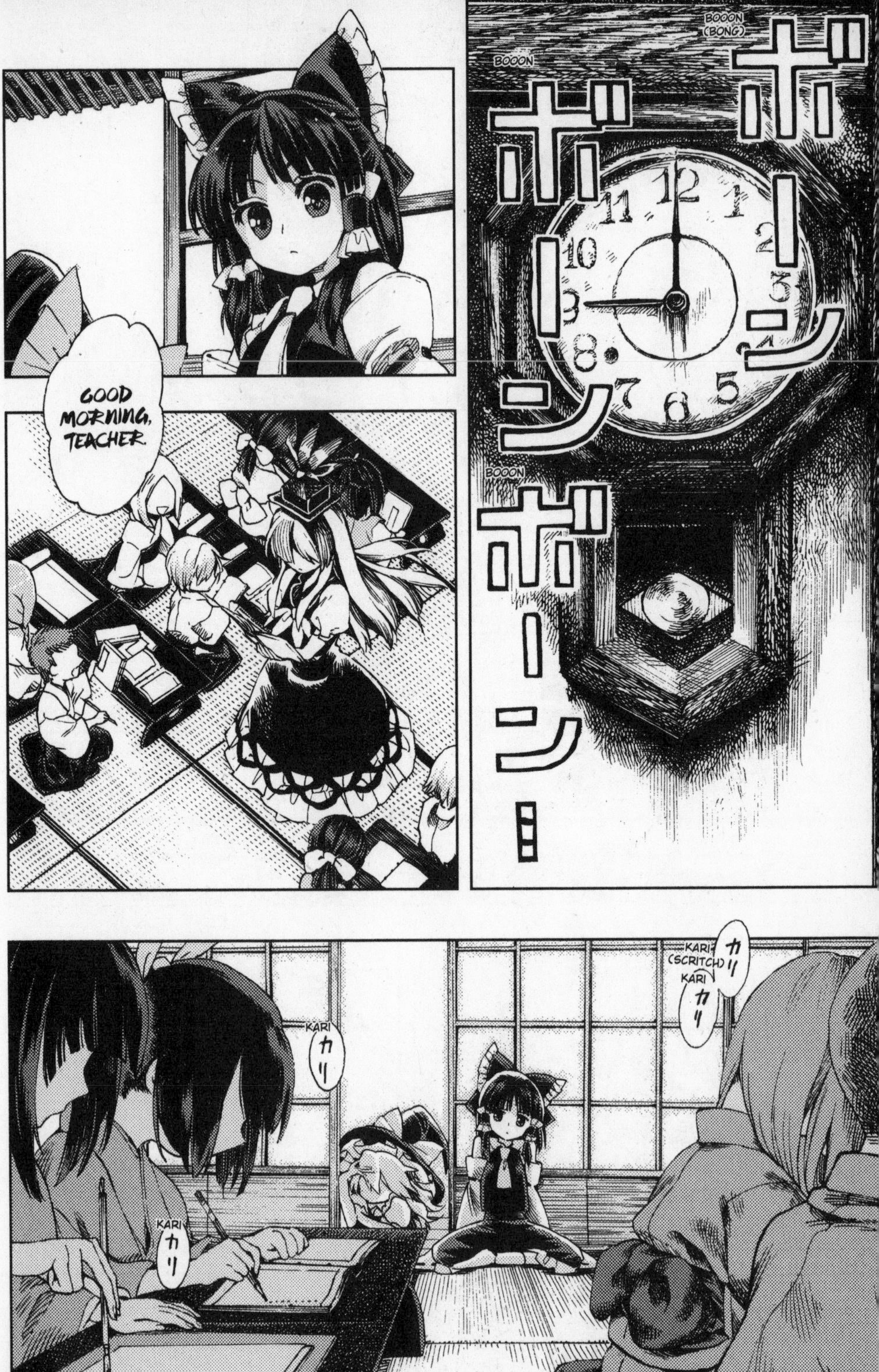

BOOON (BONG)
ボーン
BOOON
ボーン
BOOON
ボーン…
GOOD MORNING, TEACHER.
KARI (SCRITCH)
カリ
KARI
カリ
KARI
カリ
KARI
カリ

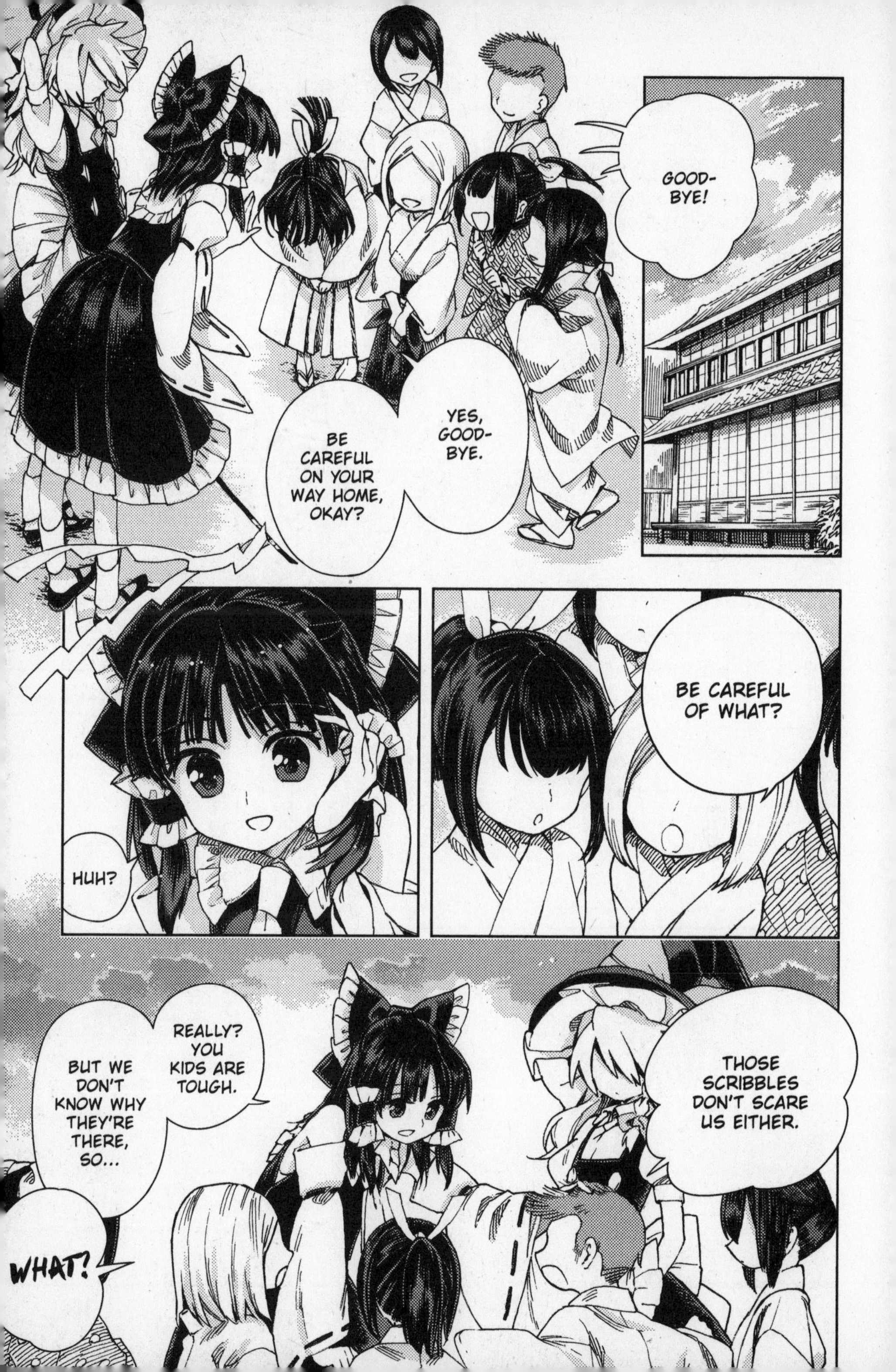
GOOD-BYE!
YES, GOOD-BYE.
BE CAREFUL ON YOUR WAY HOME, OKAY?
BE CAREFUL OF WHAT?
HUH?
THOSE SCRIBBLES DON'T SCARE US EITHER.
REALLY? YOU KIDS ARE TOUGH.
BUT WE DON'T KNOW WHY THEY'RE THERE, SO...
WHAT?!

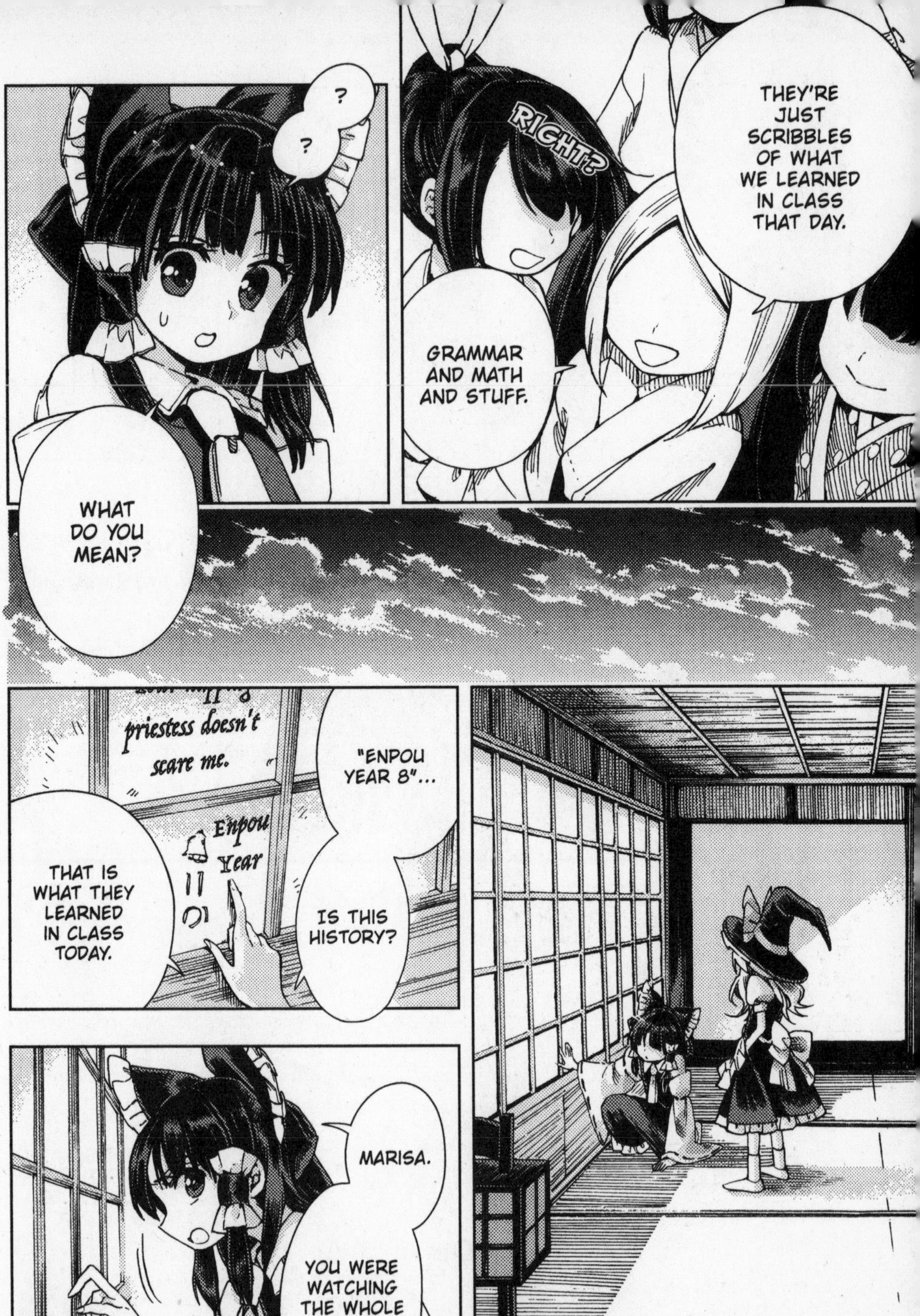
THEY'RE JUST SCRIBBLES OF WHAT WE LEARNED IN CLASS THAT DAY.
RIGHT?
GRAMMAR AND MATH AND STUFF.
?
?
WHAT DO YOU MEAN?
priestess doesn't scare me.
Enpou Year
"ENPOU YEAR 8"...
IS THIS HISTORY?
THAT IS WHAT THEY LEARNED IN CLASS TODAY.
MARISA.
YOU WERE WATCHING THE WHOLE TIME, RIGHT?

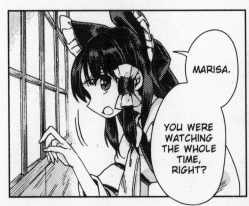

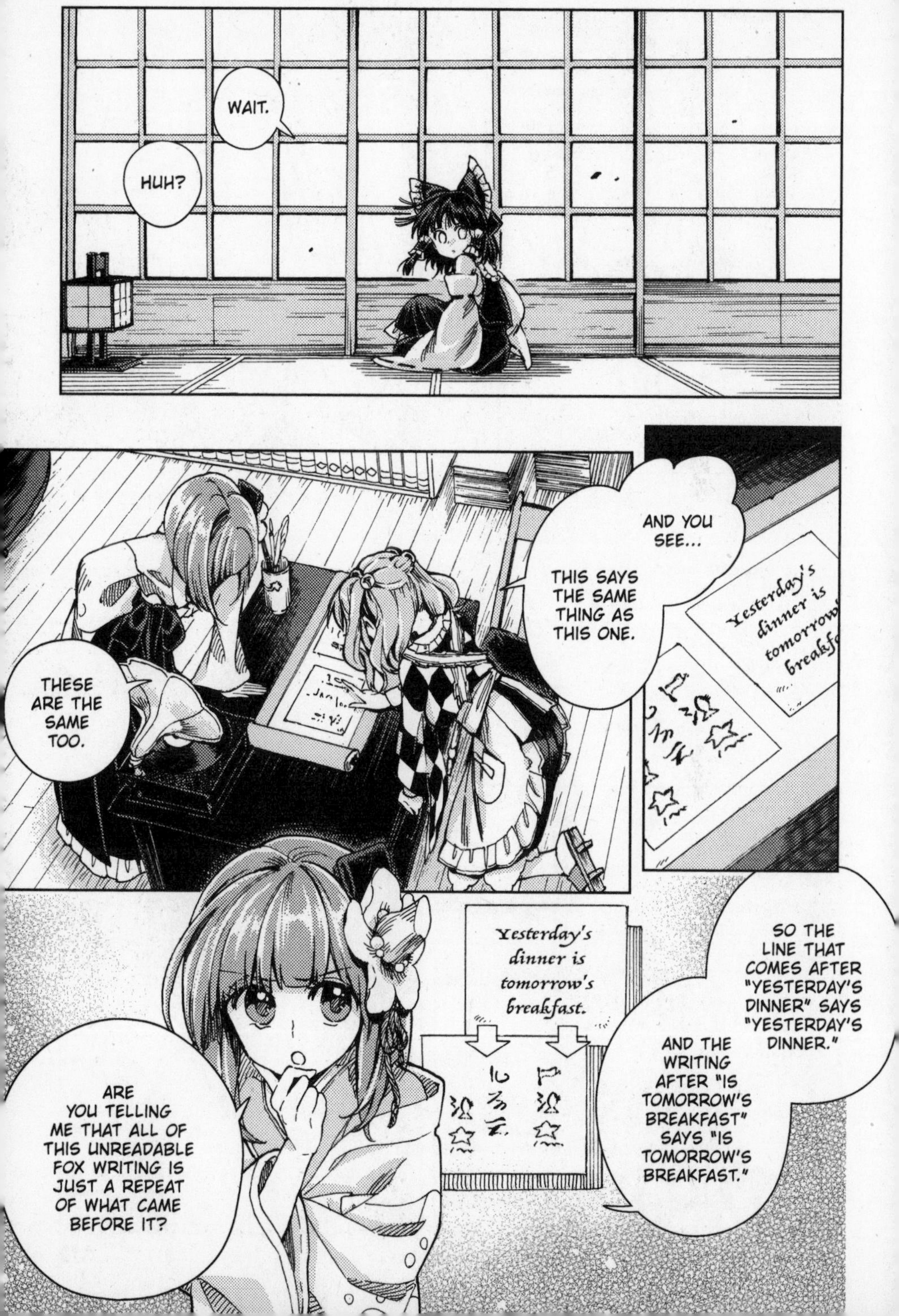
WAIT.
HUH?
AND YOU SEE...
THIS SAYS THE SAME THING AS THIS ONE.
THESE ARE THE SAME TOO.
Yesterday's dinner is tomorrow's breakfast.
SO THE LINE THAT COMES AFTER "YESTERDAY'S DINNER" SAYS "YESTERDAY'S DINNER."
AND THE WRITING AFTER "IS TOMORROW'S BREAKFAST" SAYS "IS TOMORROW'S BREAKFAST."
ARE YOU TELLING ME THAT ALL OF THIS UNREADABLE FOX WRITING IS JUST A REPEAT OF WHAT CAME BEFORE IT?

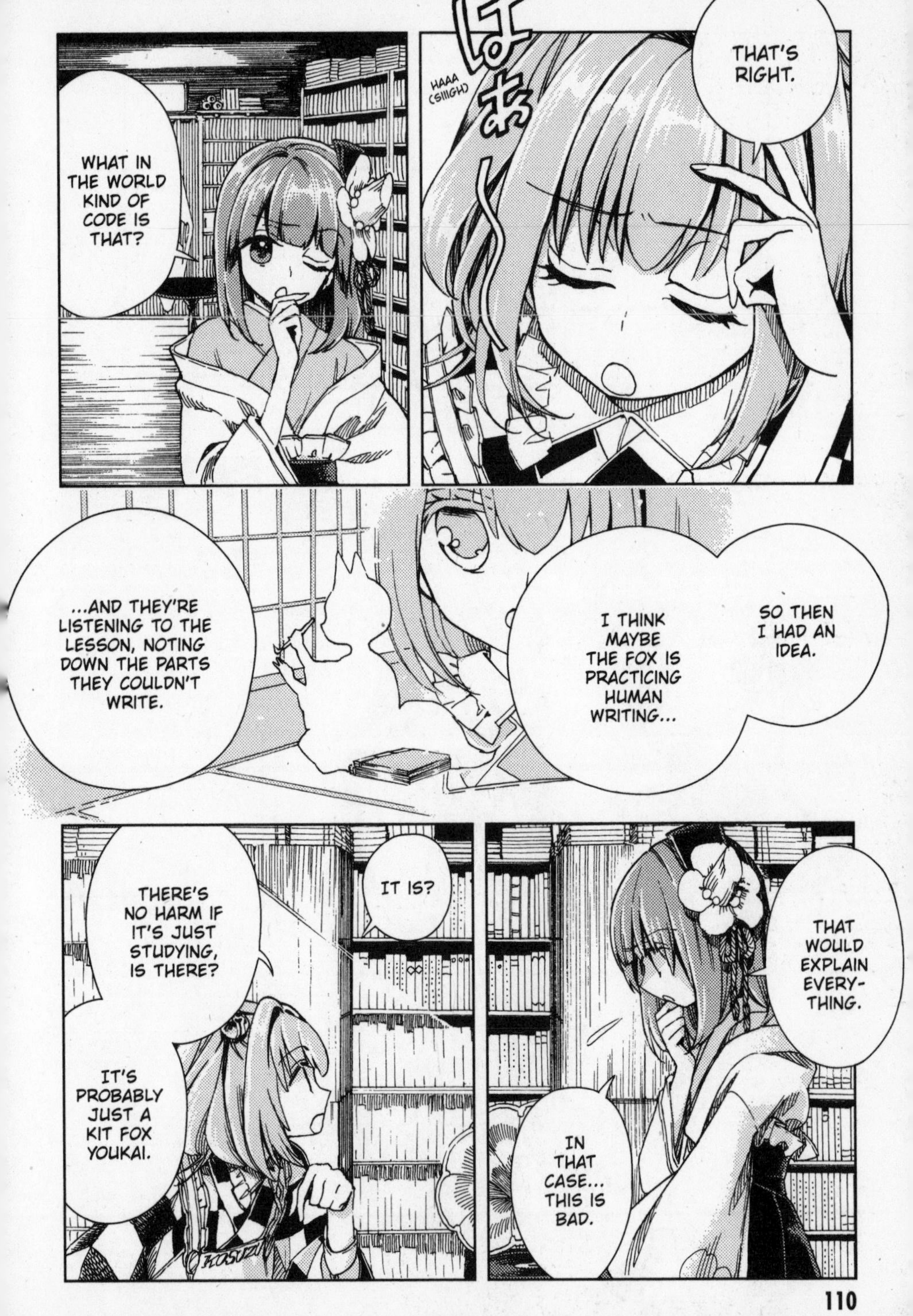
はあ
HAAA (SIIIGH)
THAT'S RIGHT.
WHAT IN THE WORLD KIND OF CODE IS THAT?
SO THEN I HAD AN IDEA.
I THINK MAYBE THE FOX IS PRACTICING HUMAN WRITING...
...AND THEY'RE LISTENING TO THE LESSON, NOTING DOWN THE PARTS THEY COULDN'T WRITE.
THAT WOULD EXPLAIN EVERY-THING.
IN THAT CASE... THIS IS BAD.
IT IS?
THERE'S NO HARM IF IT'S JUST STUDYING, IS THERE?
IT'S PROBABLY JUST A KIT FOX YOUKAI.
KOSUZU

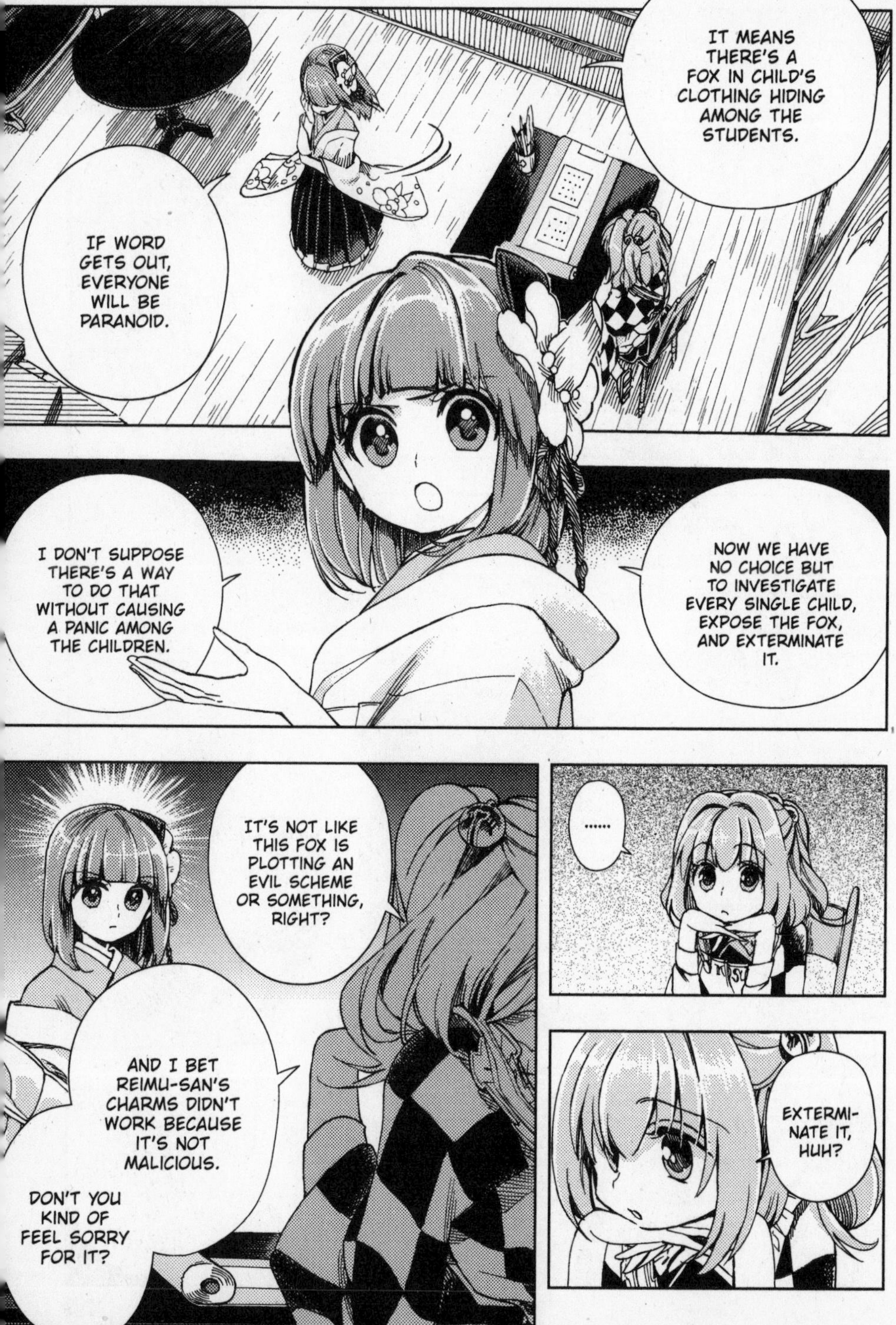
IT MEANS THERE'S A FOX IN CHILD'S CLOTHING HIDING AMONG THE STUDENTS.
IF WORD GETS OUT, EVERYONE WILL BE PARANOID.
NOW WE HAVE NO CHOICE BUT TO INVESTIGATE EVERY SINGLE CHILD, EXPOSE THE FOX, AND EXTERMINATE IT.
I DON'T SUPPOSE THERE'S A WAY TO DO THAT WITHOUT CAUSING A PANIC AMONG THE CHILDREN.
......
EXTERMINATE IT, HUH?
IT'S NOT LIKE THIS FOX IS PLOTTING AN EVIL SCHEME OR SOMETHING, RIGHT?
AND I BET REIMU-SAN'S CHARMS DIDN'T WORK BECAUSE IT'S NOT MALICIOUS.
DON'T YOU KIND OF FEEL SORRY FOR IT?

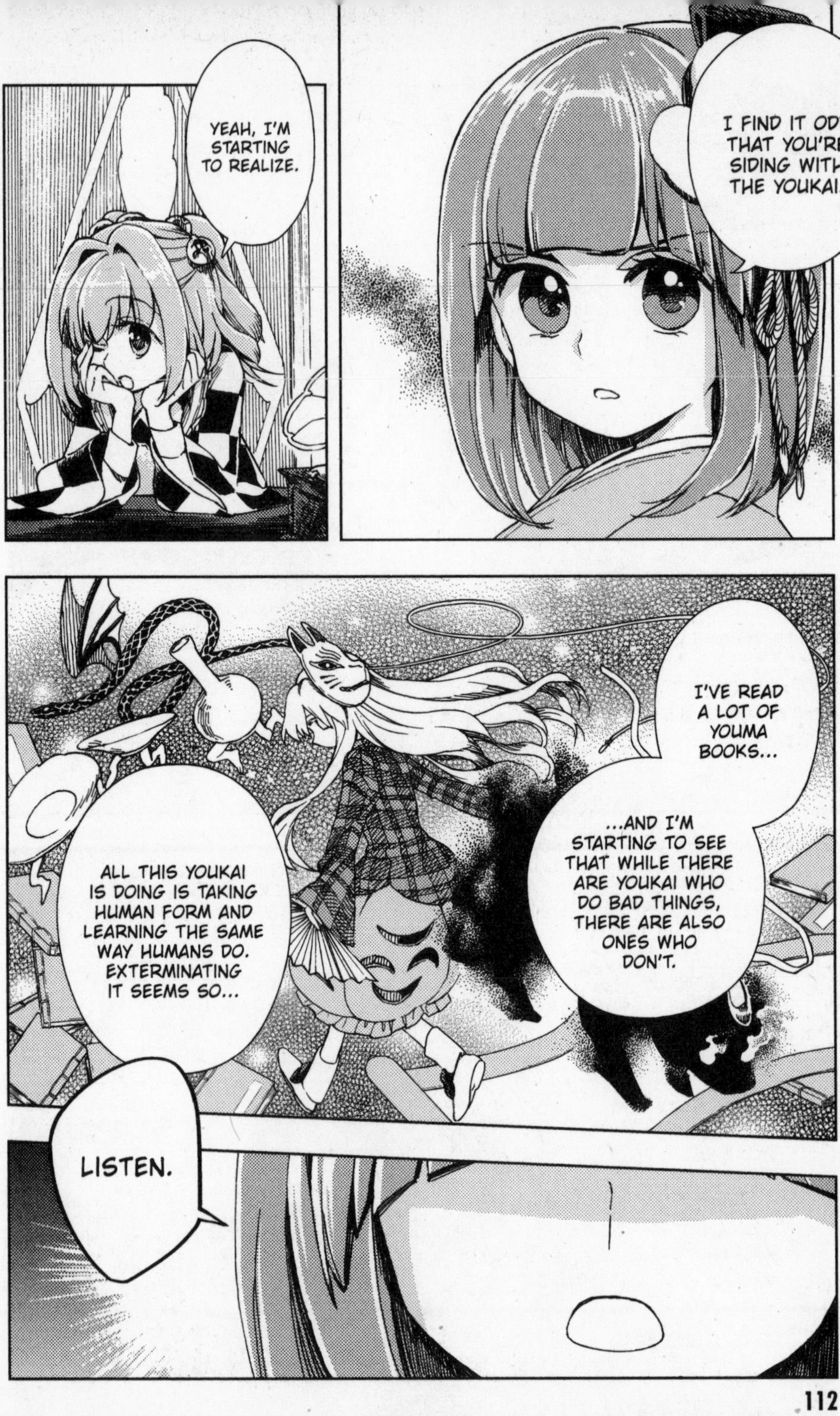
I FIND IT ODD THAT YOU'RE SIDING WITH THE YOUKAI.
YEAH, I'M STARTING TO REALIZE.
I'VE READ A LOT OF YOUMA BOOKS...
...AND I'M STARTING TO SEE THAT WHILE THERE ARE YOUKAI WHO DO BAD THINGS, THERE ARE ALSO ONES WHO DON'T.
ALL THIS YOUKAI IS DOING IS TAKING HUMAN FORM AND LEARNING THE SAME WAY HUMANS DO. EXTERMINATING IT SEEMS SO...
LISTEN.

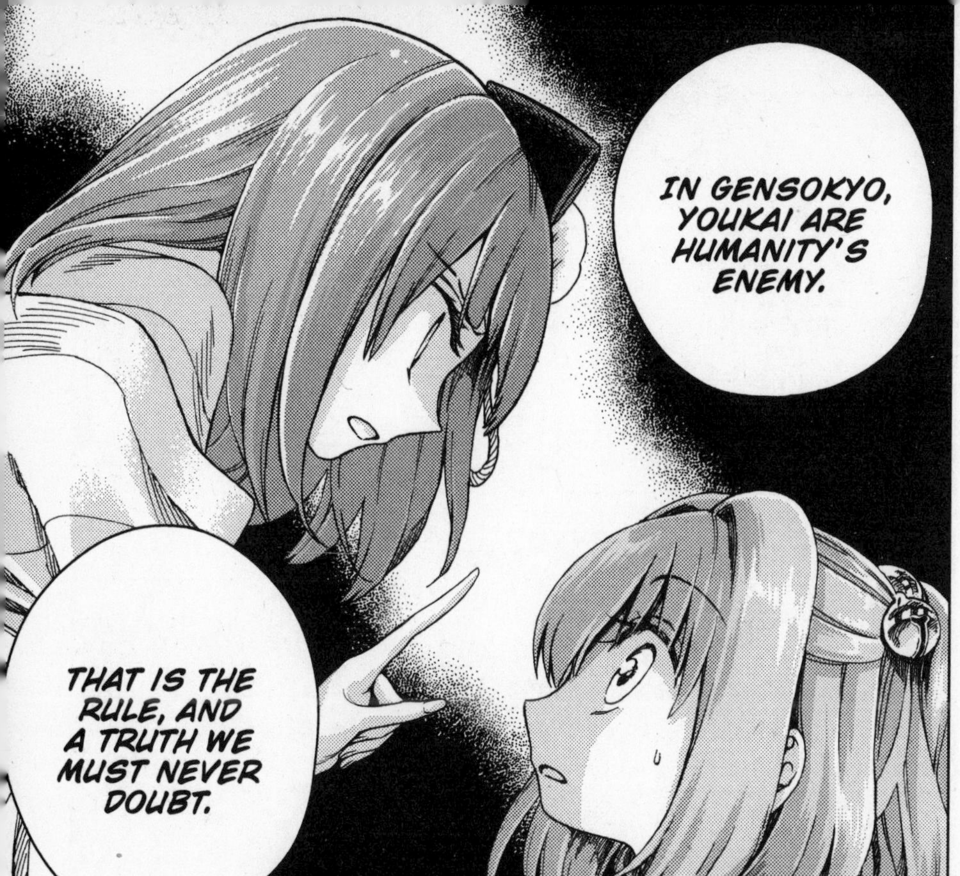
IN GENSOKYO, YOUKAI ARE HUMANITY'S ENEMY.
THAT IS THE RULE, AND A TRUTH WE MUST NEVER DOUBT.

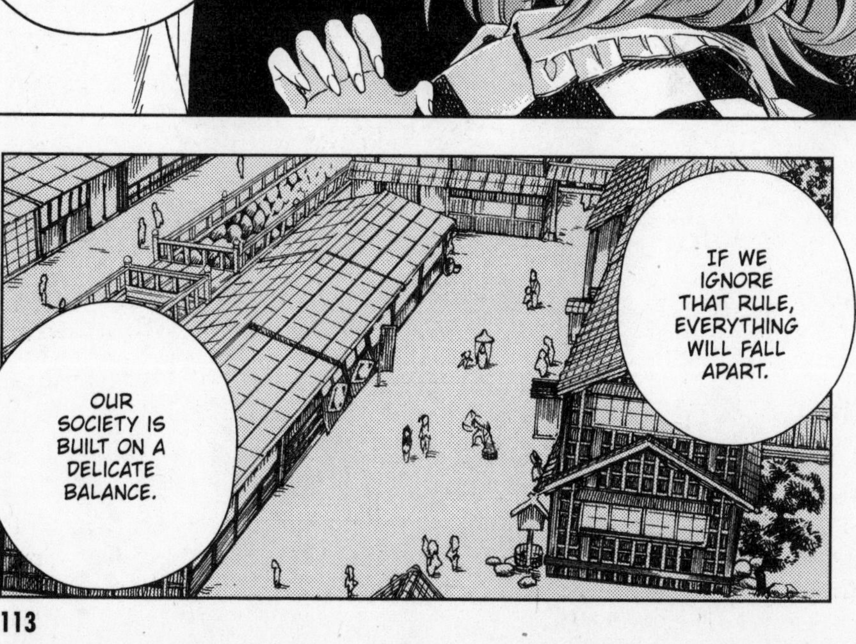
IF WE IGNORE THAT RULE, EVERYTHING WILL FALL APART.
OUR SOCIETY IS BUILT ON A DELICATE BALANCE.

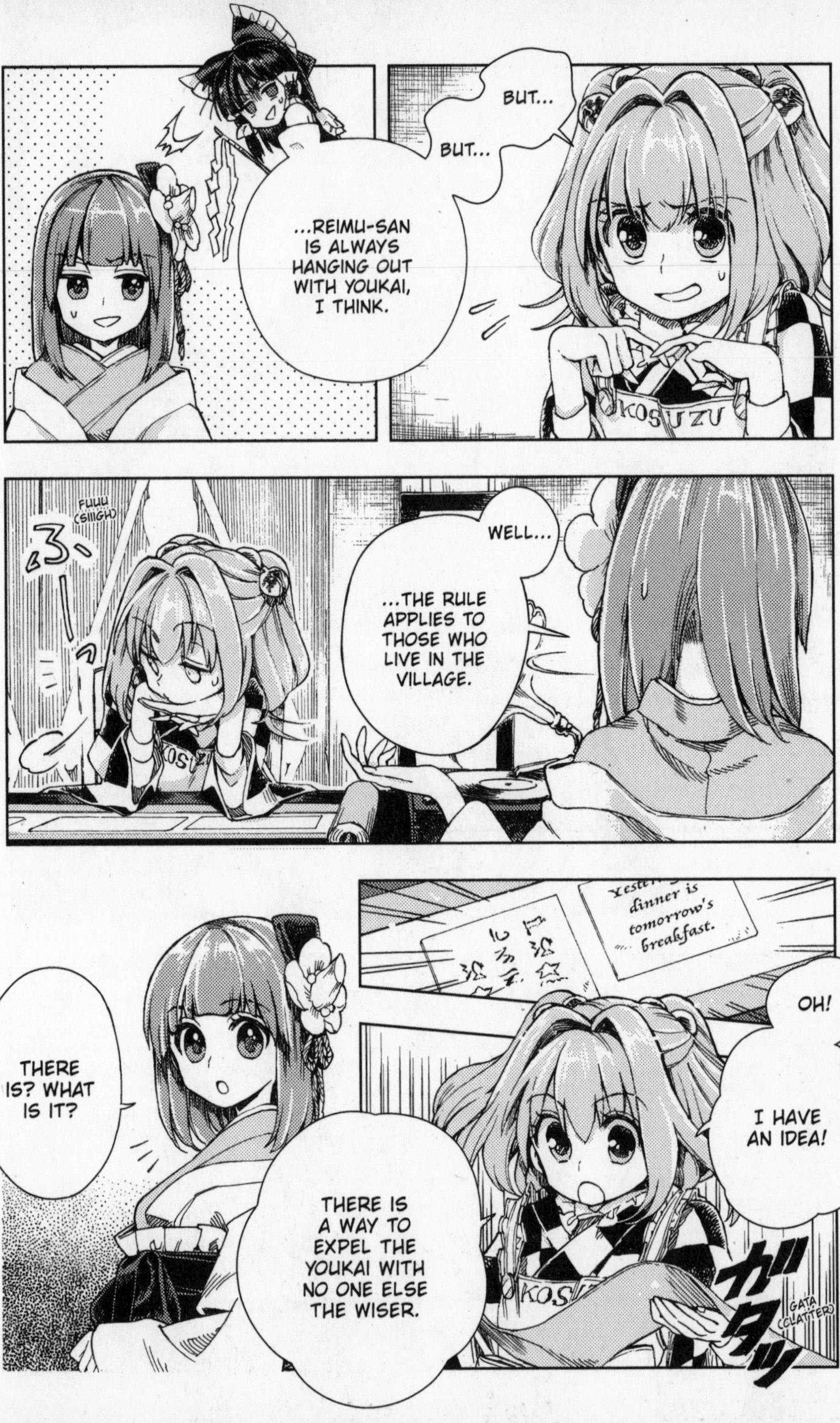
BUT...
BUT...
...REIMU-SAN IS ALWAYS HANGING OUT WITH YOUKAI, I THINK.
WELL...
...THE RULE APPLIES TO THOSE WHO LIVE IN THE VILLAGE.
FUUU (SIIIGH)
dinner is tomorrow's breakfast.
OH!
I HAVE AN IDEA!
GATA (CLATTER)
THERE IS A WAY TO EXPEL THE YOUKAI WITH NO ONE ELSE THE WISER.
THERE IS? WHAT IS IT?

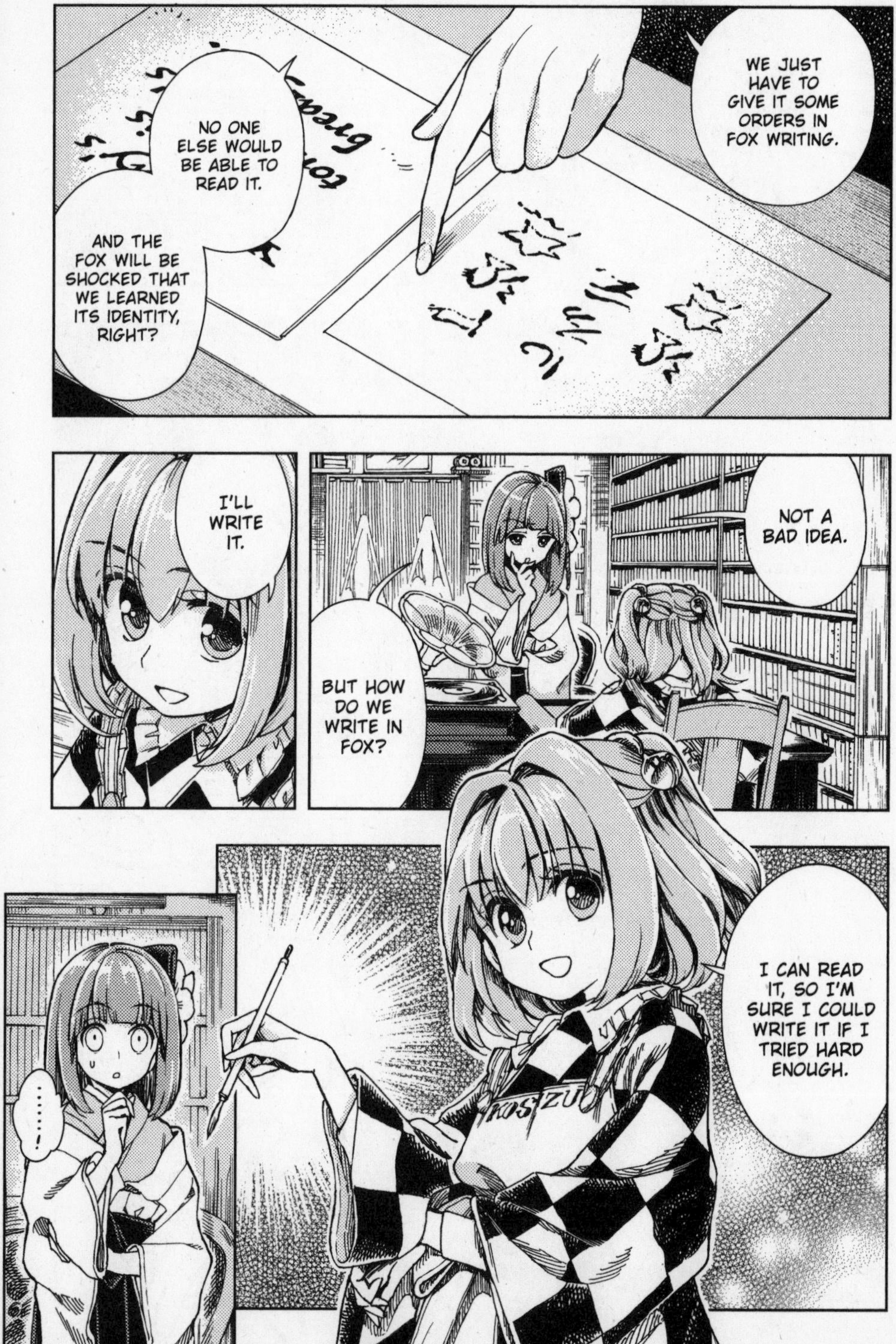
WE JUST HAVE TO GIVE IT SOME ORDERS IN FOX WRITING.
NO ONE ELSE WOULD BE ABLE TO READ IT.
AND THE FOX WILL BE SHOCKED THAT WE LEARNED ITS IDENTITY, RIGHT?
NOT A BAD IDEA.
BUT HOW DO WE WRITE IN FOX?
I'LL WRITE IT.
I CAN READ IT, SO I'M SURE I COULD WRITE IT IF I TRIED HARD ENOUGH.
......!

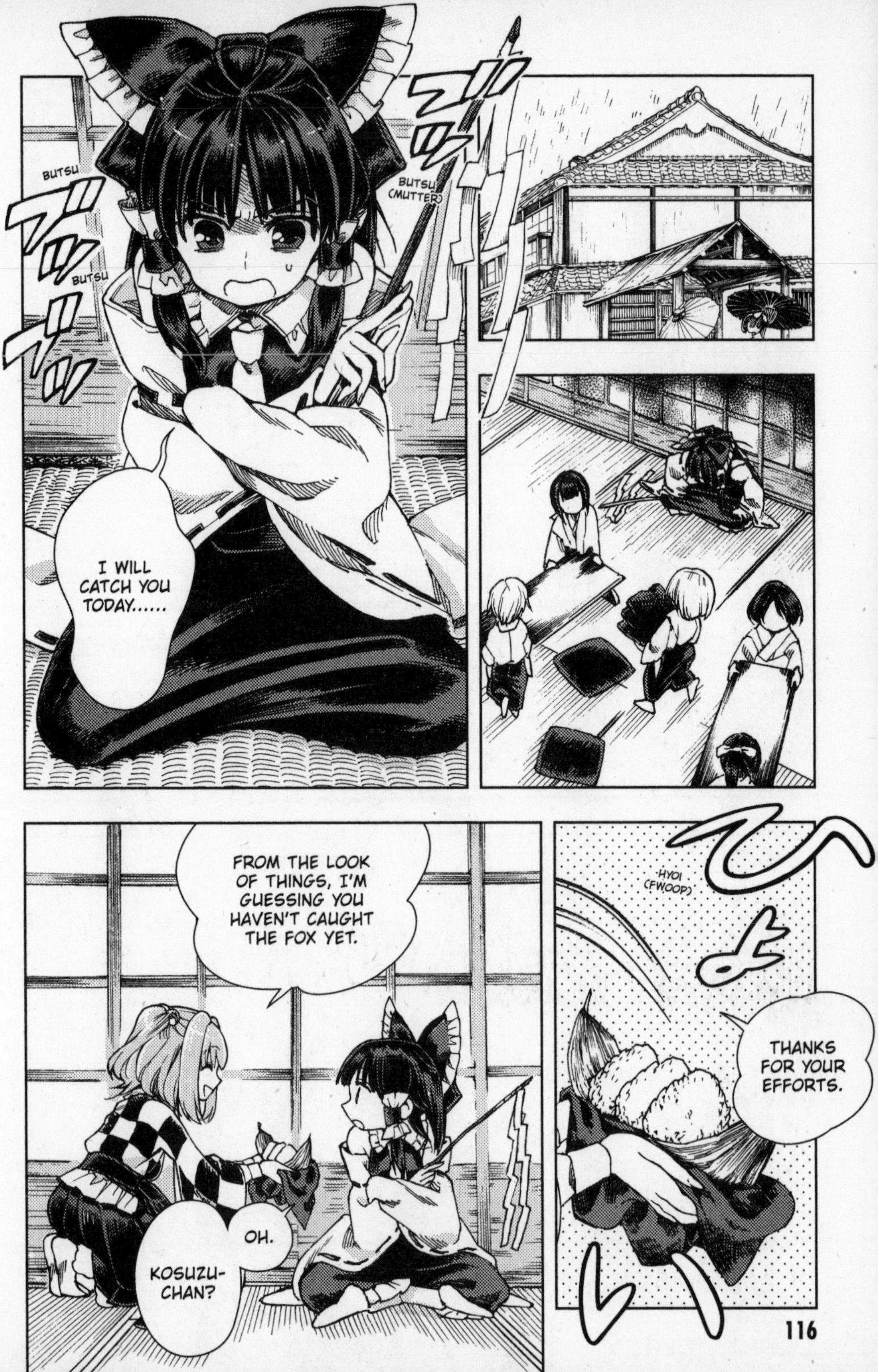
BUTSU (MUTTER)
BUTSU
BUTSU
I WILL CATCH YOU TODAY......
HYOI (FWOOP)
THANKS FOR YOUR EFFORTS.
FROM THE LOOK OF THINGS, I'M GUESSING YOU HAVEN'T CAUGHT THE FOX YET.
OH.
KOSUZU-CHAN?

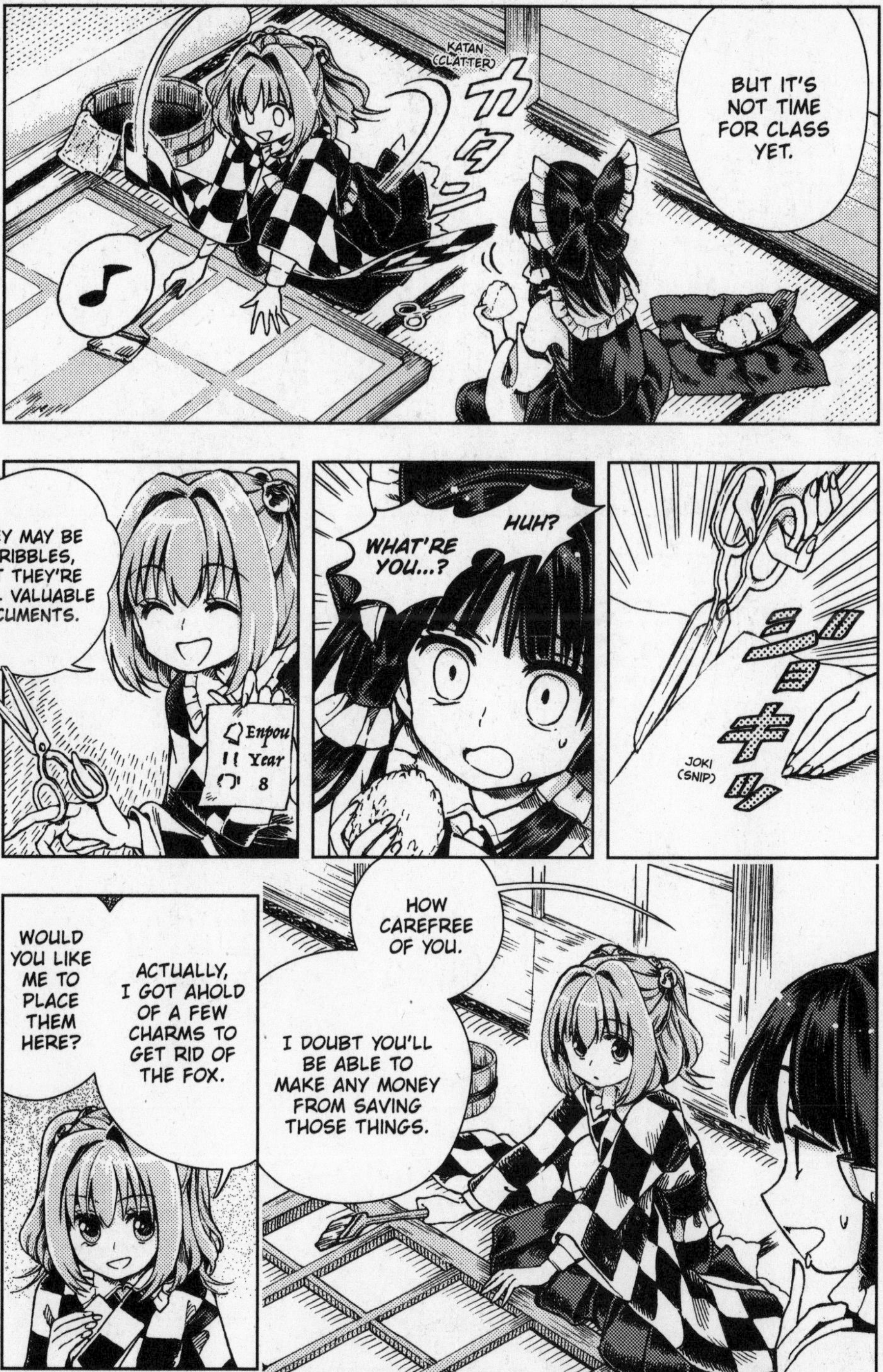
BUT IT'S NOT TIME FOR CLASS YET.
KATAN (CLATTER)
カタン
♪
ジョキッ
JOKI (SNIP)
HUH?
WHAT'RE YOU...?
THEY MAY BE SCRIBBLES, BUT THEY'RE STILL VALUABLE DOCUMENTS.
Enpou Year 8
HOW CAREFREE OF YOU.
I DOUBT YOU'LL BE ABLE TO MAKE ANY MONEY FROM SAVING THOSE THINGS.
ACTUALLY, I GOT AHOLD OF A FEW CHARMS TO GET RID OF THE FOX.
WOULD YOU LIKE ME TO PLACE THEM HERE?

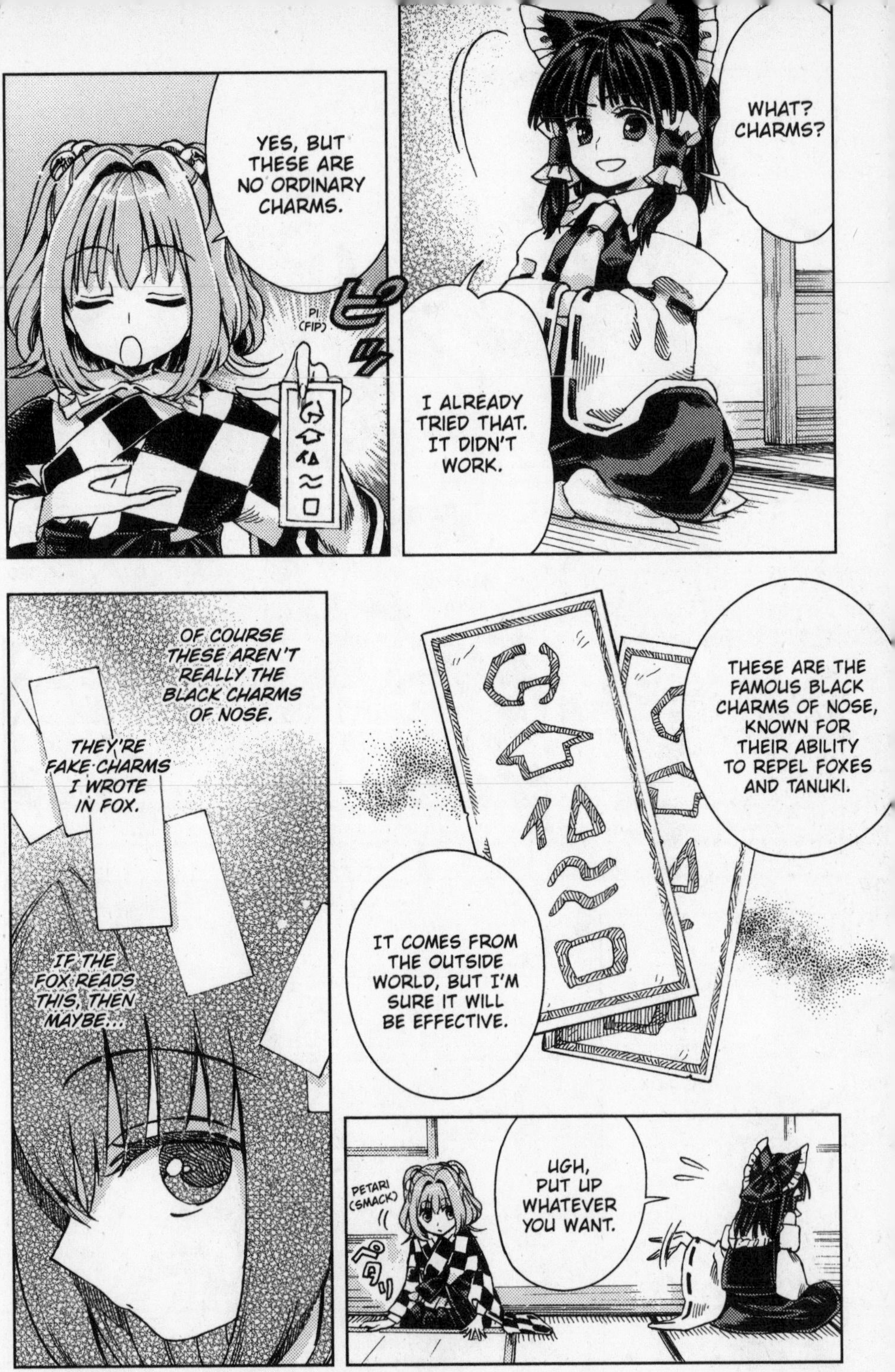
WHAT? CHARMS?
I ALREADY TRIED THAT. IT DIDN'T WORK.
YES, BUT THESE ARE NO ORDINARY CHARMS.
PI (FIP)
THESE ARE THE FAMOUS BLACK CHARMS OF NOSE, KNOWN FOR THEIR ABILITY TO REPEL FOXES AND TANUKI.
IT COMES FROM THE OUTSIDE WORLD, BUT I'M SURE IT WILL BE EFFECTIVE.
UGH, PUT UP WHATEVER YOU WANT.
PETARI (SMACK)
OF COURSE THESE AREN'T REALLY THE BLACK CHARMS OF NOSE.
THEY'RE FAKE CHARMS I WROTE IN FOX.
IF THE FOX READS THIS, THEN MAYBE...

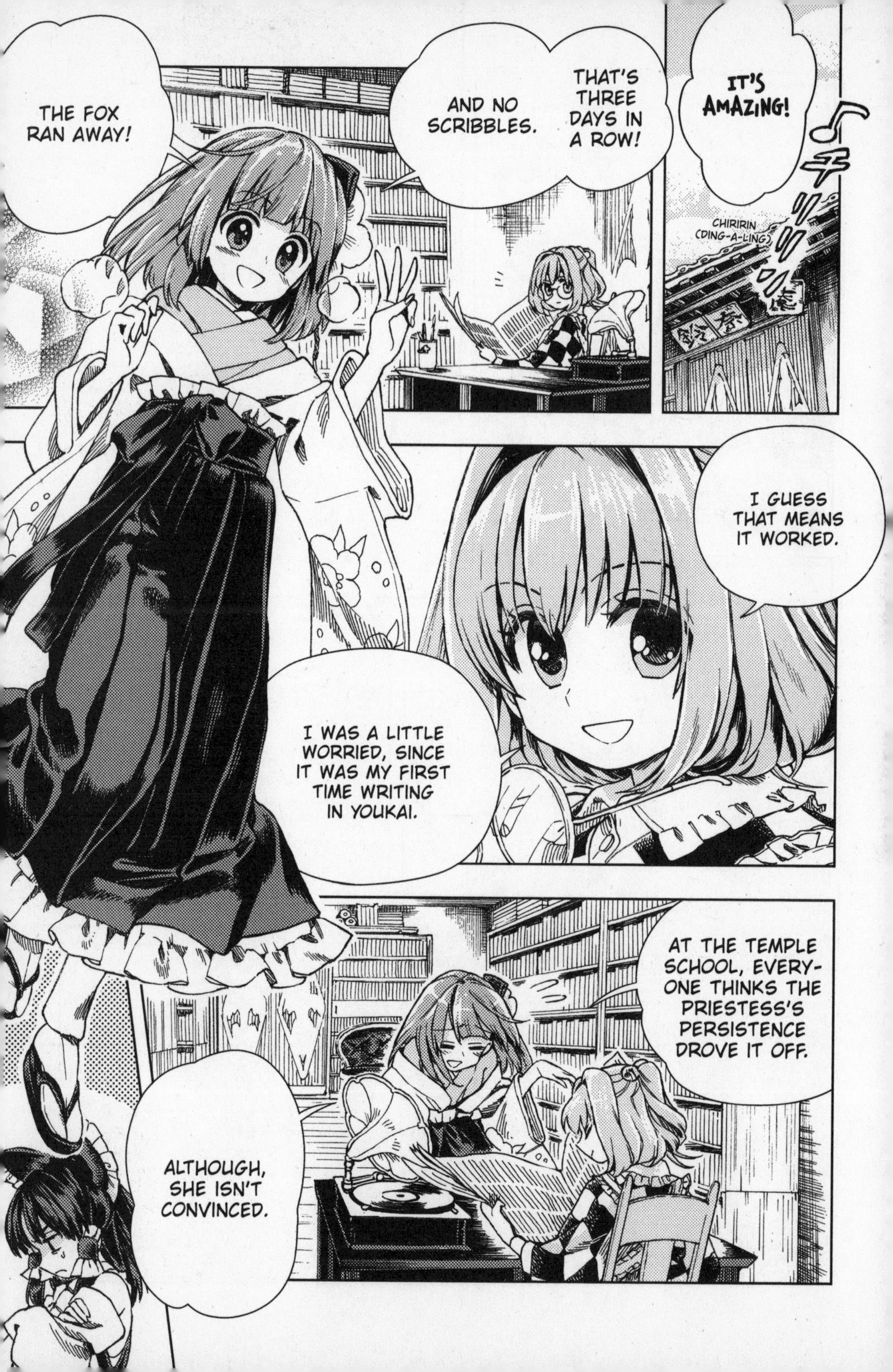
IT'S AMAZING!
CHIRIRIN (DING-A-LING)
THAT'S THREE DAYS IN A ROW!
AND NO SCRIBBLES.
THE FOX RAN AWAY!
I GUESS THAT MEANS IT WORKED.
I WAS A LITTLE WORRIED, SINCE IT WAS MY FIRST TIME WRITING IN YOUKAI.
AT THE TEMPLE SCHOOL, EVERY-ONE THINKS THE PRIESTESS'S PERSISTENCE DROVE IT OFF.
ALTHOUGH, SHE ISN'T CONVINCED.

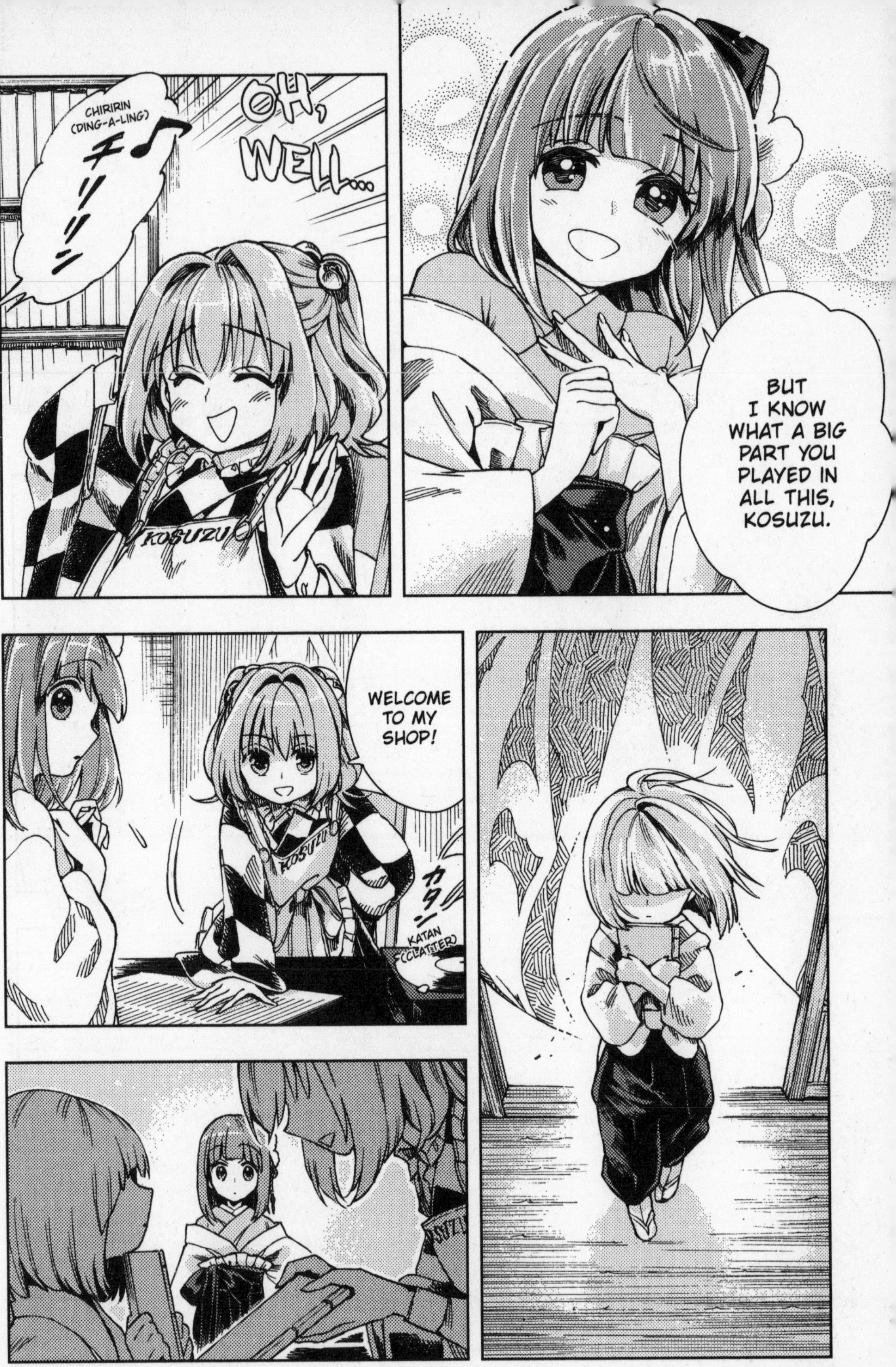
BUT I KNOW WHAT A BIG PART YOU PLAYED IN ALL THIS, KOSUZU.
CHIRIRIN (DING-A-LING)
チリリリン♪
OH, WELL...
KOSUZU
WELCOME TO MY SHOP!
KOSUZU
カタン
KATAN (CLATTER)

THAT'S A VERY STUDIOUS CHILD.

CHECKING OUT BOOKS LIKE THAT.

WHAT BOOK WAS IT?

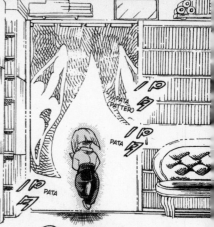

PATA (PATTER)

PATA

PATA

OH, UH.

APPARENTLY, THERE WAS SOMETHING IN CLASS TODAY THAT WAS HARD TO UNDER-STAND.

......

KOSUZU

WELL ...

...WHATEVER. AS LONG AS THE LITTLE ONE WORKS HARD.

HAA (SIGH)

YES, MA'AM!

NEXT TIME, I HOPE YOU'LL ADD A PLUG FOR MY BOOK.

IT SHOULD PROVIDE SOME WORKING KNOWLEDGE ...

...ON SOME THINGS THE CHILDREN CAN'T LEARN AT SCHOOL, LIKE HOW TO AVOID YOUKAI.

KOSUZU

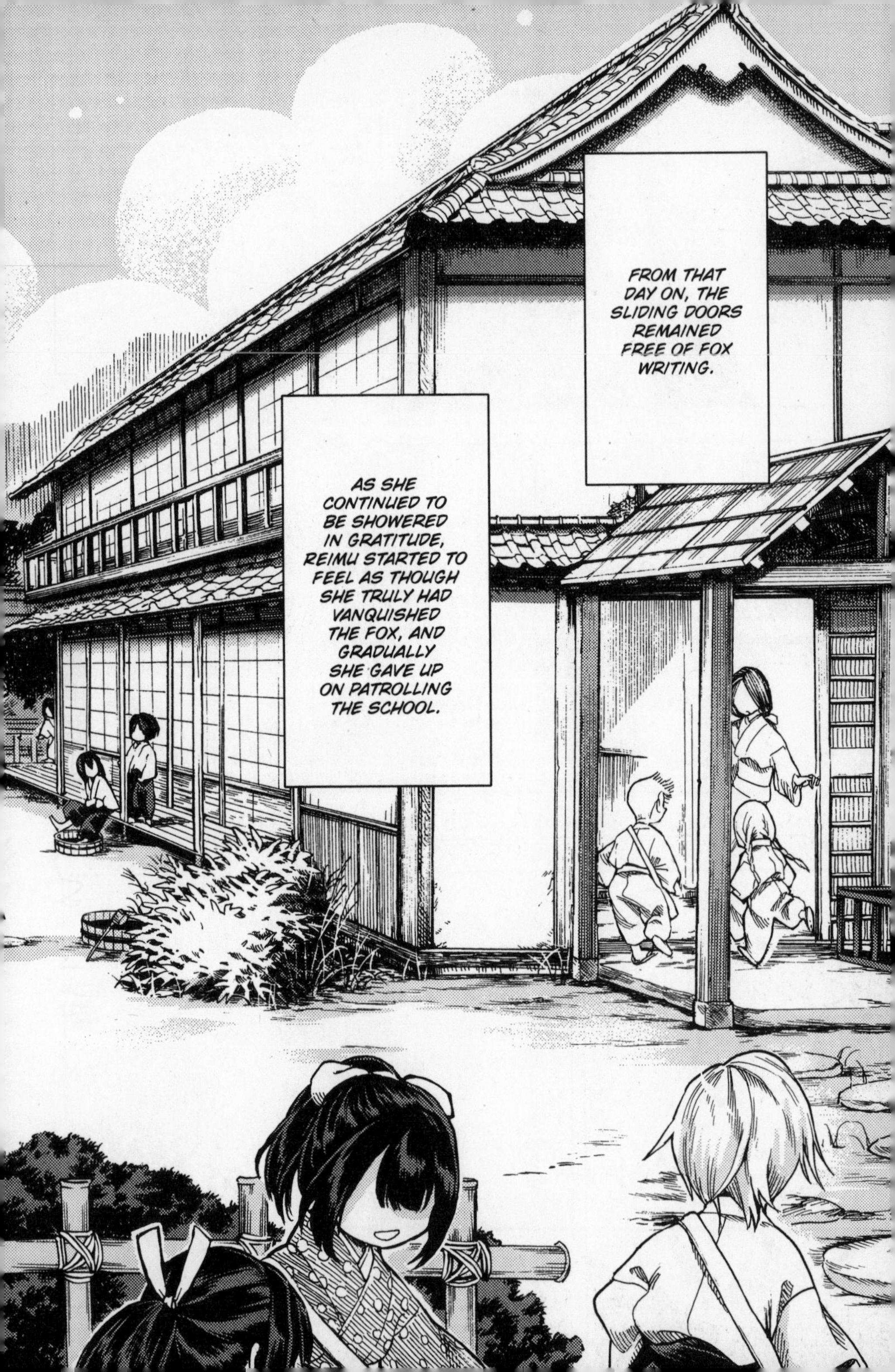
FROM THAT DAY ON, THE SLIDING DOORS REMAINED FREE OF FOX WRITING.
AS SHE CONTINUED TO BE SHOWERED IN GRATITUDE, REIMU STARTED TO FEEL AS THOUGH SHE TRULY HAD VANQUISHED THE FOX, AND GRADUALLY SHE GAVE UP ON PATROLLING THE SCHOOL.

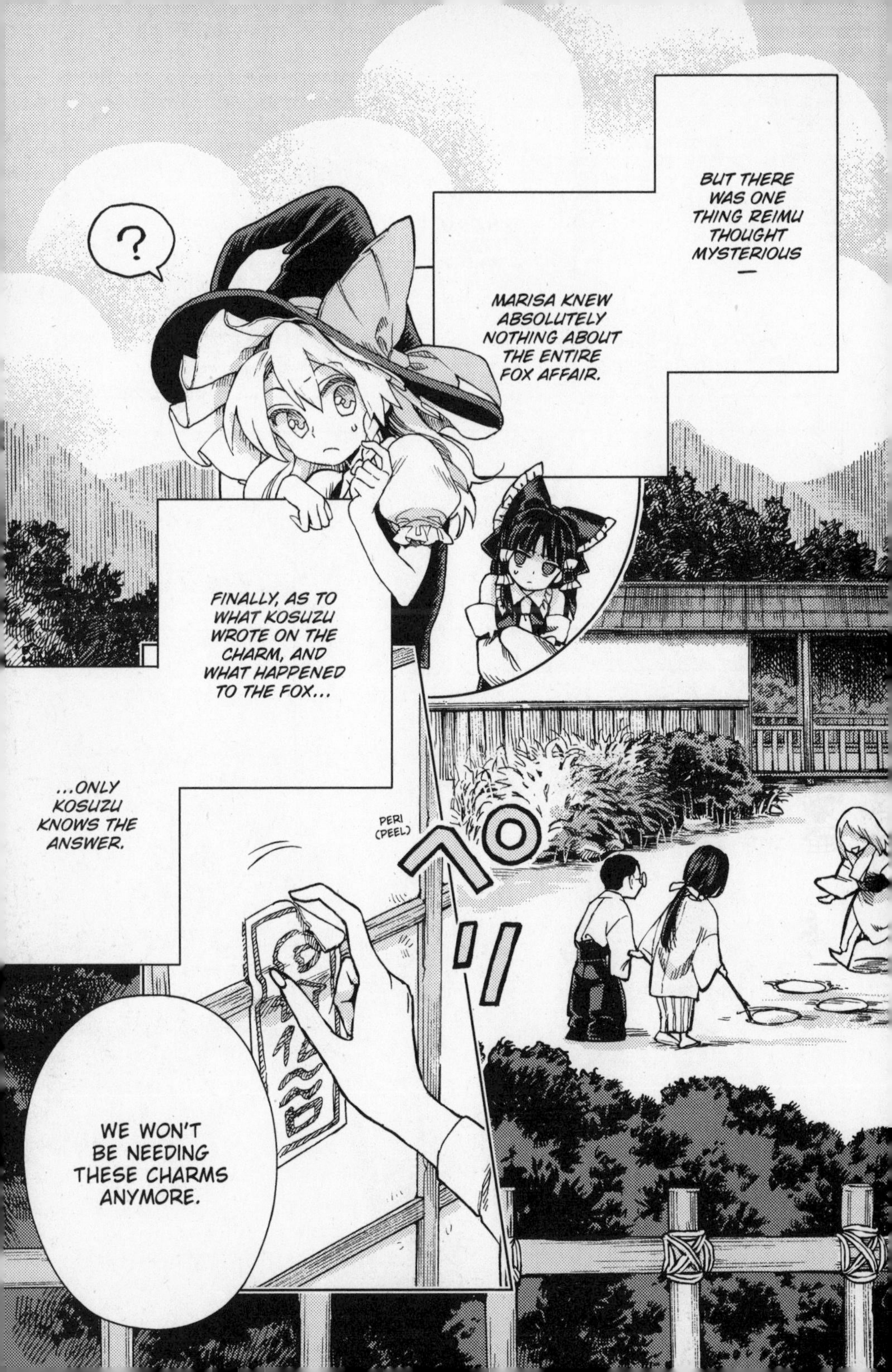
BUT THERE WAS ONE THING REIMU THOUGHT MYSTERIOUS —
MARISA KNEW ABSOLUTELY NOTHING ABOUT THE ENTIRE FOX AFFAIR.
?
FINALLY, AS TO WHAT KOSUZU WROTE ON THE CHARM, AND WHAT HAPPENED TO THE FOX...
...ONLY KOSUZU KNOWS THE ANSWER.
PERI (PEEL)
WE WON'T BE NEEDING THESE CHARMS ANYMORE.

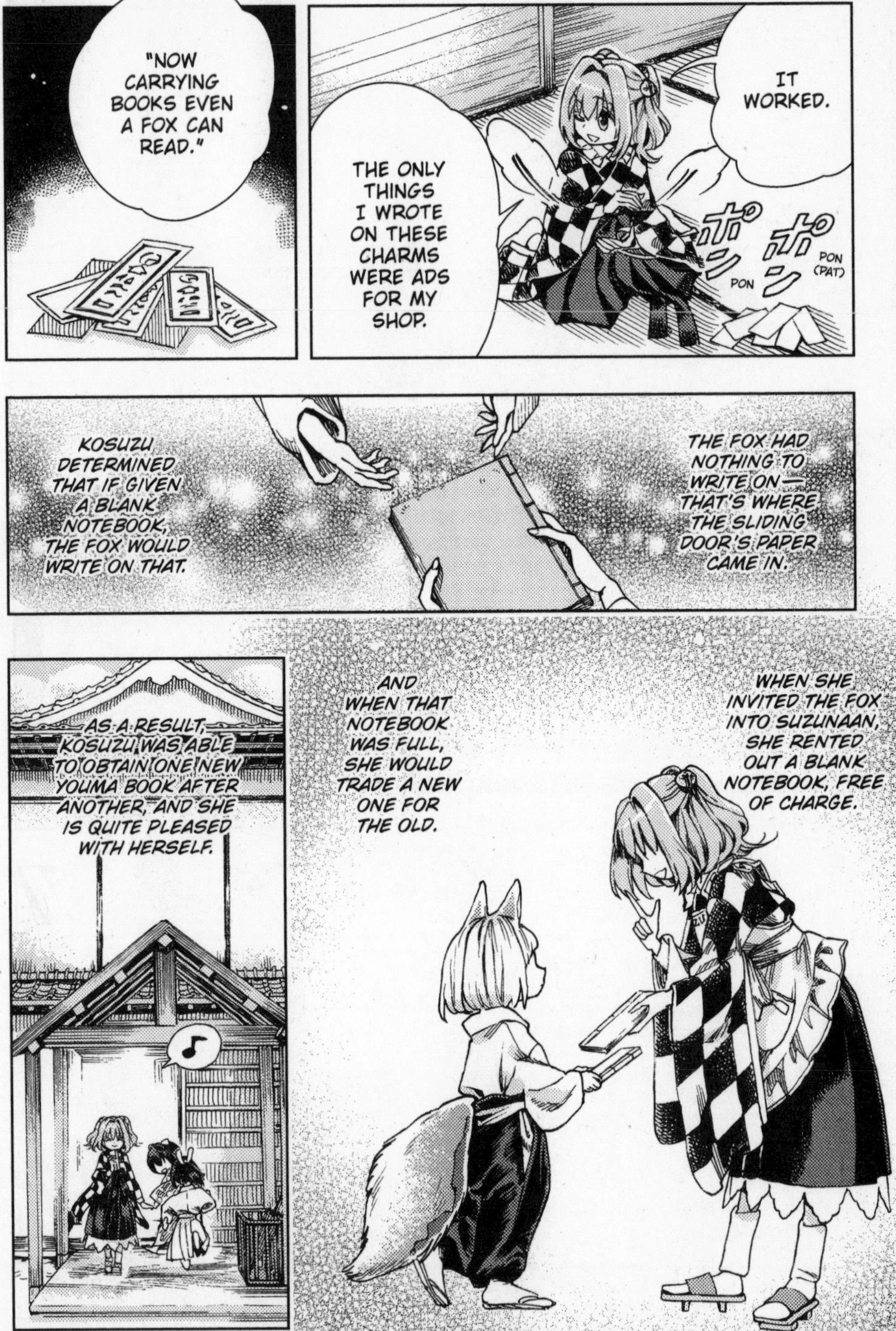
IT WORKED.
THE ONLY THINGS I WROTE ON THESE CHARMS WERE ADS FOR MY SHOP.
ポン ポン
PON (PAT)
PON
"NOW CARRYING BOOKS EVEN A FOX CAN READ."
THE FOX HAD NOTHING TO WRITE ON—THAT'S WHERE THE SLIDING DOOR'S PAPER CAME IN.
KOSUZU DETERMINED THAT IF GIVEN A BLANK NOTEBOOK, THE FOX WOULD WRITE ON THAT.
WHEN SHE INVITED THE FOX INTO SUZUNAAN, SHE RENTED OUT A BLANK NOTEBOOK, FREE OF CHARGE.
AND WHEN THAT NOTEBOOK WAS FULL, SHE WOULD TRADE A NEW ONE FOR THE OLD.
AS A RESULT, KOSUZU WAS ABLE TO OBTAIN ONE NEW YOUMA BOOK AFTER ANOTHER, AND SHE IS QUITE PLEASED WITH HERSELF.

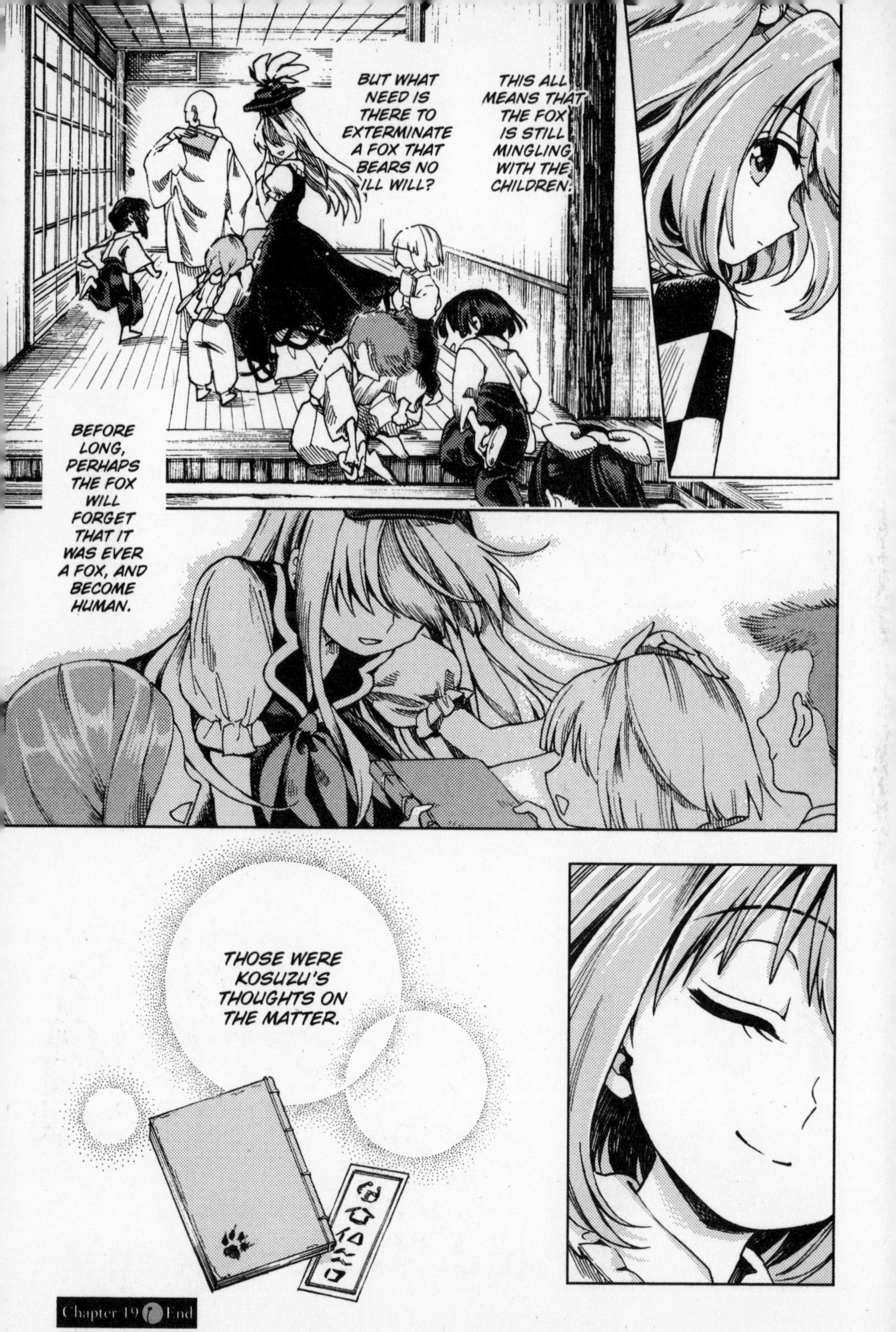
THIS ALL MEANS THAT THE FOX IS STILL MINGLING WITH THE CHILDREN.
BUT WHAT NEED IS THERE TO EXTERMINATE A FOX THAT BEARS NO ILL WILL?
BEFORE LONG, PERHAPS THE FOX WILL FORGET THAT IT WAS EVER A FOX, AND BECOME HUMAN.
THOSE WERE KOSUZU'S THOUGHTS ON THE MATTER.

Chapter 19 End

Forbidden Scrollery🐾

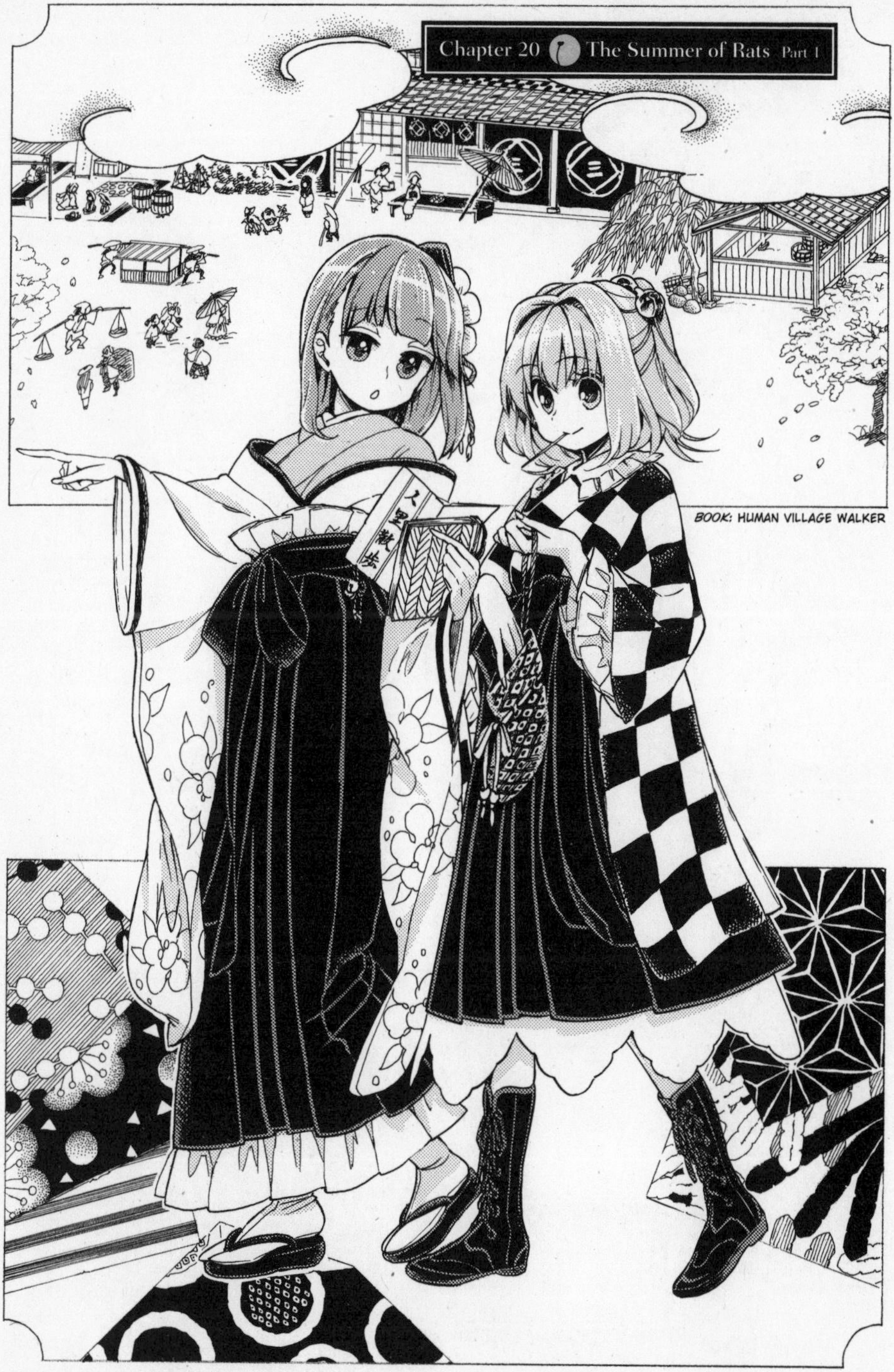
Chapter 20 The Summer of Rats Part 1
人里散歩
BOOK: HUMAN VILLAGE WALKER

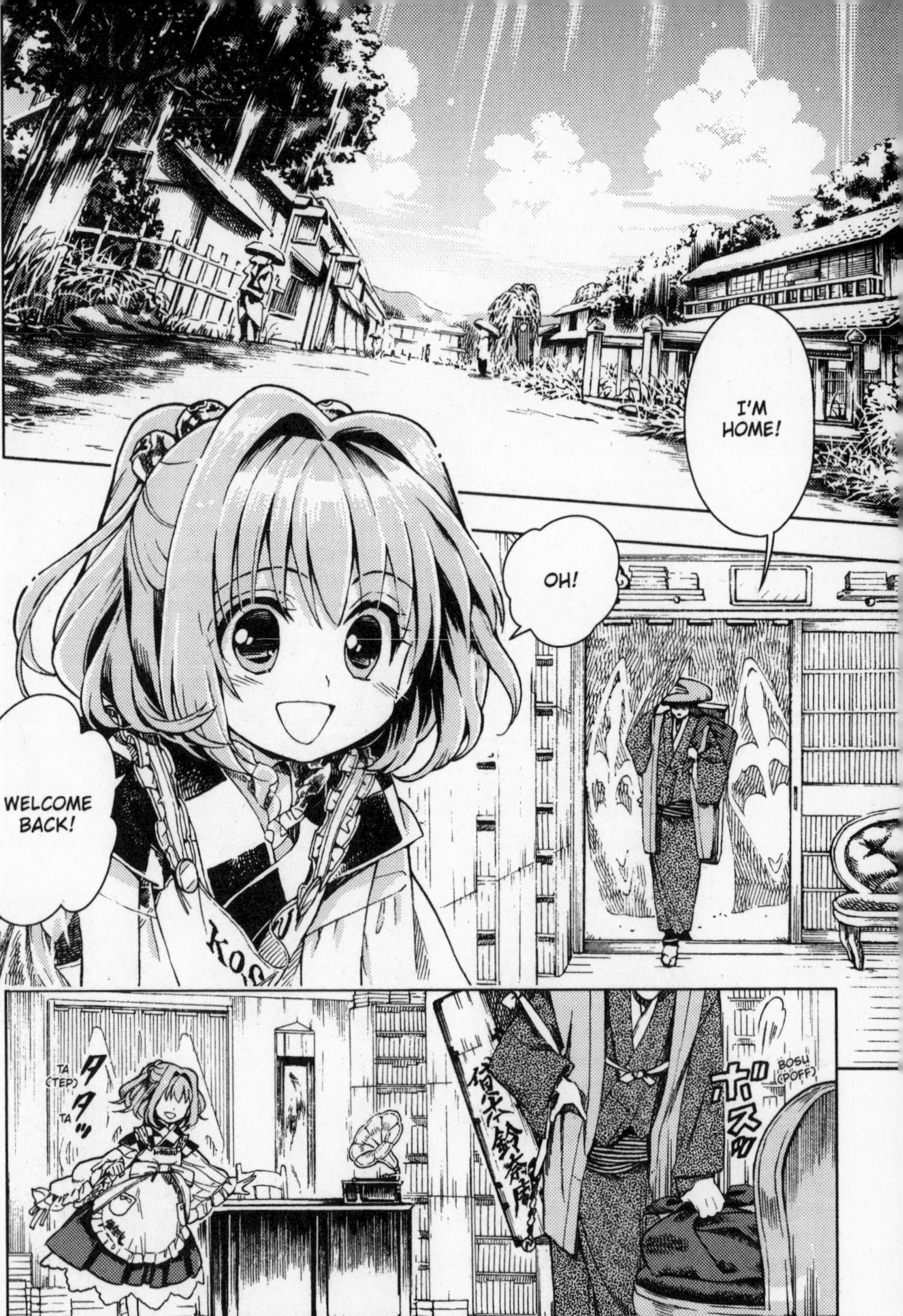
I'M HOME!
OH!
WELCOME BACK!
BOSU (POFF)
TA (TEP) TA

SIGN: SUZUNAAN BOOK RENTALS

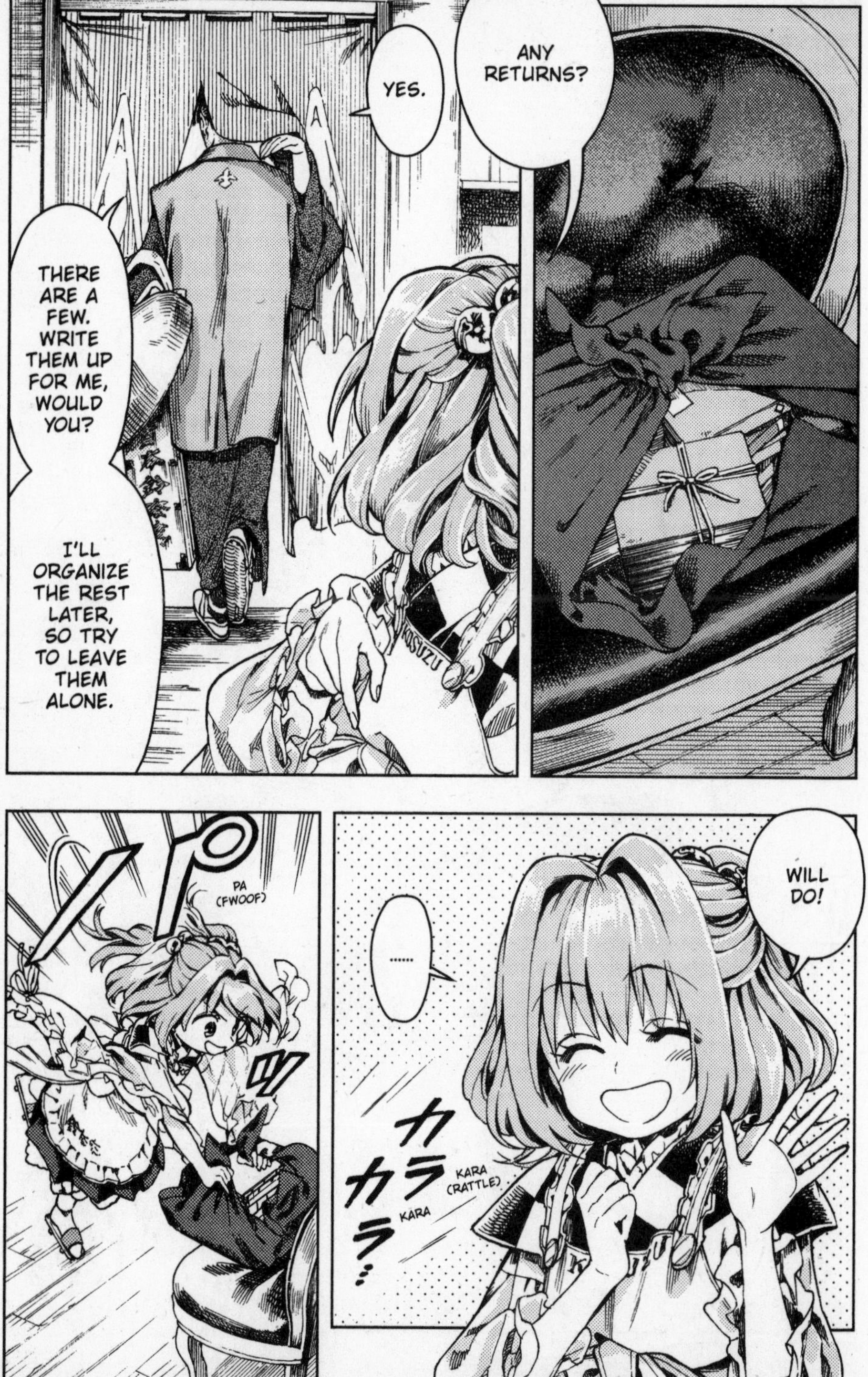
ANY RETURNS?
YES.
THERE ARE A FEW. WRITE THEM UP FOR ME, WOULD YOU?
I'LL ORGANIZE THE REST LATER, SO TRY TO LEAVE THEM ALONE.
WILL DO!
......
カラカラ
KARA (RATTLE)
KARA
PA (FWOOF)

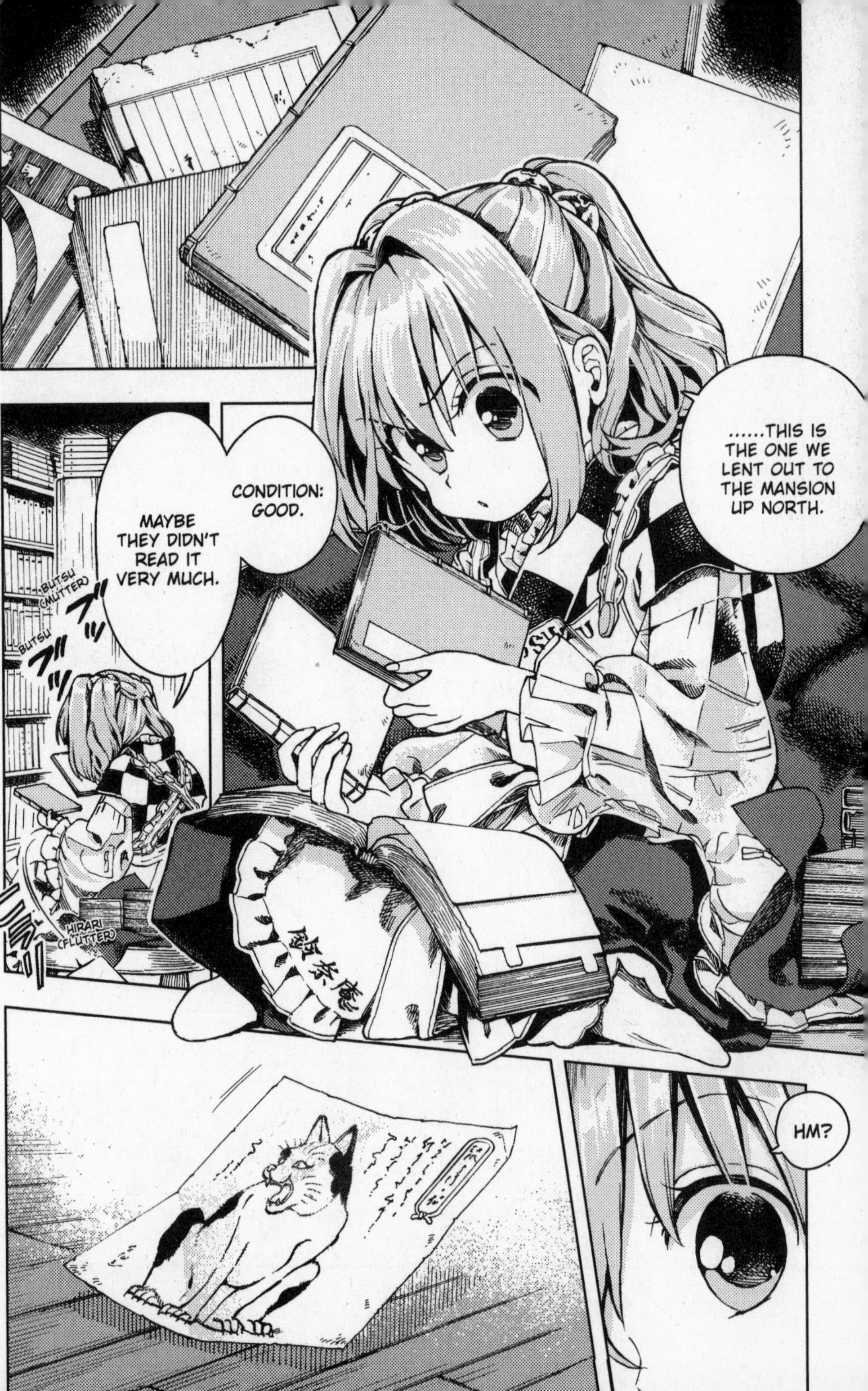
......THIS IS THE ONE WE LENT OUT TO THE MANSION UP NORTH.
CONDITION: GOOD.
MAYBE THEY DIDN'T READ IT VERY MUCH.
BUTSU (MUTTER)
BUTSU
HIRARI (FLUTTER)
HM?

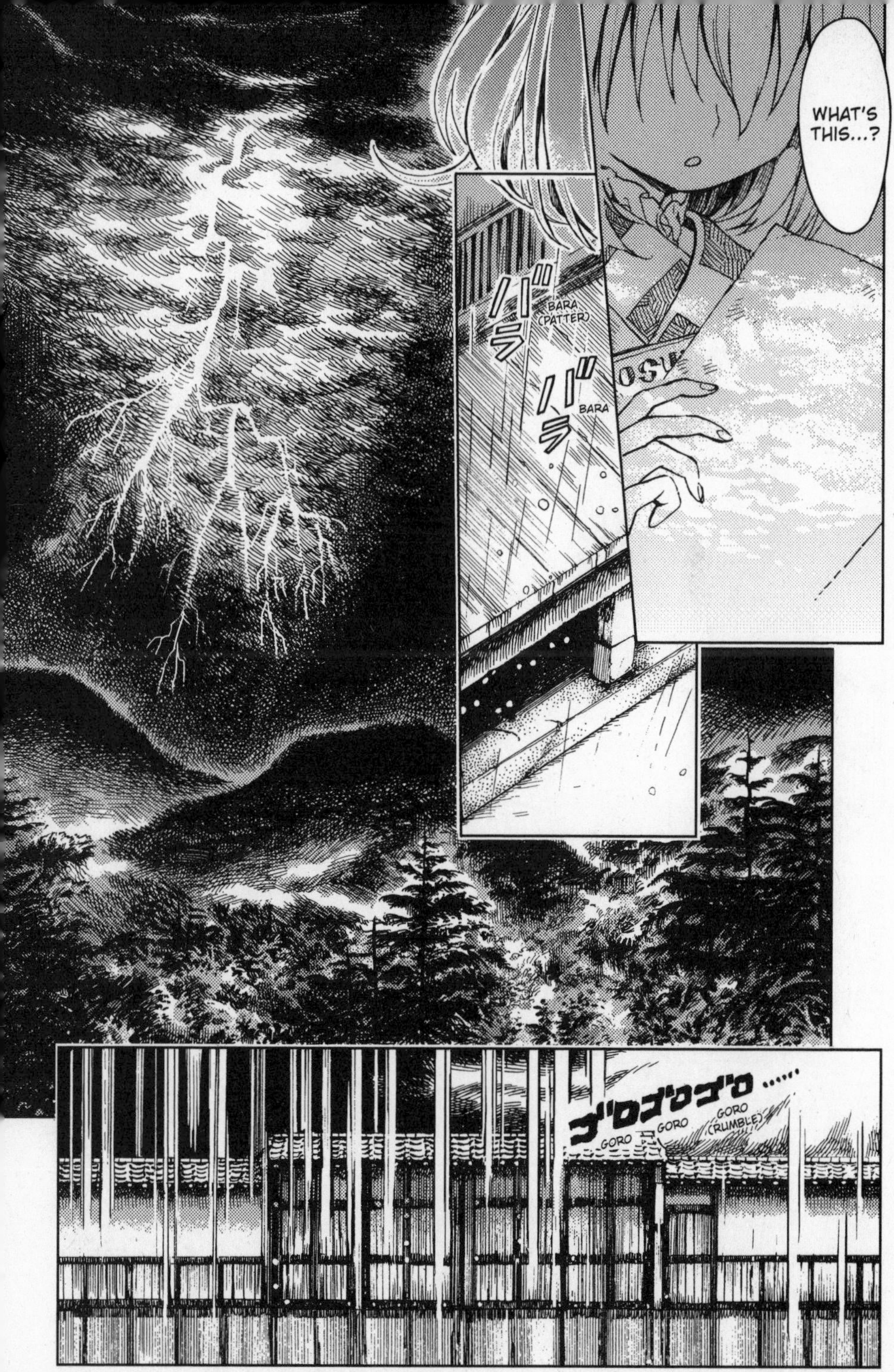
WHAT'S THIS...?
バラ
BARA (PATTER)
バラ
BARA
ゴロゴロゴロ……
GORO GORO GORO (RUMBLE)

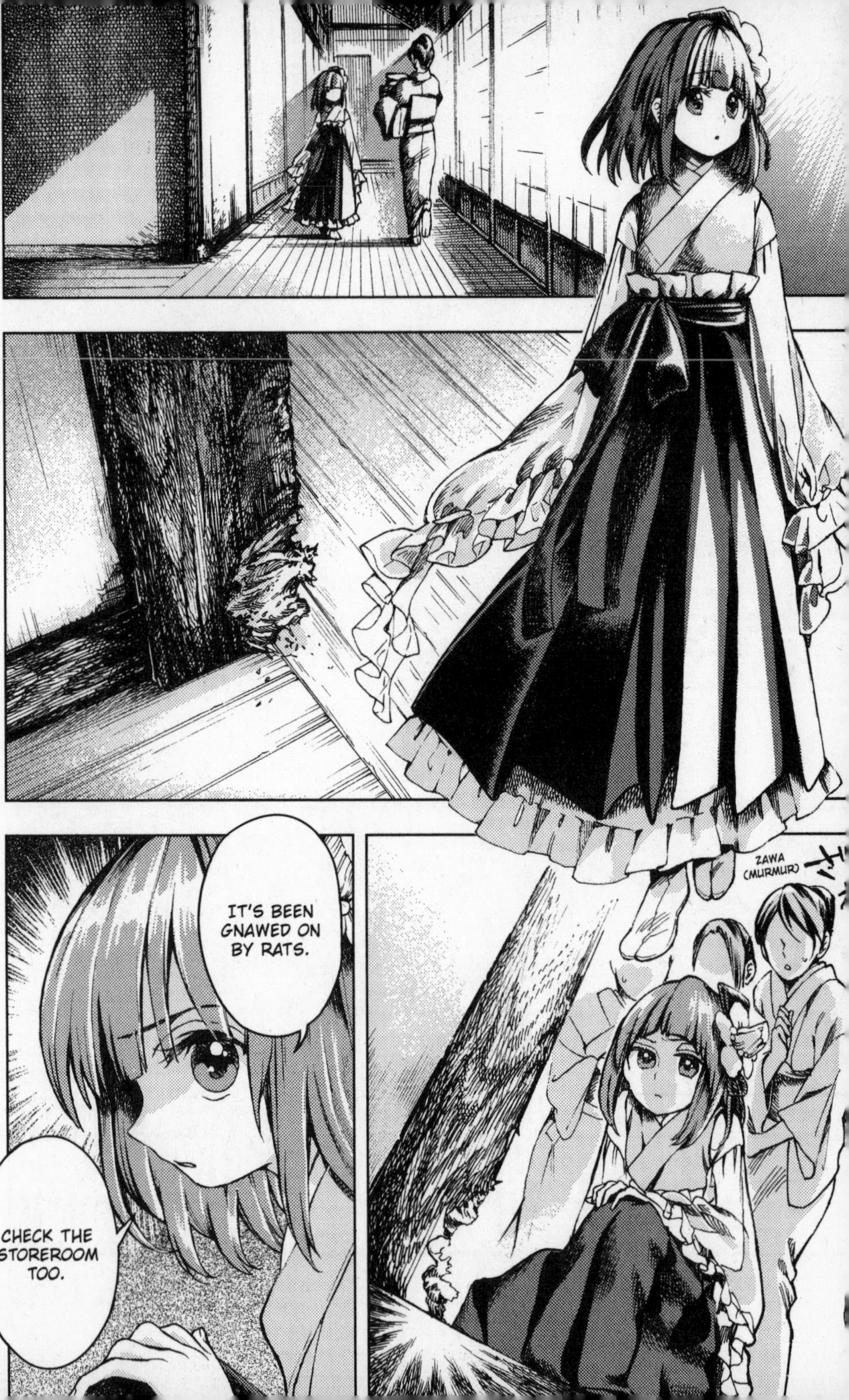
ZAWA (MURMUR)
IT'S BEEN GNAWED ON BY RATS.
CHECK THE STOREROOM TOO.

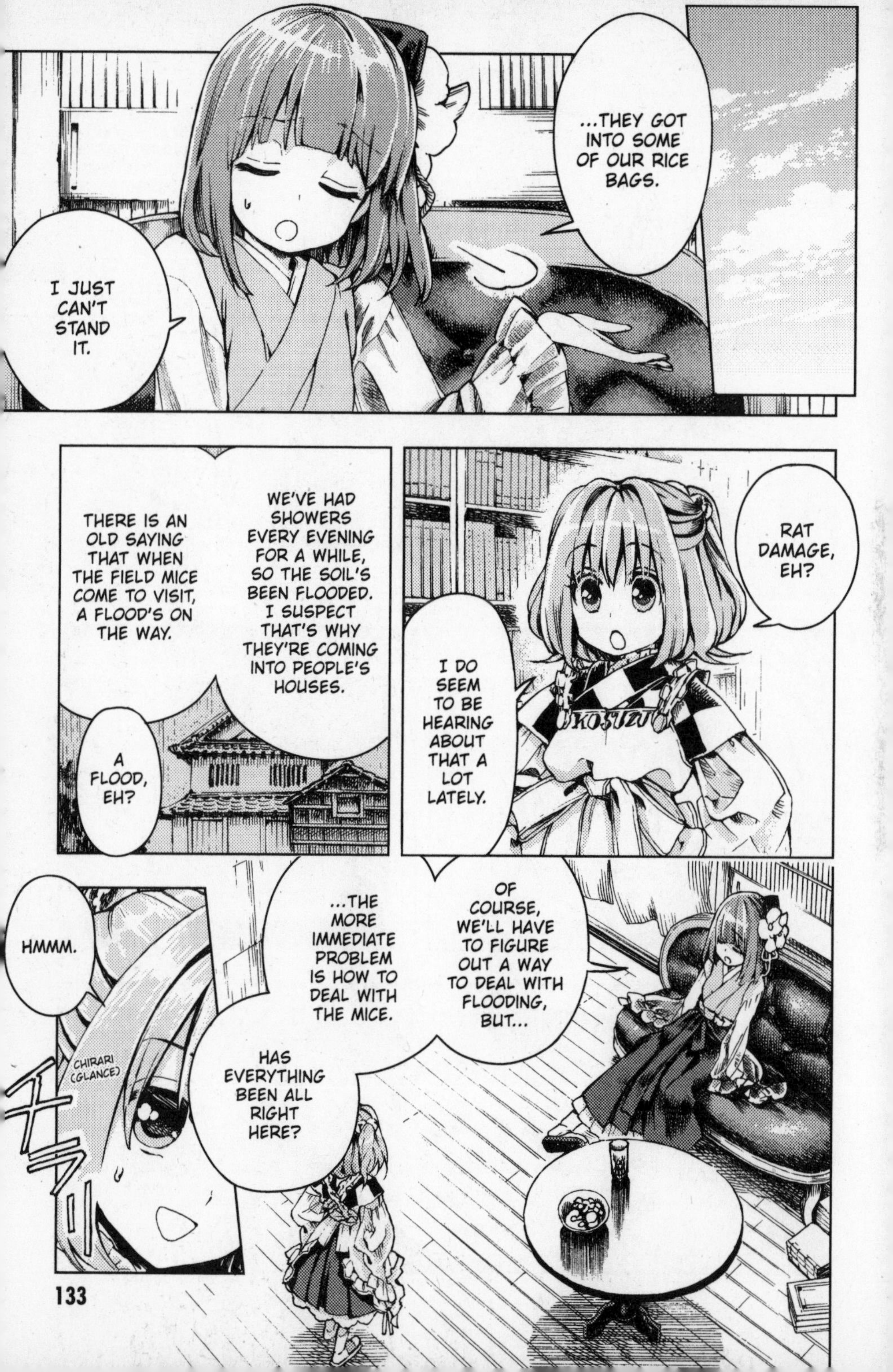
...THEY GOT INTO SOME OF OUR RICE BAGS.
I JUST CAN'T STAND IT.
RAT DAMAGE, EH?
I DO SEEM TO BE HEARING ABOUT THAT A LOT LATELY.
WE'VE HAD SHOWERS EVERY EVENING FOR A WHILE, SO THE SOIL'S BEEN FLOODED. I SUSPECT THAT'S WHY THEY'RE COMING INTO PEOPLE'S HOUSES.
THERE IS AN OLD SAYING THAT WHEN THE FIELD MICE COME TO VISIT, A FLOOD'S ON THE WAY.
A FLOOD, EH?
OF COURSE, WE'LL HAVE TO FIGURE OUT A WAY TO DEAL WITH FLOODING, BUT...
...THE MORE IMMEDIATE PROBLEM IS HOW TO DEAL WITH THE MICE.
HAS EVERYTHING BEEN ALL RIGHT HERE?
KOSUZU
HMMM.
CHIRARI (GLANCE)

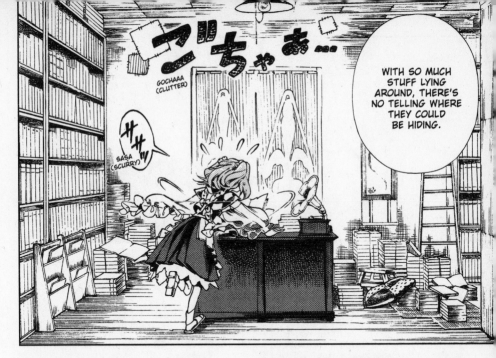

WITH SO MUCH STUFF LYING AROUND, THERE'S NO TELLING WHERE THEY COULD BE HIDING.
ゴちゃあ…
GOCHAAA (CLUTTER)
ササッ
SASA (SCURRY)
カサ
KASA (RUSTLE)
UH.
OH YEAH.
I FOUND THIS IN THE BOOKS MY PARENTS BROUGHT IN YESTERDAY.
A PAINTING OF A CAT?

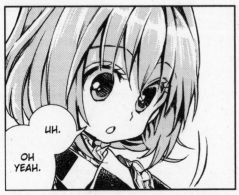

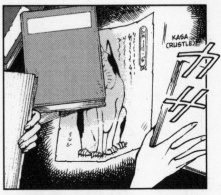

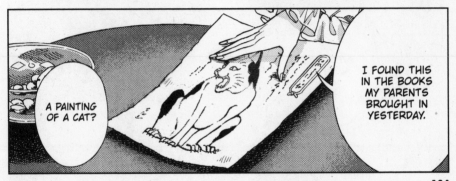

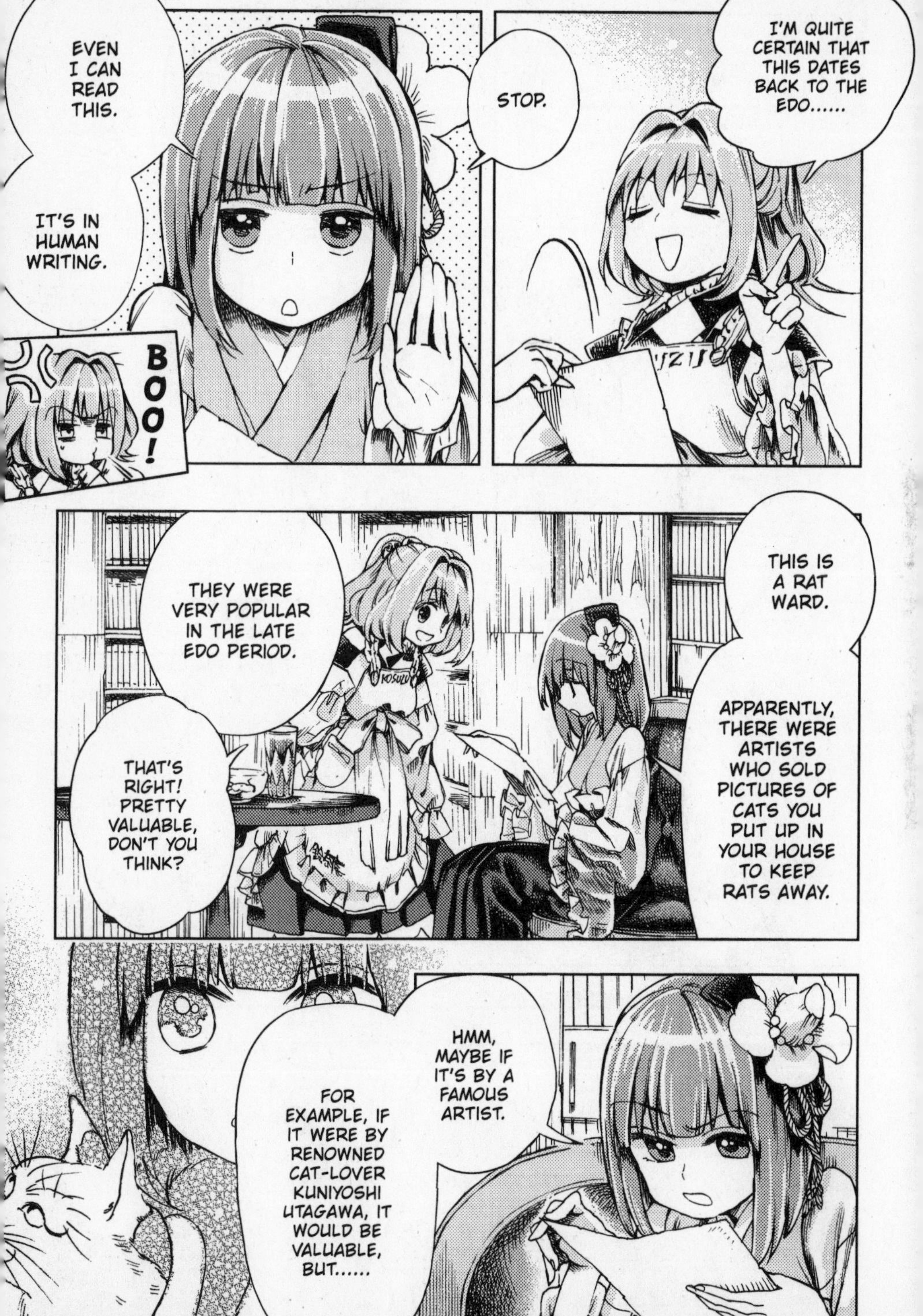
I'M QUITE CERTAIN THAT THIS DATES BACK TO THE EDO......
STOP.
EVEN I CAN READ THIS.
IT'S IN HUMAN WRITING.
BOO!
THIS IS A RAT WARD.
APPARENTLY, THERE WERE ARTISTS WHO SOLD PICTURES OF CATS YOU PUT UP IN YOUR HOUSE TO KEEP RATS AWAY.
THEY WERE VERY POPULAR IN THE LATE EDO PERIOD.
THAT'S RIGHT! PRETTY VALUABLE, DON'T YOU THINK?
HMM, MAYBE IF IT'S BY A FAMOUS ARTIST.
FOR EXAMPLE, IF IT WERE BY RENOWNED CAT-LOVER KUNIYOSHI UTAGAWA, IT WOULD BE VALUABLE, BUT......

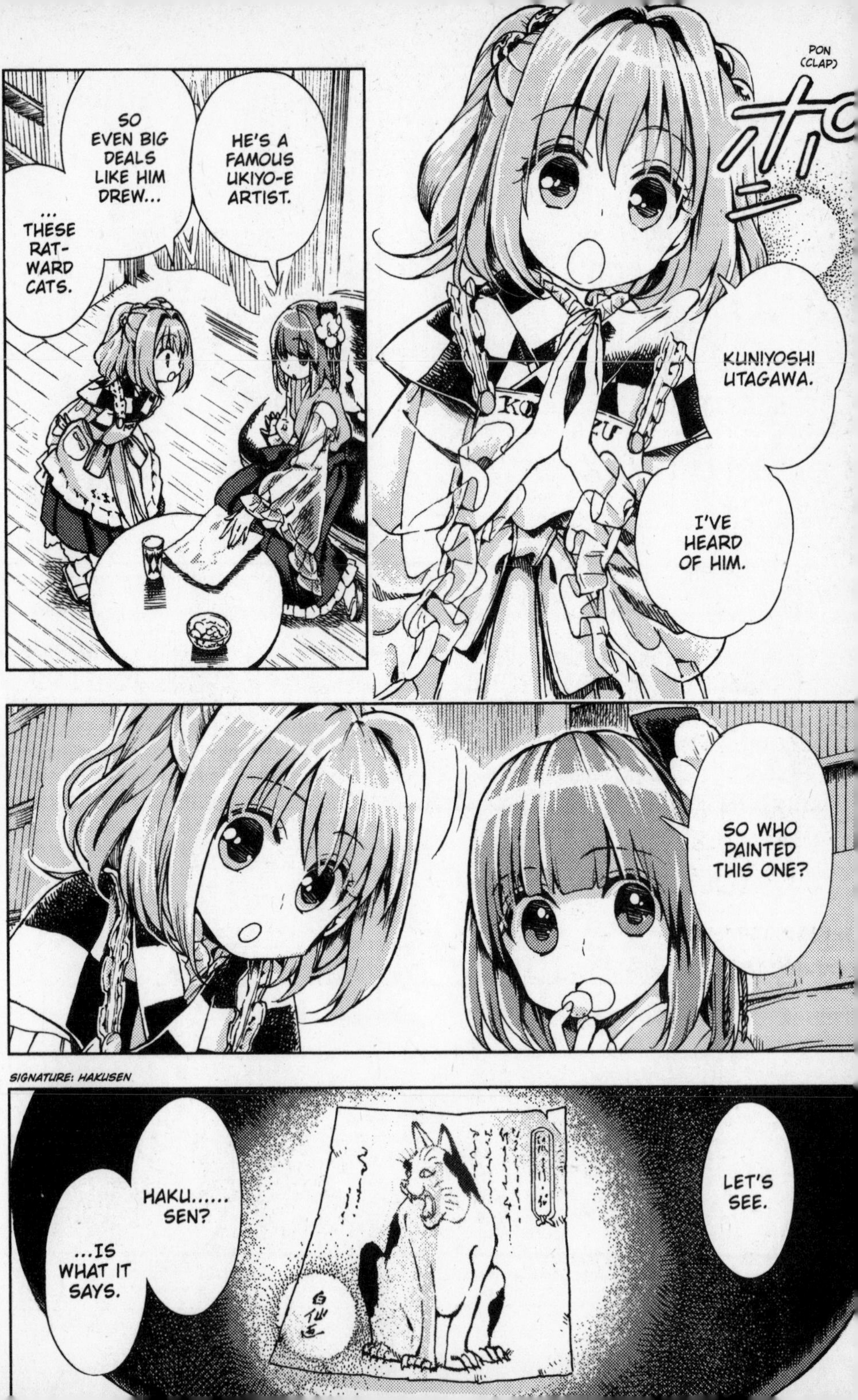
PON (CLAP)
KUNIYOSHI UTAGAWA.
I'VE HEARD OF HIM.
HE'S A FAMOUS UKIYO-E ARTIST.
SO EVEN BIG DEALS LIKE HIM DREW...
...THESE RAT-WARD CATS.
SO WHO PAINTED THIS ONE?
SIGNATURE: HAKUSEN
LET'S SEE.
HAKU...... SEN?
...IS WHAT IT SAYS.

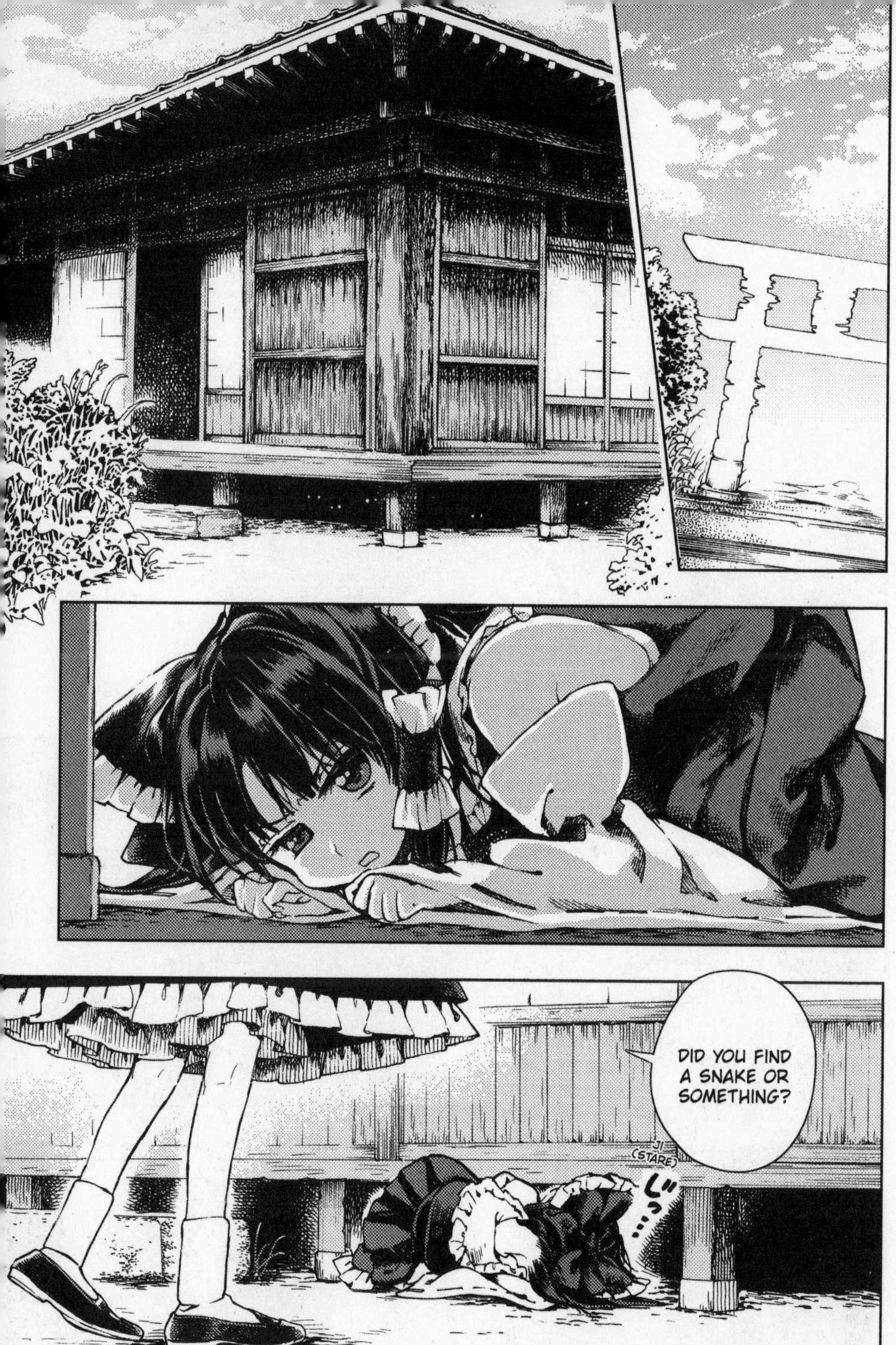
DID YOU FIND A SNAKE OR SOMETHING?
JI (STARE)

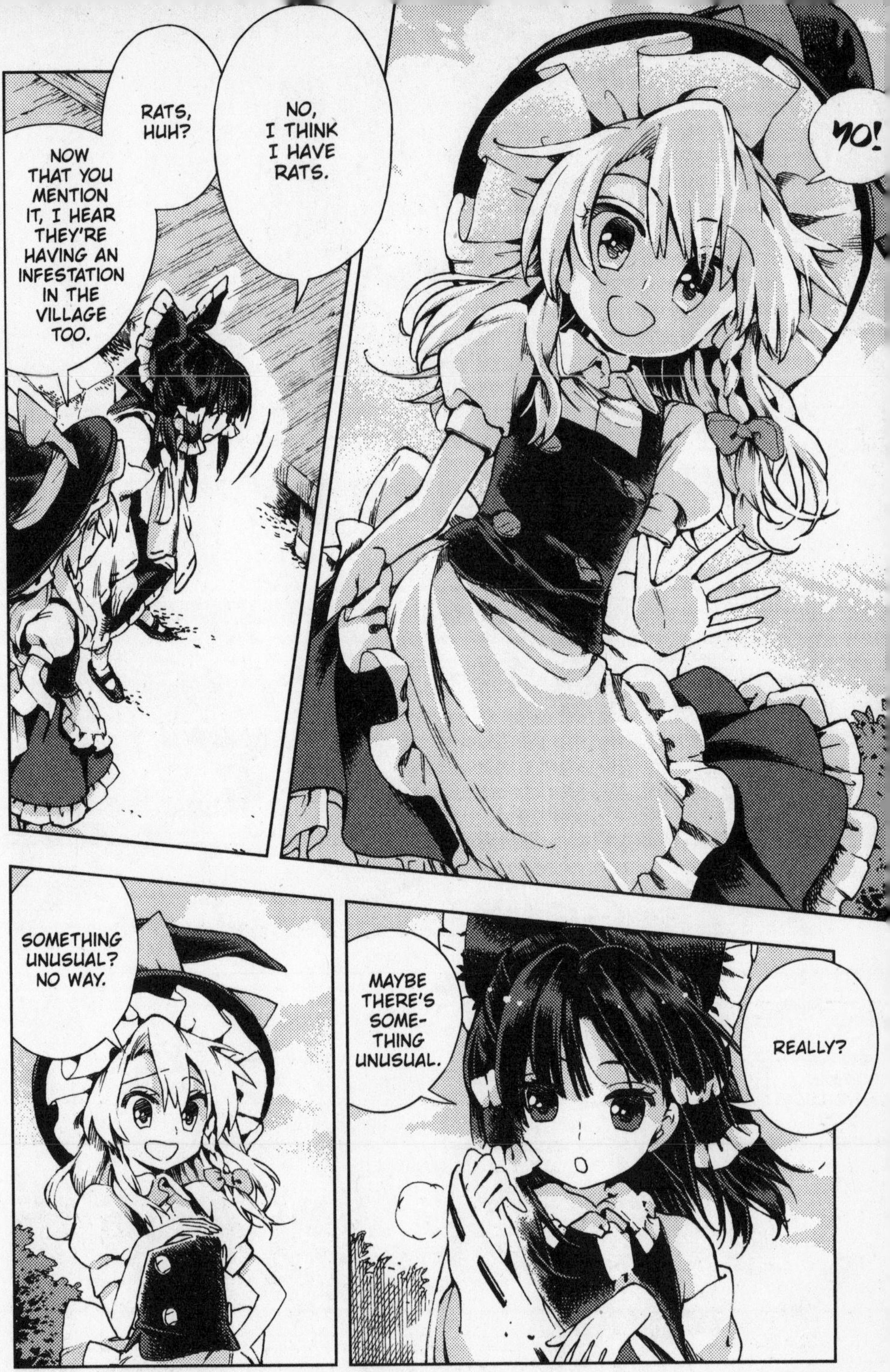
NO!
NO, I THINK I HAVE RATS.
RATS, HUH?
NOW THAT YOU MENTION IT, I HEAR THEY'RE HAVING AN INFESTATION IN THE VILLAGE TOO.
REALLY?
MAYBE THERE'S SOME-THING UNUSUAL.
SOMETHING UNUSUAL? NO WAY.

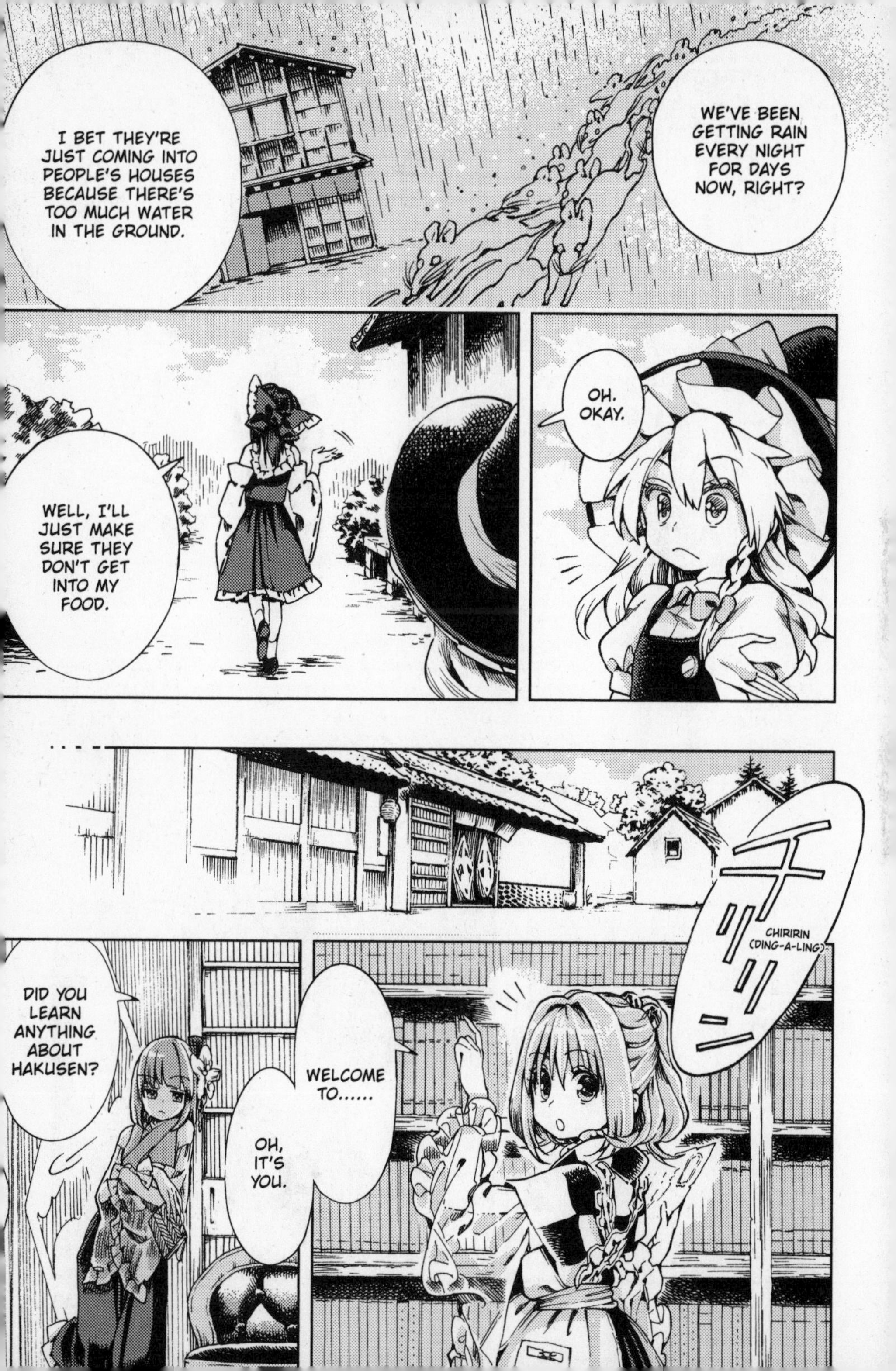
WE'VE BEEN GETTING RAIN EVERY NIGHT FOR DAYS NOW, RIGHT?
I BET THEY'RE JUST COMING INTO PEOPLE'S HOUSES BECAUSE THERE'S TOO MUCH WATER IN THE GROUND.
OH. OKAY.
WELL, I'LL JUST MAKE SURE THEY DON'T GET INTO MY FOOD.
CHIRIRIN (DING-A-LING)
WELCOME TO......
OH, IT'S YOU.
DID YOU LEARN ANYTHING ABOUT HAKUSEN?

*A WRITER FROM THE EDO PERIOD. ALSO WENT BY SHOKUSANJIN.

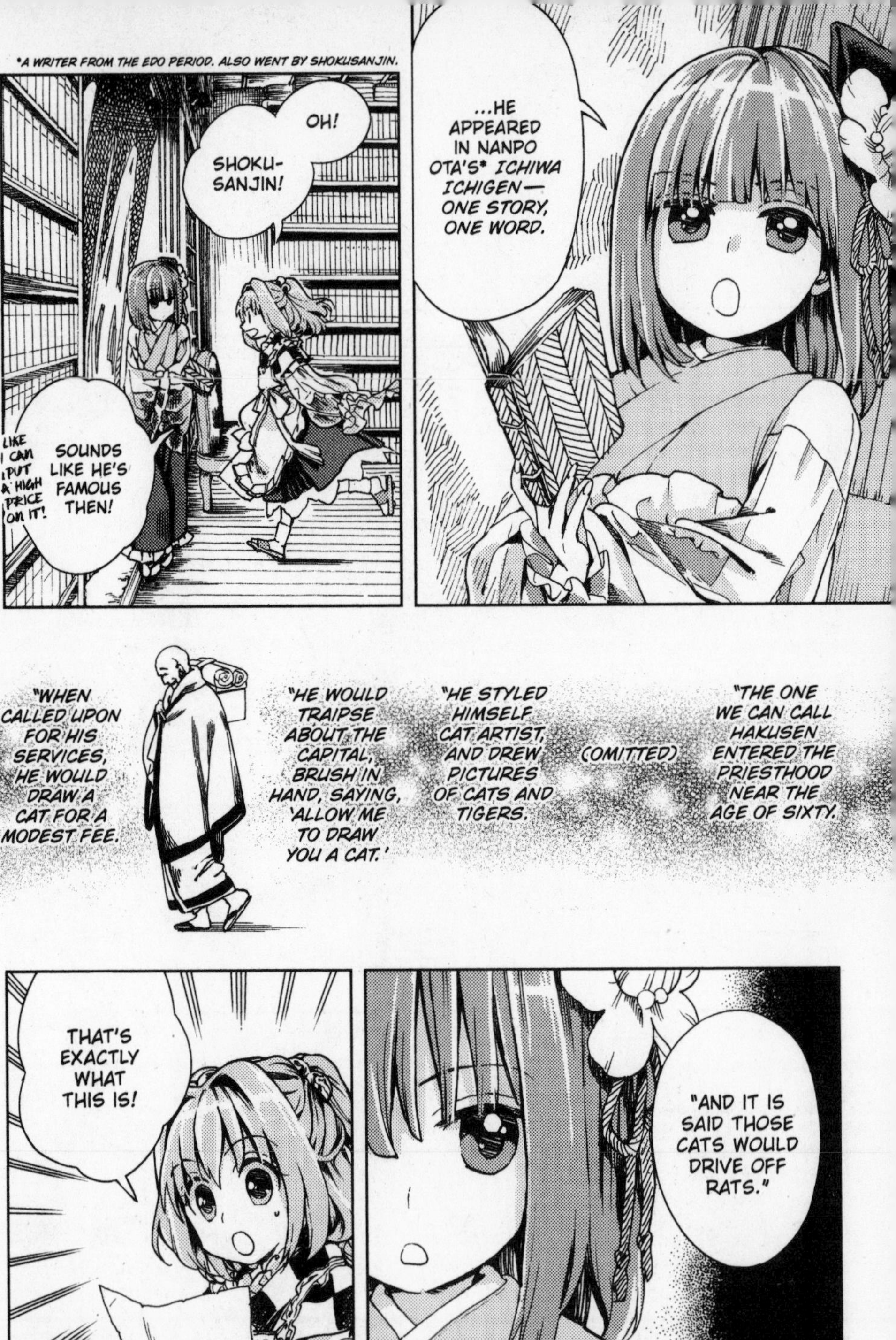

...HE APPEARED IN NANPO OTA'S* ICHIWA ICHIGEN—ONE STORY, ONE WORD.
OH!
SHOKU-SANJIN!
SOUNDS LIKE HE'S FAMOUS THEN!
LIKE I CAN PUT A HIGH PRICE ON IT!
"THE ONE WE CAN CALL HAKUSEN ENTERED THE PRIESTHOOD NEAR THE AGE OF SIXTY.
(OMITTED)
"HE STYLED HIMSELF CAT ARTIST, AND DREW PICTURES OF CATS AND TIGERS.
"HE WOULD TRAIPSE ABOUT THE CAPITAL, BRUSH IN HAND, SAYING, 'ALLOW ME TO DRAW YOU A CAT.'
"WHEN CALLED UPON FOR HIS SERVICES, HE WOULD DRAW A CAT FOR A MODEST FEE.
"AND IT IS SAID THOSE CATS WOULD DRIVE OFF RATS."
THAT'S EXACTLY WHAT THIS IS!

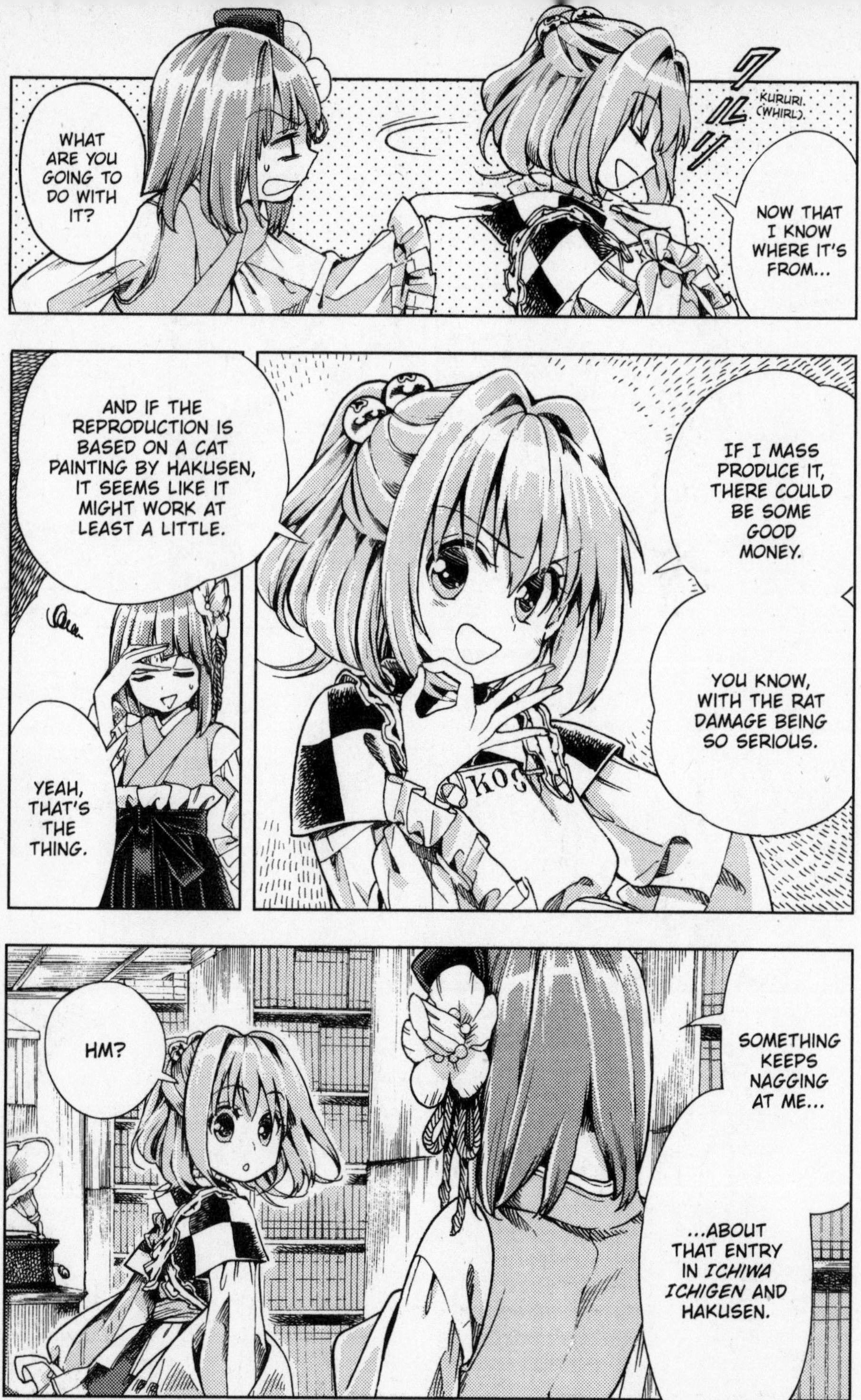
WHAT ARE YOU GOING TO DO WITH IT?
KURURI. (WHIRL).
NOW THAT I KNOW WHERE IT'S FROM...
IF I MASS PRODUCE IT, THERE COULD BE SOME GOOD MONEY.
YOU KNOW, WITH THE RAT DAMAGE BEING SO SERIOUS.
AND IF THE REPRODUCTION IS BASED ON A CAT PAINTING BY HAKUSEN, IT SEEMS LIKE IT MIGHT WORK AT LEAST A LITTLE.
YEAH, THAT'S THE THING.
SOMETHING KEEPS NAGGING AT ME...
...ABOUT THAT ENTRY IN *ICHIWA ICHIGEN* AND HAKUSEN.
HM?

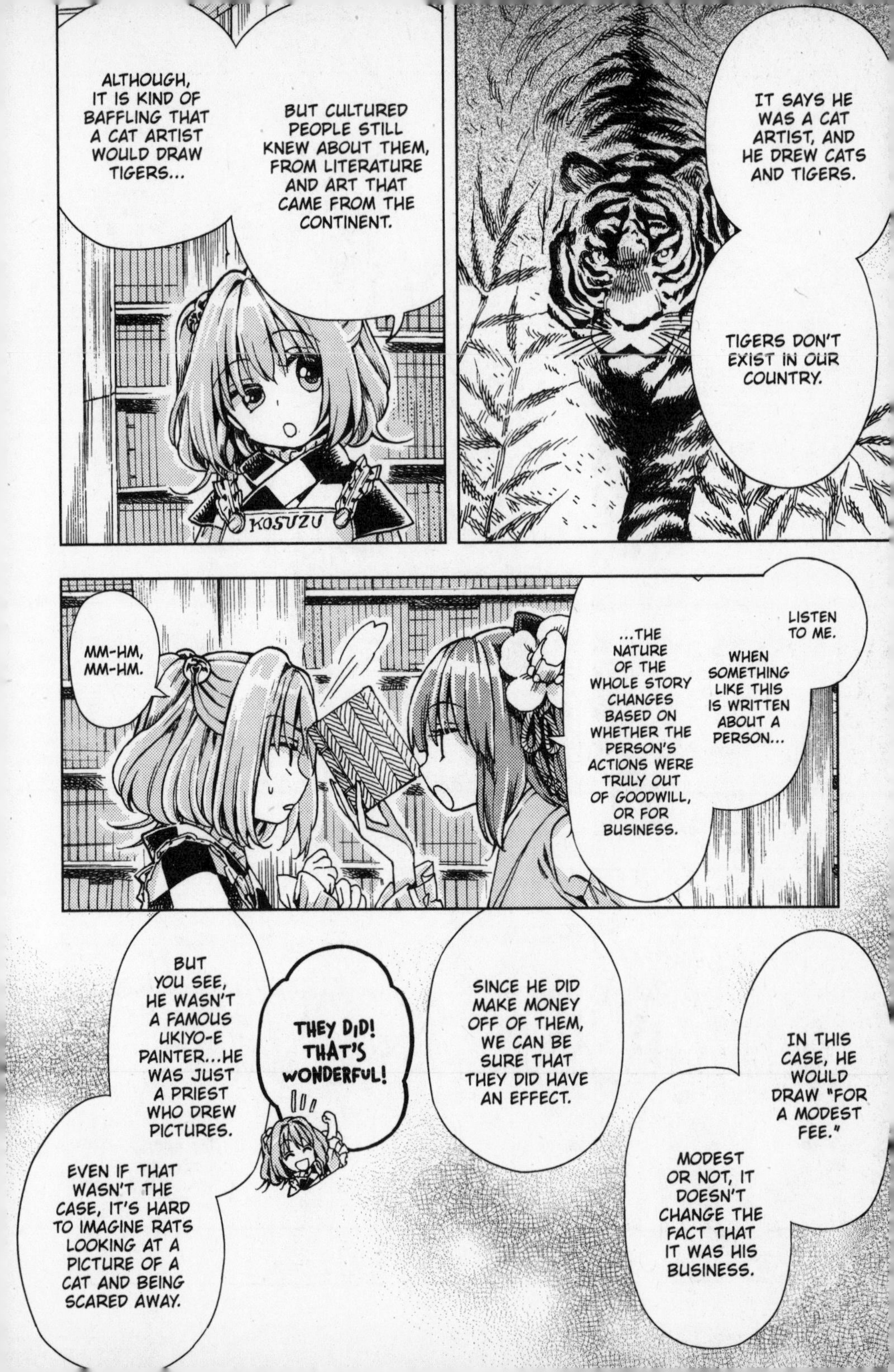
IT SAYS HE WAS A CAT ARTIST, AND HE DREW CATS AND TIGERS.
TIGERS DON'T EXIST IN OUR COUNTRY.
BUT CULTURED PEOPLE STILL KNEW ABOUT THEM, FROM LITERATURE AND ART THAT CAME FROM THE CONTINENT.
ALTHOUGH, IT IS KIND OF BAFFLING THAT A CAT ARTIST WOULD DRAW TIGERS...
KOSUZU
LISTEN TO ME.
WHEN SOMETHING LIKE THIS IS WRITTEN ABOUT A PERSON...
...THE NATURE OF THE WHOLE STORY CHANGES BASED ON WHETHER THE PERSON'S ACTIONS WERE TRULY OUT OF GOODWILL, OR FOR BUSINESS.
MM-HM, MM-HM.
IN THIS CASE, HE WOULD DRAW "FOR A MODEST FEE."
MODEST OR NOT, IT DOESN'T CHANGE THE FACT THAT IT WAS HIS BUSINESS.
SINCE HE DID MAKE MONEY OFF OF THEM, WE CAN BE SURE THAT THEY DID HAVE AN EFFECT.
THEY DID! THAT'S WONDERFUL!
BUT YOU SEE, HE WASN'T A FAMOUS UKIYO-E PAINTER...HE WAS JUST A PRIEST WHO DREW PICTURES.
EVEN IF THAT WASN'T THE CASE, IT'S HARD TO IMAGINE RATS LOOKING AT A PICTURE OF A CAT AND BEING SCARED AWAY.

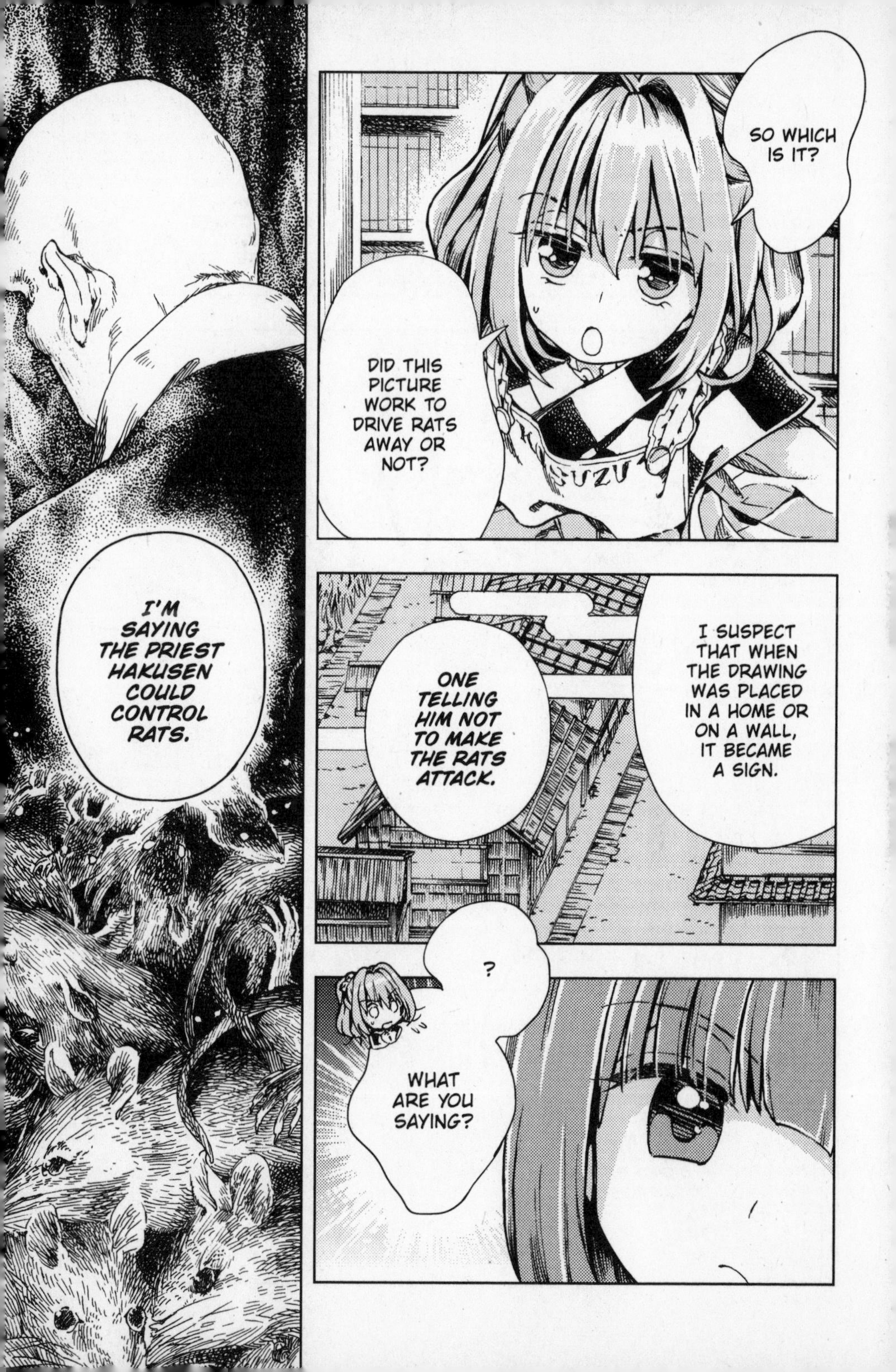
SO WHICH IS IT?
DID THIS PICTURE WORK TO DRIVE RATS AWAY OR NOT?
I SUSPECT THAT WHEN THE DRAWING WAS PLACED IN A HOME OR ON A WALL, IT BECAME A SIGN.
ONE TELLING HIM NOT TO MAKE THE RATS ATTACK.
?
WHAT ARE YOU SAYING?
I'M SAYING THE PRIEST HAKUSEN COULD CONTROL RATS.

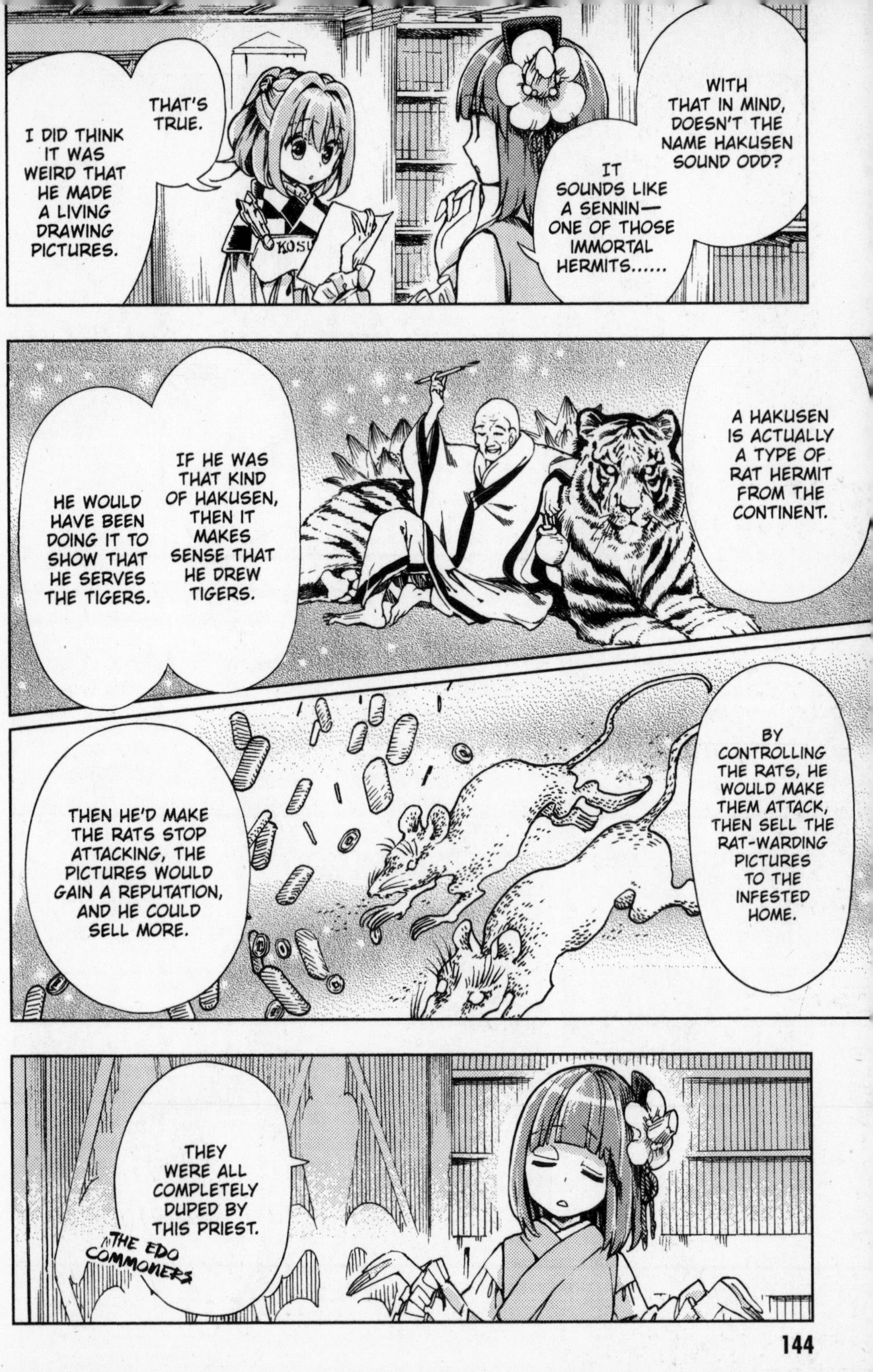
WITH THAT IN MIND, DOESN'T THE NAME HAKUSEN SOUND ODD?
IT SOUNDS LIKE A SENNIN—ONE OF THOSE IMMORTAL HERMITS......
THAT'S TRUE.
I DID THINK IT WAS WEIRD THAT HE MADE A LIVING DRAWING PICTURES.
A HAKUSEN IS ACTUALLY A TYPE OF RAT HERMIT FROM THE CONTINENT.
IF HE WAS THAT KIND OF HAKUSEN, THEN IT MAKES SENSE THAT HE DREW TIGERS.
HE WOULD HAVE BEEN DOING IT TO SHOW THAT HE SERVES THE TIGERS.
BY CONTROLLING THE RATS, HE WOULD MAKE THEM ATTACK, THEN SELL THE RAT-WARDING PICTURES TO THE INFESTED HOME.
THEN HE'D MAKE THE RATS STOP ATTACKING, THE PICTURES WOULD GAIN A REPUTATION, AND HE COULD SELL MORE.
THEY WERE ALL COMPLETELY DUPED BY THIS PRIEST.
...THE EDO COMMONERS

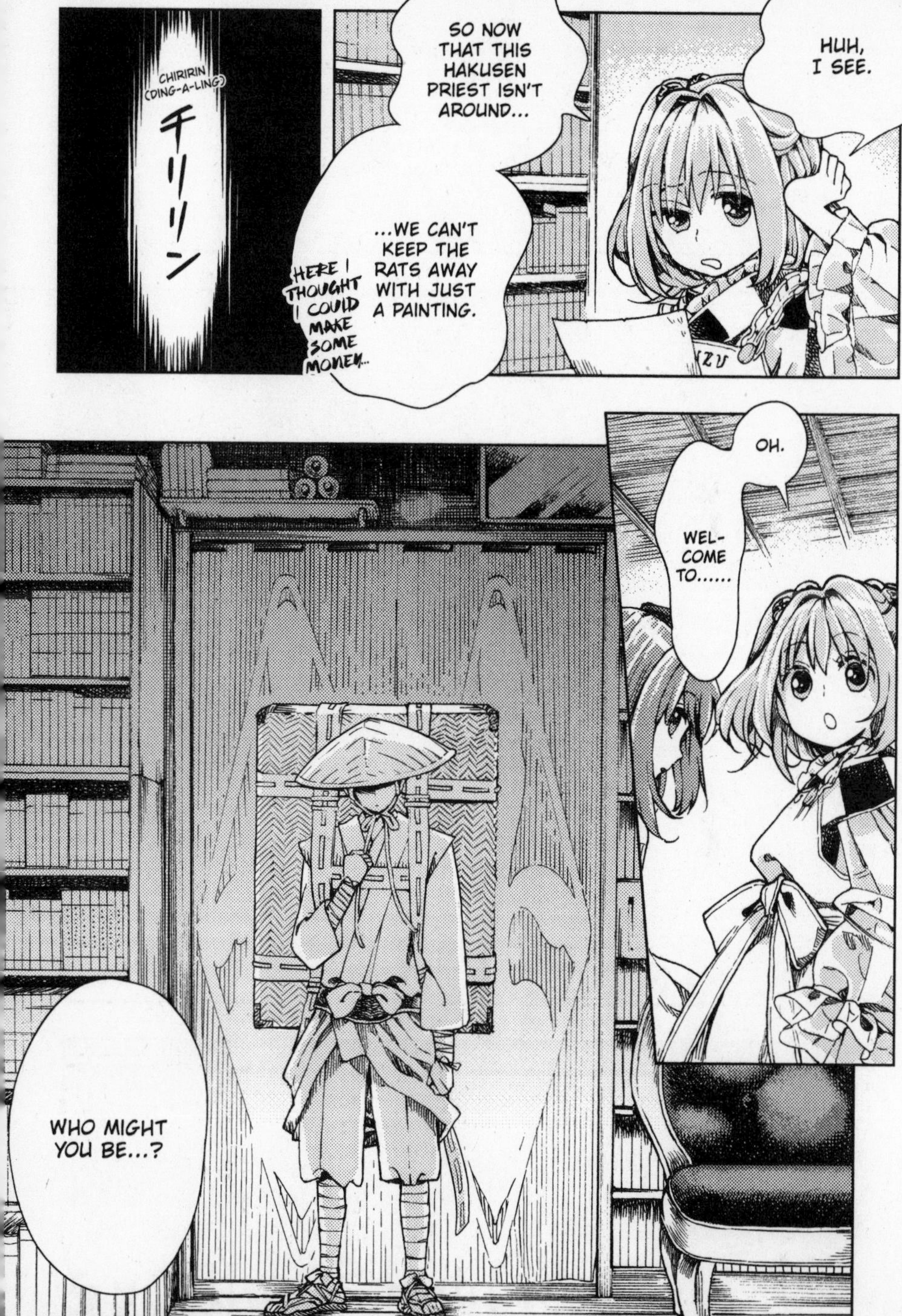
HUH, I SEE.
SO NOW THAT THIS HAKUSEN PRIEST ISN'T AROUND...
...WE CAN'T KEEP THE RATS AWAY WITH JUST A PAINTING.
HERE I THOUGHT I COULD MAKE SOME MONEY...
CHIRIRIN (DING-A-LING)
チリリン
OH.
WEL-COME TO......
WHO MIGHT YOU BE...?
Chapter 20 To be continued

Forbidden Scrollery

WARDS: HAKUREI

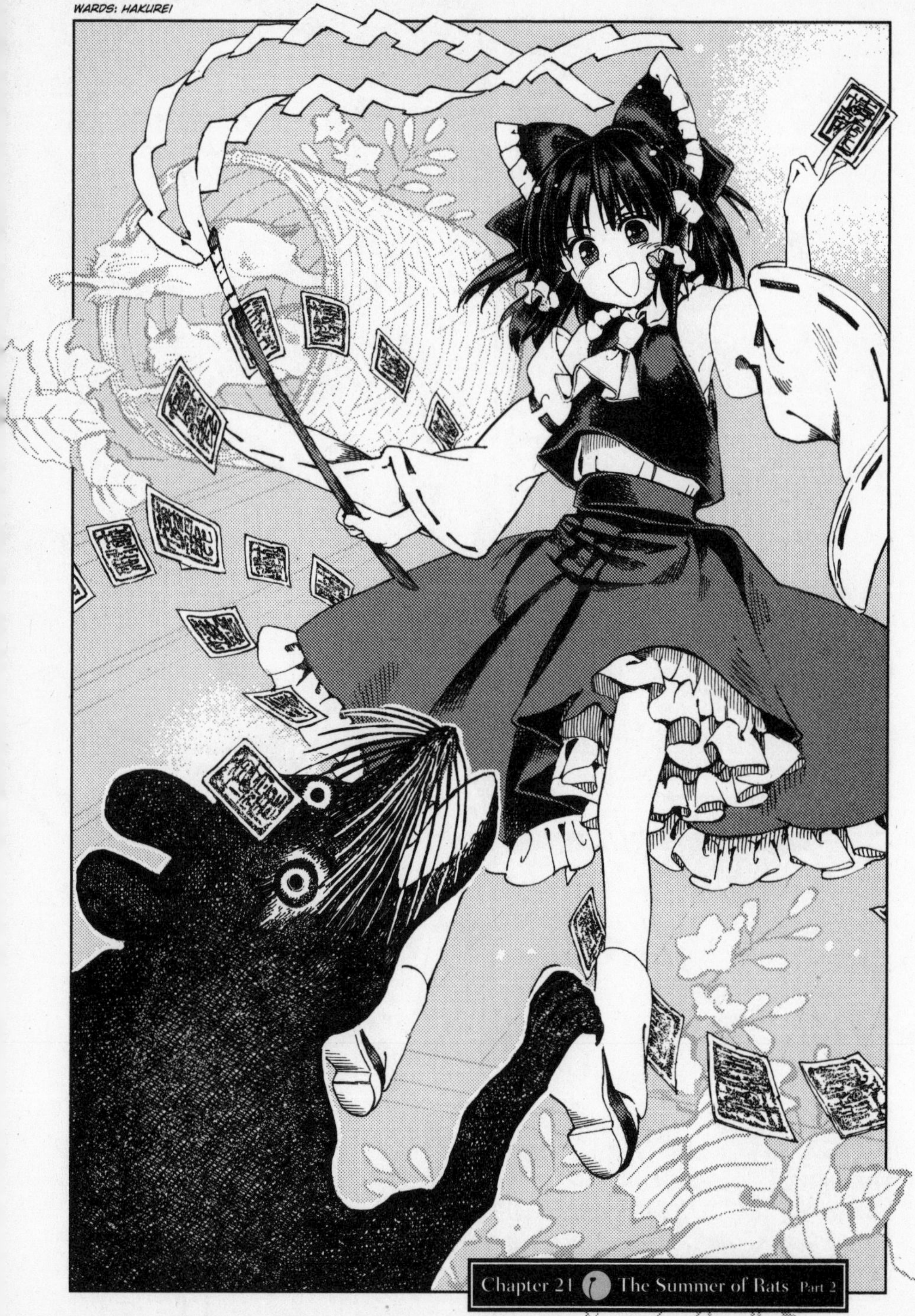

Chapter 21 The Summer of Rats Part 2

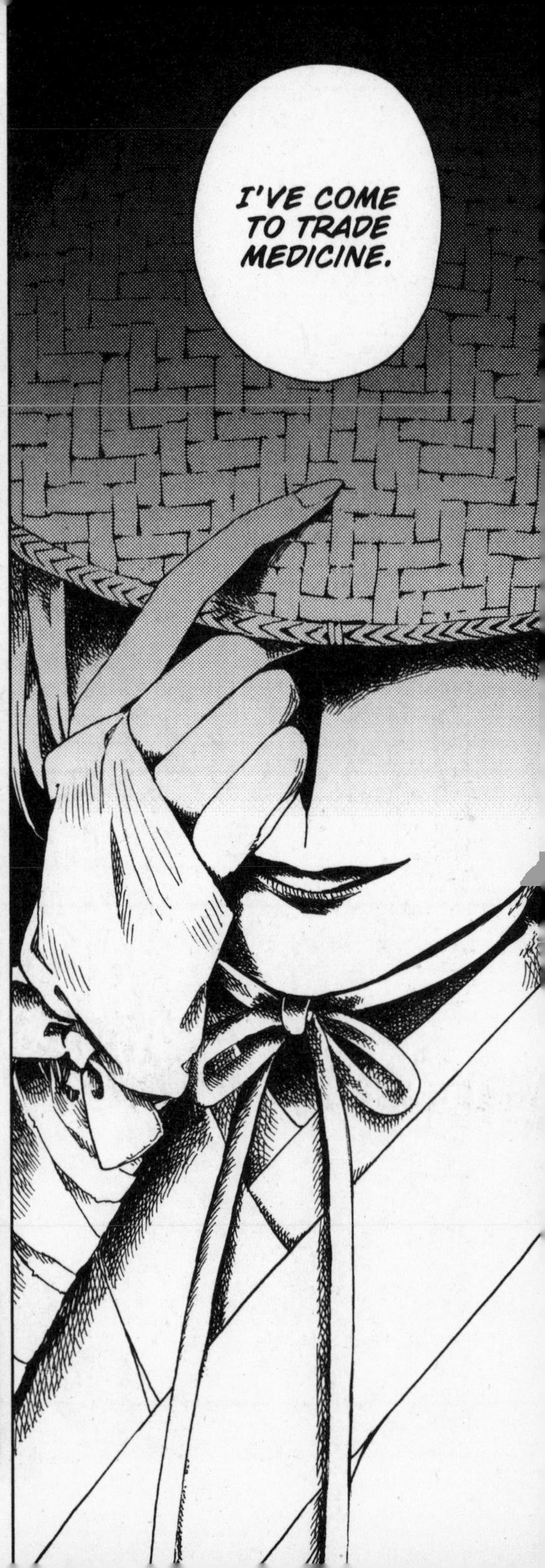
I'VE COME TO TRADE MEDICINE.

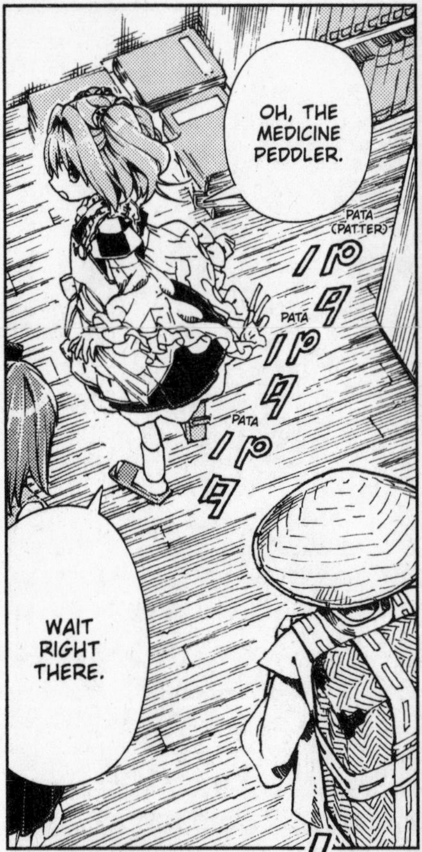
OH, THE MEDICINE PEDDLER.
PATA (PATTER)
PATA
PATA
WAIT RIGHT THERE.

BOX: MEDICINE BOX

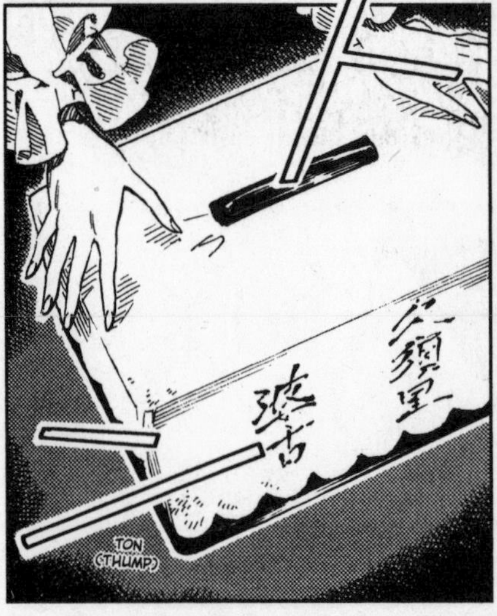
TON (THUMP)

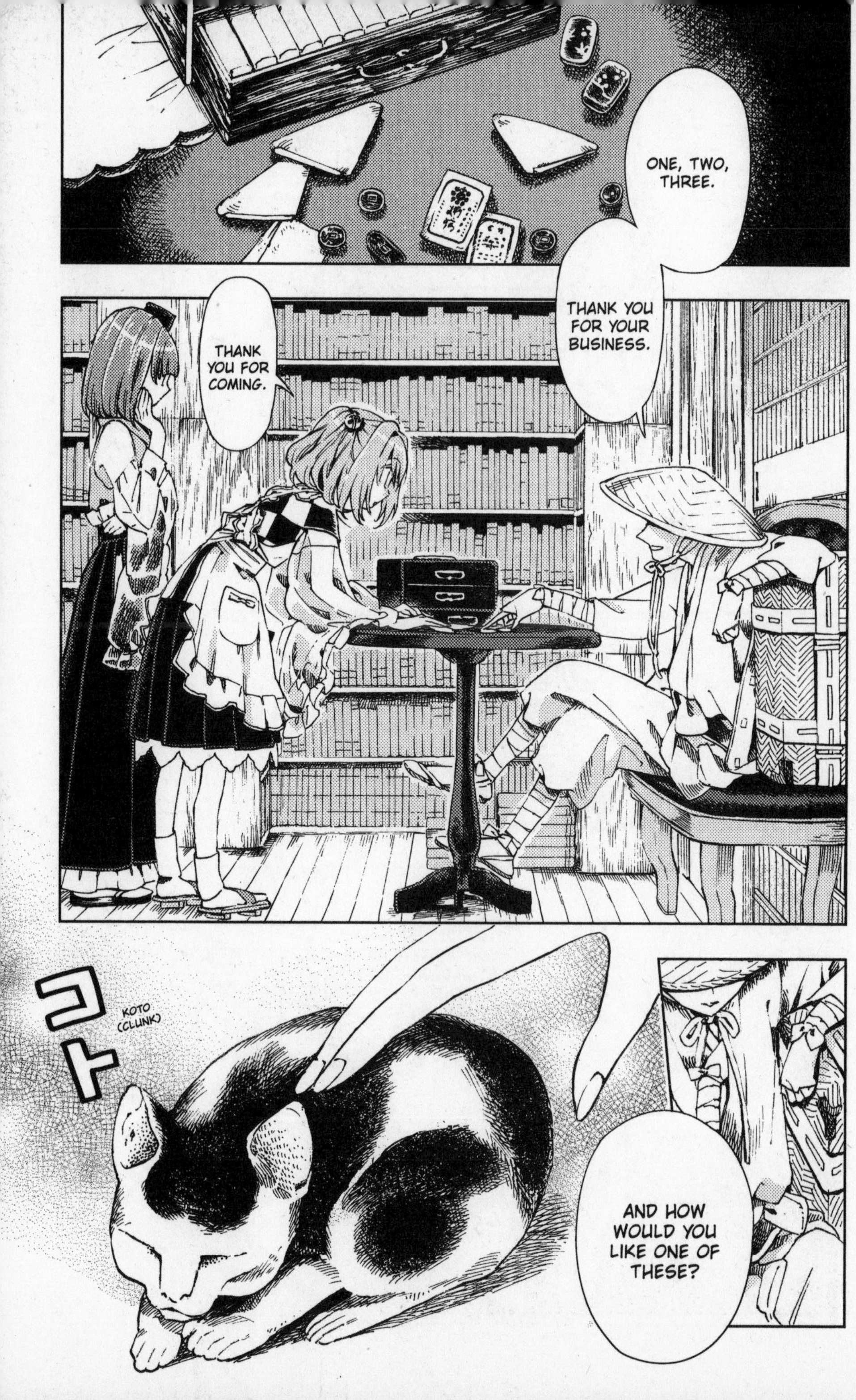
ONE, TWO, THREE.
THANK YOU FOR YOUR BUSINESS.
THANK YOU FOR COMING.
AND HOW WOULD YOU LIKE ONE OF THESE?
コト
KOTO (CLUNK)

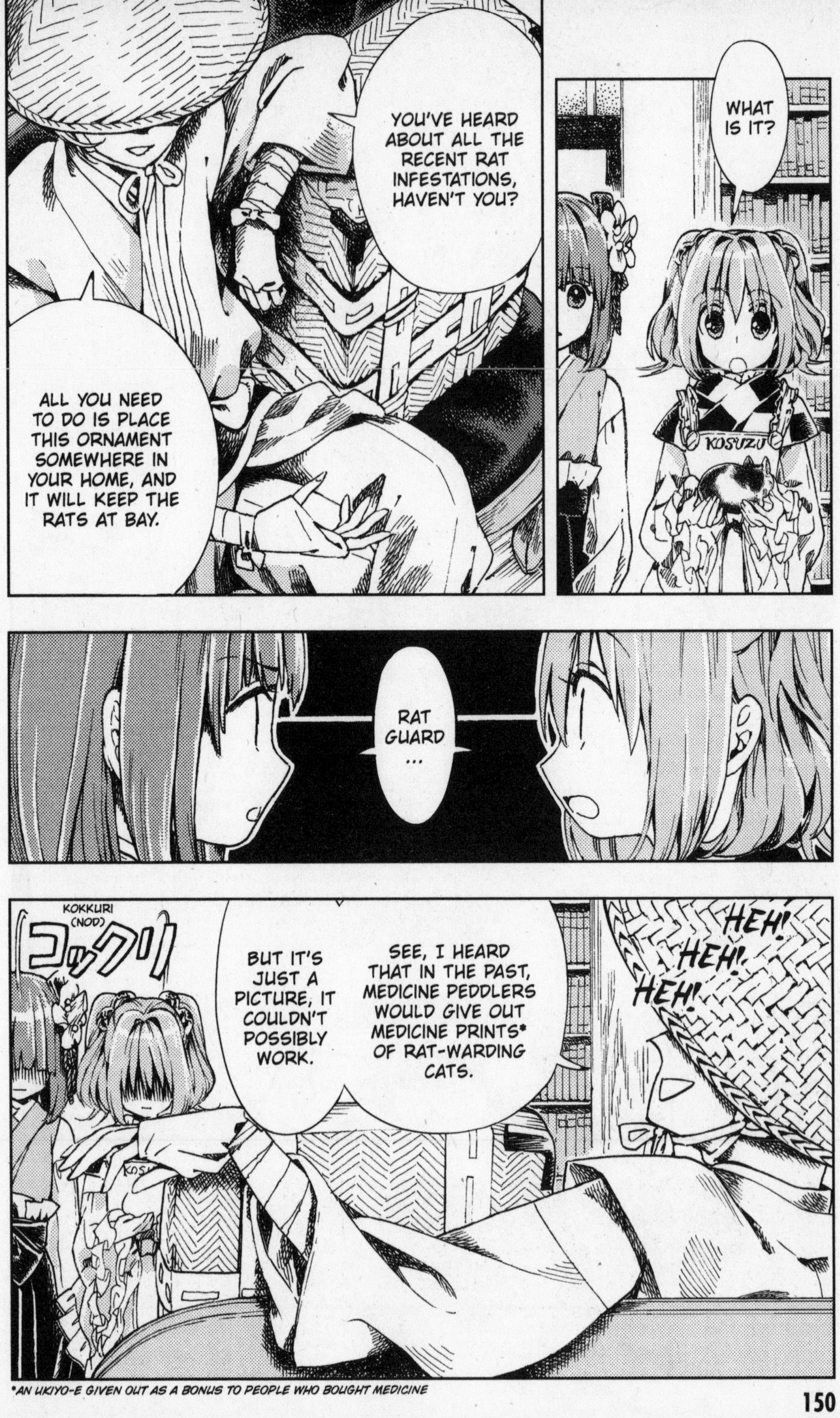
WHAT IS IT?
YOU'VE HEARD ABOUT ALL THE RECENT RAT INFESTATIONS, HAVEN'T YOU?
ALL YOU NEED TO DO IS PLACE THIS ORNAMENT SOMEWHERE IN YOUR HOME, AND IT WILL KEEP THE RATS AT BAY.
KOSUZU
RAT GUARD ...
HEH! HEH! HEH!
SEE, I HEARD THAT IN THE PAST, MEDICINE PEDDLERS WOULD GIVE OUT MEDICINE PRINTS* OF RAT-WARDING CATS.
BUT IT'S JUST A PICTURE, IT COULDN'T POSSIBLY WORK.
KOKKURI (NOD)
コックリ

*AN UKIYO-E GIVEN OUT AS A BONUS TO PEOPLE WHO BOUGHT MEDICINE

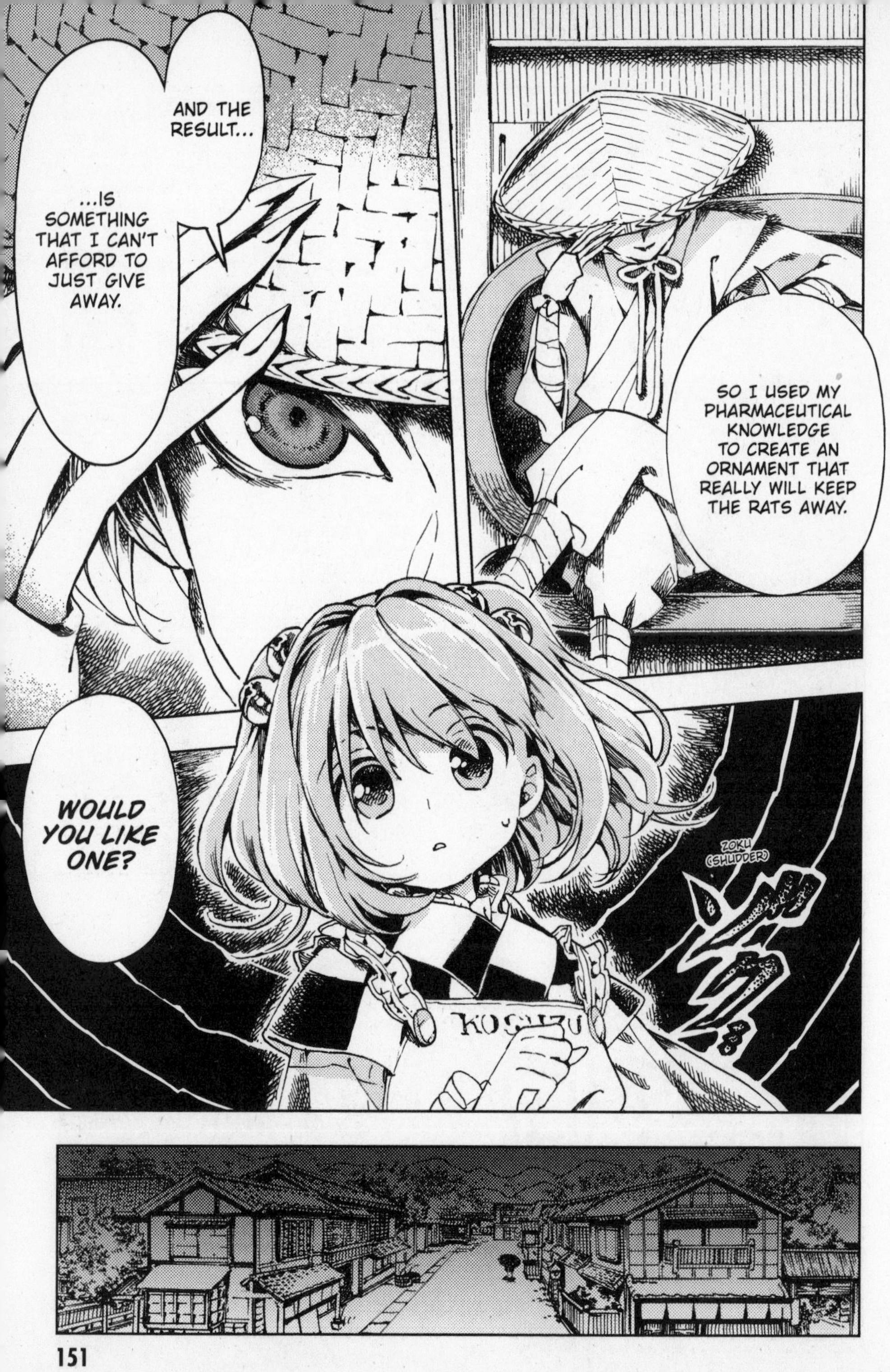
SO I USED MY PHARMACEUTICAL KNOWLEDGE TO CREATE AN ORNAMENT THAT REALLY WILL KEEP THE RATS AWAY.
AND THE RESULT...
...IS SOMETHING THAT I CAN'T AFFORD TO JUST GIVE AWAY.
ZOKU (SHUDDER)
WOULD YOU LIKE ONE?
KOSUZU

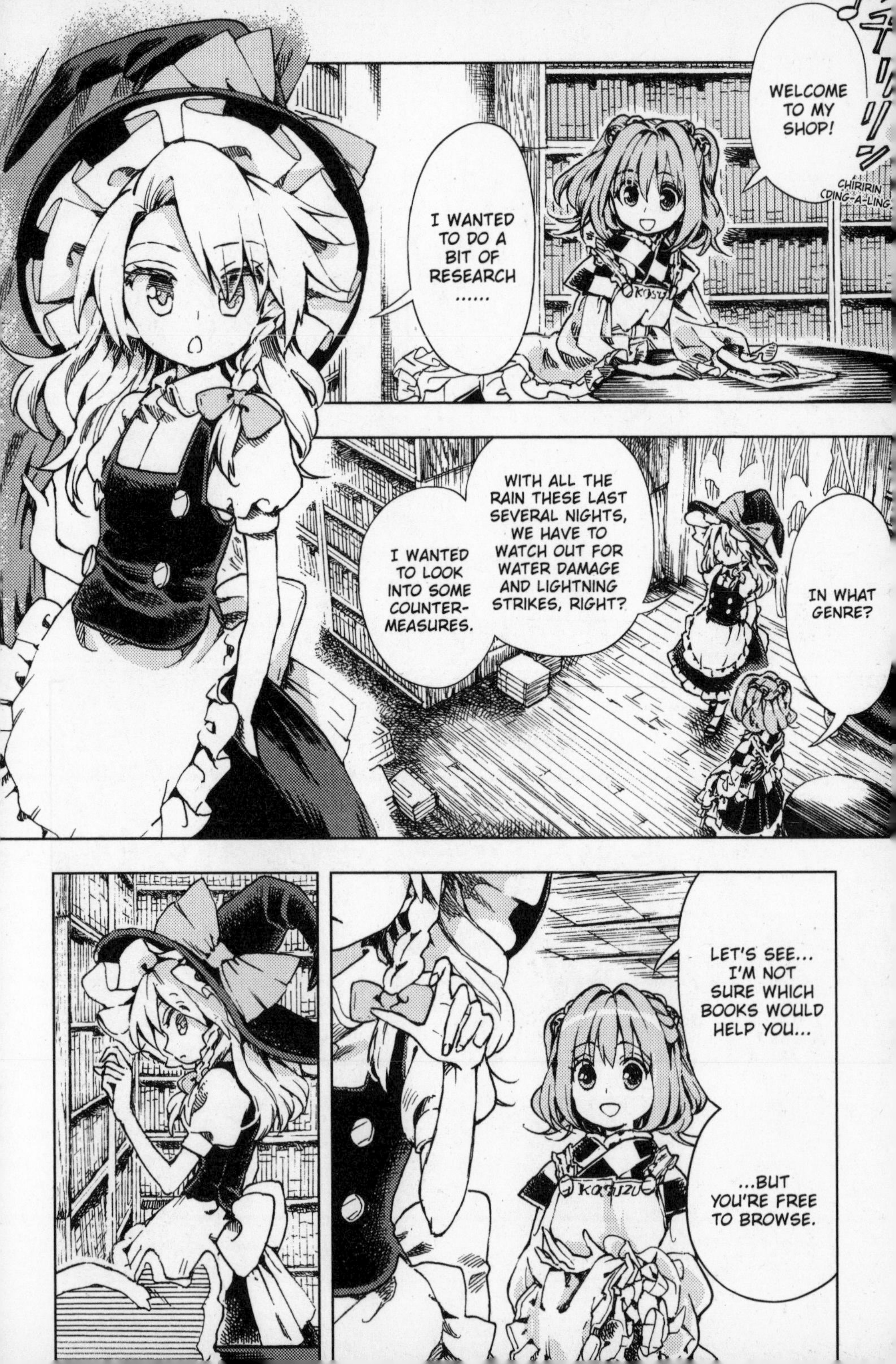
CHIRIRIN
(DING-A-LING)
WELCOME TO MY SHOP!
I WANTED TO DO A BIT OF RESEARCH......
IN WHAT GENRE?
WITH ALL THE RAIN THESE LAST SEVERAL NIGHTS, WE HAVE TO WATCH OUT FOR WATER DAMAGE AND LIGHTNING STRIKES, RIGHT?
I WANTED TO LOOK INTO SOME COUNTER-MEASURES.
LET'S SEE... I'M NOT SURE WHICH BOOKS WOULD HELP YOU...
...BUT YOU'RE FREE TO BROWSE.

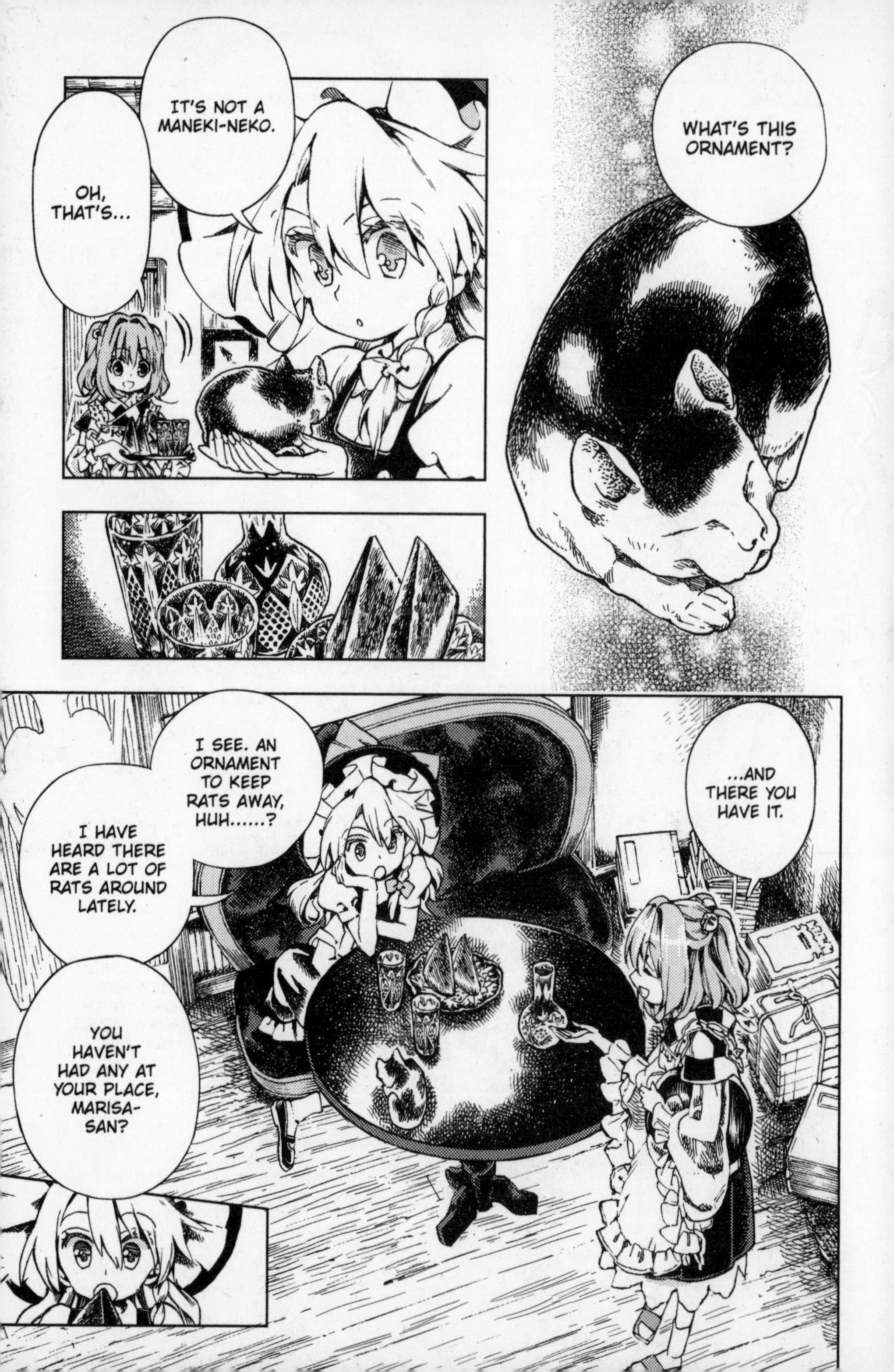
WHAT'S THIS ORNAMENT?
IT'S NOT A MANEKI-NEKO.
OH, THAT'S...
...AND THERE YOU HAVE IT.
I SEE. AN ORNAMENT TO KEEP RATS AWAY, HUH......?
I HAVE HEARD THERE ARE A LOT OF RATS AROUND LATELY.
YOU HAVEN'T HAD ANY AT YOUR PLACE, MARISA-SAN?

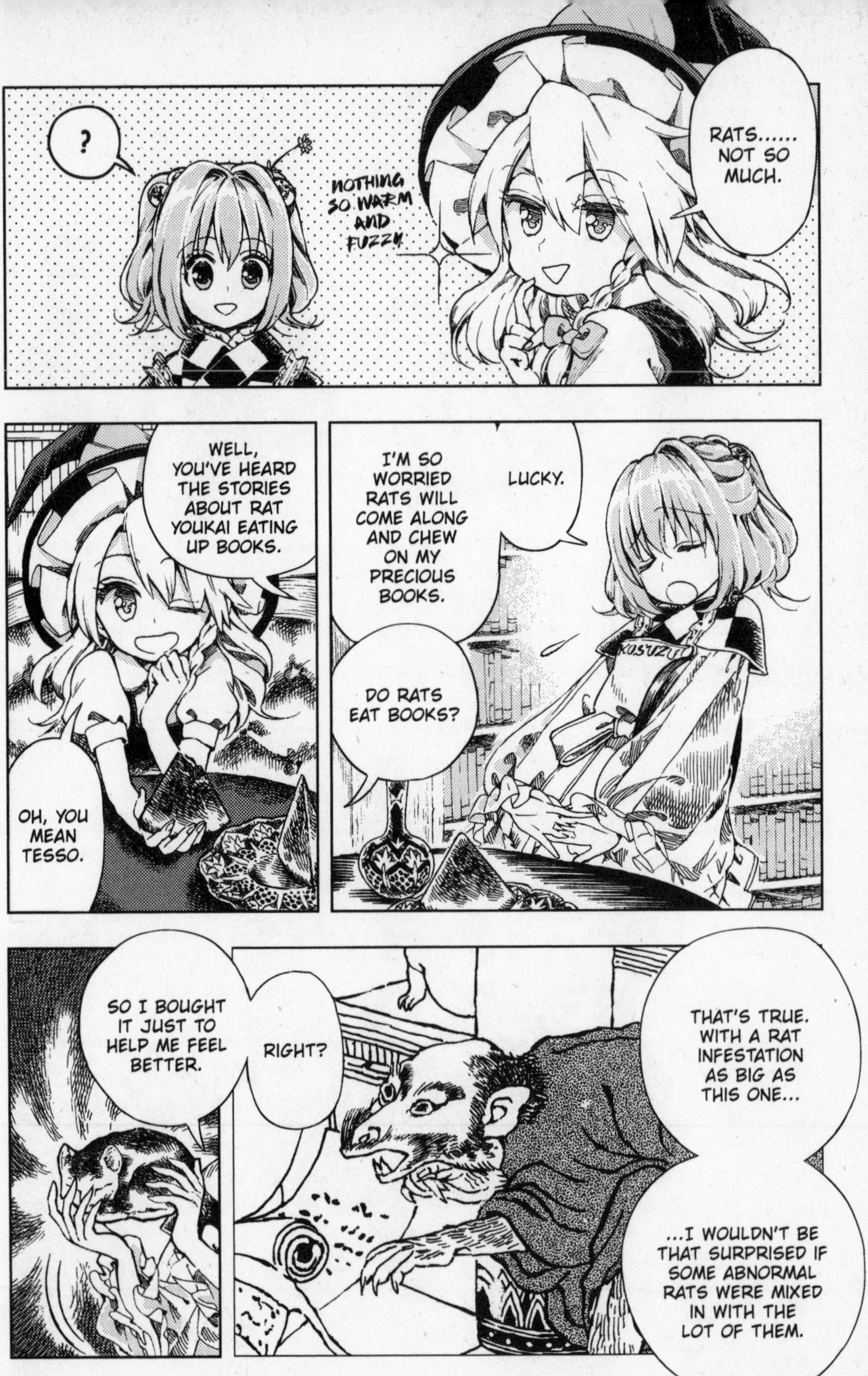
RATS...... NOT SO MUCH.
NOTHING SO WARM AND FUZZY.
?
LUCKY.
I'M SO WORRIED RATS WILL COME ALONG AND CHEW ON MY PRECIOUS BOOKS.
DO RATS EAT BOOKS?
WELL, YOU'VE HEARD THE STORIES ABOUT RAT YOUKAI EATING UP BOOKS.
OH, YOU MEAN TESSO.
THAT'S TRUE. WITH A RAT INFESTATION AS BIG AS THIS ONE...
...I WOULDN'T BE THAT SURPRISED IF SOME ABNORMAL RATS WERE MIXED IN WITH THE LOT OF THEM.
RIGHT?
SO I BOUGHT IT JUST TO HELP ME FEEL BETTER.

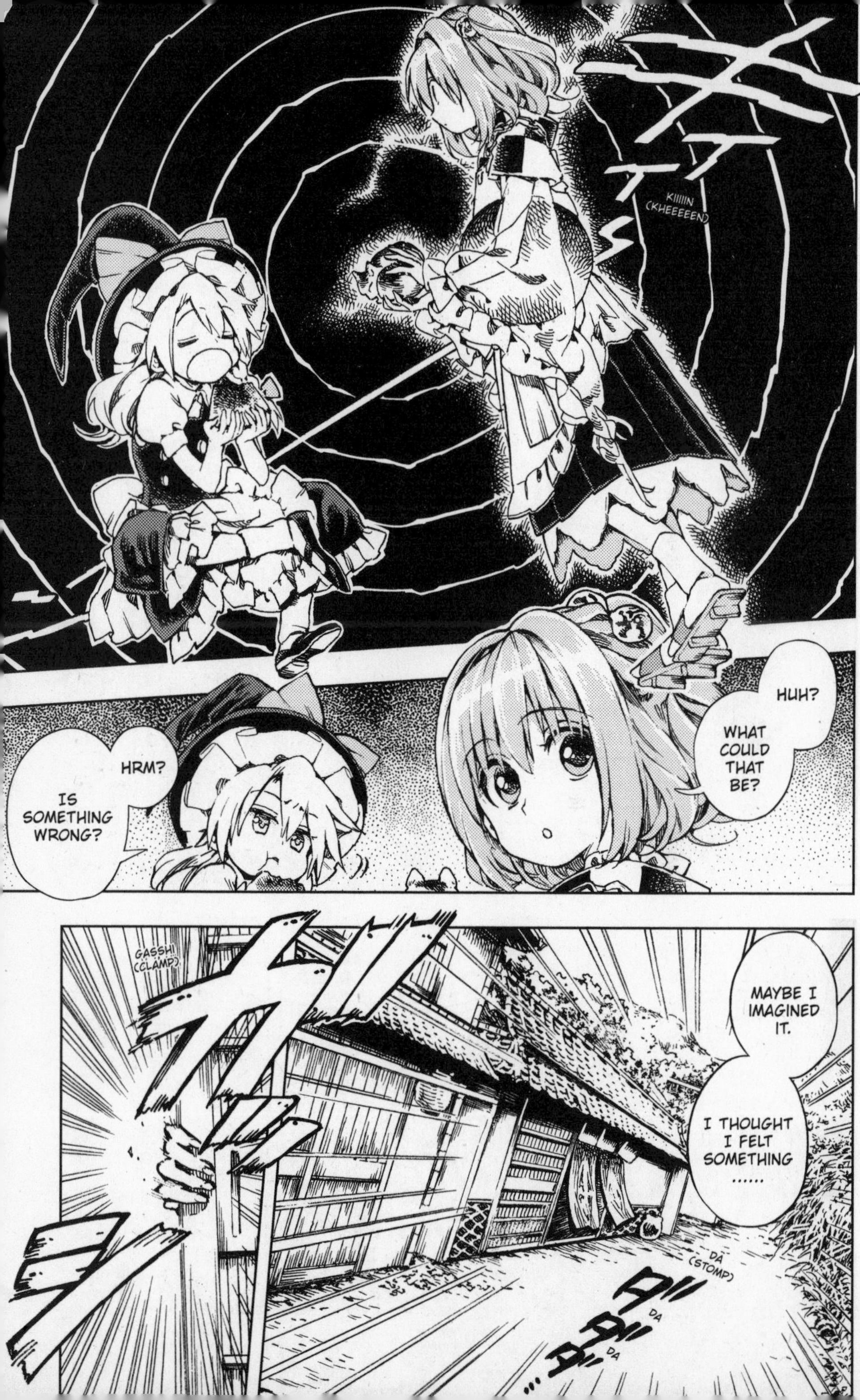
KIIIIN
(KHEEEEEN)
HUH?
WHAT COULD THAT BE?
HRM?
IS SOMETHING WRONG?
MAYBE I IMAGINED IT.
I THOUGHT I FELT SOMETHING ......
GASSHI
(CLAMP)
DA
(STOMP)
DA
DA
DA

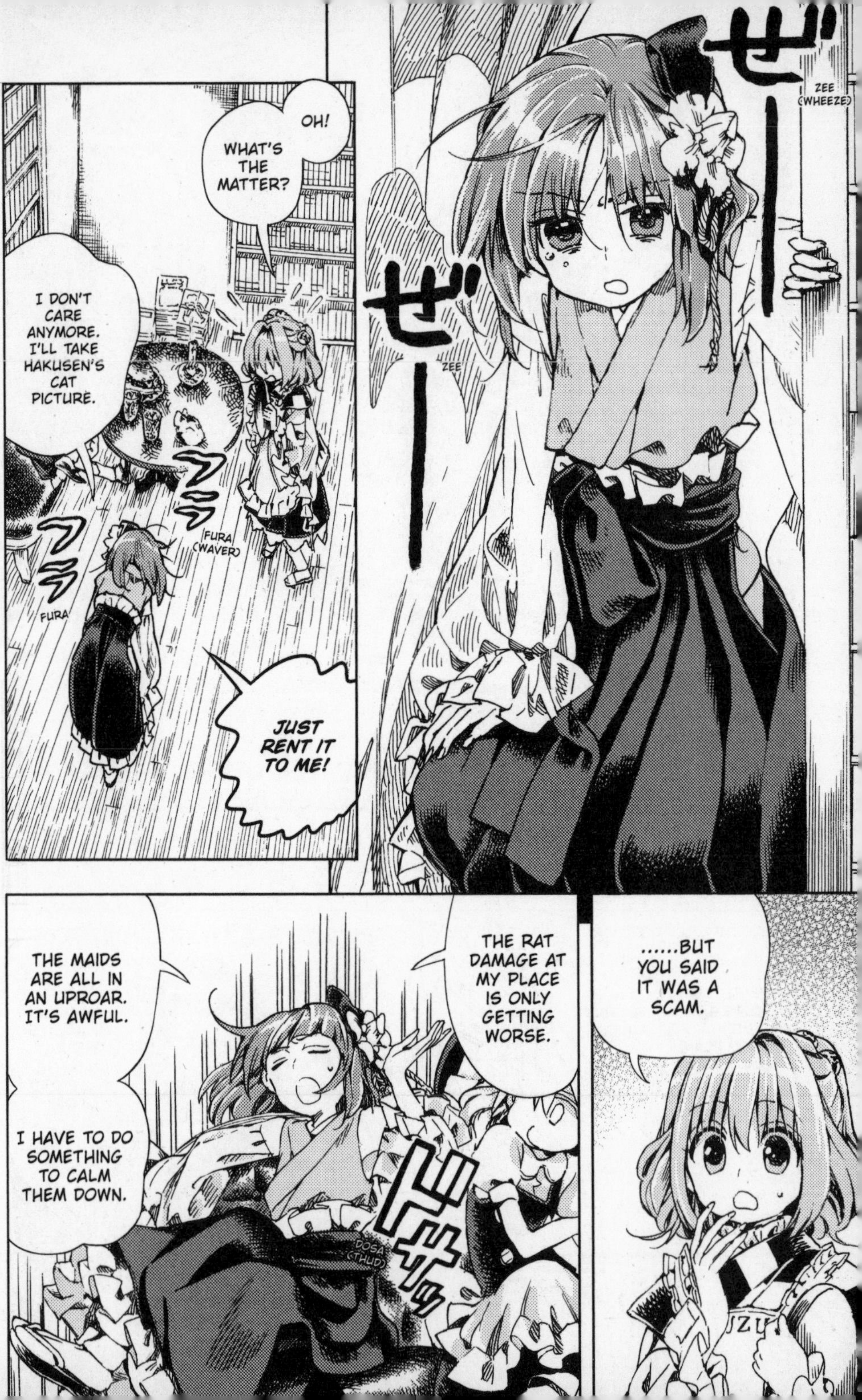
ZEE (WHEEZE)
ZEE
OH!
WHAT'S THE MATTER?
I DON'T CARE ANYMORE. I'LL TAKE HAKUSEN'S CAT PICTURE.
FURA (WAVER)
FURA
JUST RENT IT TO ME!
......BUT YOU SAID IT WAS A SCAM.
THE RAT DAMAGE AT MY PLACE IS ONLY GETTING WORSE.
THE MAIDS ARE ALL IN AN UPROAR. IT'S AWFUL.
I HAVE TO DO SOMETHING TO CALM THEM DOWN.
DOSA (THUD)

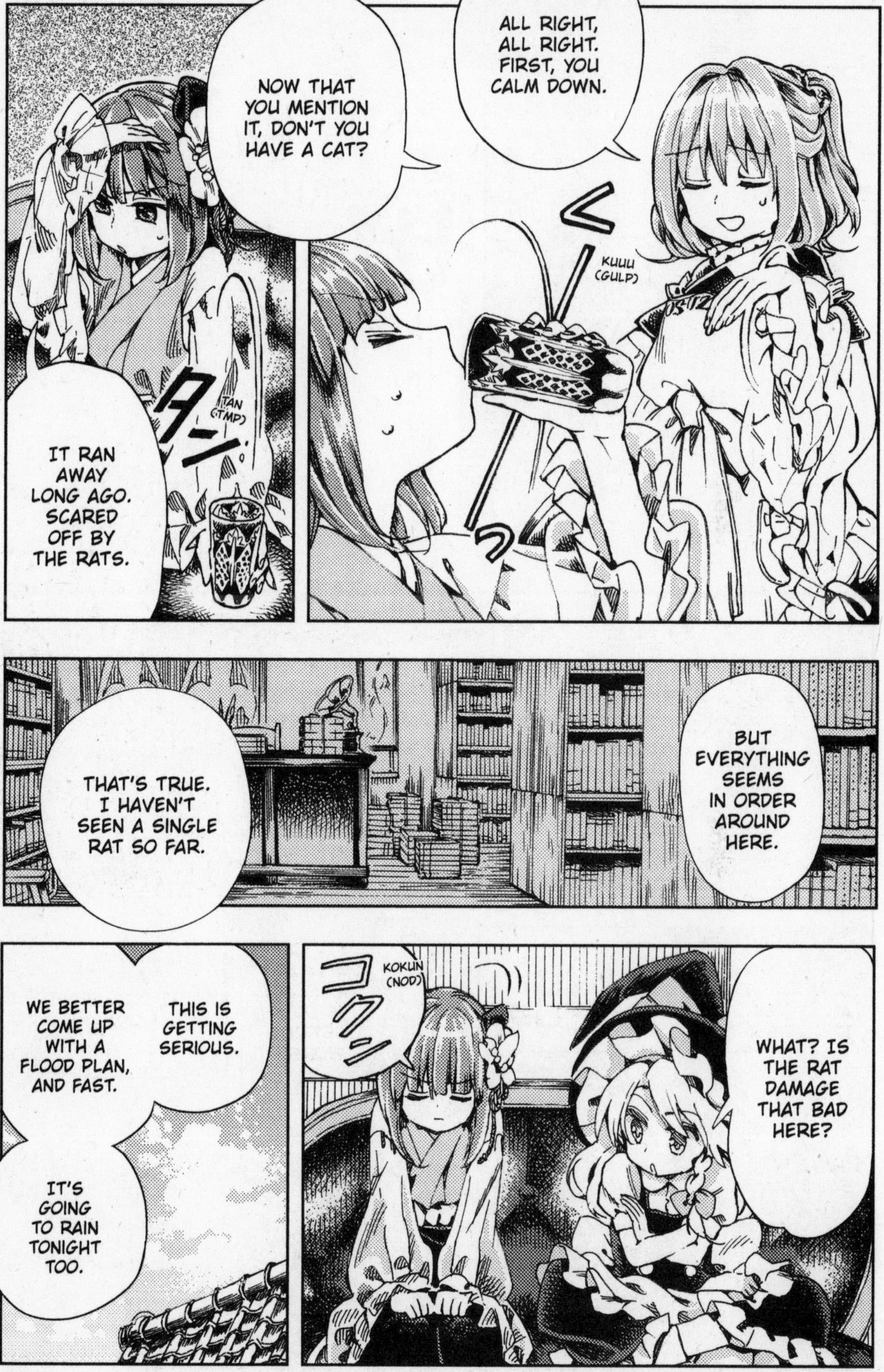
ALL RIGHT, ALL RIGHT. FIRST, YOU CALM DOWN.
KUUU (GULP)
NOW THAT YOU MENTION IT, DON'T YOU HAVE A CAT?
TAN (TMP)
IT RAN AWAY LONG AGO. SCARED OFF BY THE RATS.
BUT EVERYTHING SEEMS IN ORDER AROUND HERE.
THAT'S TRUE. I HAVEN'T SEEN A SINGLE RAT SO FAR.
WHAT? IS THE RAT DAMAGE THAT BAD HERE?
KOKUN (NOD)
THIS IS GETTING SERIOUS.
WE BETTER COME UP WITH A FLOOD PLAN, AND FAST.
IT'S GOING TO RAIN TONIGHT TOO.

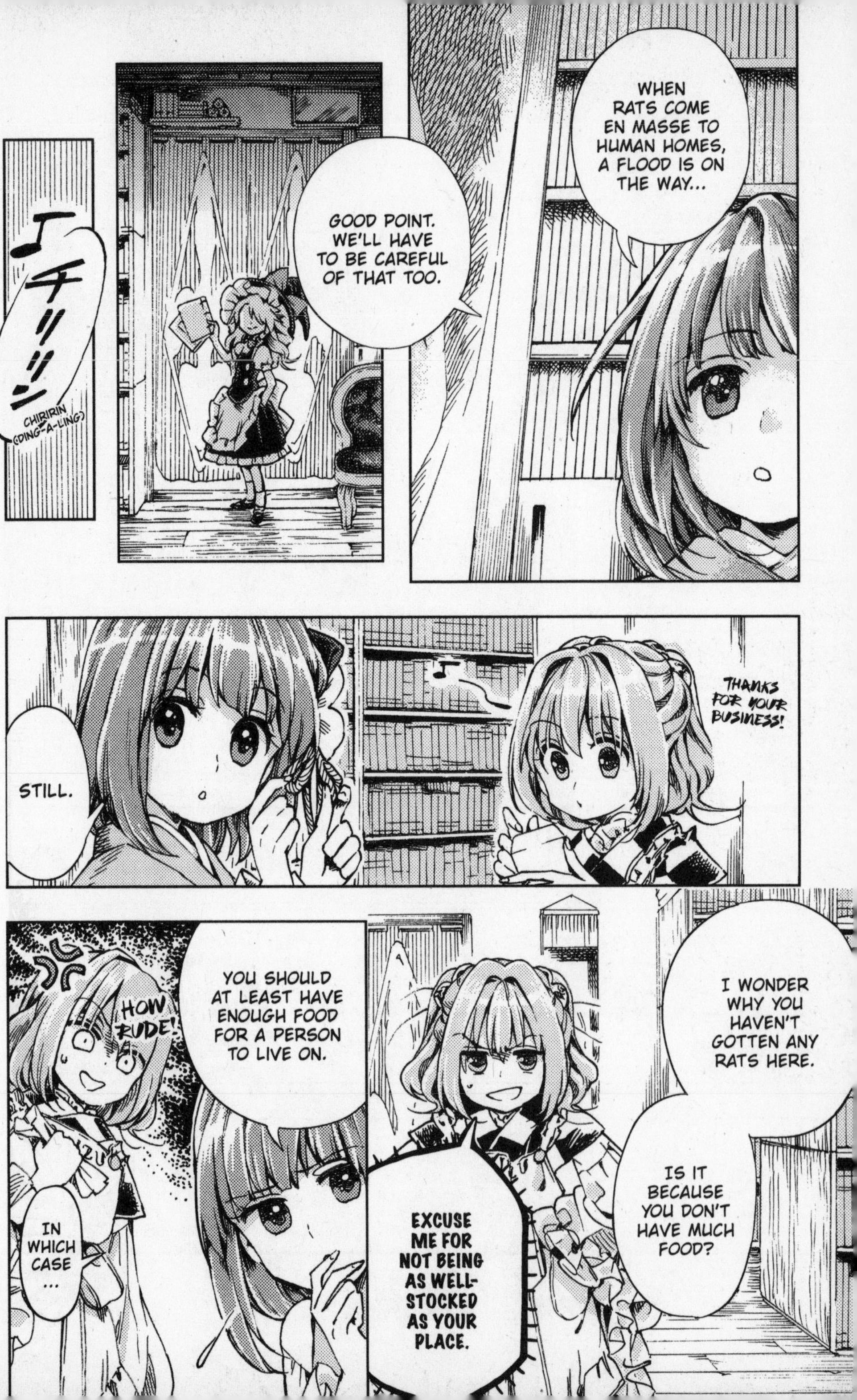
WHEN RATS COME EN MASSE TO HUMAN HOMES, A FLOOD IS ON THE WAY...
GOOD POINT. WE'LL HAVE TO BE CAREFUL OF THAT TOO.
チリリン
CHIRIRIN (DING-A-LING)
THANKS FOR YOUR BUSINESS!
STILL.
I WONDER WHY YOU HAVEN'T GOTTEN ANY RATS HERE.
IS IT BECAUSE YOU DON'T HAVE MUCH FOOD?
EXCUSE ME FOR NOT BEING AS WELL-STOCKED AS YOUR PLACE.
YOU SHOULD AT LEAST HAVE ENOUGH FOOD FOR A PERSON TO LIVE ON.
HOW RUDE!
IN WHICH CASE...

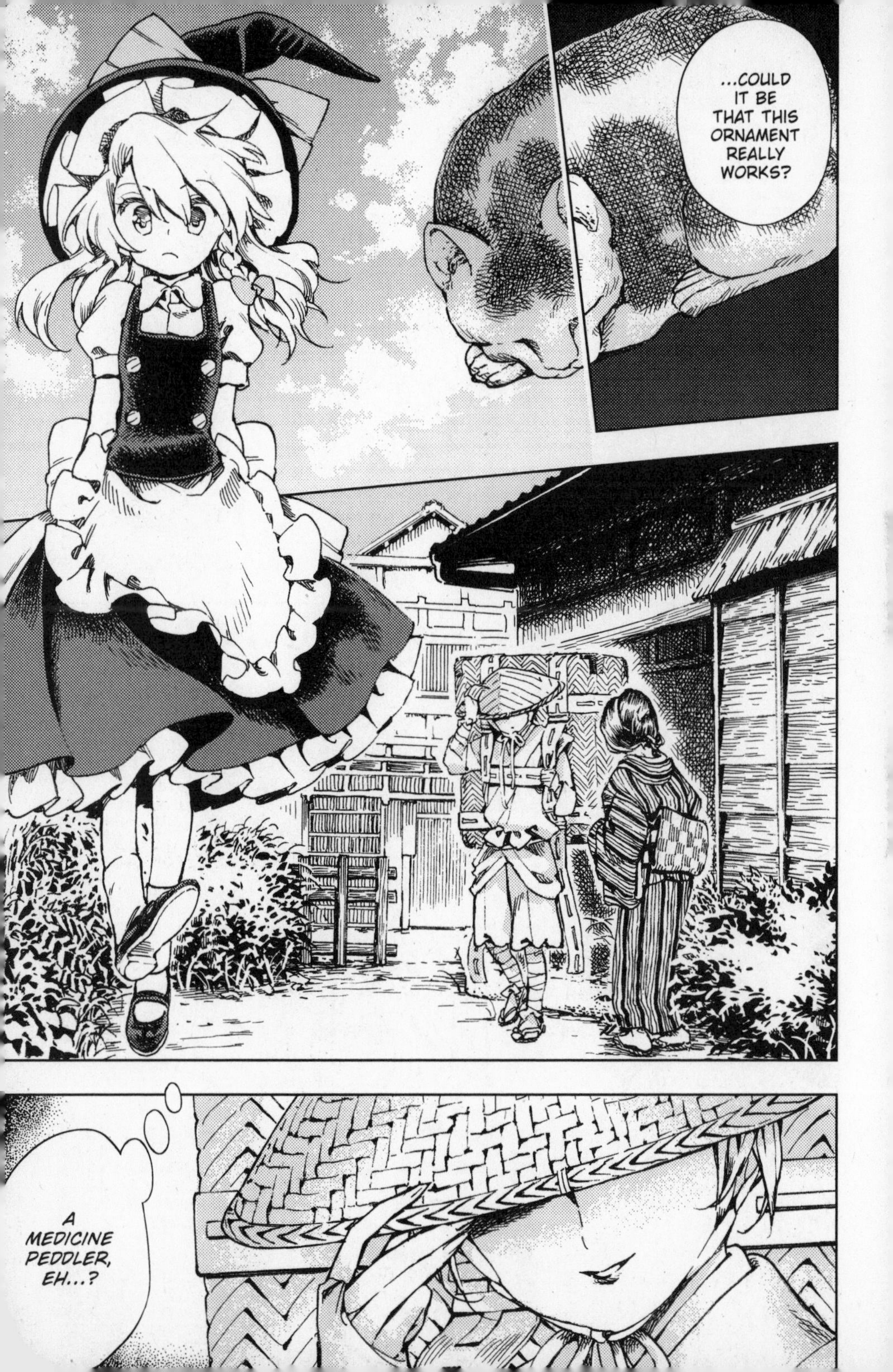
...COULD IT BE THAT THIS ORNAMENT REALLY WORKS?
A MEDICINE PEDDLER, EH...?

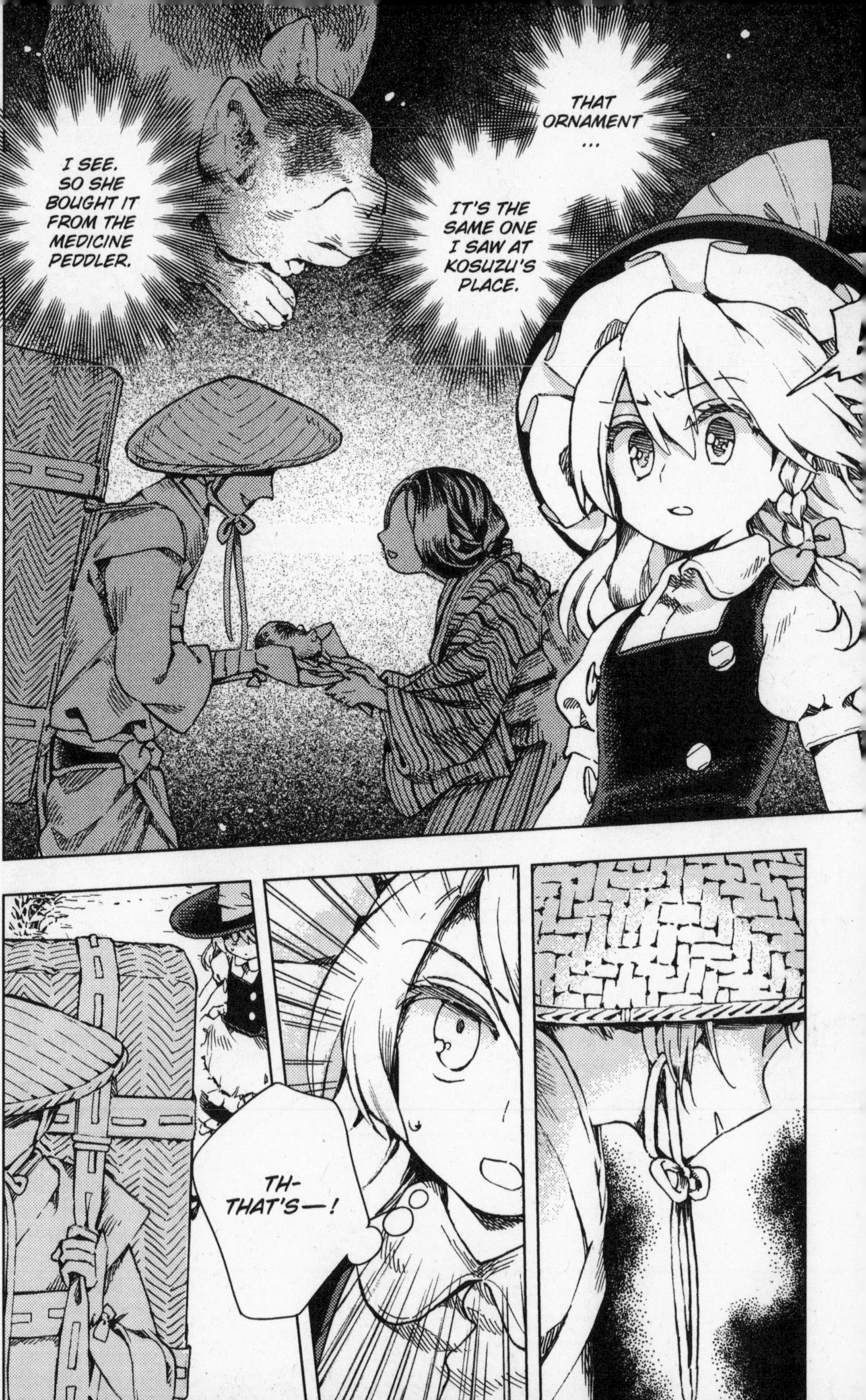
THAT ORNAMENT ...
IT'S THE SAME ONE I SAW AT KOSUZU'S PLACE.
I SEE. SO SHE BOUGHT IT FROM THE MEDICINE PEDDLER.
TH- THAT'S—!

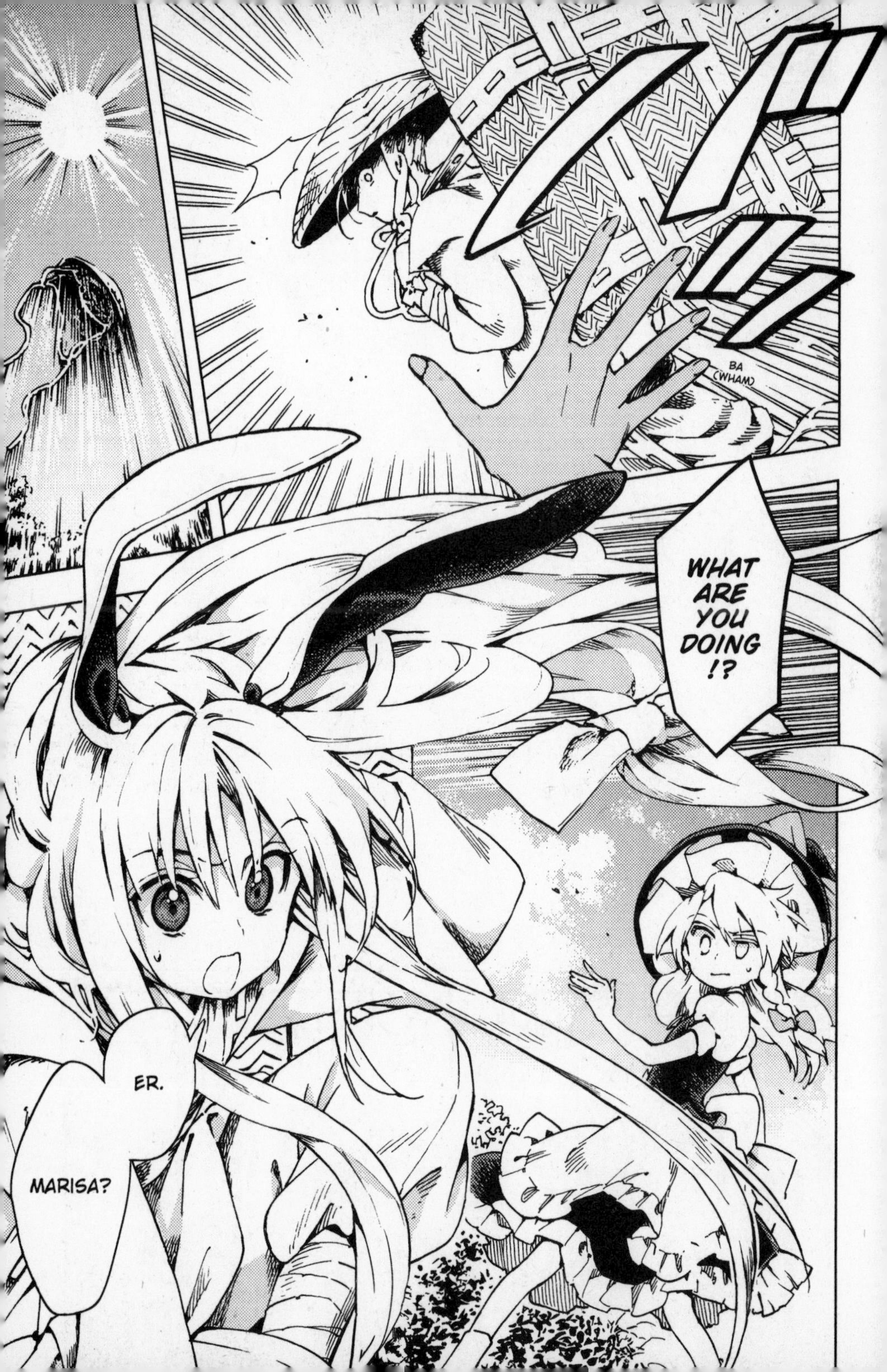
BA
(WHAM)
WHAT ARE YOU DOING!?
ER.
MARISA?

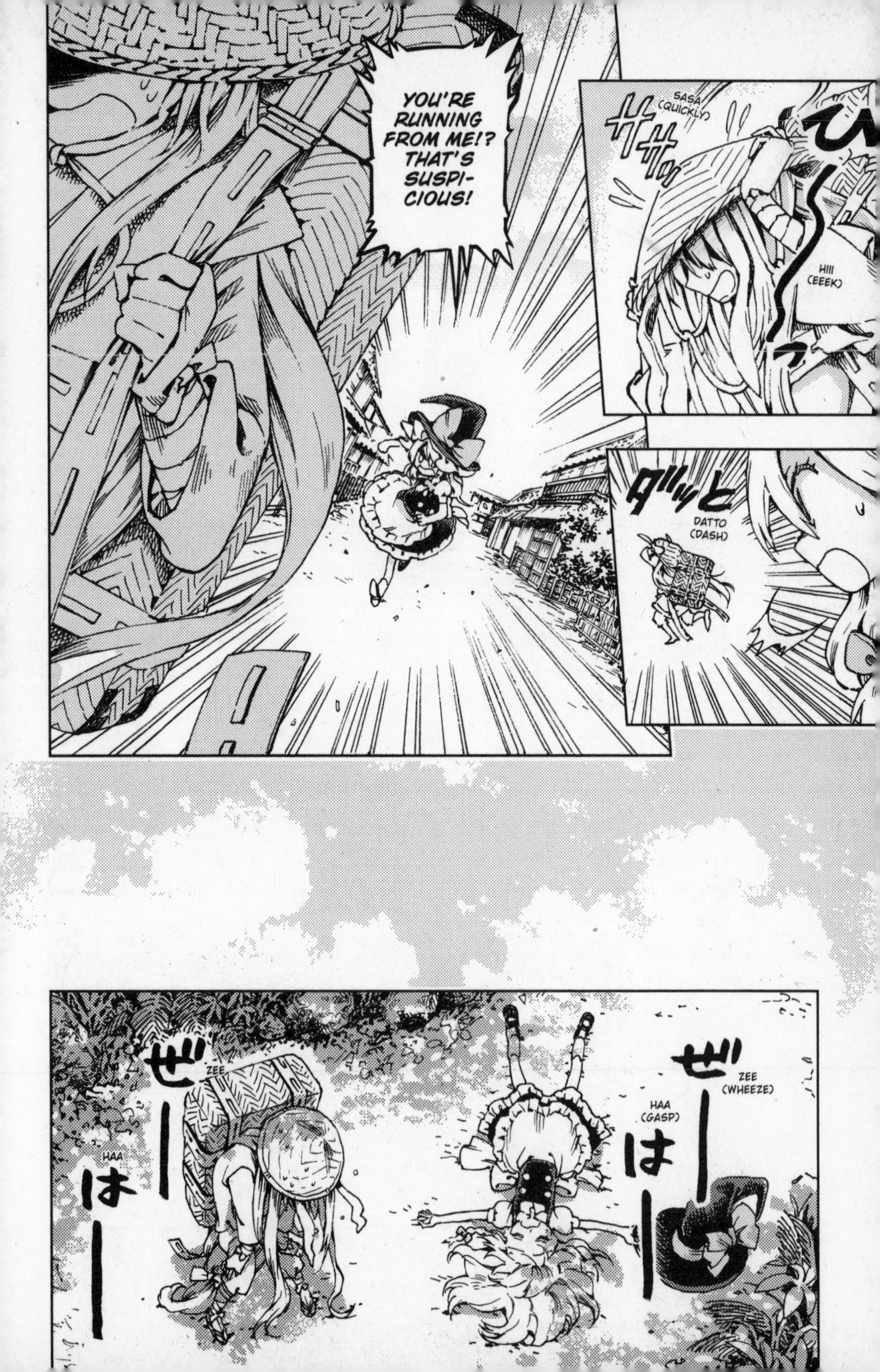
ササッ
SASA (QUICKLY)
ひぃ
HIII (EEEK)
ダッと
DATTO (DASH)
YOU'RE RUNNING FROM ME!? THAT'S SUSPICIOUS!
ぜーはー
ZEE (WHEEZE)
HAA (GASP)
ぜーはー
ZEE
HAA

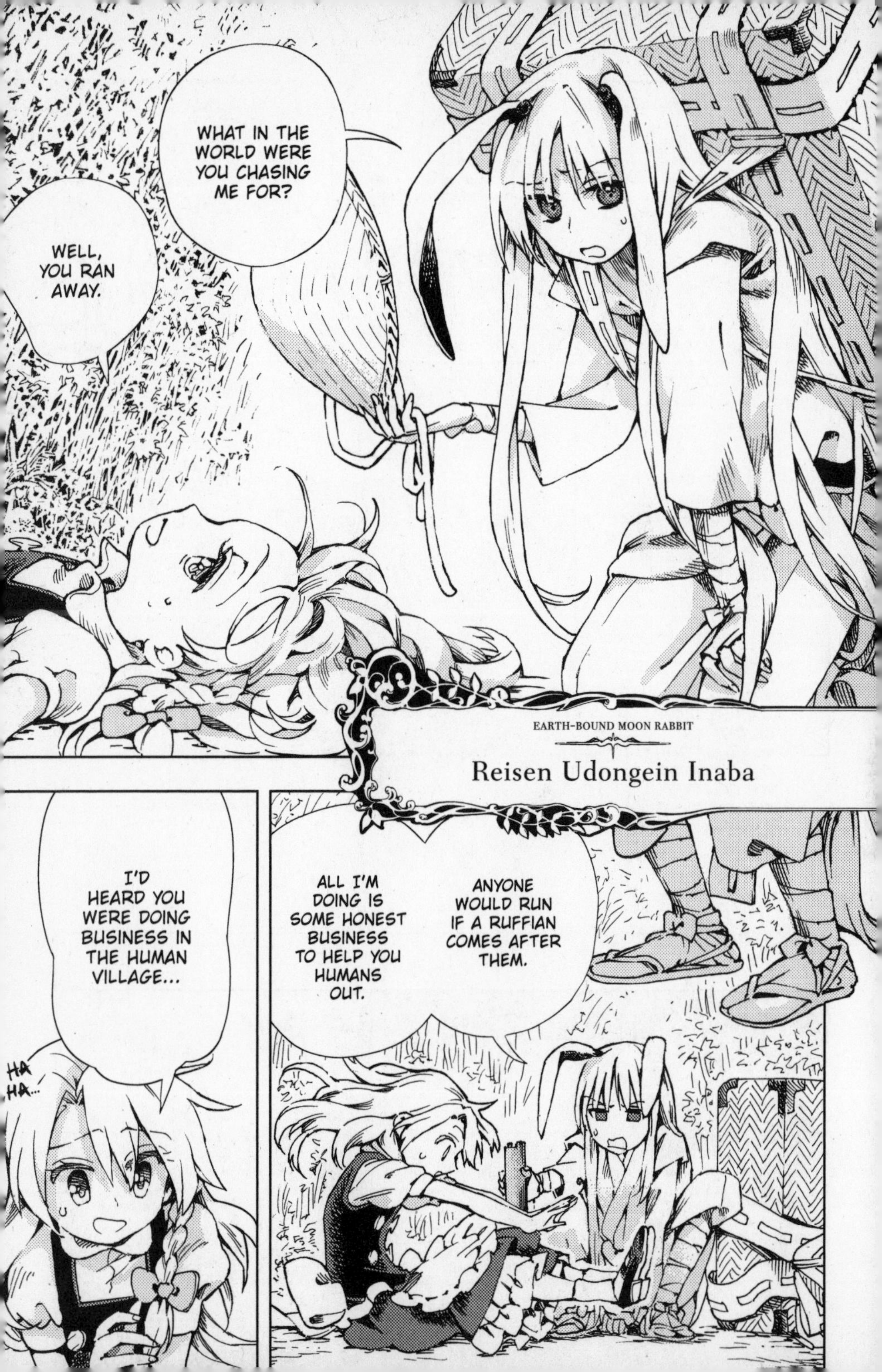
WHAT IN THE WORLD WERE YOU CHASING ME FOR?
WELL, YOU RAN AWAY.
EARTH-BOUND MOON RABBIT
Reisen Udongein Inaba
ANYONE WOULD RUN IF A RUFFIAN COMES AFTER THEM.
ALL I'M DOING IS SOME HONEST BUSINESS TO HELP YOU HUMANS OUT.
I'D HEARD YOU WERE DOING BUSINESS IN THE HUMAN VILLAGE...
HA HA...

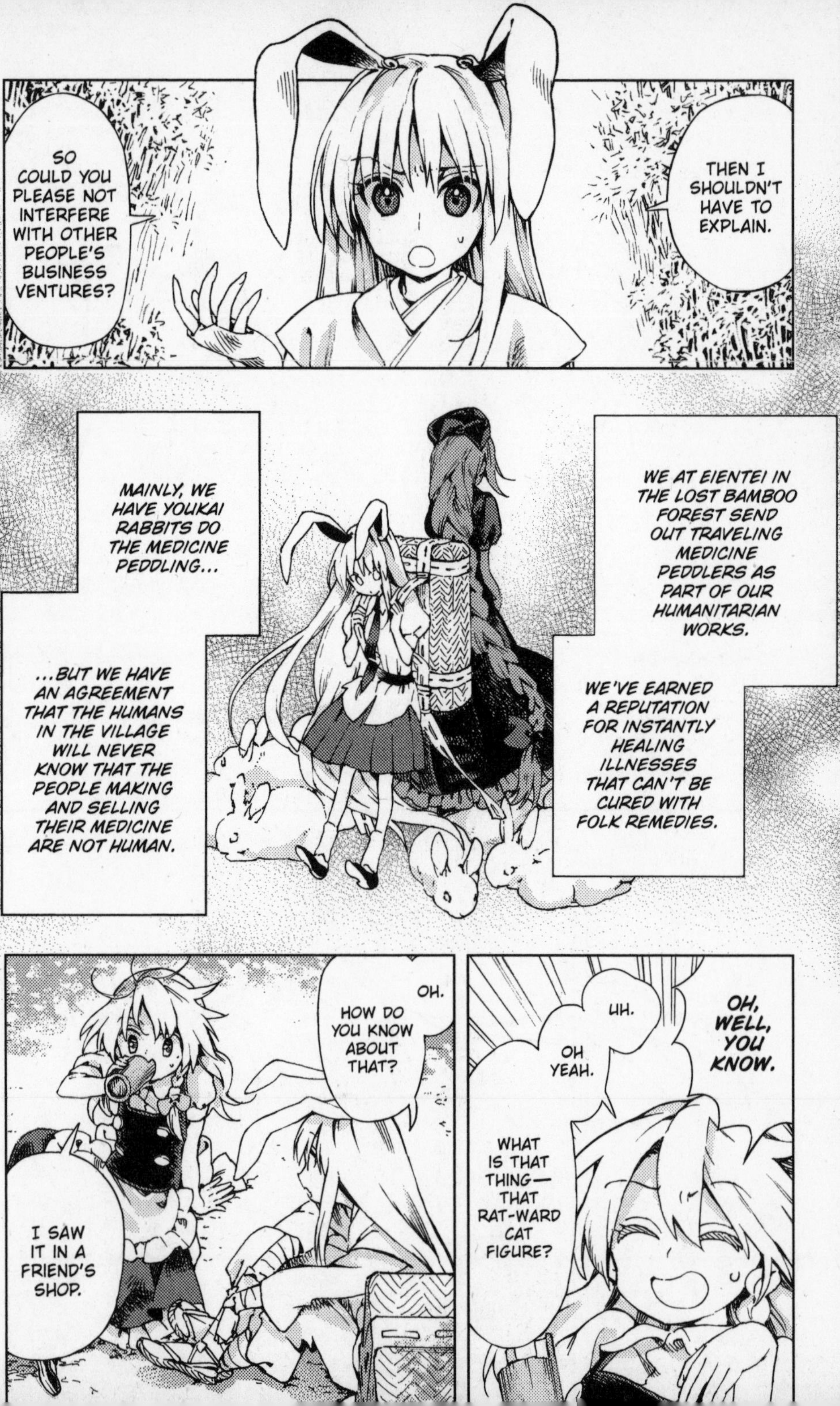
THEN I SHOULDN'T HAVE TO EXPLAIN.
SO COULD YOU PLEASE NOT INTERFERE WITH OTHER PEOPLE'S BUSINESS VENTURES?
WE AT EIENTEI IN THE LOST BAMBOO FOREST SEND OUT TRAVELING MEDICINE PEDDLERS AS PART OF OUR HUMANITARIAN WORKS.
WE'VE EARNED A REPUTATION FOR INSTANTLY HEALING ILLNESSES THAT CAN'T BE CURED WITH FOLK REMEDIES.
MAINLY, WE HAVE YOUKAI RABBITS DO THE MEDICINE PEDDLING...
...BUT WE HAVE AN AGREEMENT THAT THE HUMANS IN THE VILLAGE WILL NEVER KNOW THAT THE PEOPLE MAKING AND SELLING THEIR MEDICINE ARE NOT HUMAN.
OH, WELL, YOU KNOW.
UH.
OH YEAH.
WHAT IS THAT THING—THAT RAT-WARD CAT FIGURE?
OH.
HOW DO YOU KNOW ABOUT THAT?
I SAW IT IN A FRIEND'S SHOP.

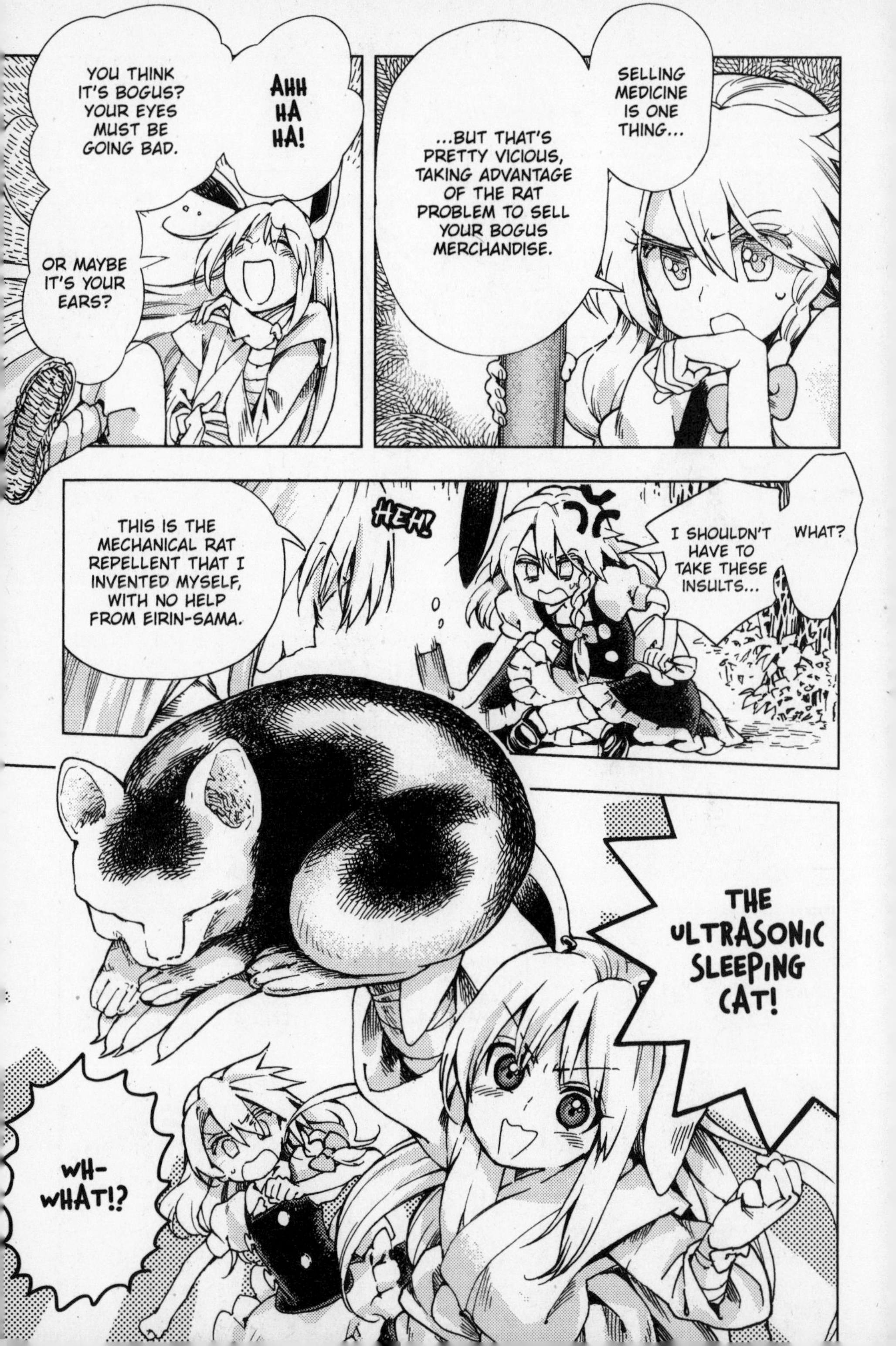
SELLING MEDICINE IS ONE THING...
...BUT THAT'S PRETTY VICIOUS, TAKING ADVANTAGE OF THE RAT PROBLEM TO SELL YOUR BOGUS MERCHANDISE.
AHH HA HA!
YOU THINK IT'S BOGUS? YOUR EYES MUST BE GOING BAD.
OR MAYBE IT'S YOUR EARS?
WHAT?
I SHOULDN'T HAVE TO TAKE THESE INSULTS...
HEH!
THIS IS THE MECHANICAL RAT REPELLENT THAT I INVENTED MYSELF, WITH NO HELP FROM EIRIN-SAMA.
THE ULTRASONIC SLEEPING CAT!
WH-WHAT!?

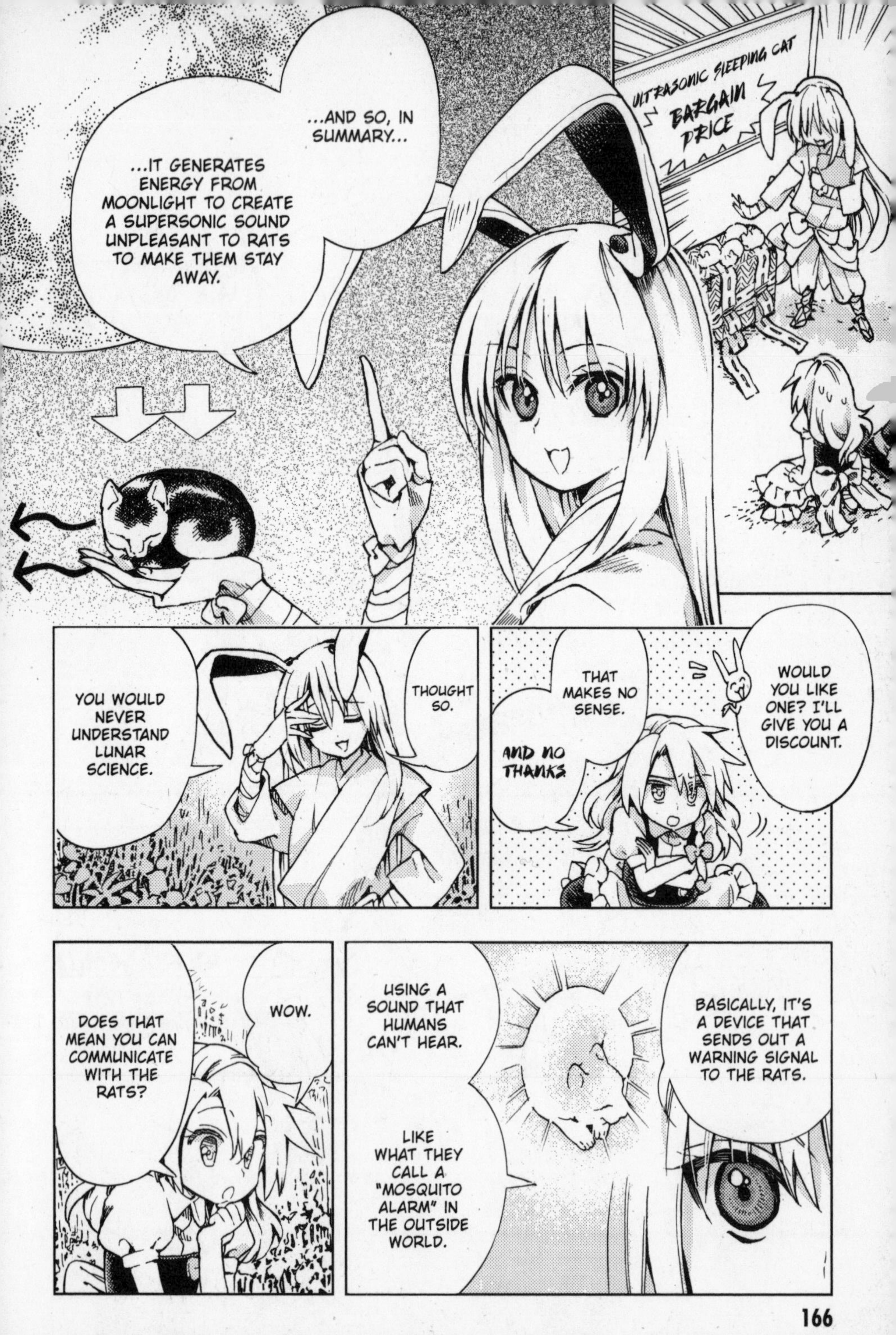
ULTRASONIC SLEEPING CAT
BARGAIN PRICE
...AND SO, IN SUMMARY...
...IT GENERATES ENERGY FROM MOONLIGHT TO CREATE A SUPERSONIC SOUND UNPLEASANT TO RATS TO MAKE THEM STAY AWAY.
WOULD YOU LIKE ONE? I'LL GIVE YOU A DISCOUNT.
THAT MAKES NO SENSE.
AND NO THANKS.
THOUGHT SO.
YOU WOULD NEVER UNDERSTAND LUNAR SCIENCE.
BASICALLY, IT'S A DEVICE THAT SENDS OUT A WARNING SIGNAL TO THE RATS.
USING A SOUND THAT HUMANS CAN'T HEAR.
LIKE WHAT THEY CALL A "MOSQUITO ALARM" IN THE OUTSIDE WORLD.
WOW.
DOES THAT MEAN YOU CAN COMMUNICATE WITH THE RATS?

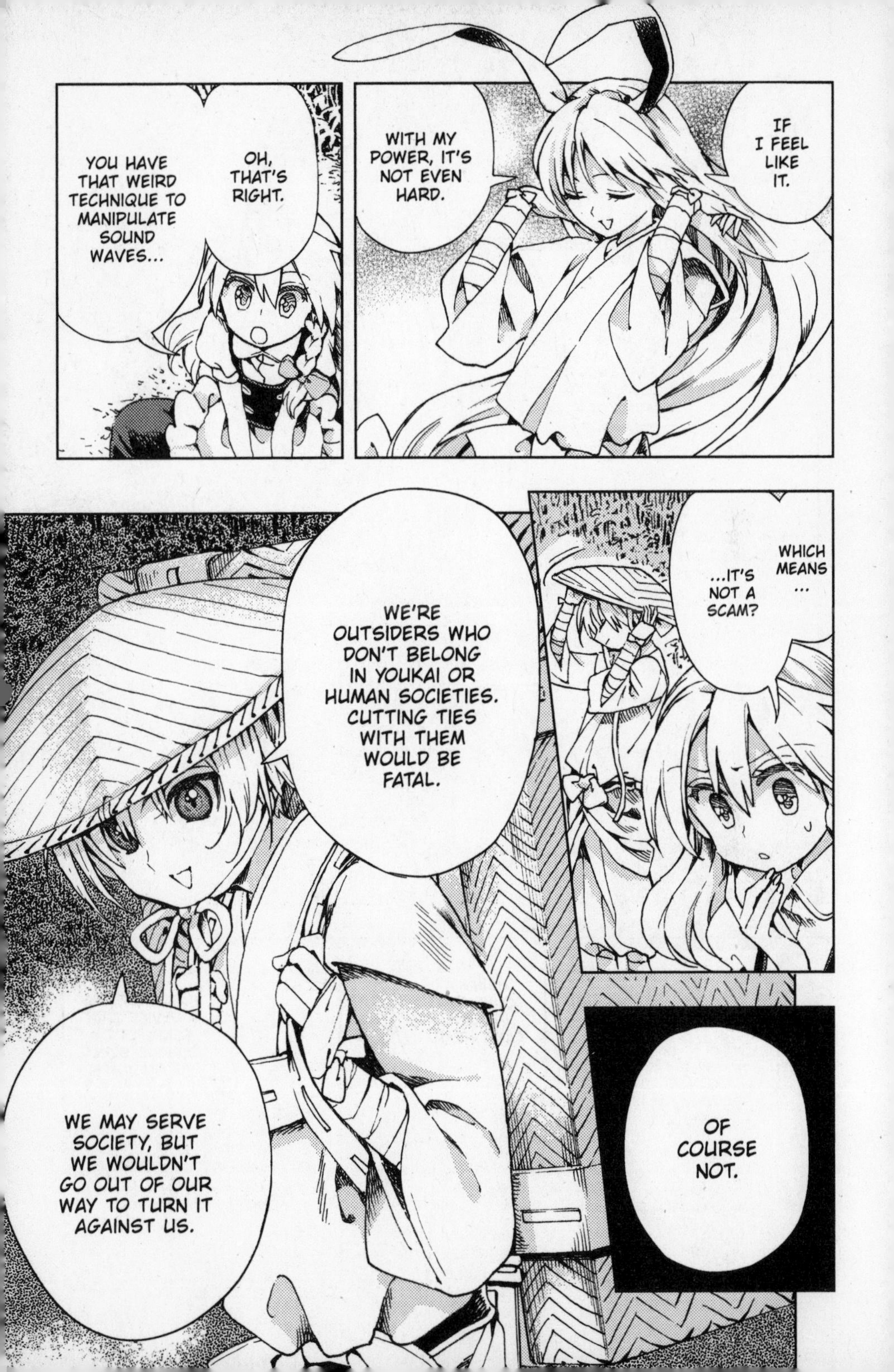
IF I FEEL LIKE IT.
WITH MY POWER, IT'S NOT EVEN HARD.
OH, THAT'S RIGHT.
YOU HAVE THAT WEIRD TECHNIQUE TO MANIPULATE SOUND WAVES...
WHICH MEANS...
...IT'S NOT A SCAM?
OF COURSE NOT.
WE'RE OUTSIDERS WHO DON'T BELONG IN YOUKAI OR HUMAN SOCIETIES. CUTTING TIES WITH THEM WOULD BE FATAL.
WE MAY SERVE SOCIETY, BUT WE WOULDN'T GO OUT OF OUR WAY TO TURN IT AGAINST US.

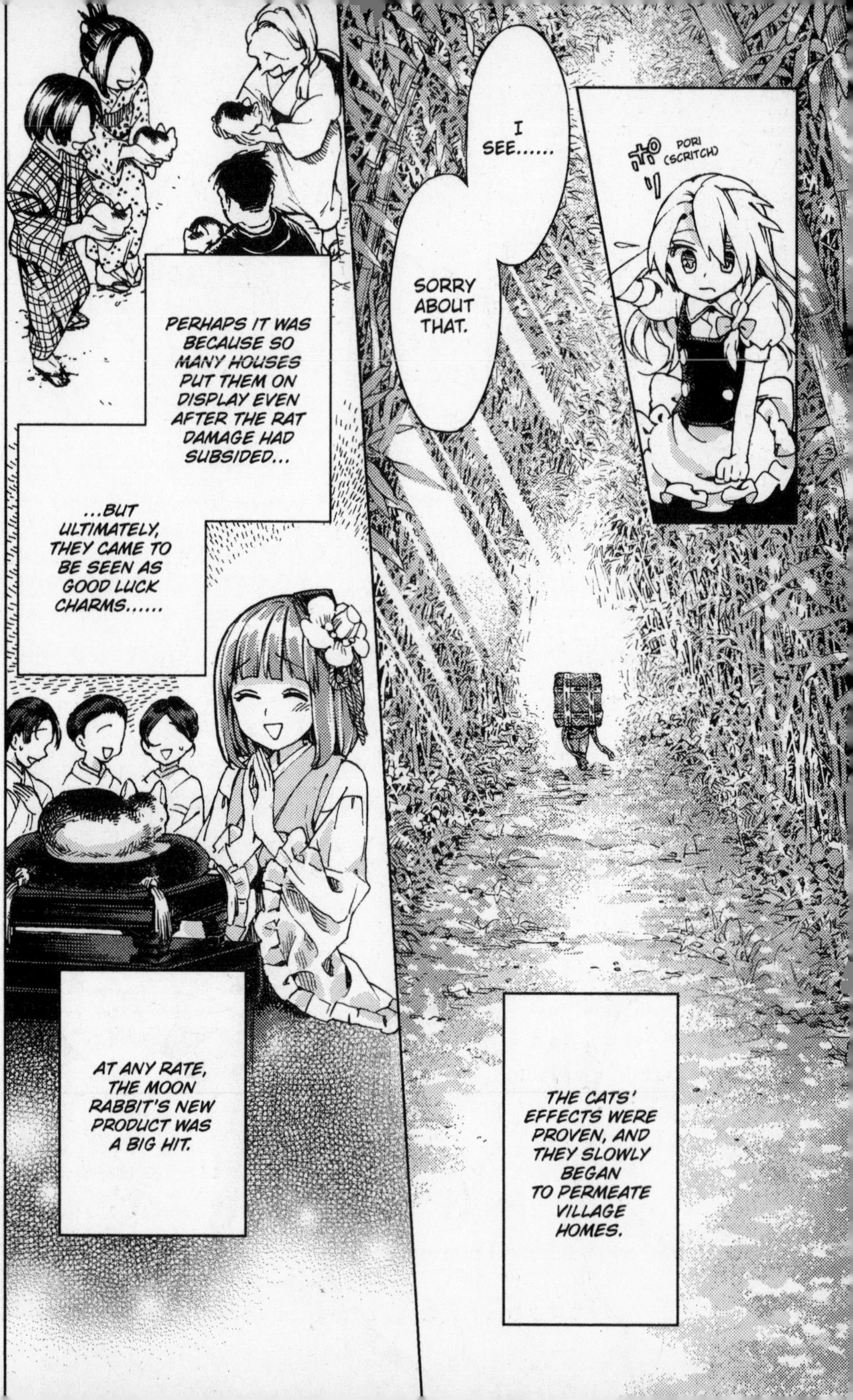
ポリ
PORI (SCRITCH)
I SEE......
SORRY ABOUT THAT.
THE CATS' EFFECTS WERE PROVEN, AND THEY SLOWLY BEGAN TO PERMEATE VILLAGE HOMES.
PERHAPS IT WAS BECAUSE SO MANY HOUSES PUT THEM ON DISPLAY EVEN AFTER THE RAT DAMAGE HAD SUBSIDED...
...BUT ULTIMATELY, THEY CAME TO BE SEEN AS GOOD LUCK CHARMS......
AT ANY RATE, THE MOON RABBIT'S NEW PRODUCT WAS A BIG HIT.

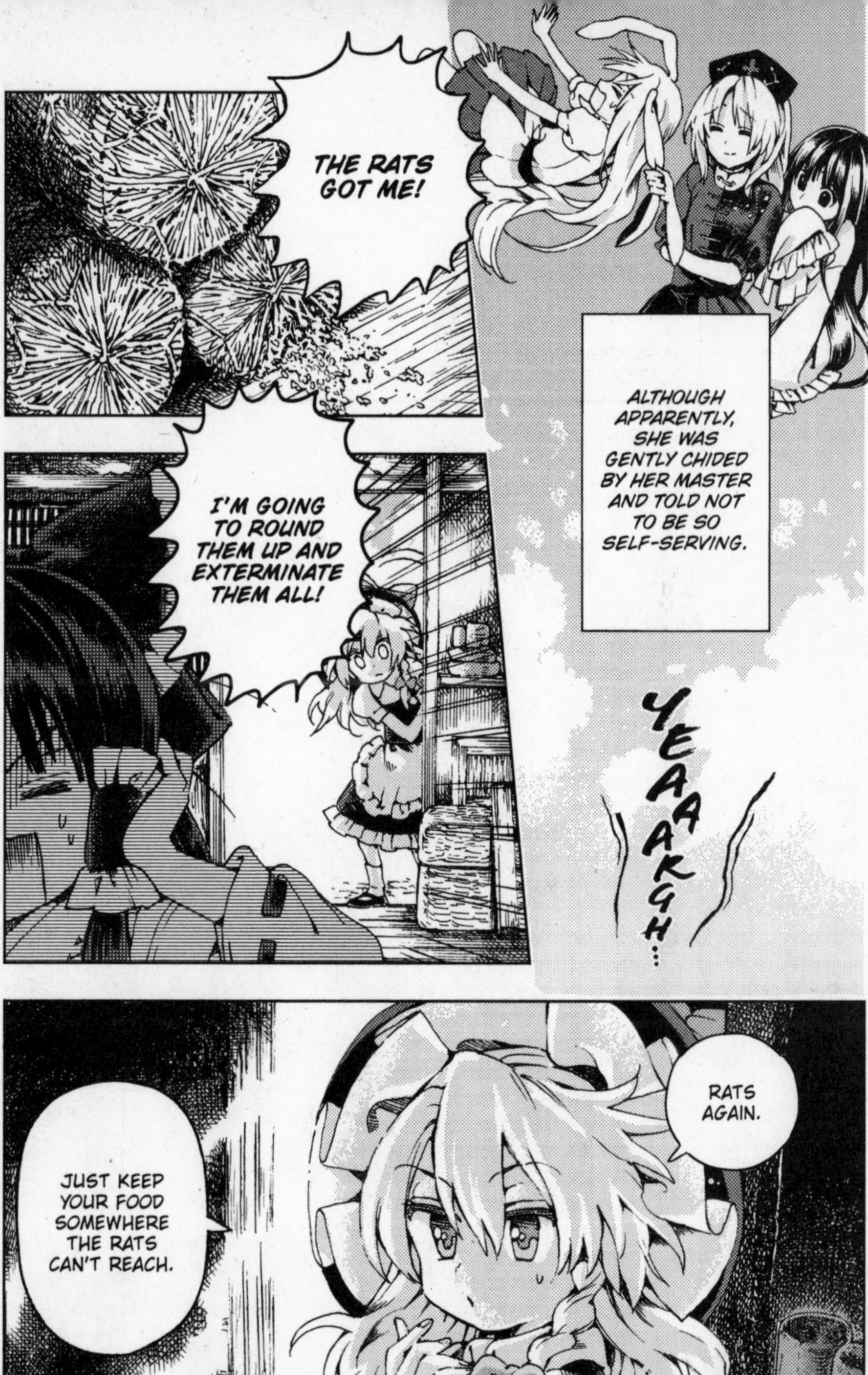
ALTHOUGH APPARENTLY, SHE WAS GENTLY CHIDED BY HER MASTER AND TOLD NOT TO BE SO SELF-SERVING.
YEAAAAGH...
THE RATS GOT ME!
I'M GOING TO ROUND THEM UP AND EXTERMINATE THEM ALL!
RATS AGAIN.
JUST KEEP YOUR FOOD SOMEWHERE THE RATS CAN'T REACH.

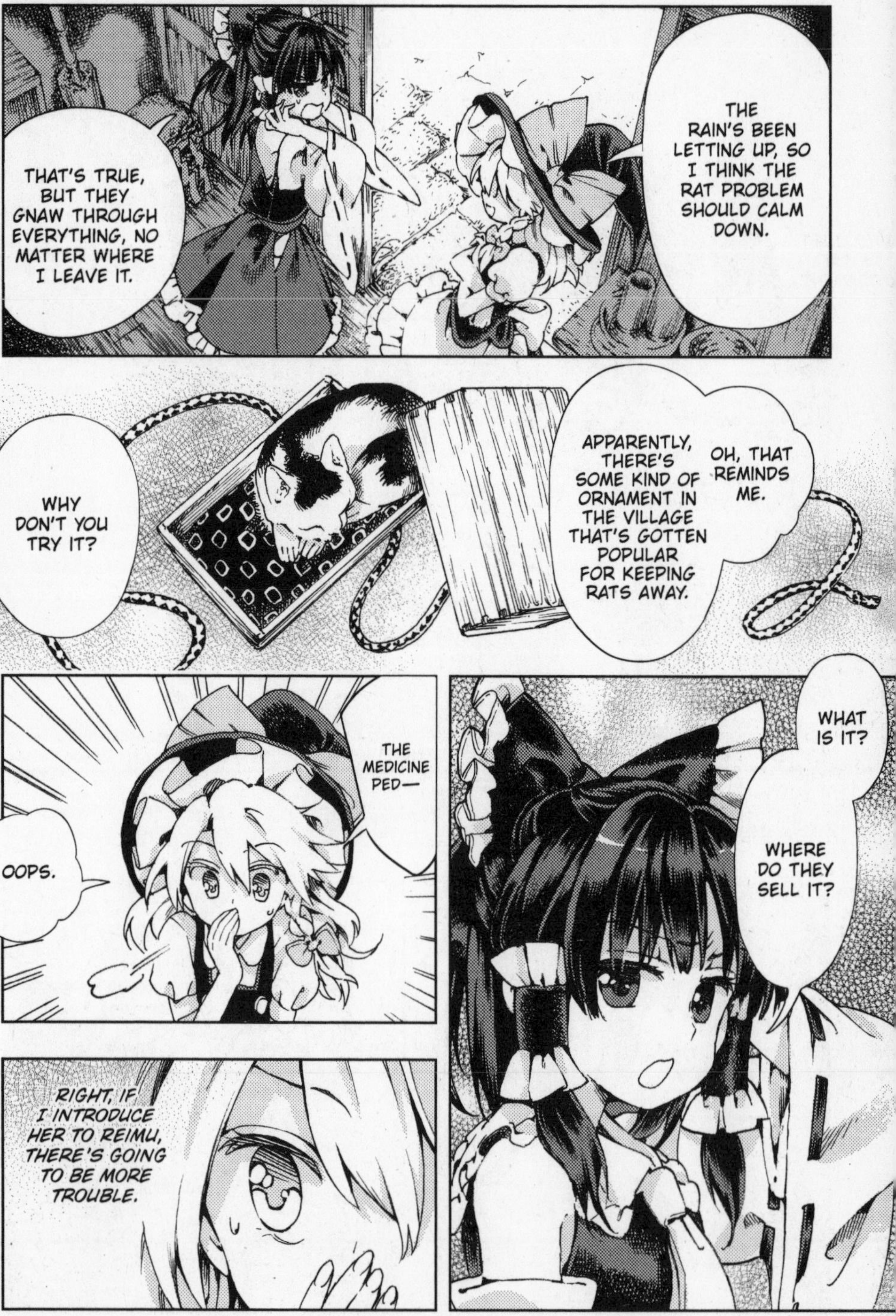
THE RAIN'S BEEN LETTING UP, SO I THINK THE RAT PROBLEM SHOULD CALM DOWN.
THAT'S TRUE, BUT THEY GNAW THROUGH EVERYTHING, NO MATTER WHERE I LEAVE IT.
OH, THAT REMINDS ME.
APPARENTLY, THERE'S SOME KIND OF ORNAMENT IN THE VILLAGE THAT'S GOTTEN POPULAR FOR KEEPING RATS AWAY.
WHY DON'T YOU TRY IT?
WHAT IS IT?
WHERE DO THEY SELL IT?
THE MEDICINE PED—
OOPS.
RIGHT, IF I INTRODUCE HER TO REIMU, THERE'S GOING TO BE MORE TROUBLE.

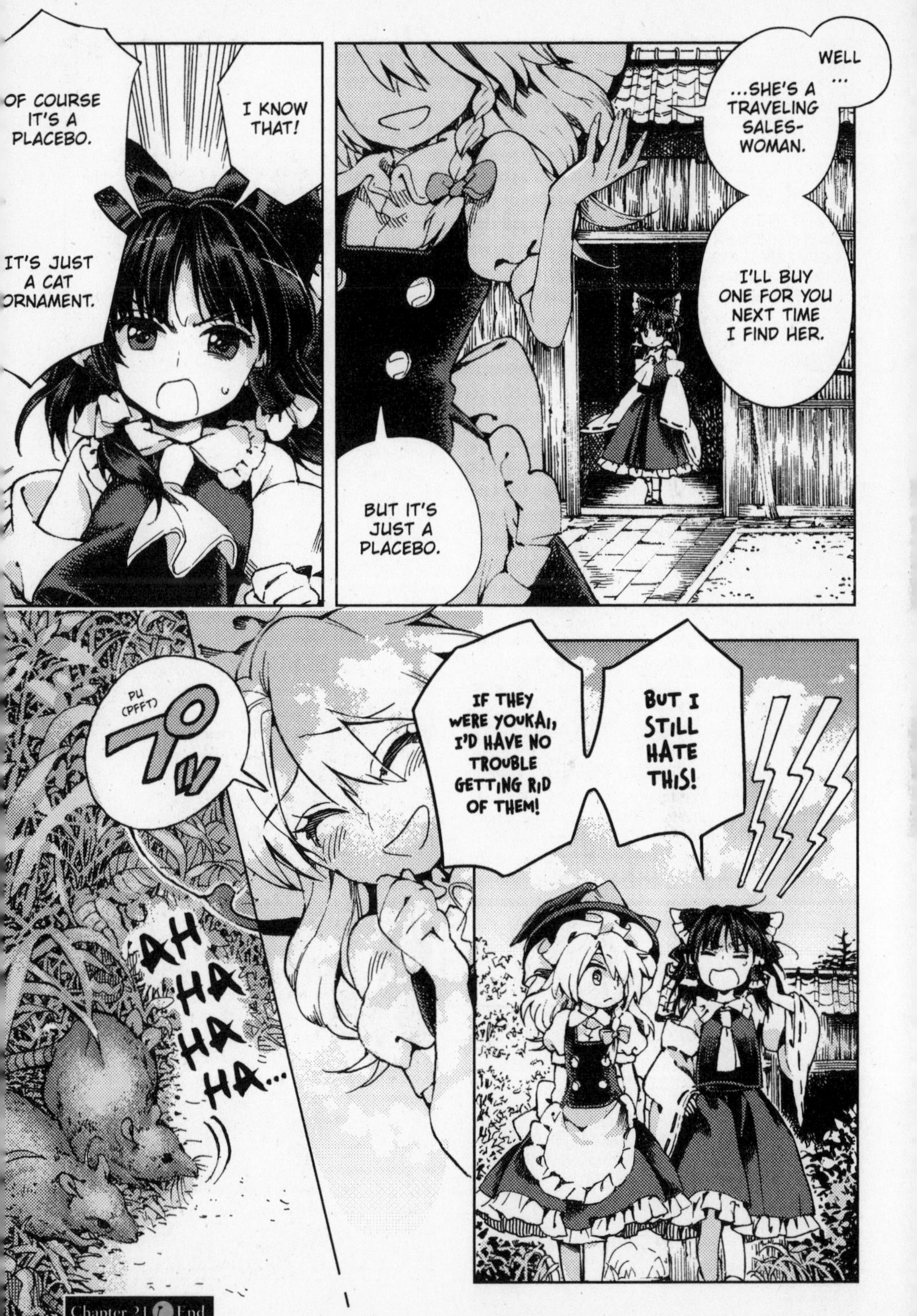
WELL ...
...SHE'S A TRAVELING SALES-WOMAN.
I'LL BUY ONE FOR YOU NEXT TIME I FIND HER.
BUT IT'S JUST A PLACEBO.
OF COURSE IT'S A PLACEBO.
I KNOW THAT!
IT'S JUST A CAT ORNAMENT.
BUT I STILL HATE THIS!
IF THEY WERE YOUKAI, I'D HAVE NO TROUBLE GETTING RID OF THEM!
PU (PFFT)
AH HA HA HA HA...
Chapter 21 End

# TRANSLATION NOTES

GENERAL

Certain character names, such as Akyu Hiedano, are also commonly rendered differently, i.e., Hieda-no-Akyu, literally "Akyu of the Hieda." This English edition renders names as given name first in order to avoid confusion.

The character names also frequently contain references or certain meanings due to how they're written in Japanese.

**Nitori Kawashiro**: Because Nitori is a *kappa*, her given name may be a reference to a line in the novel *Kappa* by Ryuunosuke Akutagawa. "Kawashiro" means "river castle," pointing to how *kappa* inhabit rivers.

**Reisen Udongein Inaba**: "Udongein" comes from *udonge*, the Japanese word for a mythical Indian tree, and is featured in the Japanese folk tale "Princess Kaguya," about a girl from the moon. "Inaba" refers to the Hare of Inaba, a Japanese hare of legend.

PAGE 6

*Oitekebori*: Meaning "leave it and go ditch," this *youkai* lives in ponds, canals, etc. It will appear in the form of a spirit, telling its victims to "drop it and go." Usually their victims are fisherman, who leave their catch and run in terror.

PAGE 8

*Okuri hyoushigi*: Meaning "sending-off wooden clappers," this phenomenon happens when the night patrol goes around hitting wooden clappers together to warn the town to be careful of fires. When the last *hyoushigi* has been clapped, more clapping will be heard, as if sending the patrol off after a job well done. But when the patroller turns to see who did the clapping, no one is there.

PAGE 20

*Okuri chouchin*: Meaning "sending-off lanterns," these lights appear late at night before people with no lanterns of their own. Wanderers would follow the lights, which vanish and return repeatedly, preventing them from catching up.

PAGE 35

*Shirikodama*: Translated roughly as "rear-end jewel," a *shirikodama* is a mythical crystal believed to exist in humans' anuses. According to legend, kappa attack people to obtain this jewel, which is a hardened form of the soul.

PAGE 47

**Shugen sect**: Known as *Shugendo* in Japanese, it's an amalgamation of various religious philosophies. Its main precept is that spiritual power can be obtained through discipline; thus, the sect's priests isolate themselves in the mountains for strict spiritual training.

PAGE 118

**Black Charms of Nose**: The Black Charms of Nose, or *Nose no Kurofuda*, really do exist and have a reputation mostly for warding off disasters, but also for driving away fox spirits.

PAGE 88

**Writing on the door**: In Japanese architecture, sliding doors called *shouji* are used. These doors consist of a wood or bamboo frame covered in sturdy paper.

PAGE 136

*Ukiyo-e*: Literally meaning "pictures of the floating world," *ukiyo-e* is a style of woodblock prints that was popular during the Edo period.

PAGE 148

**Come to trade medicine**: The practice known as *okigusuri*, or "medicine left in place," involves a medicine peddler giving a household a box of medicine for their use. The customer later pays only for the medicine that had been used since the peddler's last visit.

PAGE 151

*Maneki-neko*: Literally meaning "beckoning cat," *maneki-neko* are cat figurines used as good luck charms. They're commonly found in stores and other businesses, "beckoning" good fortune to come in.

PAGE 154

*Tesso*: Meaning "iron rat," it's the vengeful spirit of a priest who was slighted by the emperor. He died full of rage, and his spirit became a giant rat that led an army of rats to invade Kyoto, and the rats ate everything, including the sacred texts, at Enryaku Temple.

PAGE 166

**Mosquito alarm**: An anti-loitering device that emits noise at a high frequency that can be heard mostly by younger people, who are thus discouraged from loitering in the area.

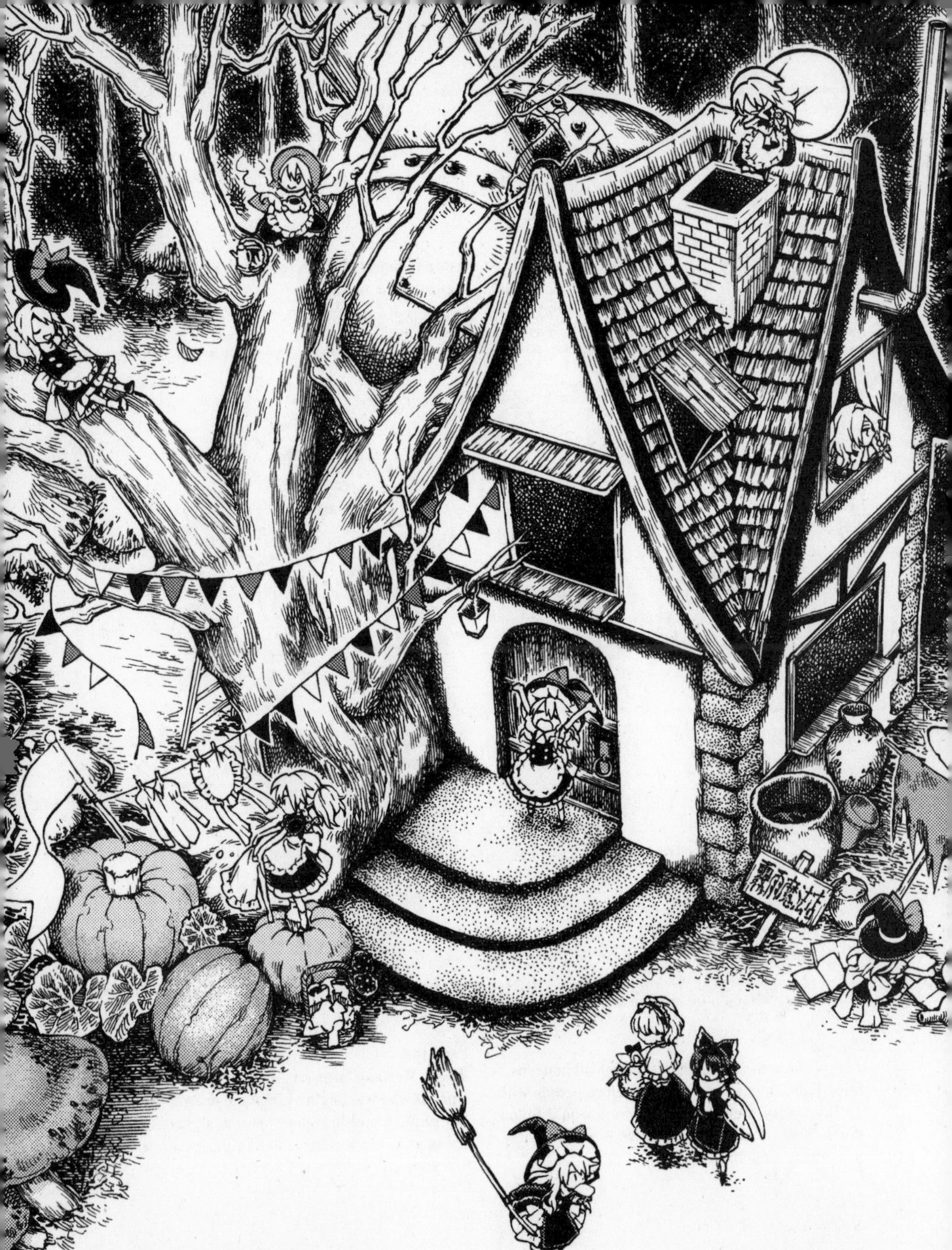

Character Design Collection

SIGN: KIRISAME MAGIC HOUSE

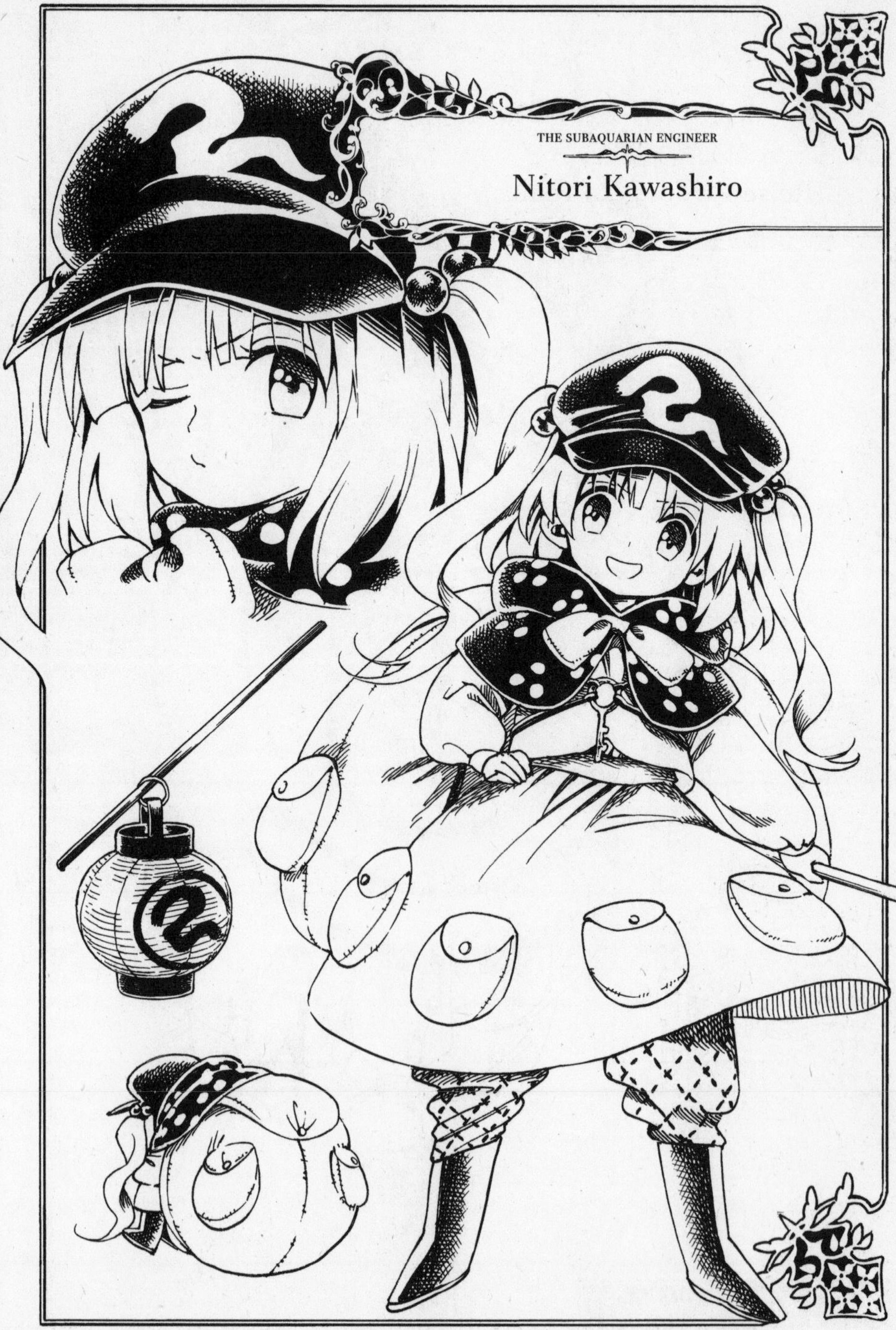
THE SUBAQUARIAN ENGINEER
Nitori Kawashiro

EARTH-BOUND MOON RABBIT

# Reisen Udongein Inaba

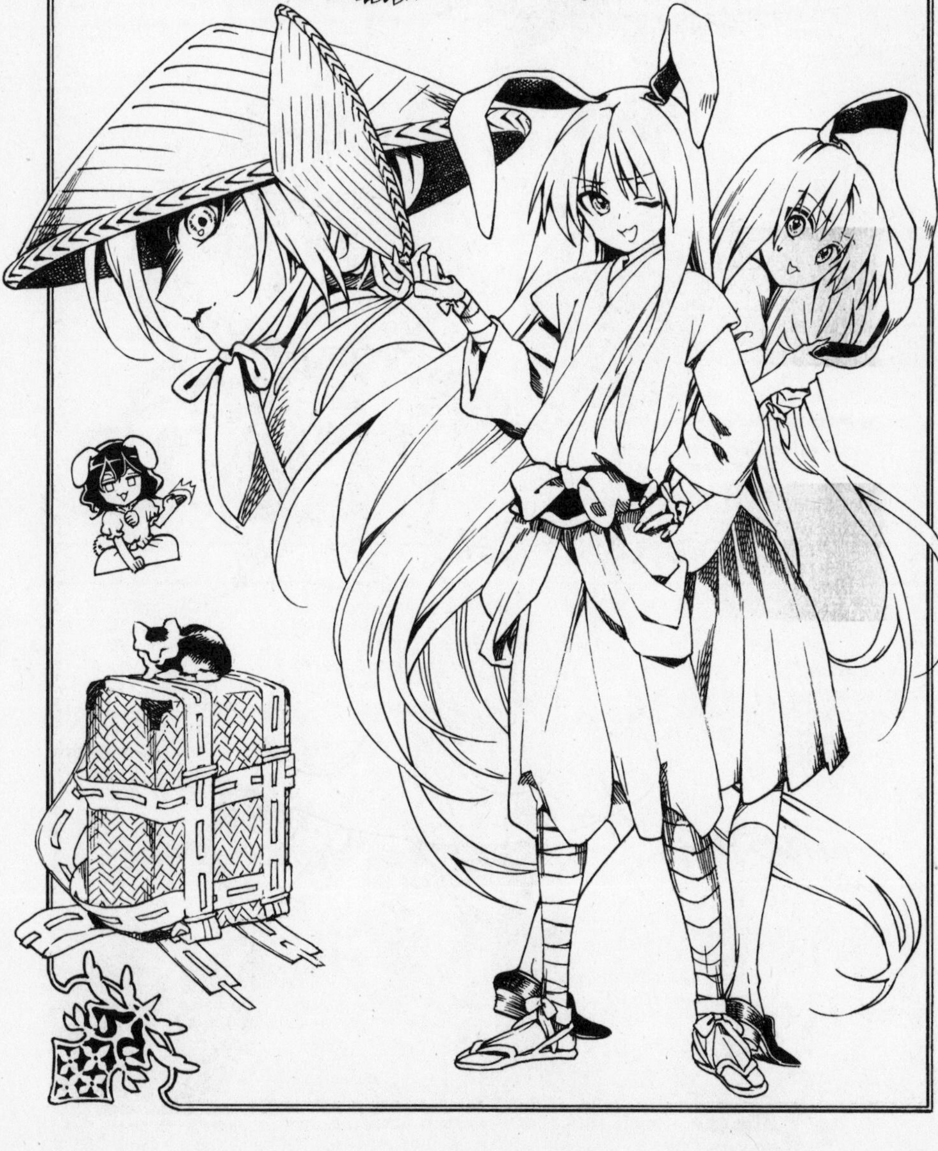

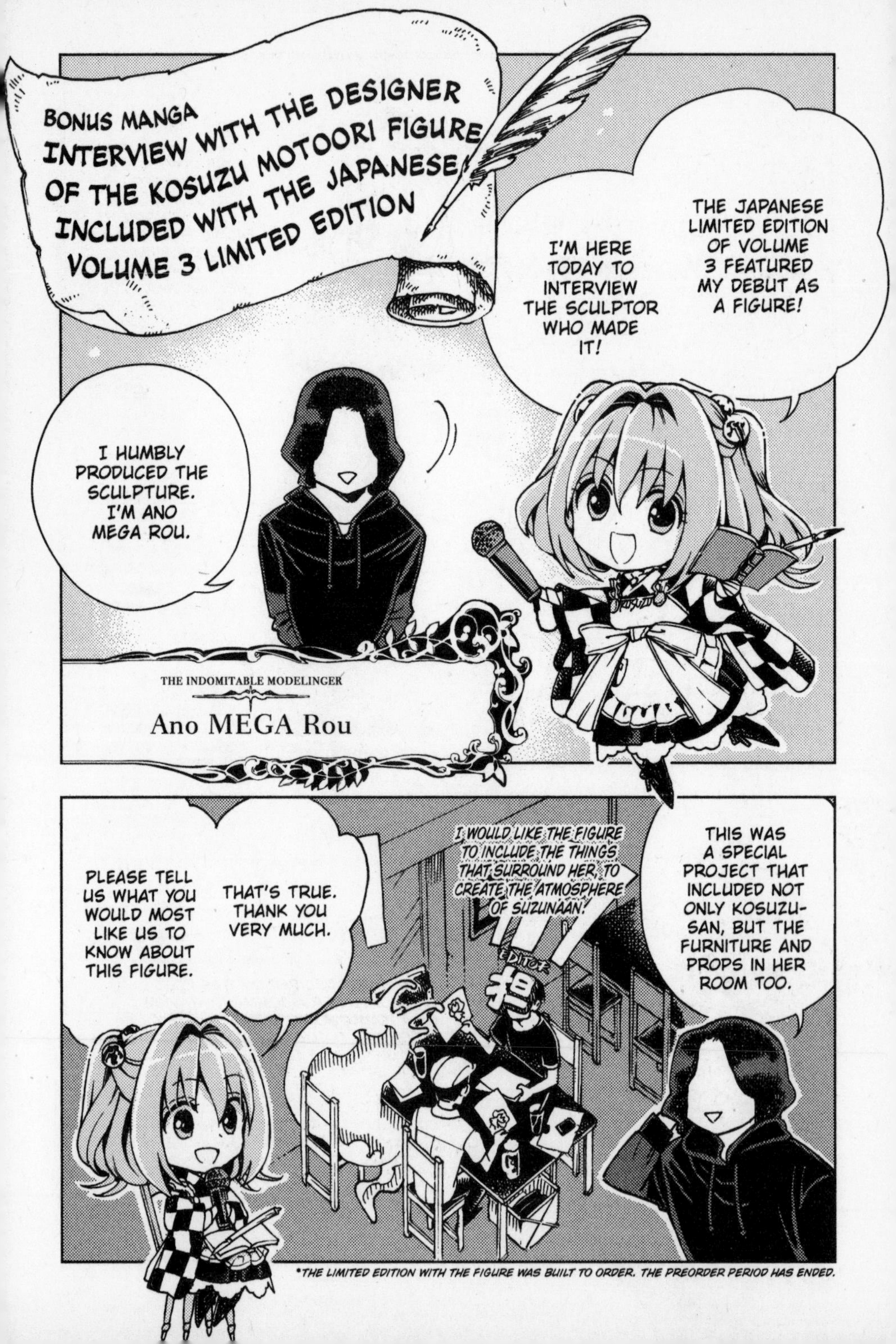
BONUS MANGA
INTERVIEW WITH THE DESIGNER OF THE KOSUZU MOTOORI FIGURE INCLUDED WITH THE JAPANESE VOLUME 3 LIMITED EDITION
THE JAPANESE LIMITED EDITION OF VOLUME 3 FEATURED MY DEBUT AS A FIGURE!
I'M HERE TODAY TO INTERVIEW THE SCULPTOR WHO MADE IT!
I HUMBLY PRODUCED THE SCULPTURE. I'M ANO MEGA ROU.
THE INDOMITABLE MODELINGER
Ano MEGA Rou
THIS WAS A SPECIAL PROJECT THAT INCLUDED NOT ONLY KOSUZU-SAN, BUT THE FURNITURE AND PROPS IN HER ROOM TOO.
I WOULD LIKE THE FIGURE TO INCLUDE THE THINGS THAT SURROUND HER, TO CREATE THE ATMOSPHERE OF SUZUNAAN!
EDITOR
THAT'S TRUE. THANK YOU VERY MUCH.
PLEASE TELL US WHAT YOU WOULD MOST LIKE US TO KNOW ABOUT THIS FIGURE.
*THE LIMITED EDITION WITH THE FIGURE WAS BUILT TO ORDER. THE PREORDER PERIOD HAS ENDED.

# Forbidden Scrollery

③

>STORY<

## ZUN

>ART<

## Moe Harukawa

### TRANSLATION: ALETHEA NIBLEY AND ATHENA NIBLEY
### LETTERING: ALEXIS ECKERMAN

TOUHOU SUZUNA AN ~Forbidden Scrollery. Vol. 3
© Team Shanghai Alice © Moe HARUKAWA 2014
First published in Japan in 2014 by KADOKAWA CORPORATION, Tokyo.
English translation rights arranged with KADOKAWA CORPORATION, Tokyo
through TUTTLE-MORI AGENCY, Inc., Tokyo.

English translation © 2018 by Yen Press, LLC

Yen Press
1290 Avenue of the Americas
New York, NY 10104

VISIT US AT YENPRESS.COM

facebook.com/yenpress  yenpress.tumblr.com
twitter.com/yenpress                 instagram.com/yenpress

First Yen Press Edition: May 2018

Yen Press is an imprint of Yen Press, LLC.
The Yen Press name and logo are trademarks of Yen Press, LLC.

Library of Congress Control Number: 2017949553

ISBNs: 978-0-316-51191-9 (paperback)
978-0-316-51201-5 (ebook)

10 9 8 7 6 5 4 3 2 1

WOR

Printed in the United States of America

## ZUN

Hello, ZUN here. We're already at Volume 3.
I used to write manga in the past, and every series ended
in three volumes, so I am deeply touched by this.

In "The Summer of Rats," we said there were a lot of evening
showers. This is a mini-disaster that takes place at around the same
time as *Touhou Ibarakasen: Wild and Horned Hermit*, which is a
manga running in another magazine. It's a miiinor crossover, so
please read that one too (plug for another publisher's manga).

Also, the team from Myouren Temple shows up in "Love Letters
with a Past," but that was just to set up the story. Byakuren Hijiri and
Yuuten Shounin have no real relation, so don't get any ideas [I guess
Byakuren gets this kind of job a lot in *Forbidden Scrollery* (ha-ha).]

Well, I hope to see you again in Volume 4 or in *Comp Ace*.

## Moe Harukawa

Hello. I am the artist, Harukawa.

There's a standard edition and a limited edition of this volume
in Japanese, and each one has a different cover. Actually,
when I drew Marisa for this cover, it was the beginning of
August, but when it hits bookstore shelves, it will be smack
in the middle of winter, won't it? According to ZUN-san,
Marisa doesn't like the cold, so I felt a little bad for her, but I
figured she could push herself to endure the short sleeves.

To ZUN-san, who writes the story outline for me every
month despite his busy schedule, my editor who extended
the deadline as far as we could possibly get away with, and
all of you who read this book, thank you very much.

I will keep doing my best.

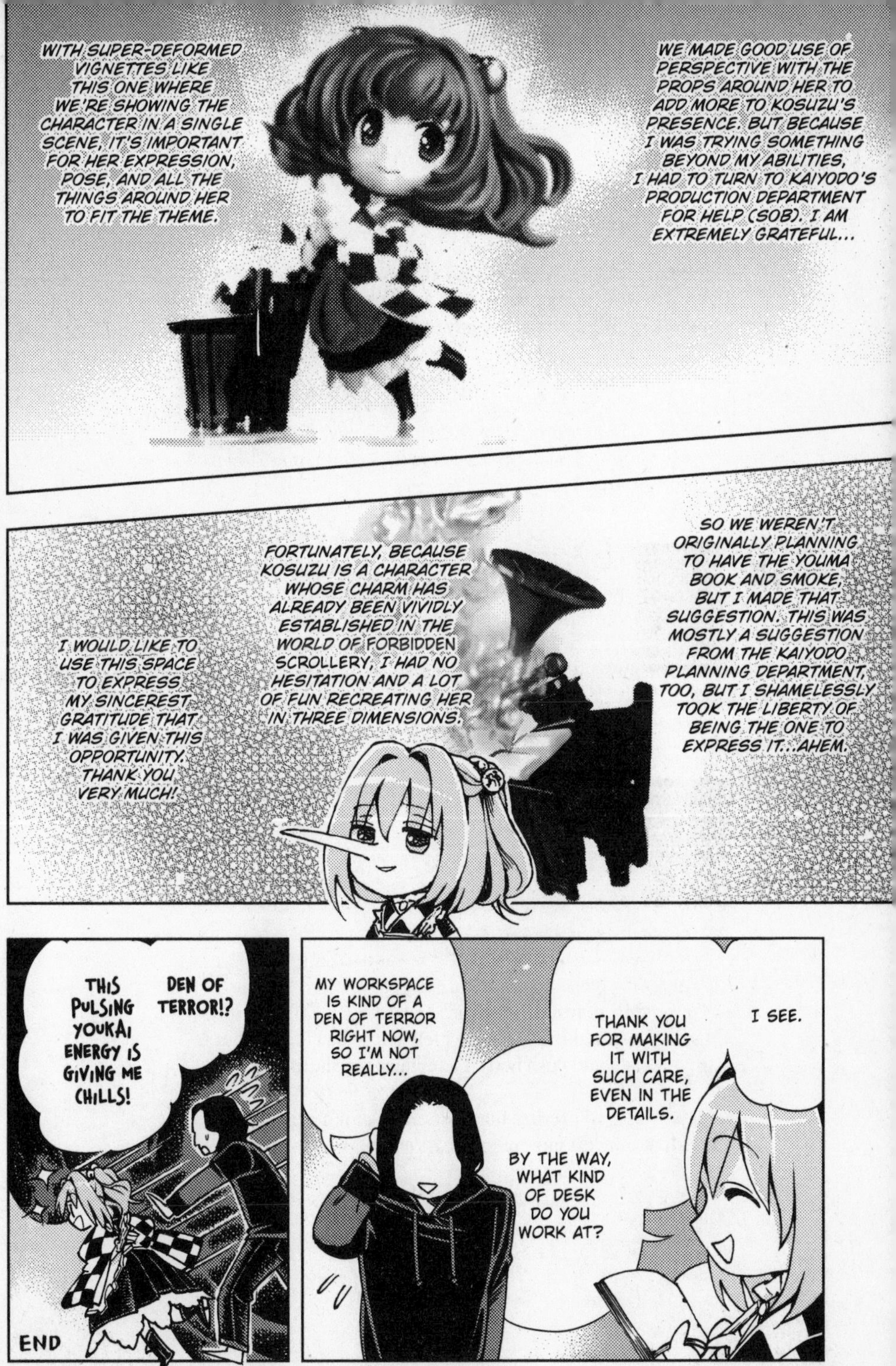
WE MADE GOOD USE OF PERSPECTIVE WITH THE PROPS AROUND HER TO ADD MORE TO KOSUZU'S PRESENCE. BUT BECAUSE I WAS TRYING SOMETHING BEYOND MY ABILITIES, I HAD TO TURN TO KAIYODO'S PRODUCTION DEPARTMENT FOR HELP (SOB). I AM EXTREMELY GRATEFUL...
WITH SUPER-DEFORMED VIGNETTES LIKE THIS ONE WHERE WE'RE SHOWING THE CHARACTER IN A SINGLE SCENE, IT'S IMPORTANT FOR HER EXPRESSION, POSE, AND ALL THE THINGS AROUND HER TO FIT THE THEME.
SO WE WEREN'T ORIGINALLY PLANNING TO HAVE THE YOUMA BOOK AND SMOKE, BUT I MADE THAT SUGGESTION. THIS WAS MOSTLY A SUGGESTION FROM THE KAIYODO PLANNING DEPARTMENT, TOO, BUT I SHAMELESSLY TOOK THE LIBERTY OF BEING THE ONE TO EXPRESS IT...AHEM.
FORTUNATELY, BECAUSE KOSUZU IS A CHARACTER WHOSE CHARM HAS ALREADY BEEN VIVIDLY ESTABLISHED IN THE WORLD OF FORBIDDEN SCROLLERY, I HAD NO HESITATION AND A LOT OF FUN RECREATING HER IN THREE DIMENSIONS.
I WOULD LIKE TO USE THIS SPACE TO EXPRESS MY SINCEREST GRATITUDE THAT I WAS GIVEN THIS OPPORTUNITY. THANK YOU VERY MUCH!
I SEE.
THANK YOU FOR MAKING IT WITH SUCH CARE, EVEN IN THE DETAILS.
BY THE WAY, WHAT KIND OF DESK DO YOU WORK AT?
MY WORKSPACE IS KIND OF A DEN OF TERROR RIGHT NOW, SO I'M NOT REALLY...
DEN OF TERROR!?
THIS PULSING YOUKAI ENERGY IS GIVING ME CHILLS!
END

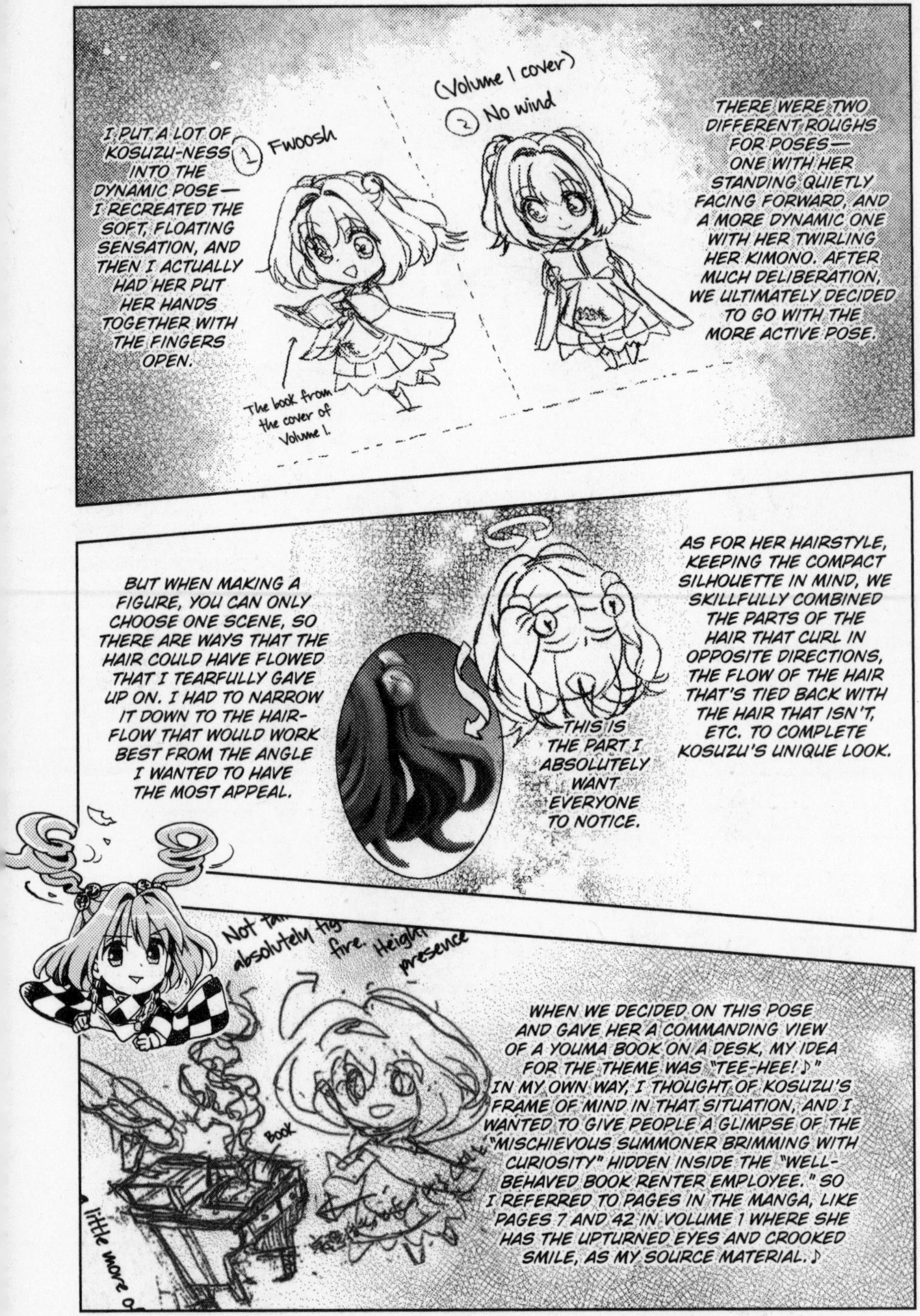
(Volume 1 cover)
2 No wind
THERE WERE TWO DIFFERENT ROUGHS FOR POSES—ONE WITH HER STANDING QUIETLY FACING FORWARD, AND A MORE DYNAMIC ONE WITH HER TWIRLING HER KIMONO. AFTER MUCH DELIBERATION, WE ULTIMATELY DECIDED TO GO WITH THE MORE ACTIVE POSE.
1 Fwoosh
I PUT A LOT OF KOSUZU-NESS INTO THE DYNAMIC POSE—I RECREATED THE SOFT, FLOATING SENSATION, AND THEN I ACTUALLY HAD HER PUT HER HANDS TOGETHER WITH THE FINGERS OPEN.
The book from the cover of Volume 1.
AS FOR HER HAIRSTYLE, KEEPING THE COMPACT SILHOUETTE IN MIND, WE SKILLFULLY COMBINED THE PARTS OF THE HAIR THAT CURL IN OPPOSITE DIRECTIONS, THE FLOW OF THE HAIR THAT'S TIED BACK WITH THE HAIR THAT ISN'T, ETC. TO COMPLETE KOSUZU'S UNIQUE LOOK.
THIS IS THE PART I ABSOLUTELY WANT EVERYONE TO NOTICE.
BUT WHEN MAKING A FIGURE, YOU CAN ONLY CHOOSE ONE SCENE, SO THERE ARE WAYS THAT THE HAIR COULD HAVE FLOWED THAT I TEARFULLY GAVE UP ON. I HAD TO NARROW IT DOWN TO THE HAIR-FLOW THAT WOULD WORK BEST FROM THE ANGLE I WANTED TO HAVE THE MOST APPEAL.
WHEN WE DECIDED ON THIS POSE AND GAVE HER A COMMANDING VIEW OF A YOUMA BOOK ON A DESK, MY IDEA FOR THE THEME WAS "TEE-HEE!♪" IN MY OWN WAY, I THOUGHT OF KOSUZU'S FRAME OF MIND IN THAT SITUATION, AND I WANTED TO GIVE PEOPLE A GLIMPSE OF THE "MISCHIEVOUS SUMMONER BRIMMING WITH CURIOSITY" HIDDEN INSIDE THE "WELL-BEHAVED BOOK RENTER EMPLOYEE." SO I REFERRED TO PAGES IN THE MANGA, LIKE PAGES 7 AND 42 IN VOLUME 1 WHERE SHE HAS THE UPTURNED EYES AND CROOKED SMILE, AS MY SOURCE MATERIAL.♪
presence
Book